INTERPRETING NEVILLE

INTERPRETING NEVILLE

edited by

J. HARLEY CHAPMAN
and
NANCY K. FRANKENBERRY

State University
of New York
Press

Chapters 8, 11, 13, and 15 appeared earlier in *The American Journal of Theology and Philosophy* 18.3 (September 1997), with the permission of the State University of New York Press and the co-editors of this volume.

Published by
State University of New York Press, Albany

Production by Susan Geraghty
Marketing by Fran Keneston

Printed in the United States of America

For information, address State University of New York
Press, State University Plaza, Albany, N.Y., 12246

Library of Congress Cataloging-in-Publication Data

Interpreting Neville / edited by J. Harley Chapman and Nancy K.
   Frankenberry.
        p.   cm.
    Includes index.
    ISBN 0-7914-4195-4 (hc : alk. paper). — ISBN 0-7914-4196-2 (pbk.
: alk. paper)
    1. Neville, Robert C. I. Chapman, J. Harley.
II. Frankenberry, Nancy K.
B945.N484I57 1999
191—dc21   98-35152
                                                                              CIP

10 9 8 7 6 5 4 3 2 1

CONTENTS

PREFACE

In the ensuing pages fifteen senior scholars from a variety of perspectives critically examine the thought of Robert Cummings Neville. Until now, aside from journal articles and a symposium or two, there has been no sustained, book-length treatment of the work of one of the most significant philosophers and theologians of our time. Long convinced of the value of Neville's profound and wide-ranging vision, we as editors invited the sympathetic but critical appraisals of experts in the several fields within which Neville works. Each of the essays that appear here has been specially solicited for this volume. Neville himself has responded to each author in a lengthly concluding essay that, to our delight, furthers the dialectic and suggests additional research projects.

A prolific writer, Neville to date has authored fourteen books beginning with his dialectically brilliant *God the Creator: On the Transcendence and Presence of God* (1968) and continuing with a series of studies testing his central metaphysical hypotheses through their applications in cosmology, ethics, social and political thought, cultural criticism, comparative religions, theology, and philosophy of religion in a global culture. Even when gravitating toward metaphysical generality, Neville does not blink at the real issues of the time, addressing the fact-value split in modern culture, postmodernism, non-Western philosophies and religions, as well as issues in biomedical ethics, capitalist-socialist debates, religion in contemporary Western culture, God, freedom, time and eternity. His work calls out for serious examination, to which this volume makes an original contribution.

We believe that the essays that follow, including Neville's, together provide a good introduction to the range and depth of Neville's thought as well as a critical commentary on significant issues, themes, and arguments. Readers with limited previous exposure to his work—an *oeuvre* that can be as daunting as it is ambitious—deserve a brief introduction here to the dimensions of Neville's overall intellectual enterprise. To grasp *how* he works is helpful for understanding *what* he says. We wish to highlight four aspects or interrelated identities: the dialectician, the hypothetical metaphysician, the comparativist, and the critic.

First of all, by temperament and as evidenced in his first book thirty years ago, Neville is a dialectician. He once quipped that there were probably only six people in the world who think the way he does. This rather unique designation is due not to his capacity for abstract thought—many intellectuals possess such a gift—but to his penchant for, and demonstrated skill at, sustained dialectical thought. Neville has a high regard for and commitment to rational faith, in the sense of seeking and offering reasoned explanations for things about which humans have genuine concern, deep puzzlement, or profound questions, even if it should mean that there is no certifying authority or simple and satisfying means of verification. The alternative to rational faith is a horrifyingly irrational display of brute force; Neville sides with Socrates over Thrasymachus. This commitment does not, however, produce an airy rationalist, who subsumes experience under a few principles but never justifies the structure of rationality. Rather, as a dialectician, Neville starts with the fundamental questions, including ultimately those of existence, and searches for what would finally and satisfyingly account for everything, including the so-called "first principles." In contradistinction to Aristotle and Kant, who interpreted dialectic as a specious form of argument, but like Plato, Aquinas, and Hegel, who saw dialectic as the highest form of reasoning, Neville believes that for a thesis to be established there must be the consideration and critique of alternative claims proffered as answers to a genuine question, which claims are, in turn, critiqued in light of the norms they presuppose. Dialectic in this and related senses—whether the consideration of alternatives in the process of self-criticism or in the social process of examination of alternative theories—is methodological. Through intellectual give-and-take, problems and their possible solutions are clarified and refined; categories initially considered are transformed into those more nearly instantiating the ideal of system. Neville pursues methodological dialectic with rigor, systematically pushing thought—his own and that of others—toward greater consistency, coherence, application, and adequacy to experience. Dialectic begins in experience generously and profoundly pondered, elucidated, organized and interpreted categorially, ramified, applied and tested. Neville's first book, *God the Creator* (1968), makes masterful use of methodological dialectic; in a later volume, *Creativity and God* (1980), he engages dialectically the writings of Alfred North Whitehead, Charles Hartshorne, and scholars in the process-theological tradition.

Yet it is the second major type of dialectic—constitutive dialectic—that more centrally gets at Neville's unique contribution: reality itself is dialectically constituted. Hegel and Marx would have agreed, but they lack the profound ontology that Neville puts forth. In this form of dialectic, there is the search for an explanation for the determinations of existence—every thing has an identity comprising both essential and conditional features—which would account for why things are together and, further, why they are at all. This search yields the explanation of the indeterminate creator (or act of creating) that accounts for all the determinations of being, including the determination of indeterminate being to the degree that it is the creating source of the world of determinations. Reality is seen as paradoxically indeterminate and determinate, infinite and finite, eternal and temporal, radically transcendent and totally present. It is the job of constitutive dialectic to trace the contours and signal the shifts in context and meaning as philosophical reflection seeks to align itself with its paradoxical subject matter. According to Neville, dialectic has not completed its work, nor rationality fully asserted its rights, unless and until it has moved from the world of contingent reality to what both grounds and transcends that world. *God the Creator* is the most sustained employment of constitutive dialectic known to us; it is a veritable tour de force. Its central arguments are repeated throughout Neville's work and can be seen especially in *Soldier, Sage, Saint* (1978), *The Tao and the Daimon* (1982), *Behind the Masks of God* (1991), *A Theology Primer* (1991), and *Eternity and Time's Flow* (1991).

In the second place, as a "speculative pragmatist," Neville operates hypothetically, that is, metaphysics is seen as hypothesis. For him, there is no absolute foundation in experience: all experiencing and all thinking involves selection, and selection entails a judgment about what is important. Other theories, of course, select different data, stimulated by different questions, categorize the selected data differently, and seek to test the hypothesis by its application to experience considered important. The ultimate test of a good metaphysical hypothesis is its ability to provide guidance in the practical affairs of life, the "issues of men (and women)," as John Dewey would have it. Inescapably, it is hypothesis all the way up and all the way down. Embracing metaphysics as hypothesis commits Neville to a radical vulnerability and fallibility. A good metaphysician, he insists, consciously puts forth a theory in such a way as to invite critique. A system, ramified and even profound, can never be certain. It is always, as William James frequently said, "ever not quite." Neville's three-volume *Axiology of Thinking* (*Reconstruction of Thinking* in 1981, *Recovery of the Measure* in 1989, and *Normative Cultures* in 1995) as well as his earlier *Cosmology of Freedom* (1974) present the argument that all thinking rests on a basis of value and that all acts of thinking are perforce evaluative.

In the third place, Neville is a comparativist. He has made it increasingly central to his thought to take in, compare, and reflect upon world philosophies and theologies. He has made a special attempt to open his thinking to the East Asian influence, especially Confucian and Buddhist philosophies. To think globally is a formidable task since philosophies incorporate widely varying cultural assumptions—aesthetic, religious, and practical. Without some categories of comparison, however, one culture cannot get close enough to assess, and be assessed by, another; yet the categories themselves may be seriously flawed and in need of radical critique. The vulnerability that Neville makes crucial to metaphysics is felt most keenly in cross-cultural comparison. Within an emerging global culture, the axiology of thinking must run the risk of making itself even more vulnerable. Neville's comparativism is most clearly seen in *The Tao and the Daimon* (1982), *Behind the Masks of God* (1991), and *Normative Cultures* (1995).

Finally, Neville is a critic. He believes that thinking should make a difference in the time and place in which one lives. This pulls him into serious and critical engagement with the issues of the culture. This approach is seen in his dialectical assessment of philosophies and theologies, in his treatment of economic theories and political ideologies, and most recently in his sustained critique of the totalizing attitudes and moves of modernism and postmodernism alike. Neville attacks the foundationalism and the rebellion against bourgeois culture of modernism and the revolt against systematic philosophy and its replacement with a move toward edifying conversation, albeit of serious moral concern, in some important versions of postmodernism. His critical work is best seen in *The Puritan Smile* (1987) and particularly in *The Highroad around Modernism* (1992).

Further ramifying and testing his metaphysical hypotheses in the fields of hermeneutics and semiotics, Neville has continued the dialectic most recently in *The Truth of Broken Symbols* (1996) and is even now, indefatigably, projecting it into future volumes. Let this collection of critical essays, then, be the first such attempt to come to terms, at century's end, with the thought of Robert Cummings Neville. Knowing that serious responses to philosophical originality are usually slow in forming, we bequeath to the twenty-first century the next set of essays that will still be needed for the full comprehension of this one scholar's rich contribution.

We wish to offer our thanks to a number of individuals for their support throughout this project. William Eastman, former director of the State University of New York Press, gave his blessing and encouragement to the whole project. Editor Nancy Ellegate and her staff, with special mention of Susan Geraghty, deserve our deep gratitude. Earline Hefferlin expertly prepared the index. Colleagues in the American Academy of Religion, the Metaphysical Society of America, and the Highlands Institute for American Religious and Philosophical Thought have been most receptive to the project. Special thanks go to Lisa Larsen, Bob Grindrod, Jean Berglof Chapman, and Jennifer Walker-Johnson for technical assistance and moral support. Finally, we thank both Robert Neville and our essayists for their contributions to this volume.

J. HARLEY CHAPMAN
NANCY K. FRANKENBERRY

ABBREVIATIONS OF NEVILLE'S WORKS

BMG	*Behind the Masks of God*
CF	*Cosmology of Freedom*
CG	*Creativity and God*
ETF	*Eternity and Time's Flow*
GC	*God the Creator*
HM	*The Highroad around Modernism*
NC	*Normative Cultures*
PS	*The Puritan Smile*
RM	*Recovery of the Measure*
RT	*Reconstruction of Thinking*
SSS	*Soldier, Sage, Saint*
TBS	*The Truth of Broken Symbols*
TP	*A Theology Primer*

PART I

Neville's Methodology

CHAPTER 1

Thinking Axiologically

George Allan

I

Imagine playing a game of wrap-around three-dimensional chess. Your queen is threatened by a knight located two levels down and at the extreme other end of the row; it'll be III-A-8 to I-A-1 unless you take evasive action. Or imagine a Fractal Book, where the third of four points being articulated at some location in the text can be seen upon closer inspection to dissolve into four subpoints detailing it, or can be enlarged to disclose a more sweeping point of which it and its three partners are the details. It's not Alice in Wonderland, because the knight doesn't turn into a flamingo, the queen doesn't shout, "Off with your head!", and the fractal transformations are not products of chance or whim. It's Robert Neville at work, inviting us to dance the quadrille of his striking and important metaphysical trilogy, *Axiology of Thinking.*[1]

There are four parts to Neville's presentation, one for each of four themes: Imagination, Interpretation, Theory, Responsibility. These are preceded by an overview of his enterprise in a part called Foundations.[2] Foundations is organized into four chapters, each of which presents Neville's central hypothesis from an angle that antici-pates one of the parts to follow. Each of those chapters has four sec-tions, and it's the same for each of the other parts. It's not fourfolds all the way down, but it feels like it. Were you to ask Neville to clar-ify some point down deep inside one of the sections, I imagine he would respond by presenting you with a micro-fourfold of ideas about images, interpretations, formal structures, and obligations, and this would go on as long as you had questions to ask him and stamina to pursue the implications of his answers.

Neville is impatient with those who focus attention, as I am now doing, on his methodological peculiarities. He wants us to judge him by the content of what he has to say. But he is also insistent, and rightly so, that you can't understand anything he says until you've followed out the way in which it is transmuted, translated, transmogrified, and transformed by the other ways he also may have chosen to say it. No, not may; must. Like a musical quartet, all four voices must be singing for the song to be sung. The second, third, and fourth ways of saying something must be said if what the first saying says is to encompass the beauty, truth, unity, and goodness without which the fullness of its value will be misappreciated, misread, misconceived, or misused. It's annoying, having to protect your queen by looking in so many directions at once. It's perverse to find only more of the same of what you found at the top whenever you try to get to the bottom of things. But to ignore Neville's fourfolds, taking what he says in some paragraph to be saying no more than what it says there, would be foolish. It would be like thinking a statement made in one of Plato's dialogues is an assertion of some Platonic truth, forgetting to take into account the perspective of the person in the dialogue who speaks those words, where the discussion is at that point in its development, and how the whole dialogue is framed philosophically.

Neville identifies his work as "essentially postmodernist" in that "its intelligibility and value come from its being an historical project, one that attempts to alter culture" [F-2-f: *RT* 33]. He argues that everything occurs at some place at some time in some manner for some purpose within some context of influences. So it cannot be grasped or critiqued, it can neither be understood nor its relevance for us known, except in terms of those factors, plus the fact of its having emerged as their integration. Everything is from a perspective; everything is historically situated. This relativism, however, is precisely what modern Western thinking denies, advocating instead that there are ways we can transcend the limitations of our point of view, extricate ourselves from the contingency of our historical situation. So Neville's postmodernism projects itself as a direct challenge to modern culture. It asks us to pull down a flawed, failing, absolutist world and to replace it with a more worthy, more humane, but more risky one. Neville offers us not merely something different but something revolutionary. To think that thinking is axiological involves a revolutionary shift in how we feel, how we perceive, how we conceive, how we decide what is best. It means becoming a different person, a new self with a new character appropriate to a brave new world. Revolution, indeed; it's not just off with our heads but with the queen's as well. This philosophic game of chess is for keeps, with the future of our civilization as the stakes.

What's not postmodernist about Neville is that his denial of transcendental absolutes hasn't forced him to deny that there is an objective reality that is the source, ground, framework, and normative measure of our limited points of view. Modernism flounders because it has been unable to moor the world we know to an anchor not dependent on our knowing. Those usually identified as postmodernists are merely modernists who rejoice instead of despair at having been thus set adrift. They celebrate the human capacity to make worlds, pretending not to notice that without a link to reality these worlds become arbitrary and any defense of them is powerless before irrational desire, self-serving judgment, disengaged fantasy, and brute force of arms. So Neville insists that we cannot do without a mooring, but his metaphysical claims concerning that mooring are open to refutation because he claims that thinking arises from a reality to which it is responsible for its claims, claims about the world as it appears, as we engage it, as it is, and as it ought to be. So Neville smiles sheepishly as he raises the banner of his revolution, for if he is to be true to his own method he knows that his hypothesis, in all its vagueness and in all the possible routes of its interpretation, cannot claim to offer us a new absolute come to unseat the old. "For vulnerability is of the essence of truth" [1-4-4: *RT* 312]—as it is of beauty and of unity and of goodness.

So Neville's assertion that thinking is axiological is a hypothesis and consequently is refutable. But this is not a one-dimensional hypothesis, and so it is not refutable by finding an inconsistency among some of the data, a flaw in some argument, a failure to generalize something properly, a weakness in the cultural context it presumes. The only way to refute Neville is to provide a better hypothesis, in all its multidimensional complication and subtlety. Well, lots of luck. But in the meantime, the first step in any responsible critique is appreciation. We will have to become revolutionaries before we can ever be certain that the revolution has gone too far or hasn't gone far enough. Although we can never be certain. Not if thinking is historically situated, responsible for its claims about reality, and vulnerable to informed criticism. Not with all those fourfolds. Not with all the constraints of our human finitude. But let's at least try to appreciate Neville's revolutionary metaphysics. If for no other reason, because the beauty of the *Axiology of Thinking*, the elegance of its "architectonic rhythm," gives it value. And even if such a value is insufficient by itself to warrant our commitment to revolution, it is nonetheless profoundly satisfying, a good beginning. A philosophic new world well found.

"The general claim of the axiological hypothesis," says Neville, "is that thinking is founded in valuation." But what is "valuation?" What does it mean to value something? To answer these questions, let's start quite simply: "The most elementary form of [valuation] is synthesis of the components [of experience] into a field that serves as a background for focused attention" [F-1-1: *RT* 17]. According to Neville, synthesis in this sense is what imagination does. So to look at how imagination functions in thinking should provide us with an "elementary" grasp of what Neville means when he claims that valuation is the foundation for thinking. Instead of following along the full trajectory of the discussion in part 1, however, let's jump instead from chapter to chapter focusing only on the first section of each.[3] Here's what we find:

[1-1-1]: Imaginative synthesis is a process of "gathering" things into a single experience. Each of the things gathered is itself the result of a prior synthesis and therefore has value. So what the gathering gathers are realities rife with the value of their achievements: imagination is the way we "take possession" of the values of the world. This "enjoyment in gathering," the values felt and the value of feeling them, is the "primitive value" of imagination. Its product is "the bare achievement of a subjective world": a specific experience.

[1-2-1]: Experience becomes "perceptual" when this process of synthesis is governed by an intentional judgment, when the gathering occurs not for its own sake but as an interpretation of the world. Bare subjective experience is taken as having a referent; it is judged to be an experience of something. But this synthesis is never reducible to the judgment. Experience is always also feelings of elements independent of judgments, feelings of "the flowing, ongoing processes of nature and society," and in particular of "bodily feelings, memories, and associations" that provide the contextualizing background to whatever might comprise the focus of experience. My experience is "sensitive" to the extent to which the "initially felt value" of the things felt are retained in that experience rather than being eliminated.

[1-3-1]: Imagination's gathering of a manifold of feelings into a determinate experience able to "engage" the world is "fantasy." Fantasizing imagination is thus the "activity by which the world appears in experience." It involves not only the content of the perceptual focus, engages not only the external world, but involves also internal realities: bodily conditions, past experiences, biological drives, and social habits. Fashioning an appearance that engages the world also includes imagining ourselves as agents of its appearance, as "creative" and "erotic" presences responsible for the emergence of something of value, the measure of which is "beauty."

[1-4-1]: The forms by which we effect a synthesis able to engage the world are "images." They have been experienced as how some particular experience was organized, but they are then found to be generalizable. They could organize other experiences as well, and when they do the resulting experiences are to that extent linked together by a common

form, organized by it as a collective unity. A sequence of experiences is stabilized by the recurrence of the same images even amid shifting contents. We are responsible for how we engage the world insofar as we have control over the images by which it can be stabilized or destabilized. The failure to utilize relevant images, hence not to actualize the norms relevant to their possible use, results in a synthesis that has omitted what the excluded images would have included. So, for instance, my failure to engage the world through the images that focus those values of feeling constituted by pleasure and pain will result in my experiences being devoid of any awareness of such feelings. I can be said to have become "alienated" from my feelings, to be suffering "anesthesia." The "true nature" of beauty is not the effecting of just any synthesis but rather of one that gathers, as fully as the world engaged permits, the whole range of available external and internal feelings, organizing them by their images now creatively generalized into an appearance that retains those inherited values while augmenting them with the new value of the emergent synthesis.

Notice the cumulative effect of Neville's recurring phenomenological explorations of imagination. Imagination, as the process of gathering into a unity, provides a monadic immediacy that becomes dyadic when claimed to be about the world, triadic when that claim is set within a theory of reality, and quadratic when the image, self, and world are contextualized by the cultural milieu out of which they arise. Aesthetic appreciation is the precondition for assertions of fact, facts for the deployment of systems of warranted belief, and the envisionment of a common world for the constitution of societies of mutually responsible persons. Thinking as the gathering of beauty into truth into unity into responsible action—a gathering that creates these values and is judged by them—begins, develops, and culminates imaginatively. In order to agree with Neville that "thinking is founded in valuation" we must have firmly grasped all these layers of what he means.

By skimming along so close to the ground, however, leaping over considerations of interpretation, theory, and responsibility except as these form the sequential background to our focus on the phenomenology of imagination, we have missed important dimensions of Neville's discussion. We haven't followed his dialectic of pros and cons as he distinguishes his interpretation of imagination from Kant's. Nor have we attended to the conceptual distinctions Neville is always carefully making—for example, differentiating concrete appearance, image, schema, and normative measure. We've neglected the cosmology he deploys as a framework and foundation for his arguments, and we've ignored almost everything he has to say about culture, community, and responsibility. We've focused on none of these within the horizon circumscribed by our attending to imagination, much less focused on them as defining, each in their turn, the horizon for attention.

It would be interesting to suggest another approach, to move across the same terrain but this time at the highest rather than the lowest of the fourfold of levels, exploring what imagination reveals concerning responsibility. We would find ourselves focusing on religion and art, as dimensions of social existence in which imagination is most central. But that's something you can do on your own nickel. I've attempted to gather for you a few of the important elements in Neville's explorations concerning imagination. This has meant having to ignore most of his discussion and condense the rest far too radically. I've suggested that Neville's methodological framework is a good roadmap for finding your way around in the complexities of his thought, and that there is more than one route to take and more than one destination to have in mind. If something of Neville's enterprise has in this way become apparent, enough so for you to begin to appreciate the elegance and significance of what he has accomplished, I will be satisfied.

II

Interpret Neville as a Whiteheadian. Past actualities grasped selectively as the data for a newly emerging actuality, creatively integrated by means of formal patterns inherited and original, issuing in a determinate quantum of reality available to be grasped by successor emerging actualities—this is Whitehead's notion of concrescence and Neville has made it the central integrating image for his metaphysical system.

Neville's use of this image must be taken, however, in a manner appropriate to his understanding of what metaphysical systems are and how they function. The structure comprising the concrescence of any actual occasion, elaborated in considerable detail by Whitehead in *Process and Reality*, is not imported into Neville's work as a description of how the fundamental units of reality are actualized. Nor is concrescence a model in the usual sense of that term: a template for picking out features by which a number of different things can be compared or by reference to which they should be constructed, developed, and evaluated. Concrescence for Neville is a metaphysical image, an idea of the most basic and vague sort possible. The concrescence image, indeed, is Neville's primary metaphysical notion, a notion he also expresses in Platonic language as the Form of the Good. It's his "root metaphor": vague, general, summative. From it all his other ideas derive through various processes of selective specification.

Whitehead proposed the theory of concrescence as an analysis of what must go on if the cosmos is taken to be composed fundamentally of organically related events rather than enduring substances externally related in space and time. Whitehead's vocabulary is highly technical because he takes his account of the concrescence of an actual occasion to be a very precise presentation of a very complex idea. Neville rejects the adequacy of that account as a cosmological theory. But he retains concrescence as a metaphysical first principle, which on Peircean (and, indeed, Whiteheadian) grounds, requires it to be extremely vague. This liberation of concrescence from an inappropriate specificity then becomes a powerful tool in Neville's axiological metaphysics, guiding his development of a cosmological theory that can make sense of a theory of knowledge adequate to human experience and to the reality of things.

What Neville wants, and the image of concrescence provides, is a way to explicate our experience of the world as genuinely "of" it. He wants the world we think we know to actually be ingredient in our knowing, such that by appeal to it what we claim to be the case can be judged true or false. This means that what characterizes a thing in the world must be "carried over" into the character of our experience of it. The thing experienced and the subject experiencing it must be yoked together, else we are left with a content of experience that has no necessary connection to the world external to experience. For "the entire European tradition . . . the problem of truth seems to be a leap outside the mental sphere to compare representations with a measuring external reality. That leap plops into the abyss" [2-4-3-2: *RM* 287].

The only way to leap the abyss is to show there is none to leap. But the only way to remove the epistemological gap is to remove the ontological gap as well, to interpret the human knower's relation to the world as the same in key respects to the knowledge relation. Neville needs a theory of persons and a theory of the cosmos that are consonant with his theory of knowledge, theories in all three cases that are abyssless. The concrescence image meets these requirements, for the modalities of its specification yield under Neville's shaping hand a naturalistic theory of interpretation, a theory asserting that the process of knowing has a formal structure that also characterizes the emergence of "temporally thick" entities and the development in some of them of personal identity. Neville also argues that the transformations of space-time that comprise the adventures of such entities severally and of the cosmos holistically are structured in the same manner. From the whole cosmos to a flitting moment of triviality, from a metaphysical system to a flash of emotion, the structure of concrescence is refracted under varied contexts and specifications. As Neville would put it, it's concrescence all the way up and all the way down.

Neville's epistemological hypothesis is that "truth is the properly qualified carryover of value from the object of interpretation into the interpreting experience" [2-1-3-f: *RM* 54]. Carryover is dyadic: something in the object is relocated in the experience, making it the case, therefore, that the experience is true of, true to, the object. The assertion that there is this carryover is triadic, however. An aspect of any object is a sign standing for that object, and when in experience it is taken to be such, a truth relation is asserted. The interpreting experience is a "second sign" taken by the interpreter as exhibiting a correspondence between the "first sign," the aspect, and the object of which it is an aspect.

Remember that for Neville the object of any experience is a thing in the world resulting from a process of integration, the value of which is determined by the complexity of what is integrated and the simplicity of the resulting unity. Suppose that the aspect under which that objective thing is experienced as an element for a new process of integration is the form by which that prior integration was effected. The aspect would therefore replicate the thing's value; the aspect would be a form identical to the form of that of which it is an aspect. But the relation between the forms would not be one of original and copy. It would be a relation between the specific formal character of a thing and a potential for how another thing might be similarly characterized formally. The two forms would be, at a proper level of vagueness, the same reality: in one case made fully determinate within a particular synthesis, in the other case to some degree indeterminate but ingredient, now necessarily, as a conditional feature of whatever the new synthesis might be.

The value carried over into experience is never the twin of the value of the object, however, because the experience is always contextually conditioned. As human beings, we are biological creatures whose physical makeup sets limits to what and how we can experience things and organizes them in hierarchies of importance influencing our attention. We see with our eyes, but our eyes only detect objects that have features emitting or refracting energy within the visible light spectrum, and that detection can be inhibited or heightened by the extent of our health and alertness, the complexity of the information, and the like. We are also creatures of a culture that orients our expectations and channels our responses through beliefs and habits that filter what we think we are experiencing and how we characterize it. Our experience is further shaped by language, by the linguistic structure of thinking as such and by the peculiarities of whatever actual languages we inhabit. A fourth contextual condition is that of our own specific purposes: the intentional orientation we bring to every experience, the values we expect or are working to realize, both right now and over the longer run, values to which we are trying to be true and values we imagine are original or innovative.

These biological, cultural, semiotic, and purposive "vectors" [2-4-3-2: *RM* 285] are determinant influences on what we take as signs of objects and on which signs we take as signifying a specific object. Vectors are signs for objects and structures of objects that we must take account of in determining the signs that will, if taken as of the objects experienced, permit us to effect a cognitive or actional outcome of some sort. Some of these vectors are overweening determinants: our spatiotemporal location is a matrix of interdependencies we can alter only at the margin. Other vectors are easily trivialized and made all but irrelevant: we may be supremely indifferent to the influence of Mozart on our ways of appreciating intentionally ordered sound patterns. But the totality of the vectors qualifying our experience and the objects of our experience— and hence qualifying truth as the carryover of value into their relationship—is always significant, its influence preponderant.

Neville's hat trick, which fully justifies his claim that his theory of interpretation is "a serious innovation" [2-1-3-3: *RM* 65], is that although "we never get at reality except through interpretation," nonetheless this reality is "the measure of our interpretations" [2-4-4-4: *RM* 324]. An assertion of truth is a judgment, a claim that what is represented in experience truly depicts the real world in some fashion because the value of the representation preserves some aspect of the value of the world represented. We may gainsay that judgment, arguing that the value is not a carryover from the object it is claimed to represent or that the carryover and hence the representation are too partial to be conceptually or practically useful. Our gainsaying is also a judgment, of course: an interpretation concerning the adequacy of another interpretation. But we are not trapped into an infinite regress of interpretations, left wandering in an endless network of meanings where the meaning of anything can only be traced to other meanings. "Network meaning" is crucial to interpretation, to be sure, for it is the web of conditions—the context—that has shaped what we take to be signs of things and take as the signs by which we effect those takings. These internal relations among things, their coherence, is fundamental for Neville's axiology. "Content meaning" is just as crucial, however, and logically prior, because it is the meaning that network meanings condition. It may be true that "a content representation deficient in network meaning" would be "unclear, brute, not well-formed or thought out," but it is equally true that "a network representation" alone would be "formally efficient but empty, and therefore deceptive" [2-4-2-3: *RM* 273]. The correspondence of meaning to an objective content is what grounds the endless layerings of interpretation. The measure of truth rests ultimately with the value comprising the determinateness of objects and carrying over into our experience of them. The spider's web is tethered to the bush and thereby its network is pulled taut, forming a net in which the spider can catch its food. Without the tethering the net is no longer a net but only a worthless pile of thread.

Neville appeals to our "intuition" that the values appreciated in experience derive from the objects experienced and can be asserted truly to represent them. He also appeals to the "common sense" conviction of our ancestors that truth "had to do with being faithful to the realities about them" [2-f: RM 9]. But above all his appeal is to the adequacy of his theory of nature and his theory of personhood, since if their truth is rooted in the same metaphysical image that roots his theory of interpretation then their validation validates his epistemological claims as well. This may seem at first blush to be Neville capitulating to a coherence theory of truth, but as long as any turn to network meaning is balanced by an exploration of the correlative content meaning he remains true to his interpretation of how interpretations at any level work.

Consider Neville's ideas about what it is to be a person. Identity of any sort will need to satisfy two criteria: it will need to take account of the "conditional features" comprising the myriad ways in which a thing is qualified by its context and it will need to take account of the "essential features" comprising the ways by which the conditional features are worked together into a thing, a fully determinate specifically located harmony. Without conditional features a thing would be a self-contained contextless monad; without essential features, a thing would only be a convenient shorthand for its relationships. So for things to be different from each other and different from nothing at all, they must be at once relational and unique. And in this regard, all things are equal: "with respect to reality, all things have ontological parity" [2-2-1-4: RM 109].

Things are "discursive actualities" if their harmony of conditional and essential features becomes temporally thick, if the features integrated and the features of the integration are sustained through time. This occurs whenever the past features conditioning a thing include the features comprising its past identity and these latter features are taken not merely as conditional but also as essential. The present "reenacts" past achievement because "the structural potential generated by the past achievement" leaves little or no room for variation; the inherited potential for achievement delimits sharply the relevance of novel possibilities [2-3-2-3: RM 193]. A "discursive individual" or "person" has emerged when the enduring structure is sufficiently developed with respect to hierarchical complexity to provide a relatively stable context within which harmonies can be reenacted, when the values achieved by that structure appear as obligations that evoke commitment to their reenactment, and yet where the person's future appears as possibilities for realizing values not limited to those reiterative values. This permits two enlargements in identity: an account of self-identity involving changes in the person's past self-identity, and an identity that includes achievements beneficial to other individuals and actualities that share the person's past and present and may share its future or its successors' future. For its past and future to be essential in this sense, a person must be appropriating those conditions interpretively: in addition to the carryover of value being qualified by bodily and purposive factors, cultural and semiotic constraints emerge as also relevant. The resulting discursive actuality, the individual, is a "tighter" enduring harmony than the harmony that characterizes nonhuman actualities.

So the structure of personhood expresses the concrescence image at a less vague level, and insofar as what it articulates enlightens better than alternative theories our sense of how persons develop, sustain, and lose their self-identity, it confirms the adequacy of Neville's theory of interpretation. And vice versa. Similarly, my interpretation of Neville's theories of interpretation, person, and nature has sought to image in a few pages the complexity of over three hundred pages of argument set within the context of another six hundred pages of the *Axiology* trilogy and the thousands of pages of Neville's other philosophical writings. Insofar as I have been able to grasp his ideas in a way that other readers will think carries over his points into my way of presenting them, and insofar as I can shape my comments coherently in a sustained and maybe even persuasive argument, I will have accomplished two things: I will have provided a reasonable interpretation of Neville's theory of interpretation, and I will have shown it at work.

III

Theorize and we destroy, for we murder not only to dissect but also to unify. As Neville's theories of imagination, interpretation, and nature make clear, the process of gathering things together synthetically, the process of making meaningful assertions about the world, and the processes by which the things of the world emerge and endure, all involve, and necessarily, selection. Some of the old must be destroyed—eliminated, trivialized, distorted—in order that the new might be born. Theoreticians, especially revolutionary ones, should know what any good cook knows: the best casseroles blend their ingredients so that the particularities of each are sacrificed to a more savory emergent totality.

Neville can theorize with the best of them, of course. If he's anything he's a philiotheorist: a systematizer, a categorizer, a distinction maker. That's what philosophers do and Neville is, prolifically, a philosopher: for him, it's theory all the way down. Take, for instance, his theory of time [2-3: RM 169–85]. For each of the three modalities of time Neville makes a distinction between its "timeliness" or essential features and its "temporality" or conditional features. The temporality of the present involves its relation to past potentialities and future possibilities as conditions for present determination. Past and future are similarly conditioned each by the other two modalities, and then time, understood as the unity of past, present, and future, has its own timeliness and temporality, providing for the togetherness of the modes and disclosing the nontemporal creative act that grounds time in its modal complexity.

Neville's "doctrine"—as we philosophers are wont to term any such complex categoreal assertion—is deployed with serious intent. His theory of time is no tour de force; it's not a labyrinth he's deployed to test the intellectual acumen of his readers. Neville needs all these distinctions, these wheels within wheels, in order to escape from the problematic consequences Whitehead drew from the theory of concrescence. Whitehead was so focused on making sense of how momentary actualities emerge that he couldn't make convincing sense of enduring actualities. Neville uses vague metaphysical categories concerning identity, being, value, and harmony to braid temporal connections thick enough to support temporally thick things. His discursive actualities are very similar to Whitehead's enduring objects, but with one difference. An enduring object is a society, an abstract structure of common features shared by certain actual entities, whereas a discursive actuality is a primary structure accumulating across synthetic accomplishments. But this one difference makes all the difference. Neville's fugue on the categoreal complexities of time makes it possible for us to interpret reiteration of form not as a merely derivative notion but as an essential feature of actual things.

Despite this strong sense of theory and its importance, however, Neville is vividly aware of the limitations of theory. He's very much a fallibilist regarding his own work. His axiological theories are identified as "hypotheses" and he insists that his ideas, that anyone's ideas, be "vulnerable to correction" [3-4-4: NC 101]. This is in part a judgment on the limited capacities of the human intellect and in part an appreciation that the world is incredibly varied, that there are more things in heaven and earth than can possibly be contained in our philosophies. Moreover, Neville is unusually well versed, for a modern Western metaphysician, in the beliefs and practices of other cultures, especially Chinese culture. This has made him quite sensitive to the complaint that the bearers of Western culture are prone to imposing preconceived structures on whatever they encounter, that Western theorizers are as imperialistic as their political and economic counterparts. Neville is no metaphysical Napoleon or Genghis Khan. His primary motive for attempting an axiological interpretation of things is to counter the modern Western interpretation, which he thinks inadequate for many reasons, including its imperious tendencies toward epistemological certainty and ontological absolutism. He wants us to heed other traditions than our own, to give Neo-Confucianism the same respect we accord Platonism or Aristotelianism. Nor will he rest with this as merely a personal exhortation. Neville wants a theory concerning theorizing that will justify the skepticism he advocates toward theories, yet without denigrating their importance.

In the first two parts of *Axiology of Thinking*, Neville's celebration of value-creation is wrapped in the recognition that achievements of beauty, truth, unity, and sociality are hard to come by, difficult to sustain, and doomed eventually to perish. Since without synthesis there can be no value, Neville emphasizes harmony: the determinate results of imagining and interpreting, of making a work of art, a religious practice, a descriptive assertion, a personal character. In the third part of his trilogy, however, Neville inverts the emphasis, playing down the synthetic "importances" and underscoring the "singular value" of the particulars to be synthesized. Unities are characterized as "tragic" and particulars are said to deserve our "pious deference."

This inversion seems unjustified. Because every thing is a harmony of essential and conditional features, it is arbitrary to defer piously to one such harmony rather than to the component particulars from which it is synthesized or to the wider harmony of which it is a synthesized component. Neville responds by distinguishing "singularity" from other kinds of unity. A singular thing, like any thing, is "unique" in that it is a determinate harmonization of the "congeries of roles or natures" that define it [3-1-1: NC 21], a finite value to be treasured as such and for its relevance to other finite values. But a singular thing is also "absolutely particular," possessed of a "thisness" or "haecceity" that can in no way be reduced to its roles and natures, to its conditional features, or to the unity effected by its essential features. There is "an ontological infinity of value in each thing" [3-4-1: NC 89], Neville argues, that roots in the "ontological togetherness" things have in addition to the togetherness forged through their mutual relationships. Because things can be truly different only if they are not exhaustively definable in terms of their relation to the things from which they are different, there must be a ground, an "ontological context of mutual relevance" [2-2-2-1: RM 112] that provides the necessary context for their togetherness. This particular and that particular share a common ground that unites them over against sheer non-

Being, contrasts them as a plurality of distinct things that are together existing rather than not existing. Each particular thus has as one of its values the "value of being in the ontological context of all the other things" [3-4-1: NC 89]. That context or ground is infinite. Neville's hypothesis is that it is God, Being, Brahman, the Dao that cannot be named: "the singular creative act the end-products of which are the various determinate beings with their cosmological connections ontologically together in the act itself" [3-4-1: NC 89].

Hence each thing has infinite value because it is together ontologically with other things as the expression of an infinitely creative act. And so, metaphysically, each finite creation has infinite value not because the harmony it fashions is infinite but because the particular things it harmonizes have infinite ontological value, to which its finite unification is an added value. Furthermore, the formal components by which any harmony is effected are infinite in number and each is analyzable into an infinity of subelements, so from a cosmological perspective as well, the unity achieves an infinite value. To these "infinitely dense" particulars we must therefore defer when theorizing about them or in any other manner attempting to incorporate them within some synoptic accomplishment.

I'm not so sure that Neville has resolved the seeming arbitrariness of deferring to some things rather than others. But he's at least turned it into an insightful paradox. Each thing has infinite intrinsic worth, which we must honor and protect at all costs from the selective hegemonic drive of the synthesis into which that thing is in danger of being swallowed. But this synthesis is itself a thing of infinite intrinsic worth that we are to honor and protect. The fish swallowing the smaller one and being swallowed by the bigger one is both victimizer and victimized: a destroyer of infinite value for the sake of creating infinite value, which value is in turn destroyed by the emerging of other infinite value. Krishna, come as Destroyer of the nations and as their Creator. A tragic vision, yes:

> Actualization itself is invariably tragic with regard to those diminished or excluded by actual achievements and all history is tragic from the standpoint of those might-have-beens. The tragedy in theorizing is a species of the tragedy of actualization. [3-3-1: NC 60]

But a vision that grasps tragedy as a necessary condition of creation. Loss of value, including loss of infinite value, is what makes addition of value, including additional infinite value, possible.

The challenge for theorizing, and similarly for all other creative acts, is how to preserve this paradoxical double vision. The individual is to be respected as a value beyond price, an infinite good to which we are to defer unconditionally. Yet the individual must be slighted, its achievement modified, its truth destroyed, for other individuals to arise who also deserve our deference. Neville can sound at times as though neither theories nor social institutions express singular value, that they have importance but not infinite density. He seems to want our theories properly subordinated to the flesh-and-blood persons and the real concrete objects about which they theorize. But that's an anti-intellectualism as wrongheaded as the overintellectualism that willingly sacrifices persons and particular things to an idea, institution, ideology, or mystic vision. Neville's notion of pious deference does not justify anarchy. The theory that must defer to the individuals about which it theorizes is also in its own right a thing that deserves our deference.

Neville eases the tension in this paradox by proposing three ways to engage in theory-making while fully respecting the particular values of things. The first is to be sure to represent in the theory the values each thing has in its "site": the importances it has determined within its unique harmonized actuality. The synoptic field deployed by a theory should contain a "field of sites." It should be "capable of representing the various sites of importance of the things in its subject matter." This means that each particular should be represented on its own terms, not merely as an instance of some category predefined by the theory. Particulars should be represented within a field that allows them in the full plenitude of their singularity to be compared with each other [3-2-4: *NC* 55]. An anthropologist would call a well-sited synoptic field an empathetic description, an account of a thing—for example, a culture—from within the point of view of its members, in terms of their own values and meanings. But the appropriation from the inside is in terms of values of importance, which are values capable of generalization, of expression at various degrees of vagueness, and so permit comparison with other cultural sitings. The inclusion of the sites in the theory restrains the imperialistic tendency of the theory to reduce the data, to force the facts into the categoreal schema of its hypothesis. But siting the sites within the synoptic field legitimates the aim of the theory at synoptic reduction.

The problem is how to pull this off. Neville's second suggestion is that neither the individual sites nor the theoretical categories should be privileged with respect to the other, and that the making of a theory should be understood "dialogically." The theory should always be open to criticisms originating at the sites of importance: complaints that a sited value is not being acknowledged adequately or that a category obscures or overemphasizes a form of integration. The various sites should similarly be open to being compared and to acknowledging the legitimacy of generalizations that translate their concrete beliefs, practices, and ideals into a vaguer but more inclusive language. Neville points out that one of the important implications of his hypothesis that categories of under-standing can be arrayed in nested hierarchies running from extremely vague metaphysical ideas to minimally vague local-site expressions is that it permits inclusion without distortion. The including category is the vague one, translating into the same formal concept a number of incom-mensurable and less vague concepts. The concretely unique values of dif-ferent sites are not denigrated by being reexpressed at another level as identical, because the unifying level is more vague than the differentiat-ing level and so "tolerates" various and not necessarily compatible "expressions" [3-3-1: NC 63]. Two worlds can become one without loss of their differences if translation, in both its generalizing and instantiat-ing directions, is understood in this nonreductive manner.

Neville's third way to protect the value of the individual sites within a synoptic field is to give metaphors the same standing as abstract con-cepts. Metaphors can do what concepts cannot: they are able to express the value of singulars and the reality of the unconditioned ground of the togetherness of such values. So metaphors bring into the synoptic field the infinite values that values of importance cannot capture. They do this by showing instead of saying, by presenting what escapes conceptu-alization because it is not a function of the formal patterns of concep-tual integration. Metaphors like concepts can be translated into gener-alizing categories, those categories expressed metaphorically rather than by concepts. But Neville recommends the use of "metaphoric overlay": the "piling on of tropes" that "set up resonances and contrasts that together say more than could be said by any one or a disjunctive set of them taken serially" [3-4-1: NC 85].

So as Whitehead famously remarked,

> Philosophy is akin to poetry, and both of them seek to express that ultimate good sense which we term civilization. In each case there is reference to form beyond the direct meanings of words. Poetry allies itself to metre, philosophy to mathematic pattern.[4]

Neville neglects this obvious reference, probably as part of his campaign to distance himself from Whitehead, although like the monkey trying to flee Krishna the distancing simply isn't possible. What is possible, and should be actualized, is for philosophers to take poetic expression as a legitimate form for asserting truths about the world. But is it possible to subject judgments of truth in metered form to the same kind of rigorous critique and dialogical development accorded judgments utilizing math-ematic logical pattern? Neville's answer is yes, although in this trilogy he only hints at how such an undertaking might be accomplished.

So the value of individuals in their haecceity can be protected against theory. Neville is equally solicitous of theory, however, as the protector of individuals and their singular value. "Without theorizing, deference is at the whim of chance metaphor" [3-4-4: *NC* 106]. Theory, like the conditional features of any determinate thing, is what makes temporally thick meanings possible and so locates us in a world of enduring values without which our singular value would be a value without purpose, without wider resonance. But enduring values are finite. They are crucial to the infinite values of the haecceities but they are fragile achievements, difficult to sustain, and all too easily perishing. Theories are as precious as individuals, even though for different reasons and in different ways.

Neville beautifully expresses this poignant judgment about the value of theory in his recurrent metaphor of a "maelstrom." For instance, after analyzing the cosmological features that provide the causal underpinnings to the permanences we experience—"inertial force, regularities, and systems"—and after criticizing Whitehead for giving these "tendency"-making features short shrift, Neville notes nonetheless that

> the mixtures of our lives are between order and chaos, and in those moments when the shades of illusion are rolled away, we alternatively struggle to cope and to relax into the maelstrom of causes. Finding the Tao, the true cause of mixture, is not attaching to a super-order, as some have thought, but is finding a center to orient the haecceities of life in that maelstrom. [2-3-4-2: *RM* 230]

Synoptic vision, including the theories by which it comes to be specified, is not our access to realities that lie beyond the flux of things, offering us dry land safe from the roiling sea. Nonreductive theories are boats with rudders and sails fashioned in the midst of the maelstrom in order to save ourselves from drowning. They orient us, allowing us to imagine enduring worthwhile purposes and to pursue them responsibly. For the nonce.

IV

Be responsible. Act not just for your own good but for the common good, in response to the needs of others: your family and friends, your community, humanity in general, all living things, the cosmos itself. This is a familiar ethical admonition, but Neville has inverted its usual presuppositions. Social contract theories presume that in a state of nature persons seek only their own good, and that the difficulties of doing so lead them to trade some of their freedom to define and pursue their own ends for the security of membership in a group. Societal obligations are historically emergent, an improvement on the state of nature created by acts of will and sustainable only insofar as the members of the group continue to reaffirm their original commitment to one another. Neville turns this relation on its head, arguing that in a state of nature everyone is already interrelated and responsible for all the mutual obligations thereby entailed. Everything that should be done to preserve and enhance the common good is everyone's responsibility to carry out. What is historically emergent is a condition in which particular persons in particular contexts have no social obligations, where it is morally acceptable for them to attend to their own interests and ignore the common good.

Neville's idea is bold, but there's nothing arbitrary about it. His views are not merely idiosyncratic notions with which to tweak the establishment. They are deeply rooted in his metaphysics, some of the most important consequences of the axiological hypothesis. They are a key salient in his revolution.

The basic thesis of Neville's axiology is that to be a thing is to be a determinate synthesis of conditional and essential features, a harmony. But the harmonies achieved vary in the complexity of their conditional and essential components, the extent to which their initial values are carried over into the harmony, and the intensity with which they are integrated. Therefore values lie on a continuum from most trivial to most important. Hence for any given situation with its context of conditions and possibilities, there is always some maximal value that could be realized in the emergent determinate harmony. For any determination of a given situation, the synthesis actually achieved is simultaneously contrasted with the best harmony possible for it. This best harmony, like any harmony, is finite, however. Every synthesis is constrained by the limitations inherent in what it is initially given and by the possible ways what is given might be brought together. These finite maximal possible harmonies are what Neville calls "normative measures," and they are all over the place. Every achievement, no matter how trivial or important, is measured by the ideal of what could have been achieved. The measures are necessarily relative to the given context, but for each context there is necessarily such a measure.

Values and their normative measures are categoreally organized in accord with the fourfold structure of experience. Imaginative syntheses are judged with respect to beauty; interpretive syntheses, with respect to truth; theories, by the synoptic unity they achieve; societies, by their goodness [F-1-3: *RT* 17–29]. A human community, for example, whether the family or the nation-state, whether a narrow-focused voluntary organization or a whole civilization, is a determinate being marked at any moment of its existence as a discursive entity by some achieved enduring harmony. Consequently it has some value not reducible to the value of the persons and creatures and other things comprising it. This unique communal value is a value having to do with goodness, one which is more or less trivial, more or less important, positive or negative, with respect to the ideal goodness for that society on that occasion, which ideal objectively measures the actual goodness the society has achieved.

Now add another of Neville's basic assumptions: that it is good to seek the better harmony, and better to seek the best harmony available. It follows that norms not only measure our achievements but also have the authority to command them. The realization in each situation of its ideal harmony is an obligation for whatever entities in that situation have the opportunity and capacity to make a difference in what is achieved. Whatever contributes conditional or essential features it could have contributed differently has the responsibility to contribute those most conducive to the best possible outcome. Hence the members of any human community are responsible for meeting the obligations defined by the ideal value normative for that community in that situation. And since people are members of various human and nonhuman communities simultaneously, they live in a complex network of obligations for which they are responsible.

The normative measure of an action is vaguer than the action itself. It describes a possibility for realization, but possibilities are necessarily vague and so can be realized in more than one way. The freedom of persons, a prerequisite for moral obligation, not only involves affirming a possibility as normative, as commanding a proper response, but also means inventing a determination of that possibility: imagining a resolving synthesis, judging whether it might be effective, ascertaining its appropriateness to the wider contexts in which it will likely be embedded, and fashioning with these tools a determinating course of action. As the obligation to act becomes more general, abstracting from the peculiarities of place, time, and intent, the person able to respond to the obligation is no longer predetermined, and the creativity required to actualize a relevantly determinate response becomes more difficult. The responsibility for keeping the promise I just made to give you the object in my hand is clearly mine to fulfill and the ways for doing so clearly delimited. But the responsibility for keeping the current generation's implicit promise to its elders that it will pass on the ancestral values to the rising generation is vague regarding who should do what for whom, and when and where, and in what way.

The vaguer obligations are more encompassing and therefore include the more important obligations, those that if not fulfilled threaten the communal fabric. But their vagueness means that the persons who must act are intersubstitutable. Everyone is obliged but anyone can be the agent for the others in actually performing the needed action. In some cases "anyone" means whoever is at hand, whoever is well positioned to do what is required. In other cases, the "anyone" has been specified as anyone assigned by the community the particular role of being the one to do such things. Only someone who is a lifeguard is the one designated to take responsibility for the safety of the swimmers, although in an emergency anyone able to rescue the drowning person should do so. Only citizens can vote in elections, and for that role there are no substitutes; but only the officials thereby elected may then vote in the legislature, and they are obliged to do so. The more complex the community, the more likely its collective obligations are sorted out into roles, formal and informal, by which some persons take responsibility, freeing the others to focus their energies on the fulfillment of other obligations. This division of labor is efficient, opening up possibilities for realization not otherwise possible or even conceivable, which if actualized improve often dramatically the quality of persons' lives, but if not actualized increase the disparity between is and ought. The pathos of life is that often we attain to the realization of ideals in situations that are trivial, painful, or widely destructive. The tragedy of life is that just as often we fall far short of ideals, even betraying them purposefully, in situations that are important and that if properly realized could have enhanced individual and community harmonies.

An obvious question is whether there are normative measures broad and deep enough to describe the obligations incumbent on us as human beings. Such norms would be extremely vague, to be sure, but they would have to do with the most general communities to which we belong: the community of entities with its ground in Being, the community of Earth's beings as grounded by the ecosphere, the community of culture-bearing beings with its regulative ideal of a Kingdom of God, Realm of Ends, or Classless Society. Neville has warned us against overdetermining such visions, however, and has recommended piling up cultural metaphors and myths rather than devising universal principles. We are to stop with the comparison of alternative models and historical achievements rather than attempting to meld them into one grand holistic social theory. Hence "normative cultures" rather than "natural law" is the arena within which to critique the shortcomings and potentialities of Western civilization and to propose what should be done that we might be saved.

Neville offers some general norms, or "meta-obligations": the obligation all of us have to do whatever we can to foster the development of societal conditions that increase the possibilities for value, including the nurture of a public discourse that contains "ways of representing what is important to all those involved" [4-4-1: NC 200], since what cannot be imagined and publicly expressed cannot become an object of aspiration relevant to societal purposes. And we have a similar obligation with respect to the possibilities for realizing these possibilities: enhance the ends, enhance the means.

One of the more distinctive features of Neville's discussion is his emphasis on social rituals. The comparison of cultures, of the lives of peoples participant in traditions other than that of Western civilization, yields features crucial to the survival and enhancement of those cultures that are neglected, to its detriment, by the West. One of these is the role played by explicit rules of interaction in shaping the ways by which people understand themselves, others, and their mutual responsibilities. Neville discusses the Confucian emphasis on ritual, its place in traditional Chinese culture, noting the benefit to society of well-established forms for interactions from the most trivial to the most significant. Where the ritual forms at each level resonate with those at the other levels, where they are "hierarchically dense," young people develop an appreciation for their culture and a commitment to its ideals that then gives a deep sense of purpose to their adult lives, a sense that they have a proper destiny that is being fulfilled in the roles they play within their family, among friends, in their jobs, and as citizens. "Rituals of a highly civilized level," because they nurture "elementary human endowments to harmonious fulfillment," "function as a platform from which the other activities of civilized life are possible" [4-3-1: NC 175, 177].

Not that Neville advocates substituting ancient Confucian practices for our contemporary Western practices. The problems with which we struggle cannot be resolved by aping others, as though alien gods or imported mercenaries could do our work for us. But our problems cannot be solved merely by applying the same old familiar methods with renewed resolve. Nor is the solution simply to fantasize a new metaphysical possibility for breaking us free from the problem-inducing mechanistic presuppositions in our Western intellectual heritage. Encountering the Other, honoring the Ancestors, and dreaming of Utopia all have their place, but none are sufficient or even essential to meet the challenge confronting us. So what is? The purpose in undertaking a comparison of normative cultures is to find differences in cultural practices, in the concrete rituals of human interactions in societal contexts. When these are translated into categories of appropriate vagueness they reveal homologies that critique and enlighten our concrete beliefs and practices by expressing alternative enhancing possibilities. So, says Neville, we need responsible people who take their responsibility to be more than "virtuous habit," more than fulfilling the specific expectations instantiated in the accustomed cultural practices. Our practices themselves must change, and this means changing the concrete ways in which we express our identity, locate our significance, and take up our responsibilities. We need new rituals for the new world in which increasingly we find ourselves. "We need rituals for public life in a pluralistic society. . . . We need rituals for family structures shaped by a highly mobile, meritocratic society. . . . We need rituals for friendship in an age of vastly increased mobility and communication across long distances" [4-3-1: *NC* 180].

But new rituals cannot be made *ex nihilo*; they are always made from the old by transforming it. We need people able to move up the hierarchy of increasingly vague forms for action and thought until they feel the bite of formerly unappreciated meta-obligations and the lure of previously unknown synoptic visions. We need people with imaginations sufficiently fertile and critical judgments sufficiently acute to carry over the value inherent in those uncovered vague obligations and visions into freshly made new harmonies, moving back down the hierarchy of increasingly more concrete forms for action and thought. We need rituals that attune us, as our current rituals do not, to the normative ideals undergirding our culture, ideals that we have betrayed but that when re-invoked can find creative expression in theories, beliefs, commitments, and institutions that enable concrete practices that can realize values wider, deeper, and more enduring than our present ones. In this sense, Neville correctly insists that "the invention and inculcation of good rituals is one of the most important normative tasks of any culture, and one of the most revolutionary" [4-3-2: *NC* 185].

We have an obligation to do whatever we can to save our culture from its growing aimlessness and sin. One of the many ways to accept this responsibility is to study seriously books that thrust us onto the barricades, critiquing our familiar world and proposing a new world we are asked to help actualize. Neville offers us such a revolutionary possibility in his *Axiology of Thinking*, in a manner that goes far beyond the merely programmatic calls of many another self-styled metaphysical revolutionary. But like any genuine revolution, the one to which he calls us is not really the invention of a brave new world but the redemption of our old one, a "recovery" of its unrealized ideals and their creative "reconstruction."

That the new is the old redeemed, Neville acknowledges. At the very end of his books, he identifies his radical transvaluation of modern values as an affirmation of "a major and lasting contribution of the Enlightenment": that we must, each of us, take responsibility for our actions, for the worlds we make, and that we must, each of us, take responsibility for our place, our "homes," for the natural and social environments in which willy-nilly we are supported and constrained in what we make and how we make it.

The quality of our homes reflects the trust we have from the history of the cosmos as well as from our forebears. The quality of our homes in this large sense is also our legacy to the future. So we should attend to the consequences of nature, of our institutions, and of our actions. Without exaggerating the extent of our potential influence, without minimizing the blind trajectories of cosmic forces, without overestimating our capacities to discern what is good and bad; our highest activities our excellences, our greatest joys, consist in taking responsibility for consequences [4-4-4: NC 221].

Nor is Neville's "we" royal or rhetorical. The we is you and I, philosophers and religionists, friends and family, clans and nations, brothers and sisters of this Earth and cosmos. We must take responsibility for the obligations that measure our shared reality. And reading thoughtfully *Axiology of Thinking* is not unimportant among the ways of that taking.

NOTES

1. Robert Cummings Neville, *Axiology of Thinking* (Albany: State University of New York Press). In three volumes: *The Reconstruction of Thinking*, 1981, hereafter, *RT*; *Recovery of the Measure: Interpretation and Nature*, 1989, hereafter, *RM*; and *Normative Cultures*, 1995, hereafter *NC*.

2. Citations will be to the parts, but in defiance of Neville's misleading and often inconsistent numbering system they will be identified as follows: part F for his part 1 (Foundations) and part 1 for his part 2 (Imagination), comprising *The Reconstruction of Thinking*; part 2 for his part 3 (Interpretation), comprising *Recovery of the Measure*; part 3 for his part 4 (Theory) and part 4 for his part 5 (Responsibility), comprising *Normative Cultures*. These designations will be followed by numbers for the subdivisions of each part, starting over with each shift in level, whereas Neville numbers the chapters in a volume consecutively, doesn't number the subsections of chapters in *The Reconstruction of Thinking*, and adds an additional level (Divisions) in *Recovery of the Measure*. Any introductory material to a chapter or section I will identify by an "f," and I will follow these numbers by an indication of volume and page. For example, "1-1-1: *RT* 139" refers to a citation found in the first section of the first chapter of the first postintroductory part, page 139 in *The Reconstruction of Thinking*—even though in Neville's numbering this is part 2 (Imagination), chapter 5 (Imagination as Synthesis: Religion), and the unnumbered opening section of that chapter (Phenomenology of Synthesis).

3. Neville gives us permission to read him in this way: "If one squints so as to blur the details, one can observe that in each part, the first chapter focuses mainly on the imaginative aspect of the topic. . . . Still squinting, one can observe that in each chapter the first section is an imaginative phenomenology. . . . The generally interested reader can read only the first section in each chapter and still derive a coherent account both of the book's presentation of the problems of

reconstructing thinking and of its positive suggestions." But Neville reminds his readers that the trilogy is written to be read, preferably, in "rhythmic" fashion, moving away from phenomenology to other topics and then returning, moving away again, returning again: "reconsidering issues and proposals from different angles and with increasing complexity." [F-1-4: *RT* 30].

4. Alfred North Whitehead, *Modes of Thought* (New York: The Free Press, 1968 [1938]), p. 174.

CHAPTER 2

Re-reading Neville:
A Postmodern Perspective

Edith Wyschogrod

It is now not as easy as it had been for hard-nosed analytic philosophers to dismiss alternative views, those of Americanists, certain comparativists and feminists, as well as process and continental philosophers—postmoderns figure among them—with the apothegm: "This is not philosophy." No longer marginalized, these philosophers are gaining attention, in no small measure because of the intellectual rigor and imagination with which they recontextualize ontological and epistemic questions. It was therefore with some surprise that I learned from Neville's *Highroad around Modernism*[1] that philosophers who thought of themselves as postmodern dwelt in the same philosophical nether world as analytic types, not through some taxonomical quirk but rather because Neville sees philosophical analysis and postmodernism as versions of program philosophy, philosophy that does not allow the results of investigations in one or several of its areas to modify its original suppositions, that delegitimates and ignores rather than refutes its competitors. The problem with some program philosophies, phenomenology, for example, is their foundationalism; the problem with all program philosophies is their intolerance and tolerance is for Neville a fundamental virtue. Epistemic intransigence is, he thinks, also a primary defect of modernism, defined as "the family of cultural responses to the panic of Europeans about the collapse of their religion and values in the face of modern science" (*HM* 171).

Intolerance is what links various modes of high modernism, from Kantian philosophy to certain fixed construals of religion, to more recent versions of program philosophy such as deconstruction. Analytic philosophy becomes programmatic in Neville's sense when it dissolves into its subsets, for example, cognitive science and ethical case studies, thereby losing sight of its presuppositions, whereas deconstructionists do so by floating in gnostic isolation above circumscribed regional embodiments. Neither conduces to conversation. The best hope for philosophy is an ongoing reworking of process thought (Whitehead and his heirs) and American philosophy (especially Peirce, but also Dewey) that can bypass modernism and its legacy to philosophy and Western religion.

I should like however to show that Neville and I (something of a postmod) can, in fact, be philosophical friends. In spite of significant differences, such friendship would not be a *mésalliance* but an important step forward for thinking. To be sure, postmoderns do not define themselves since to do so is to return to a philosophy of essences. Yet certain lineaments of postmodern thinking are not difficult to discern: the delegitimation of modernity's master narratives, especially Enlightenment accounts of knowledge whether speculative or empirical; the notion that the diffraction of time is obscured in acts that attempt to render what is absent as present and the related claim that truth cannot be said to result from acts of re-presentation; attentiveness to the question of alterity, especially to the otherness of gender, and non-Western cultures and peoples. In addition, it is argued by many postmoderns that contemporary existence is posthistorical and is characterized by media-created images that blur the boundary between the real and what putatively represents it, a feature described in Jean Baudrillard's famous quip that the map precedes the territory.

Like the features of a long-lost cousin in whom one discovers unsuspected resemblances, Neville may be closer to postmodern responses to modernity's account of knowledge and being than he suspects. In both his *Highroad around Modernism* and *Normative Cultures*,[2] Neville's critique of postmodernism prevents him from perceiving these affinities on several grounds: First, Neville's view of what philosophy is deters him from appreciating Heidegger's account of being and truth, one that provides an indispensable entryway into postmodern thinking as well as the strengths of Heidegger's reading of the Western philosophical tradition, crucial for most postmoderns. Second, by identifying postmodernism largely with deconstruction, he fails to appreciate the range of postmodern thinking while at the same time neglecting some subtleties of deconstruction that might, in the light of his account of broken symbols, render him more sympathetic to it. Finally, systems philosophy, the amalgam of semiotic and process thought that Neville endorses, is closer to some versions of postmodernism, especially that of Gilles Deleuze whose historical forebears include Spinoza and Bergson, than may be immediately apparent. If these affinities are borne out, there may be grounds after all for rapprochement.

NEVILLE, HEIDEGGER, AND THE RIGOR OF THOUGHT

It is likely that Neville would find congenial Heidegger's claim that we do not yet know what being educated or uneducated in thinking means. In endorsing Aristotle's assertion: "'For it is uneducated not to have an eye for when it is necessary to look for a proof and when this is not necessary',"[3] Heidegger, like Neville, points to the confusion between philosophical thought and scientific thinking in which proofs are needed. To be sure, Heidegger sometimes refers to thinking as questioning back (*Rückfragen*), whereas Neville's account of thinking is forward-looking and is committed to the corrigibility of conceptual structures when new phenomenological evidence appears. Yet, like Neville, the early Heidegger does not eschew rigor. Reflecting the influence of Husserlian phenomenology in which the concept of *Philosophie als strenge Wissenschaft* is presupposed, Heidegger of the Marburg lectures of 1927 speaks of philosophy as the *science* of being. "For the future we shall mean by 'philosophy' scientific philosophy and nothing else," he avers.[4] Philosophy thus defined is distinguished from the nonphilosophical positive sciences, each of which carves out its own niche, its specific domain of research: that of mathematics, physics, biology, history, and the like. Philosophy's task is not to relate to the beings in these specific realms but rather to focus upon something like the question of Being in general.

Still, it is not enough simply to discern that both Heidegger and Neville posit a difference between thinking and scientific inquiry without considering their interpretations of this difference. In fact, Neville's account of thinking as theorizing seems far removed from Heidegger's recasting of philosophy as fundamental ontology in *Being and Time* (1927) and other works of that period. Does not Neville's identification of thinking and theory already presuppose a view of being that derives from the outlook of the positive sciences? But even if thinking is linked to theorizing, it is clear that Neville means nothing like systematic thinking in a formal or deductive sense. To be sure, theorizing aims at a "synoptic vision of some subject matter" (*NC* 3). But, like Heidegger, Neville peels away accretions of meaning that attach to the term *theory* to show that the Greek term from which it derives means seeing from a vantage point, a claim that does not necessarily entail seeing everything at once. Instead, what is perceived are the connections, the ligatures of things. Synoptic vision is a gathering of constructs that orient people to things and projects.

Postmoderns might find persuasive Neville's powerful critique of an all-embracing methodological positivism, one that attempts to foist upon theory *qua* theory what holds only for certain types of theory: reductive theories, those that can be either true or false in the sense that their subject matters are as stipulated by the theory's formal terms; and instrumental theories, which are true when their formal terms fulfill a stated purpose. Both types are useful in specific contexts, "filter out" what they are not designed to interpret and must be distinguished from what Neville calls "a theory of theories" (NC 18–21).

INTERPRETATION AND THE
LOWROAD OF POSTMODERNISM

The expression "theory of theories" is redolent of the all-encompassing views of being and thought embodied in Spinoza and Hegel, what Heidegger and some postmoderns excoriate as ontotheology. But theories that are totalizing systems and that imply closure without the possibility of emendation do not exemplify Neville's view of systematicity. For him, phenomenological evidence may pull a theory up short and force corrections. But does this latter approach not borrow its mode of validation from the positive sciences? Is Neville not trapped between the Scylla of theory embodied in rational deductive systems and the Charybdis of a narrow positivism? Neville's escape route, what is striking and innovative in his account, is the mechanism by means of which conceptual change occurs. It is not the mere appearance of new raw data that necessitates either the stretching or the scotching of a theory, but rather the entry of both metaphor and acts of valuing into theory formation. "Value-blindness is a significant deficiency in a theory and reflects the way in which values might be missed or differ from those it registers" (NC 44). Thus a theory of theories is not governed by the necessity predicated of causal relations in many scientific theories, but with Dewey, Neville might say, "Necessary means needed; contingency means no longer required—because already enjoyed."[5] Heidegger, allergic to axiological thinking, sees valuing acts as bound up with the exercise of will and with the philosophy of the subject, a modernist legacy he repudiates. While rejecting the term, he insists that language points to what we prize or hold dear. Neville believes that we arrive at what is prized through interpretive acts: "Metaphor has the special advantage of highlighting the fact that things have singular values by always taking their rise from an act of interpretation" (NC 102). Thus metaphor, "a trope that represents indirectly" (NC 90) assures the sinuosity of theories through its power to alter value and also, conversely, through value's seeking out, as it were, ever more forceful linguistic embodiment.

Heidegger thinks interpretation must not be confused with predication or production in the technological sense, but rather is bound up with an act of unveiling "as letting that which is talked about in an assertion be seen."[6] For Neville, the meaning of a phenomenon cannot be interpreted exhaustively in any theory because certain types of value are lost in theories. The "infinite and unique worth of each thing," what Neville calls "singular value," is understood as an "infinite density of value [that] by virtue of its infinity can never be represented in a theory" (*NC* 45). If singular things resist conceptual formulation and, what is more, their components can be broken down into an infinite number of subcomponents, the singular thing for Neville is what it is by virtue of simple accretion, the adding on of properties. Should there not be instead a radical shift in each property as its relations change so that, in the end, there are no fixed properties but only relations? For Heidegger, truth comes to pass between Dasein and the world with which it transacts, thus dispensing with both modernity's subject/object distinction and with an ontological atomism of properties.

Before the Heidegger connection is too thinly stretched, recall that, for Neville, interpretation is the application of a sign to an intentional referent so that interpretation relies upon a semiotic code. Yet Neville does not forget that metaphors are related to signs by existential acts of interpretation that determine value or importance. This two-sidedness imposes upon Neville and many postmoderns an antinomy of Nietzsche's thought. On the one hand, Nietzsche holds a perspectivalism that identifies thought not as a quest for truth but as a conferring of value and, on the other, identifies interpretation with the genealogical analyses of linguistic science.[7]

This doubleness is manifested in Neville's retention of systematicity that, even after the age of the great systems builders, remains one of philosophy's crucial characteristics. The notion of system, no less than that of theory, would seem to match the profile of technological/scientific thinking that Heidegger designates as calculative, for example, a system of logic that can be defined in terms of axioms and/or rules of inference that govern truth functional operators and quantifiers and against which the validity or invalidity of arguments can be measured. Such a system is deductive, deployed in the interest of making valid inferences. Yet, even at his most "objective," Neville interprets systematicity broadly as a network of meanings that are imbricated in one another. Thus, for Neville, systems are open and, in the case of cultures, include not only the social, economic, and political behaviors of peoples but also their motives and intentions.[8] System does not signify a single formal structure but rather is an "investigation of the subject from every angle imaginable" (*NC* 21).

Unlike Hegel's system which unfolds rationally, its parts deducible from the vantage point of the Absolute, Neville's systems are fissured wholes subject to constant alteration. Far from remaining bound to unchanging axioms, system in this sense encourages the acquisition of fresh perspectives on metaphysical, axiological, and aesthetic matters, the discovery of new connections through examining the implications of categories that had been obscure, discerning what is important from some new angle of vision. Whitehead, for example, was able to construct an imaginative speculative system that surmounted the old fact/value and mind/body distinctions by developing a notion of prehension such that coming-to-be includes both the finished fact, the physical dimension of the process, and intention or decisiveness associated with mentality.

If Neville's use of the terms *theory* and *system* still remain sticking points in pressing conceptual homologies between himself and Heidegger, the matter appears in a somewhat different light when, like Heidegger, Neville does not excoriate Newtonian science, a pinnacle of modernity, but shows that many phenomena cannot be explained in terms of the physical definition of motion. Neville notes that "emotion, the movement of thought and social processes all were forced into being mere metaphors of motion in the legitimate sense of three-dimensional bodies with mass moving from place to place" (*NC* 4). While the attempt to commensurate complex metaphors is perilous, the human comportments just mentioned as inexplicable in Newtonian terms evoke the Heideggerian notions of mood, of thinking in its numerous guises, and of the *Mitsein* or social world respectively.

Neville appeals to the Confucian conception of ritual, *li*, the habits of a traditional society, as offering a pretheoretical access to a theory of theories, one that could take account of poetry and theology. The chain of metaphors employed by the later Heidegger including building a cabinet, dwelling, uttering a poetic word, all depend upon collusions between a preexisting element or milieu, wood, earth, and language, with human being-in-the-world and, as embedded in traditions, might be reinscribed in Neville's Confucian terms. To be sure, the programmed behaviors of contemporary Western societies are interpreted negatively by the Heidegger of *Being and Time* as ontic manifestations of more primordial relations to Being, whereas *li* is ritual that civilizes in the Confucianism that Neville admires. Like Heidegger, Neville remains wary of the potential for the reification of ritual into social roles, while Heidegger, like Neville, writes nostalgically of the civilizing capacity of ritual in his account of the Greek gods who have fled and are no longer ceremonially encountered.

Neville is also likely to concur with Heidegger's comments in an infrequently cited conversation with a Japanese friend in which each dialogue partner speaks from a different linguistic site and whose differences must be respected.[9] The danger that Europeans and East Asians inhabit different metaphysical languages, Heidegger and his Japanese friend agree, means that something must be kept back, something indefinable that, paradoxically, must not slip away but must display its force as the conversation unfolds. Genuine dialogue is not a communicating of information, but as Heidegger's Japanese friend suggests, "an intermingling of cherry blossom and plum blossom on the same branch."[10] Neville astutely recognizes the uniqueness of cultures when he comments: "There is no higher-than-all-cultures ritual or conceptual language to compare different cultures" (*NC* 16). Neville goes on to say that the "overlaying of meanings is the way rituals pile on one another" and pinpoints this process as another Confucian theme (*NC* 17).

The rich notion of deference that Neville develops and the later Heidegger's attentiveness to the piety of thinking suggest further affinities. In one of his most arcane yet often cited assertions, Heidegger claims that "unconcealment is . . . the element in which being and thinking and their belonging together exist. *Aletheia* is named at the beginning of philosophy but afterwards it is not explicitly thought as such by philosophy."[11] As opening and as letting be seen, *aletheia* is not to be confused with truth but may be its precondition, a matter Heidegger proposes for thinking. The failure to discern the opening that both conceals and reveals can be construed as heedlessness, an impiety of thought. "Presence as such and the opening granting it, remain unheeded."[12] Yet concealment itself is part of the process of the opening of presence, one that always already hides itself, a self-concealing that shelters. In a 1936 lecture on Hölderlin,[13] Heidegger sees the poet as the one who calls attention to the destitution of our time, a time in which we are unable to heed the concealing-revealing of *aletheia*.

Like Heidegger, Neville envisages certain orders of thought as more primordial than others: "[To understand] is to see that the description of phenomena is a poetic act. Poetry in this sense is not the mere metaphorical representation of something but the attempt to say what is most important and valuable about it by overlaying metaphoric and other description" (*NC* 94). Neville warns against the indiscriminate substitution of metaphor for other modes of theoretical description but exempts from this stricture, the dialogical process of theory formation as well as theories of religious symbolism.

THE PEIRCEAN CONNECTION

To read Neville as a Peircean is pertinent to my claim for the consanguinity of Neville and postmodernism. With Peirce, Neville holds that thought is fallible, that in the absence of certainty there can be no unquestionable habits of thought but only those that have not yet been questioned, a claim that rules out nondialogical philosophies or religions as thinking. Moreover thinking is not a private affair but the achievement of a community, even if that community consists of a single individual's multiple perspectives. Equally important, Neville's metaphysics and construal of religion is Peircian in its stress on the emergence of a nonteleologically driven novelty.

For Neville, it is the uncomplicated categories of Peirce's metaphysics that appeal: firstness, anything that is what it is regardless of anything else, that is indiscriminable, original, and free, the monadic element of the world; secondness, a mode of being acquired by being other than something else, the actuality of things; thirdness, that which mediates between subjects assuring their continuity and intelligibility.[14] Peirce's semiotic reflects this ontological structure. Because immediate intuitive knowledge of the world is precluded, any object we know is a sign, which, in turn, is interpreted by another sign. Within the order of signs, object, sign and interpretant imbricate the triadic structure of the metaphysical categories.

Peirce's logic especially commends itself to Neville's antifoundationalism in that Peirce's notion of vagueness introduces a kind of tolerance at the deepest metaphysical level. Contrasting generality (a property of a category such that it applies without further interpretation to all its instances) with vagueness, Peirce writes: "Vagueness leaves for some other sign or experience the function of completing the determination. . . . The vague might be defined as that to which the principle of contradiction does not apply."[15] A category is a descriptive sign that may be complex or simple. Vague categories require intermediate specifications before they can be applied to individuals and can bypass the law of excluded middle. A vague category is enhanced by its ability to accommodate specifying categories so that the more it is stretched the more its breadth is determined by the specific categories it accounts for, an epistemological doubleness that also binds and separates postmodern thinking from modernity.[16] For Neville, vagueness means that systematicity need not entail that what is predicated of objects at higher levels of abstraction must hold for more restricted levels, nor must different subsets of a system dealing with a common problem agree with one another. It is enough that each subset be illuminating and self-justifying. If the result of multiple angles of vision yields contradictory conclusions, this could imply philosophical richness rather than sloppy thinking. No longer need intercultural conversation result in consensus reached on terms laid down by the more powerful participants or, per contra, as a concession to the weaker.

It would seem that Neville's Peirce-like link to Heidegger disappears in the interpretation of philosophy's history. Neville faults Heidegger's reading of that history for its arbitrary selectiveness, for "reducing Western culture to a single story, totaliz[ing] it and mak[ing] it possible for the whole thing to be rejected" (*HM* 8), a serious charge if true. But far from repudiating that history, Heidegger insists that the task of philosophy is to ponder what remains unthought in Western thinkers. But beyond this difference there is still another philosophical link between the Peircean side of Neville and Heidegger, in that they (and many postmoderns) share an interpretation of a key theme in the history of Western thought. This similarity is inherent in the treatment of the crisis of nominalism to which Peirce, Neville, and Heidegger are heir. Each takes the philosophy of Duns Scotus as an important starting point for his own thought. To be sure, Peirce affirms the reality of generals and ties this claim to a logic of possibility, whereas Heidegger turns to difference and the special reading he gives to what he calls the Same as different from the identical or general (a topic to be considered below). But both reject objectivity as interpreted in modern sensationist and mechanistic empiricisms and subjectivity as exemplified in the Cartesian cogito, the subject as knower. For Heidegger, the mistake of the nominalist is to identify thinking with asserting something about something such that one thing is differentiated from another. Peirce makes a comparable point when he declares:

> The modern philosophers . . . recognize but one mode of being, the being of an individual thing or fact, the object's crowding out a place for itself in the universe . . . and reacting by brute force of fact against all other things. (1.21)[17]

Heidegger believes that we can make no progress in resolving the problem of nominalism so long as ontology is subordinated to logic, a position Peirce could hardly endorse, but much hangs on the extent to which being and existence mirror the ontology of science in Peirce's logic.[18] Suffice it to say that, for both Peirce and Heidegger, the Scotist account of the relation of a thing's general character to its haecceity (individuating property), is determinative for their readings of the epistemological crisis of modernity, a crisis reflected in the self-understanding of modernist social sciences.

DERRIDA AND DECONSTRUCTION

In his reading of deconstruction in *The Highroad around Modernism*, Neville endorses David Ray Griffin's charge that for deconstruction no worldview can be subject to informed criticism because any critical vantage point that leans on rational argument is exposed to the charge of logocentrism, the use of traditional categories of logic and grammar that privilege present time. If no worldview counts more than any other, nothing counts and deconstruction is left open to the charge of nihilism. Griffin's accusation requires more than the trivial response that the truths of everyday life retain their force for Derrida just as they did for Hume: "Put your finger in the fire and you will say 'Ouch'." Rather what is at stake is the construal of a broad range of philosophical frameworks.

Griffin's challenge is best confronted by returning once again to Heidegger country. Like Heidegger, the deconstructionist peels away specific arguments to expose how being and nothing are grasped in whatever philosophical assertions are in question, to see what has been said before anything is said, to understand what is always already intrinsic to an argument, its social and political as well as its metaphysical commitments. Applying Heidegger's strategy to a Heideggerian problem in "How to Avoid Speaking: Denials," Derrida ponders Heidegger's discussion of modern nihilism in *Zur Seinsfrage*. There Heidegger proposes that the word Being be written under erasure in the form of a crossing out so that the word remains readable but the crossing out solicits decipherment. The term Being written in this way is not to be confused with a being, an existent, that which can be represented. In this *Durchstreichung*, Being is not effaced but still read. Yet how is one to think erasure in the context of negation, to gain access to the place of the nothing? Derrida writes: "The nothing should also be *written*, that is to say *thought*. Like Being, it should also be written and read under erasure 'Wie das Sein, so musste auch das Nichts geschreiben und d.h. gedacht werden.'"[19]

With Heidegger, Derrida calls attention to what has been overlooked in Western thought. Deconstruction does not demolish philosophical metaphors. In keeping with Nietzsche's view that philosophical metaphors are like worn-out coins but are the only currency we have, deconstruction could not dispense with philosophical language, even if it chose to do so. This assertion can be applied to Neville's interpretation of religious symbols, signs of the divine that include religious narrative, concepts, and artifacts and generally embody ancient traditions that we need not read in a traditional manner even if we could recover a symbol's origin.

Such openness of interpretation would appear to validate Neville's anti-Derridean worry that there is no *hors texte*, that there is no world apart from texts. For Neville, symbols are not the measure of one another but rather reality is their measure. Yet Neville also says "in religious matters . . . the infinite is the measure of our finite symbols" (*TBS* xii). Because the finite can never become commensurate with the infinite, it is virtually assured that symbols will be broken so that we are both drawn in by them yet grasp their limitations. Thus Neville: "The insistence on the brokenness of religious symbols is to protect and highlight their apophatic reference to the transcendent or infinite" (*TBS* 243).

Put off by Derrida's expansion of the idea of textuality,[20] Neville does not notice that the brokenness of religious symbols can be interpreted as their effraction, as marked by difference in both Heidegger's and Derrida's sense. Heidegger conceives of difference as ontological, what holds between Being and beings. It cannot be represented, as if difference were a relation added on to Being and beings that could be grasped by the understanding.[21] Always already there prior to any effort to represent it, we must step back in order to think difference. Like Neville's symbols that relate us to the infinite, for Heidegger difference is not anywhere but rather "grants and holds apart the between" as the condition of bestowing identity and difference. In this context, Heidegger speaks of the Same as the belonging together of what differs. Contrasting the Same with the identical, the reductive subversion of difference, Heidegger is unlikely to see a paradox in speaking of Being and beings as differentiated by virtue of the Same.[22]

Derrida's by now familiar term *différance*, neither word nor concept, neither origin in the sense of cause nor creative source, nevertheless generates meaning. Drawing upon the double meaning of the French *différer*, Derrida describes *différance* as a separating that is both temporal and spatial. "It is because of *différance* that the movement of signification is possible. . . . An interval must separate the present from what it is not [the past or the future] in order for the present to be itself, thereby also dividing everything that is thought on the basis of the present, that is in our metaphysical language, every being and singular substance or the subject."[23] Would it not be worthwhile to consider the brokenness of symbols as a difference that defers and distances, that establishes proximity and otherness between the holiness of the divine and the human condition as Neville sees them? In Neville's more technical register, "for religious symbols to be at all apophatic, to take back what they seem to assert, to suggest that the divine is more than is said, or not quite what is said, is for them to be indexical" (*TBS* 41).

DETERRITORIALIZING THOUGHT
IN DELEUZE AND NEVILLE

To think with Deleuze and Guattari is truly to teeter at the brink of an abyss. Their *Anti-Oedipus: Capitalism and Schizophrenia* has been com-

pared to the works of R. D. Laing and Thomas Szasz, critics of orthodox psychoanalysis, a practice construed by them as the puppet of establishment social forces. As Brian Massumi notes, Deleuze and Guattari's
work was first regarded as "short-circuiting the connection between
psychoanalysis and the far-left parties."[24] This reading, faithful in a limited sense, fails to note that theirs is a post-Nietzschean open system
incorporating the thought of Lucretius, Hume, Spinoza, and Bergson, a
"synthesis" already presaged in Deleuze's magisterial studies of Bergson
and Spinoza. Deleuze and Guattari's open system is postmodernism's
contribution to systems philosophy with an attentiveness to the limitations of modernism already built into its free-moving, nontotalizing relational a/metaphysical account of the patterning of forces. Here there is
a parting of the ways between Heidegger and a postmodernism that
repudiates the connection of philosophy to Greek thought. Because Heidegger's Greeks are autochthons rather than free citizens and
autochthony is reminiscent of National Socialism, Heidegger "betrays
the movement of deterritorialization because he fixes it . . . between the
Greek territory and the Western earth that the Greeks would have called
Being."[25]

Consider first the systematicity of the socio/psychological/economic
complex of *Anti-Oedipus: Capitalism and Schizophrenia.*[26] Reinterpret-
ing received notions of desire, the authors see it not as lack inherent in
an individual subject, but as force, the production of states of intensity
that circulate within an economy and are socially apportioned in accordance with specifiable laws of distribution. Thus desire, an affect and an
economic resource, is an erotic ideality that is interpreted as a com-
modity. In neo-Marxist terms, desire is capital and needs to be redis-
tributed. What is more, psychoanalysis has become so embedded in
recent Western culture that the individual interiorizes its mode of dis-
tributing desire. For the authors (as for Heidegger), Being in our epoch
has become mechanism so that psychic life is envisaged as a production
process: machines both produce and interrupt or cut into a society's
material flow. The factuality of desiring machines is understood as an
amalgam of their social and material natures. (Matter itself is socially
produced.) *Homo natura* is thus not primary in this process but always
already preceded by *homo historica.*

Desiring machines are not free floating but attach themselves to
what the authors call bodies without organs, the nonplace of counter-
production, breakdown, and death, the surface upon which production
is recorded. When the body's organs that articulate production seem to
drop away, they leave an undifferentiated mass. As presently arranged,
the organs of the body cause the body suffering in that the body takes
on the character of the mode of production projected upon it, for exam-

ple, the body of earth in "primitive" societies. There is an energy that courses through the body without organs that is not something fixed but manufactured through one's desiring practices, not a fundament that can be reached but a limit that, like a Kantian regulative ideal, is always in the process of attainment.

If this potpourri sounds like a mix of Marx, Freud, Artaud, and Lacan, consider the following reading of Spinoza by Deleuze in *A Thousand Plateaus: Capitalism and Schizophrenia*[27] and check for affinities with my description above of Deleuze's own system:

> There is [this] aspect to Spinoza. To every relation of movement and rest, speed and slowness grouping together an infinity of parts, there corresponds a degree of power. To the relations composing, decomposing, or modifying an individual there correspond intensities that affect it, augmenting or diminishing its power to act. . . . Affects are becomings. Spinoza asks: What can a body do. We call the latitude of a body the affects of which it is capable at a given degree of power. . . . In the same way that we avoid defining a body by its organs or functions, we will avoid defining it by species and genus characteristics; instead we will seek to count its affects. This kind of study is called ethology, and this is the sense in which Spinoza wrote a true Ethics.[28]

Will Spinoza ever be the same again in the light of such readings? In *A Thousand Plateaus*, Brian Massumi (the work's translator) invites the reader to move from plateau to plateau, entering the system at any point. "What counts is not Is it true? But: does it work? What new thoughts does it make it possible to think? What new emotions does it make it possible to feel?"[29] Are these not Neville's Peirce-like and Deweyan questions to both philosophy and the world's religions?

NOTES

1. Albany: State University of New York Press, 1992. Hereafter cited in the text as *HM*.

2. Albany: State University of New York Press, 1995. Hereafter cited in the text as *NC*.

3. Aristotle, *Metaphysics* 1066ff., as cited in Martin Heidegger, "What Calls for Thinking," in *Basic Writings*, ed. David Farrell Krell (New York: Harper & Row, 1977), p. 392.

4. Martin Heidegger, *Basic Problems in Phenomenology*, trans. Albert Hofstadter (Bloomington: Indiana University Press, 1982), p. 13.

5. John Dewey, *The Early Works*, ed. Jo Ann Boydston (Carbondale and Edwardsville: Southern Illinois University Press, 1969–72) 4: 29. I am indebted for this citation to Larry Hickman's review in *Transactions of the Charles S.*

Peirce Society 23.3 (Summer 1987), of R. W. Sleeper, *The Necessity of Pragmatism: John Dewey's Conception of Philosophy* (New Haven: Yale University Press, 1986). Sleeper argues that Dewey (contra Peirce) believes we should get our logic from our ontology rather than the converse (p. 47). If Neville is closer to Dewey in this respect, he is also closer to Heidegger in his privileging of ontology.

6. Martin Heidegger, *Basic Problems in Phenomenology*, p. 214.

7. The antinomy in Nietzsche is identified by Jean Granier in his "Perspectivism and Interpretation," in *The New Nietzsche*, ed. David Allison (Cambridge: MIT Press, 1980), pp. 196–97.

8. Robert Cummings Neville, *The Truth of Broken Symbols* (Albany: State University of New York Press, 1996), pp. 22–23. Hereafter cited in the text as *TBS*.

9. Martin Heidegger, "A Dialogue on Language," in *On the Way to Language*, trans. Peter D. Hertz (San Francisco: Harper & Row 1971), pp. 50–51.

10. Ibid., p. 53.

11. Martin Heidegger, *On Time and Being*, trans. Joan Stambaugh (New York: Harper & Row, 1972), p. 69.

12. Ibid., p. 71.

13. Published as "Hölderlin und das Wesen der Dichtung." Translated as "Hölderlin and the Essence of Poetry," trans. D. Scott in *Existence and Being*, ed. Werner Brock (London: Vision Press, 1959), esp. pp. 312–13.

14. James K. Feibleman, *An Introduction to the Philosophy of Charles S. Peirce* (Cambridge: MIT Press, 1969), pp. 157–68.

15. Ibid., p. 314.

16. Although Derrida repudiates the notion that *différance* is a master concept and Deleuze rejects a similar attribution to deterritorialization, it could be argued that something like vagueness can be ascribed to these terms although such an effort lies beyond the scope of these remarks.

17. Charles Sanders Peirce, *Collected Papers of Charles Sanders Peirce*, ed. Charles Hartshorne and Paul Weiss (Cambridge: Harvard University Press, 1935). Citation is by volume and paragraph number according to convention.

18. See note 5.

19. *Derrida and Negative Theology*, ed. Harold Coward and Toby Foshay (Albany: State University of New York Press, 1992), pp. 125–26. Neville's intercultural conversation in its engagement with negation, e.g., the śūnyatā of Buddhism, might benefit from a Derridean reading. Robert Magliola, David Loy, and Harold Coward have made a good beginning in these matters as has David Dilworth's taxonomy of world philosophies.

20. Derrida has often denied that intratextual openness is a denial of extratextual reality.

21. *Identity and Difference*, trans. Joan Stambaugh (New York: Harper & Row, 1969), p. 62.

22. Ibid., p. 65.

23. Jacques Derrida, *Margins of Philosophy*, trans. Alan Bass (Chicago: University of Chicago Press, 1982), p. 13.

24. Brian Massumi, *A User's Guide to Capitalism and Schizophrenia* (Cambridge: MIT Press, 1992), p. 3.

25. Gilles Deleuze and Felix Guattari, *What Is Philosophy?* trans. Hugh Tomlinson and Graham Burchell (New York: Columbia University Press, 1994), p. 95.

26. Trans. by Robert Hurley, Mark Seem, and Helen R. Lane (New York: Viking Press, 1977).

27. Trans. and foreword by Brian Massumi (Minneapolis: University of Minnesota Press, 1987).

28. Ibid., pp. 256–57.

29. Ibid., p. xv.

PART II

Neville and Western Philosophy

CHAPTER 3

Neville's Use of Plato

Patricia Cook

In a famous passage in the *Sophist,* Plato reflects that two views on the nature of reality have dominated the history of philosophy.[1] The faction called "giants" are materialists. The opposing faction, the "friends of the *eidē,*" have a view of a transcendental reality that is largely akin to that of Plato. The Friends of the Forms are called gods. Plato would no doubt have recognized Robert Neville as one of the "Friends of the Forms." Everyone who is acquainted with Neville's work notices that Neville considers himself to have a debt to Plato. Although Neville cannot be said to be a Platonist without qualification, and although Neville's scholarly work does not dwell on Platonic exegesis, there is an important sense in which Neville carries on the inquiry that Plato began.

Having said this, we should immediately note that the Platonic spirit of Neville's work is somewhat elusive. Neville's direct treatment of Platonic doctrine is confined to several articles written early in his career.[2] Neville makes use of some of Plato's metaphysical and cosmological ideas in *God the Creator: On the Presence and Transcendence of God* (University of Chicago Press, 1968), and he deals obliquely with Socratic ideas in *The Tao and the Daimon: Segments of a Religious Inquiry* (SUNY Press, 1982). The only extended references to Platonic teachings in more recent work occur in *Recovery of the Measure: Interpretation in Nature* (SUNY Press, 1989), where Neville makes significant use of the categories of reality that appear in Plato's *Philebus.* Given that Neville has been a prolific philosophical writer for nearly thirty-five years, it would seem that Neville's explicit dedication to Plato has been more attenuated than is generally thought. Although Plato belongs to the phalanx of thinkers who have inspired and influenced Neville—Confucius, Whitehead, Buddha, C. S. Peirce, Hegel, Jesus—along with his teachers Paul Weiss, John Smith, and Robert Brumbaugh—Plato does not, on the face of things, occupy a privileged place.

I

Fidelity to Neville's thought thus seems to dictate that we proceed by a sort of *via negativa* and note the ways in which Neville explicitly departs from Plato. A fundamental divergence lies in the significance that each attributes to the philosophical enterprise. Since his earliest writings Neville has insisted on a public role for philosophy.[3] About this Plato is quite ambivalent. The *Republic*, the *Apology,* and the *Crito* emphasize an inescapable tension between philosophy and politics. On the one hand, society cannot countenance the relentless questioning of the philosopher; although societies in some ways profit from self-examination, the philosopher's scrutiny is motivated by ideals and is ultimately subversive. A political entity requires some unquestioned authority for its own stability. On the other hand, insofar as the philosopher refrains from political critique he abdicates his role. Socrates would not accept political office and he would not stop "teaching" or choose exile.[4] Yet, society can never wholly tolerate the philosopher. Plato seems to insist that the human condition involves the political irony that society can thus never be receptive to the wisdom it so palpably needs.

Since the fifth century B.C.E., the vast majority of philosophers have assumed the truth of this Platonic lesson. It is not just that the philosopher should not expect a warm welcome when he returns to the cave; it is that the philosopher must remain at some distance from any political establishment to maintain his role as the critic of it. A relative minority of thinkers, including Marcus Aurelius, Machiavelli, and Confucius, have maintained contra Plato that political life need not compromise philosophical integrity. Neville belongs with this latter company. These thinkers are able to view the philosophical life as compatible with public roles in part because they do not follow Plato's puzzling insistence on specialization. The *Republic* maintains that each person has a single natural talent and a single way of contributing to the whole community.[5] It seems as though Plato thought of no alternative; he presents no argument for either side. But the Nevillean philosopher belies Plato's principle of specialization. Indeed, the Nevillean philosopher is anything but singular in his pursuits: he philosophizes from experience, and seeks to enrich it with an eclecticism that would have baffled Plato. The Nevillean philosopher can simultaneously live as public administrator, artist (of more than one kind), and religious leader.

Moreover, Neville consistently commends faithfulness to experience as against vague theoretical formulation, mysterious ideals, and formal logical analysis. Plato seems to be without this scruple.[6] The arguments of Plato's characters occasionally become so recondite and so apparently pointless that a warning against misology has to be introduced.

Plato's characters are permitted to spin likely stories, are made to dwell extensively in "a city founded only in words, that does not exist on earth," and "never will exist," and are encouraged to pursue knowledge for its own sake.[7] In this sense Plato subjugates philosophy as "the art of life" and the human need to know how to live to an intense and indecisive quest for the limits of human understanding.

This leads us to a second way in which Neville is conspicuously and importantly un-Platonic. Neville is a systematic philosopher par excellence. Plato's philosophizing is unsystematic in the extreme. This is not just a matter of style, although the elegant essay-treatise genre of Neville obviously embodies different assumptions from those of Plato's dramatic dialogues. According to Neville, "systematic philosophy is the critical attempt to comprehend everything in one discursive reflective view."[8] The point of having such an edifice is both to illuminate the connections between things and to have a ground from which to observe or express value or importance. Neville's own system ranges from a metaphysics of morals to a full-blown speculative cosmology. A system is in one sense descriptive: that is, it attempts to map out experience in such a way that it can examine relations and connections between things on the highest level of reflective abstraction as well as at the lowest level of concreteness. But such description can only be carried out intelligibly insofar as it is able to designate appropriate categories. A good or adequate system has categoreal nomenclature that can interpret any level of experience from any perspective whatsoever and can describe the conditions of the possibility of apprehension at any of these foci. Neville steadfastly maintains that systems must be accessible to, and continually exposed to, rational critique.[9] A system should be designed in principle to integrate the widest possible scope of experience and to have an answer to every difficulty that might be brought before it. It is marked by logical coherence (though this is not the hallmark of its truth) and is, like any legitimate theory, falsifiable.[10]

Plato's dialogues are emphatically devoid of any counterpart. Plato's works are not a "system."[11] They are dramatic, mimetic scenes from ordinary life in which serious subjects are discussed. The characters are not mere foils for the conveyance of arguments; they are vividly portrayed with personalities, backgrounds, and occupations. Ideas are ventured that are never fully expounded. Theses are mistakenly dismissed on the grounds of what look like faulty arguments. Lines of inquiry proceed to seemingly pointless dead ends. People occasionally laugh, are sometimes humiliated, and often (one suspects) dissemble. In no case is a positive philosophical conclusion definitively reached. T. S. Eliot once said that we are unfair to both drama and philosophy when we suppose that Shakespeare writes philosophy.[12] Something similar should be said for Plato and systematic metaphysics. The twenty-nine dialogues ought not to be thought of as a "critical attempt to comprehend everything in one discursive reflective view" merely embellished or artfully disguised.

Furthermore, Plato puts forth no "theories." Neville defines a theory as a presentation of experience "through an integral conceptual structure . . . which provide[s] explicit cognitive connections between all parts."[13] It is a unified vision "with the added dimension that the thinker takes responsibility for the unity of the world."[14] If Plato had what Neville calls "theories," he did not make them available to us. Far from "taking responsibility for the unity" of what is presented in the dialogues, Plato speaks through numerous actors whose stories are often recounted through an inscrutably complex series of narrators. The voice of "Plato himself" cannot be strictly identified with any of his characters on literary grounds. Plato deliberately confounds his own thought with that of Socrates in such a way that even these two cannot be disentangled.[15] Indeed, the dialogical nature of Plato's work refracts the unified vision that theories seek.

Those who attribute to Plato a "Theory of Forms" or a "Theory of Recollection" do not get this from Plato's own works.[16] Nowhere in the dialogues are such topics referred to as *theōriai*. When Socrates refers to them he calls them suppositions, literally, *hypotheseis*.[17] They seem to function the way (centuries later) articles of faith would function, as beliefs that permit one to understand. Hypotheses work as place holders for the unknown, so that inquiry can begin its departure. Suppositions must be acknowledged so that inquiry can begin; they do not constitute conclusions presented for verification.

In any case, Plato himself falsifies—or raises the most devastating objections against—the very "theories" that are attributed to him, within the very same dialogic pages in which they are hypothesized in the first place. If we are to attribute to Plato a system, it is riddled with self-contradictions of which he was well aware.[18] This is patently not what Neville means by "system," even if systems are continually engaged in self-scrutiny.[19]

Socrates cannot be said to have a system or to have theories either. Socrates speaks of having, at a crucial point in his life, fled to the *logoi*, abandoning the investigation of nature in order to direct his attention inward.[20] And while Socrates advocates the Delphic motto "Know thyself," his introspection yields no theory, but only the famous ignorance that the oracle would dub "human wisdom."[21] The "theory" that "knowledge is virtue" is sometimes attributed to Socrates from the *Meno* and the *Protagoras*, yet in the *Euthydemus* Socrates argues the other way around. In fact, the only claim Socrates ever makes in a dialogue that is not controverted elsewhere is that there is a difference between knowledge and belief: "That there is a difference between right opinion and knowledge is not a matter of conjecture, but something I would claim to know; there are not many things of which I would say that, but this is one of them."[22]

II

Neville's consanguinity with Plato may be found, after all, in the dialectical method. In the *Cratylus*, Socrates says that the dialectician is one who knows how to ask and how to answer (390c): this, Neville certainly does. In another place, dialectic is described as a kind of "sorting through" speech, culling it for interconnections.[23] Does Neville do exactly that? This question becomes quite literally Academic, since scholars have never reached a consensus on exactly what dialectic means for Plato, and the term "dialectic" has since had a philosophical career of its own. But Neville is as clear as Plato in saying that it is proper to philosophizing.

Broadly conceived, dialectic seems to be constructive question and answer. It seems to be the opposite of working out one's views and then presenting them in finished form to those who would then memorize or intuit them. When Aristotle gets hold of this term (which was first used in a technical sense by Zeno of Elea) he uses it to refer to a process of introducing and weighing commonly held beliefs (as well as received philosophical opinions) and subjecting them to mutual cross-examination. Aristotle seems always to suppose that these various views contain some element of truth that is worth preserving. Moreover, his resolution of conflicting traditional views always includes an account of why the erroneous view had been adopted. All of this seems to me to describe precisely what Neville does in creating a system and moving among its articulations in the "persistent attempt to discover whether anything has been left out."[24] Neville's works are so expansive in their inclusion of "commonly held beliefs" from many cultures and the philosophical opinions that have accrued over two and a half millennia that we must really see him as engaged in a level of Aristotelian dialectic of which Aristotle never dreamed. In this same vein, it is noteworthy that Aristotle only assumed that there was a problem to be solved when traditional views were in conflict with one another. At least Neville, working in the cacophony of postmodernity, can make short work of that assumption.

Of course, this is not the end of the story of dialectic. The term is barely recognizable after Kant gets through with it.[25] By the end of the nineteenth century it has been worked over by Hegel and Marx until it is nearly effete. Neville does not truckle to this. Neville argues that

Hegelian dialectic, if understood by the Stace formula of thesis, antithesis, synthesis, would stall with a *regressus ad infinitum*.[26] Hegel's negative dialectic fails on similar grounds, that is, it misconstrues totality. For a situation to be sufficiently determinate, complete, integrated, and "whole enough to negate," it must be a totality, but if there is room to dialectically "step away" from this, then it is not a totality in the required respects. Neville calls this a "fatal flaw" and seems to conclude that Hegelian dialectic is thereby unable to engender a genuine philosophical system.

So let us return, with Neville, to the Greeks. Neville seems to employ dialectic for its "rhetorical" force as well as for its inherent propriety for moving about in a philosophical system.[27] One must think, likewise, that Plato chose the dialogue genre for philosophizing (at least in part) for its natural accommodation to dialectic. Yet when Plato deliberately tries to state what dialectic is in the *Sophist* and the *Parmenides*, he uses arithmetic as the paradigm of its structure. More revealing, perhaps, are the claims made for its power in the *Republic*: "by the power of dialectic, discourse (*logos*) can reach up to the un-hypothesized, the first principles of all that is" (509d). In other words, to arrive at insight into Being, into what is fundamentally Real, our thinking must proceed dialectically. Does Neville take dialectic to be capable of attaining to un-hypothesized first principles? Note that Aristotle does not. For Aristotle, dialectic does not yield the highest type of knowledge precisely because it does *not* rest upon absolutely certain first principles (it is based only on opinions that are commonly accepted as true).[28] Once again, Neville seems closest to the Aristotelian view. Neville finds dialectic to be the proper mode of reflection for systematic philosophizing just because it formulates questions that are addressed to particular *positions*, that is, to candidate solutions to a problem on a certain subject.[29] Neville generally uses the term "dialectic" to denote "integration with other dimensions of judgment."[30] Although he cites with approval Plato's image of the ladder of hypotheses from the *Republic*, Neville's notion of dialectic involves "*unending* stepping up" (my emphasis).[31] For Neville, the work of dialectic is never finished; a systematic philosophy is never complete.[32]

On the other hand, it may be the case that Neville has used dialectic to the end that Plato would call "un-hypothesized" when Neville's own system comes to "the ontological context of mutual relevance," also known as "divine creativity" or "God."[33] Neville says that the ontological context of mutual making admits of no distinction between creativity and what is created, and that "the creative act is immediate and has no steps." Of course, arriving at the ultimate ground does not put dialectic out of business: dialectic will always have more relations to discover, new judgments to integrate, and novel values to enjoy. But would this satisfy the paradigm of knowing that Socrates proposes to Glaucon (*noēsis*)? Does it escape the limit that Socrates says keeps geometry from occupying the topmost segment of the divided line, namely, that of mere "consistent agreement (*homologia*)"? Socrates puts the matter this way:

> Now with regard to . . . [the arts] which we say reach something of what *is*, namely geometry and those following in train with it, we see that they dream of what is, but that it is impossible for them to have a wakeful view of what is, as long as they leave unchanged the hypotheses they use and are not able to give an account of them. For if the starting point (*archē*) is unknown and the middle and conclusion are woven out of what is unknown, what contraption is ever going to change such merely consistent agreement into knowledge? (*Republic* 533b)

Knowledge would require, says Socrates, that the hypotheses as such be "destroyed";[34] and although I don't know exactly what this requirement would mean, I think these questions of Plato, that I have addressed to systematic philosophy, must stand.

III

One of Neville's core ideas is that of the Good as the ordering principle of all things. This is derived from a suggestion made by Socrates in the *Republic* (509a–b). Socrates briefly entertains the Good, not as a Form among Forms, but as some sort of culminating principle that gives all beings their vividness and propriety. He makes it the term of the famous analogy: The Good is to the Forms as the Sun is to Vision. The sun, or light, makes vision possible; it is that without which we would see nothing. The Good, then, is that without which there would be no knowledge or truth. This same Good was the advertised topic of a public lecture that Plato once gave at the Academy. Apparently this attracted quite a crowd, all eager to hear about what was really good. But the lecture turned out to be about arithmetic, and how the Good is in fact the One. According to ancient reports, the audience went away disgusted.[35]

Neville's system manages to make some sense out of Plato's strange idea. He interprets Plato as having meant that "there is only one true form, the Form of the Good. In itself, this form is wholly indeterminate, hence not structured."[36] About the Good as the One, he says, "Plato hoped that all things could be understood in numbers, or ratios." To represent value mathematically, Plato had to discover that "what is elementary is not the littleness of the stuff but the ratio of the form."[37] This is all well placed in Neville's theory of reality, which itself is based on a grasp of identity.[38] Neville's theory, in a perfect dialectical turnabout, provides a way to read another notoriously difficult Platonic passage: the discussion of whether Being is one or many in the *Sophist*. I know of nowhere that Neville takes credit for this, but here is the interpretation I think he would give. And this is what, in the end, I think makes Neville a *sympotikos* for Plato, what makes Neville a true "friend of the forms."

The Stranger is addressing Socrates' supposition that the form is not Being itself but *a* being. There is a problem: the appearances participate in the forms in such a way that these diverse beings (apparently) intersect; forms appear superimposed in one object. How is this possible? The Stranger establishes that all the forms are beings, and that they all therefore participate in the highest Form, in Being itself. But the solution to the paradox lies in the Stranger's radical suggestion that there is yet another Form in which all forms participate: Not-Being. Now, there is a way of "Not-Being" that is really just a version of Being, namely, to be Other. All beings, then, participate in the form of the Other, thereby making them other than each other, "not what the other is."[39] But then, each form should also be said to participate in the Form of Not-Other, which he calls the Form of the Same, since all have otherness in common.[40] The Form of the Same should be understood as that which gives each form its identity, its own uncontaminated nature. And because the Same is the comprehending principle for all being, it must ultimately be understood, not as itself a form among other forms, but as surpassing and lying beyond all being.

Now we have reconnected to what Plato calls the Form of the Good in the *Republic*, which is the One thing that makes even knowledge and truth what they are, and which "is not form but even transcends form in dignity and surpassing power" (509b). This now seems like just another approach to that unifying principle (i.e., the Same), comprehending but surpassing all being. It is obvious now why, from the approach of Plato's lecture, and even from the approach of the *Parmenides* (139–49), this principle is called the One.

IV

Neville's system finally goes far beyond even the most profound suggestions of Plato. There is no Platonic antecedent for Neville's view that a thing is constituted of a harmony of its essential and conditional features, nor is there one for his idea that the Being of a thing is its whole nature and context, including its interpretations (which can occur from any number of perspectives on any number of levels of abstractions).

For Plato, the Being of a thing is eidetic, and the kind of being (or "becoming") something has determines its knowability. Neville's system is dimensionally different from anything suggested by Plato because it includes a theory of time.[41] Neville maintains the reality of the past and the future, and takes into account the ideas of twentieth-century theoretical physicists, including the theory of relativity. Of course, there is no real treatment of time in Plato's dialogues, and the forms themselves dwell outside of time.[42] Time is discussed only in myths, and none of these are myths told by Socrates himself. In the *Timaeus*, it is mentioned that time arose simultaneously with the heavens as a moving image of eternity. De-mythologized, this seems to mean something like Aristotle's notion that the motion of heavenly bodies provides the measure of motion with respect to before and after; this sort of view is formally superseded by Neville's work. Another myth in the *Statesman* tells of an age when Cronos ruled and time ran backwards. Gray-haired humans are born understanding language and they grow into childhood; fruits spring ripe from the vine without cultivation; animals are born tame. In the present age, according to this myth, Cronos has let go of control and is allowing the world to unwind itself. The myth does not specify time's nature as such, although it hints that human temporality is what makes philosophy a human necessity.

Some of Neville's most important ideas pertain to the metaphysics of morals. His notions of freedom, responsibility, agency, and culture could not even have been formulated in Greek terms. Neville's system includes an understanding of the directedness of will, which he claims can be found in the *Meno*.[43] I have not been able to find it there. What I do find is Neville's idea that a moral-aesthetic intuition leads directly to action: this is Socrates' suggestion that knowledge is virtue.

I have been hinting in this chapter that Neville's philosophy might rightfully be heir to Aristotle rather than to Plato. Aristotle is the real progenitor of systematic philosophy in Neville's sense. Neville's method is the apotheosis of Aristotle's notion of dialectic. Neville and Aristotle share an emphasis on praxis. Neville has a wonderful insight about how the discussion of reality in the *Philebus* might actually have been stimulated by Aristotle.[44] The list goes on. One is reminded of the way Alfred North Whitehead's thought was for decades taken to be the great resurrection of Platonism until R. G. Collingwood suddenly looked at it another way.[45] Now we take it for granted that Aristotle taught the original process metaphysics. But in spite of the foregoing insinuations, I would not want to claim that Neville is essentially Aristotelian. I would maintain, for whatever designating such alliances is worth, that Neville's work is fundamentally Platonist. What I believe to be decisively Platonic in Neville's case is his interpretation of the Good, which includes his conviction that goodness can be aesthetically apprehended. This is an architectonic that Aristotle does not share. Indeed, from what Aristotle says in the *Nicomachean Ethics*, it seems as though he himself couldn't make any sense out of Plato's notion of the Good at all.[46]

Whatever the case, the question of lineage is not particularly significant for Neville's system. The very idea of systematic philosophy and the method by which it proceeds are synoptic. To focus for too long from one perspective—even from the genetic one—would be to miss the metaphysical point. Neville's influences are manifold, and this, in a way, is the essence of systematic thought. In another way, Neville's system lies beyond all these influences and is idiomatic, idiosyncratic, indeed, as the Greeks say, *idiōtēs*, that is, utterly singular.

With this in mind, it may be worth noting that philosophical insights might occasionally be additive, yet not reducible to a common denominator. Consider the following. Plato's dialogues constantly remind us that what it is to be human is to find ourselves in the world *in media res*, where our knowledge is invariably incomplete. The human task seems to be to discover how to live well in spite of this limited understanding but with a full recognition of it. The meaning of living with incomplete knowledge is one of Plato's most profound themes.

Now, here is the question. Can systematic philosophy ever teach us the meaning of living with incomplete knowledge? Systematic philosophy acknowledges that our vision is incomplete, but its whole emphasis is on overcoming this incompleteness. Neville knows that the systematic philosopher does not see everything "all at once";[47] but he stresses the ability of the systematic philosophizer to move by means of critical reflection from one thing to anything else. It seems that the systematic philosopher doesn't stop moving—that is, ranging around enlarging his system—long enough to reckon with the evanescence of his vision.

In short, then, it may be that the most important philosophical difference between Neville and Plato comes down to this matter of emphasis. The accent of systematic philosophy is not upon living without knowledge. Realizing that any philosophical net that is cast out will filter the reality that it gathers back in, systematic philosophy takes the human task to be that of remaining ready to cast the net again in new waters. This effort is not defined, nor is it nullified, by an awareness of what is missed, lost, forgotten, or absent. By contrast, for Plato the philosophical enterprise begins, and ends, amidst these absences and shadows. The Platonic quest is to discover what living among the shadows intimates for human life.

I think this reveals a kind of ultimate incommensurability of Neville's thought with Plato's, but not one that we would want to eliminate. Systematic philosophy would seem to be the more fulfilling, the more humanistic; it requires no resignation, and it places true knowledge within human grasp. Yet one might argue that Plato's emphasis on the superficiality of human sight accentuates, and gives direction to, the *erōs* that is the very substance of our souls. And it might turn out that all but the most vigorous of systematic philosophers would fall prey to the desolation depicted in Dürer's engraving of *Melancholia Prima*: a kind of undirected ennui even in the midst of the riches of knowledge. In any case, I think this shows that we would do well to accrue our insights from Neville and from Plato individually, as well as from their collaboration.

NOTES

1. *Sophist* 242b–249d. See also Aristotle's *Metaphysics* 987a–b.

2. "Socratic Ignorance: E. G. Ballard," *International Philosophical Quarterly* 7 (1967): 340–56; "Intuition," *International Philosophical Quarterly* 7 (1967): 556–90; and "Teaching the *Meno* and the Reformation of Character," *Teaching Philosophy* 1 (1967): 119–21. Neville also wrote a hilarious one-act play based on Plato's *Euthydemus*. The play has been performed, although it has never been published.

3. See, for examples, Robert Cummings Neville, "The Social Importance of Philosophy," *Abraxas* 1 (1970): 31–45, and *The Puritan Smile: A Look toward Moral Reflection* (Albany: State University of New York Press, 1987).

4. If we believe the *Seventh Letter,* the young Plato had planned a political career for himself, but abandoned these aspirations as he became acquainted with the corruption of Athenian politics, as described in the *Eighth Letter.*

5. *Republic* 370a–c. Note also that happiness depends upon fulfilling one's distinctive function (352d).

6. Aristotle, on the other hand, insists that the inquiry into the good be a *practical* inquiry; it is "a study whose aim is not knowledge but action" (*Nicomachean Ethics* 1095a). In this respect, Neville's work displays a kinship with Aristotle rather than with Plato.

7. *Republic* 592b.

8. Robert Cummings Neville, ed., *New Essays in Metaphysics* (Albany: State University of New York Press, 1987), p. 253.

9. See, for example, Robert Cummings Neville, "Hegel and Whitehead on Totality: The Failure of a Conception of System," in *Hegel and Whitehead*, ed. George R. Lucas (Albany: State University of New York Press, 1986), pp. 86–108.

10. See *Recovery of the Measure*, pp. 13–30, for Neville's unique understanding of Truth as such.

11. Neville himself does refer to Plato as a systematic philosopher (see, for example, *The Highroad around Modernism*, p. 137), but does not explicate this assessment. Perhaps Neville means that one can extrapolate a metaphysical or cosmological system from the dialogues. But the dialogues certainly do not present a single, coherent system, which Plato himself endorses. Even if we assume

that Plato, the man, must have had some systematic views, we cannot ignore the fact that he does not present them as such. One of the most famous passages in Plato's writing suggests that a discursive account of "the most important things" would be impossible:

> There is no treatise of mine about these things, nor will there ever be. For this can't be talked about like other subjects of learning. Yet out of much communion with this matter, and from living together, suddenly, like a light kindled from a leaping fire, it gets into the soul, and from there on nourishes itself. (*Seventh Letter* 341c)

12. "Shakespeare and the Stoicism of Seneca," in T. S. Eliot, *Selected Essays, 1917–1932* (New York: Harcourt, Brace and Co., 1932), p. 117.

13. Robert Cummings Neville, *The Reconstruction of Thinking* (Albany: State University of New York Press, 1981), p. 120.

14. "The norm of theory is *unity*." Ibid. For example, Copernican theory "is more theoretical" than Ptolemaic theory by virtue of its more unified vision, (ibid., p. 28). See also pp. 26–27.

15. I follow Guthrie and others in believing that we will never be able to satisfactorily disentangle the views of Plato from the views of the historic Socrates. We have insufficient testimonia to establish very much on philological grounds, and, of course, Socrates himself wrote nothing. Of decisive importance is the plain fact that Plato did not want his readers to be able to separate Socratic positions from his own. My own view is that Plato wanted to deter his readers from seeing him as an authority. Reason itself should be discovered to be the final arbiter of truth.

16. Of course, Aristotle may have been the first to have seen Plato in this way. But then, Aristotle essentially repeats difficulties that are already present as objections within the dialogues. In some cases, Aristotle's own account does not square with the dialogues themselves (e.g., *Metaphysics* 987b and *Parmenides* 131c–132). In any case, Aristotle *was* a systematic thinker, and was struggling to come to terms with his teacher. He cannot be taken as the ultimate authority.

17. *Phaedo* 100b.

18. Some of these are elementary logical blunders, some are obscure arguments against some abstruse conception of Being. The three major arguments against the hypothesis of the Forms (which spawned a kind of industry, beginning with Aristotle) are all clearly stated in the dialogues. What have come to be known as the lower participation problem, the problem of self-predication, and the fallacy of the Third Man are all difficulties that Socrates definitely knows about. See *Parmenides* 132d; *Republic* 597c; *Phaedrus* 251a; *Protagoras* 330c.

19. Neville says that "systematic method means to look at everything from as many angles as possible with a way of being responsible for the connections between those viewpoints" (*The Highroad around Modernism*, p. 134).

20. *Phaedo* 99d–e. See also *Phaedrus* 229c–e, where Socrates explains his lack of interest in theological speculations: "I have no time for the business [of debating stories of the gods]; I cannot as yet know myself as the Oracle enjoins, so it seems ridiculous to inquire into extraneous matters."

21. *Apology* 23a–c.

22. *Meno* 98b.

23. *Phaedrus* 266c.

24. Robert Cummings Neville, ed., *New Essays in Metaphysics*, pp. 253–54.

25. It is far from obvious how Kant's use of the term "dialectic," for example, in the "Transcendental Dialectic" in *The Critique of Pure Reason*, is related to the "dialektikē" of Zeno, Plato, or Aristotle. Similarly, when Marx uses the term to modify his doctrine of Materialism, "dialectic" seems to have only a tenuous connection to its Greek "question–and–answer" origins.

26. The argument for this is part of a sustained examination of Hegelian dialectic in *The Highroad around Modernism*, pp. 113–20.

27. See, for example, the presentation of the argument of chapter 4 in *Creativity and God: A Challenge to Process Theology* (New York: Seabury Press, 1980), especially p. 68.

28. Aristotle does say in his treatise on dialectic, the *Topics*, that dialectic is useful nonetheless for hammering out conundrums and for exposing difficulties in the middle of conversations (101a25–b4).

29. Robert Cummings Neville, "Reply to W. Christian's 'The New Metaphysics and Theology,'" *The Christian Scholar* (Winter 1967): 324–25.

30. See, for example, *The Reconstruction of Thinking*, p. 121.

31. Ibid.

32. See Neville, *The Highroad around Modernism*, p. 133ff.

33. See Neville, *New Essays in Metaphysics*, p. 259.

34. *Republic* 533c.

35. Aristoxenus, *Elements of Harmony* 2.30.

36. Neville, *Recovery of the Measure: Interpretation in Nature*, p. 140.

37. Ibid., p. 121; cf. Neville, *The Highroad around Modernism*, p. 203.

38. Ibid., pp. 95–128; see also Robert Cummings Neville, *The Cosmology of Freedom* (New Haven: Yale University Press, 1974), chap. 3.

39. *Sophist* 258c.

40. *Sophist* 254e.

41. Robert Cummings Neville, *Eternity and Time's Flow* (Albany: State University of New York Press, 1993).

42. *Phaedrus* 247b.

43. Neville, "Teaching the *Meno* and the Reformation of Character," *Teaching Philosophy* 1.2 (1975): 120–21.

44. Neville, *Recovery of the Measure*, pp. 118ff.

45. R. G. Collingwood, *The Idea of Nature* (Oxford: Oxford University Press, 1934/1960), p. 170. Ivor LeClerc's *Whitehead's Metaphysics* (New York: Humanities Press, 1957/1978) gives a complete account of the parallels between Aristotle's "potentiality/actuality"–based metaphysics and the system set out in *Process and Reality*.

46. Aristotle's critique begins in the *Nicomachean Ethics*, book 1, chapter 6.

47. Neville, *New Essays in Metaphysics*, p. 253.

CHAPTER 4

Neville and Pragmatism: Toward Ongoing Dialogue

Sandra B. Rosenthal

Two of the powerful influences on Robert Neville's thinking are classical American pragmatism and Whiteheadian process philosophy, both of which he creatively utilizes in developing his own original position. Neville's strong affinity for pragmatism, as well as his most critical comments about it, alike take as their point of departure the pragmatic focus on interpretation. The first part of this paper will explore the strong affinities between Neville's position and pragmatism, focusing on the way these involve their shared understanding of the embeddedness of interpretation in an ontologically vague processive universe and lead ultimately to Neville's unique understanding of the interpretive structures constituting philosophic systems. The second part of the paper will explore his intriguing attempt to synthesize the Whiteheadian emphasis on discreteness with the pragmatic emphasis on continuity, an endeavor that will lead directly to his understanding of time and the ongoing dynamics of a processive universe. This will involve returning to the issue of interpretation, this time to help bring into focus a fundamental divide that separates his basically Whiteheadian intuitions from those of pragmatism in the structuring of his move toward synthesis.

While Neville draws from various of the pragmatists, he relies most heavily on Peirce's thought. He sees Peirce as giving rise to two tightly interwoven lines of descent. The first is the pragmatic tradition of James, Dewey, Mead, and others. The second is the tradition of Whiteheadian process philosophy and others that draw from Whitehead's general position in their own work. These two lines Neville shows to be linked together in many shared insights, both offering non-modernist philosophies that are neither themselves postmodern nor subject to the criticisms of postmodernism. Many of these shared features will be those discussed below, though the focus will be on their relation to pragmatism.

The key to Neville's affinity with pragmatism is to be found in the opening claim of his introduction to *Recovery of the Measure,* which asserts that "none of the intellectual projects feeding our current preoccupation with interpretation sustains a developed philosophy of nature." Pointing out that the currently popular European and Anglo-American approaches all lose their grip on a sense of reality by which to measure our interpretations, he turns to the American pragmatic-process tradition, with its emphasis on a philosophy of nature, as the basis from which to derive his own theory of interpretation.

The pragmatic understanding of interpretation has several key features that are important for Neville. While both hermeneutics and pragmatism point out the theory-ladenness of observation, the basis of hermeneutics is interpretation of texts, while for pragmatism it is experimentation. All experience involves experimentation, and hermeneutical conversation is but one aspect of it. Again, in contrast to the semiotics of Saussure and the structuralist tradition, the pragmatists hold that signs have the power to grow and generalize. Ideas generalize beyond initial contexts and in doing so grow in richness. As Neville states, in a claim that anticipates his later development of the nature of metaphysics, "Growth begins with a vague, suggestive, metaphoric extension, and as the sign is actually lived with in the new mediating function, it becomes specific. The specifics are not delimitations of the initial vague sign, they are enrichments."[1] And, just as signs in human thinking and communication grow in richness and extent, so do signs in human institutions and in nature.

What is of utmost importance for Neville in pragmatism is something that is often overlooked or, worse, denied by its critics who view it as crass and materialistic. The way signs interpret their objects are in some respects selected by the purposes guiding the interpretation, and purposes are value laden and are judged by their ability to allow for the promotion of the values involved in the interpretive context. Neville's philosophic project is geared to develop categories for understanding interpretation as specifications of categories for understanding nature, and all interpretation involves valuation. Human experience and nature in general are value-laden throughout, and this is one of the keys to the way in which pragmatism as well as Whiteheadian philosophy avoid the reduction of nature to a machine and offer a "high road around modernism." The nonreductionist embeddedness of humans in nature, as well as the understanding of nature as the measure of our interpretations and as grasped through our interpretations eludes the postmodern critique of modernist philosophy.[2]

Likewise, the pragmatic conception of experience rejects dualism in favor of a view in which mind is not separated from body but understood as the guiding element of humans in their ongoing interaction with the world. This guiding, interpretive element is corrected by ongoing experience and involves creativity and imaginative reflection by which hypotheses are constructed and tested in the ongoing course of experience. This gives rise to the understanding of metaphysics as an activity involving the formation of experimental hypotheses. In this way the pragmatic focus on the experimental nature of interpretive activity leads to speculative systematic philosophy. Metaphysics does not involve a philosophy of presence but a philosophy of experimentation, the experimental formation of hypothetical claims.

Neville's understanding of metaphysical systems as well as the ontological reality to which they apply seems throughout to have more in common with pragmatism than with Whitehead. This is in part due to his extensive, creative use of Peirce's concept of vagueness. As he stresses, the position he has developed utilizing Peirce's concept of vagueness is clearer than Whitehead's about the kind of abstraction involved in systematic philosophy. Thus he expresses hesitation about Whitehead's intent: "Should Whitehead believe that philosophic abstractions are merely general, referring immediately to actual things, the system of categories might be taken to require a totality in its references which is unjustified by either our experience or our philosophic arguments."[3]

Distinguishing Peirce's understanding of the vague from his understanding of the general, Neville holds that a sign that is vague tolerates mutually contradictory interpretations. "Vagueness is not fuzziness but rather tolerance of ambiguity, confusion, and contradiction among the less abstract notions that might specify the vague ideas."[4] Vague hypotheses are highly abstract and do not dictate to or directly refer to less abstract local domains but rather must be further specified in order to have real reference, and they can be specified in varied or even contradictory manners. Thus, for example, Whitehead's event ontology of selfhood can be specified by the psychologies of Freud or Skinner. By contrast, claims that are general rather than vague refer directly without the need for further theory. For instance, Skinner's scientific theory refers directly to conditioned reflex.

This understanding of metaphysical systems as vague avoids logocentrism or categorial imperialism imposed upon local domains. It also allows diverse domains of intelligibility to communicate with each other without imposing their own claims. Metaphysics proceeds by providing a categorial system that articulates a vague world we have in common and then dialectically moving back and forth between the categorial system and its potential specification in the pockets of order that seem to be important. Moreover, it leads naturally to the fallibilism and tolerance of philosophic systems that again reflect basic tenets of pragmatic philosophy.

Neville's affinity with pragmatism is even more marked in his move from the vagueness of metaphysical systems to the ontological vagueness of the world.[5] He rejects the concept of totality implicit in Whitehead's conception of God's conditioned, consequent nature in favor of an ontological vagueness. In keeping with his understanding of the term 'vagueness', ontological vagueness means the world is potentially coherent through the harmony imposed by a finite subject, and this harmony can be imposed even in contradictory ways. The development of the enduring perspective of a civilized culture imposes an enduring unity, harmony, or coherence on the ontologically vague world, but such an enduring unity cannot be confused with absoluteness of any sort. Thus, we are brought again to the pragmatic notion of an ontologically embedded perspectivalism involving creative interpretation and allowing for a plurality of perspectives.

Drawing on the Peircean distinction between meaning and truth, Neville argues that the question of truth is not relevant to philosophic systems, but rather the important issue is whether a unified perspective creates a systematically enlarged and penetrating experience. In this way, philosophical systems provide meaningfulness rather than truth. Neville's use of pragmatism on this point is perhaps not put to the best use. In saying this, the intent is not to take issue with his interpretation of pragmatism. Such a critique would well miss the mark, for Neville is not giving an exposition of pragmatism but creatively and brilliantly utilizing pragmatic themes for his own purposes. Rather, taking notice of something such as this has validity in the context of his work only if it is understood as questioning whether or not the conclusions he reaches in particular instances best suit his purposes.

In his utilization of pragmatism here Neville develops a position that is in line with various contemporary attempts to reject any cognitive content for metaphysics while allowing it some usefulness.[6] From the pragmatic framework of an ontologically grounded perspectivalism, however, the claims of common sense, science, and philosophy alike provide meaningfulness, a way of orienting oneself to the world, before the issue of truth can emerge. If one does not confine truth to conformity or correspondence, then meaningful, creative orientation toward that reality in which we are embedded, and truth as workability, go hand in hand. At no level—common sense, science, or metaphysics— does this claim for allowing truth value to our assertions rule out pluralism or tolerance, for truth emerges from the backdrop of an interpretive context, and other interpretive contexts are possible. This point would seem particularly important given Neville's concern with "whether a theory of interpretation can acknowledge that reality is the measure of interpretive truth. Truth is the elusive but most important concept at issue."[7] To the extent that truth, according to Neville, is relative to a meaningful, perspectival context, and other meaningful contexts can give forth other truths for which reality is the measure, metaphysical interpretations, as interpretations, would seem not totally divorced from the issue of truth. And, to the extent that there is, as Neville holds, a truth about real values that transcend the various perspectives and varying nets for "catching" reality,[8] then metaphysical systems may well offer the best possibility for exposing them through the scope of the interpretive net they offer.

It would seem that Neville's understanding of the way in which reality is the measure provides as well an understanding of truth that offers a potent tool for allowing some cognitive, though vague, import to philosophic theories without lessening their role as providing "enlarging and penetrating experience." If this reconciliation is viable within his position, it may well be worth pursuing. Neville's position itself contains the seeds for this, for he discusses the way we judge some metaphysical systems as false and some as possibly true, though the notion of truth involved is implicitly a basically pragmatic one that denies correspondence or conformity.[9] Further, in drawing from the pragmatic notions not only of tolerance and engagement but also of fallibilism in characterizing philosophical systems, the notion of truth would seem to be implied. For to say that hypotheses at all levels are fallible would seem to imply that at any level they may or may not be true—though again, not in the traditional senses of truth. Neville has clearly provided a strong alternative to traditional understandings of the nature of metaphysical systems, a view of them as experimental, tolerant, and fallible. What his philosophy implicitly also offers is a strong alternative to traditional understandings of what it means for them to be judged true or false, an understanding of the emergence of truth as experimental, tolerant, fallible, and inextricably context-related, yet nonetheless measured by reality.

The key themes of pragmatism that have been seen to be operative as key themes in Neville's understanding of our access to the real and in his move toward the understanding of speculative philosophical system are:

First, interpretation does not cut us loose from an anchor in reality but rather is an endeavor that opens meanings to their fullness and richness at the fundamental level of existence. Interpretation involves the structures and processes that are constitutive of the reality of the interpreter and the reality of what is known.

Second, traditional empiricism is not empirical enough; it is not radically empirical. Experience overflows our attempts to divide it up, grasp it discretely, view it through the valueless lens of science. Experience overflows the rigid boundaries of conceptual distinctions and abstract interpretations. This 'radical empiricism'[10] regains the rich textures lost by traditional empiricism.

Third, experience is not the coming together of a separate subject and object, of a subjective realm of the contents of experience and an objective realm of nature. The entire attempt to somehow relate subjective sense data to an objective world is rejected. Rather, experience is permeated by an ontological presence, the vagueness of which we render precise through our interpretive directions.

Fourth, the view of knowledge and experience is radically nonspectator. In no way are humans merely spectators in the universe, just seeing what is there. Rather, what we experience is always a product of two factors, what is there and our interpretations or purposes or goal-oriented activities in terms of which we interact with what is there. Our purposes, what we are doing, affect the very character of what we experience.

Fifth, and as a result of the above points, there is an undercutting of the alternatives of foundationalism or nonfoundationalism and, along with this, the closely related dichotomies of objectivism or relativism, since each, in its own way, represents the alternatives of an absolute grounding of knowledge or skepticism.

Sixth, there is a reversal of the building-block model of experience and knowledge in favor of an understanding of them as holistic. We do not begin with bits and pieces that we put together. All experience and knowledge involve contextually set selectivity that is guided by our intents, purposes, and desires, and is value-laden throughout.

Seventh, philosophy must begin where we are, immersed in the world of thick experience, and from an examination of this experience, draw out certain features and dimensions. This "drawing out" or speculative extrapolation from experience involves a creative interpretation that directs the way we focus on experience and that is judged by the intelligibility it in turn introduces into the examination of experience. This allows for fallibilism, pluralism, and open-endedness; for the espousal of a method that is experimental; and for the rejection of all attempts to absolutize the contents of science, favoring instead a truly philosophic metaphysics. Further, such a metaphysics must allow for the fact that the nature we experience evinces both the precarious and the stable, activity and structure, change and order, novelty and continuity.

The remainder of this paper will turn to Neville's intriguing attempt to combine the diverse insights of pragmatism and Whiteheadian philosophy concerning the issues of continuity and discreteness. Neville finds that Whitehead's position is inadequate to account for continuities, especially the continuities involved in personal identity through time. To balance out the momentariness of process philosophy's theory of atomic occasions Neville turns to pragmatism's theory of habit. This position is very congenial to Neville's for, as he notes, habits develop and alter in responding to the environment, "not as mechanical unfoldings of previously set algorithms or the dialects of power, nor as the adventitious setting of will by fancy and whim."[11]

At its most fundamental level this attempted synthesis between continuity and discreteness goes well beyond the issue of personal identity and is embedded in the general issue of time. As Neville states, Whitehead's strength lies in "the power of his speculative vision to be anti-reductionistic at the same time that its elements are atomic micro-moments." Yet what Whitehead failed to do was to "provide an account of the structures that link the vast patterns of moments necessary for the highly developed structure embodied in a moment." In this way, Whitehead's position is ultimately "an atomism too dependent on promissory notes about connective tissues."[12] Neville holds that the pragmatic theory of habit has its own limitation, however, in that "its theory of continuity does not allow for a significant distinction of the present (in which change takes place) from either the past (which is finished) or the future (which is mere possibility)."[13] Pragmatism's weakness, however, he sees as Whiteheadian philosophy's strength. For, "The atomic theory of the present in Whitehead provides exactly the corrective needed by pragmatism."[14] Neville's theory of time, then, will attempt to synthesize the Whiteheadian focus on atomicity with the pragmatic focus on continuity.

Neville is particularly critical and dismissive of the pragmatic understanding of time, and it is in fact in this area that he offers his most intense criticism of pragmatism, holding that like most twentieth-century philosophy it cannot sustain a serious theory of temporal reality.[15] And, Neville holds that this problem evolves from the pragmatic focus on interpretation, for while the future collapses into a mere conditional projection of the present, the past has its reality only as a possible object of interpretation and is, like the future, reduced to its role in possible interpretation, which is an activity in the present. As he summarizes the problem as he sees it, pragmatism cannot handle temporal reality because it reduces metaphysics to what follows the structure of interpretation, the most unfortunate consequence of this being its inability to handle the reality of past things.[16] The problem with pragmatism, for Neville, does not lie in its theory of interpretation itself but in its "reduction of metaphysics to what follows the structure of interpretation."[17]

Yet the metaphysical model of habit-taking that Neville approvingly incorporates from pragmatism ultimately cannot be separated from the pragmatic understanding of temporality. Habit is not limited to life processes, but rather, as Neville well notes, is quite apt to describe individuals, systems of social institutions and nature.[18] Such a description brings time to the fore; for, as Neville again well stresses, time is not a container of any sort, but a characteristic of temporal things. The habit-takings of humans and nature are part and parcel of its temporal features. Thus, the disagreement between Neville and pragmatism concerning the temporal dynamics of the universe would seem ultimately to underlie their respective understanding of the dynamics of habit-taking. Moreover, human habit-takings are both the source and embodiment of concrete interpretive activities. Thus, habit-taking, interpretation, and temporality are ultimately intertwined in pragmatic philosophy, and while Neville's appropriations from pragmatic philosophy of interpretation and habit are highly constructive within his position, his attack on pragmatism's theory of temporality will be seen to bring into focus the way his attempted synthesis of Whiteheadian atomicity and pragmatic continuity aligns him throughout with Whitehead in opposition to pragmatism in a very fundamental way.

Neville's synthesis of discreteness and continuity utilizes a creative reconstruction of Paul Weiss's distinction between essential and conditional features. Before turning directly to this synthesis, these conceptual tools as well as the role of harmony must be sketched.[19] Conditional features are those that constitute how a thing is conditioned by other things. These have to do at least with causation, with context, or with order. In a rough sense, causal conditions enter a present thing from the past, contextual conditions from the present, and ordering conditions from the future. Only a total atomism or "monadology" can deny conditional features. Essential features are necessary constituents of things along with conditional features because things cannot be reduced to the influences of others and their own influences on others. These features prevent a thing's being reduced to other things. Roughly, there are three types of essential features: characteristic essential features that give a thing identity over time; decisive essential features that a thing gives itself in a present moment of self-determination; and value-making essential features that are functions of the possibilities a thing might have, possibilities of different worth. Philosophies that deny essential features cannot maintain a plurality of real and different things in the world.

Essential features are not more necessary than conditional ones. Rather, both are necessary. Determinateness requires both connection and self-sameness. Understood functionally, essential features are what the thing contributes to its conditional features to integrate them into the harmonized thing. Things are harmonies of both conditional and essential features,[20] and it is this that allows them to be determinately related to other things and to be determinately different from those other things. Harmony does not involve some higher principle that integrates its components; rather harmony in the metaphysical sense in which Neville is using it is the sheer togetherness or fit of the conditional and essential features. A harmony can be expressed without specifying any unifying principle over and above the sheer fit of the essential and conditional features. The features of a harmony have harmonies of their own, and so on. Harmonies are integrations of conditional and essential features and no more; there is no implication that they are stable integrations or that they are good ones.

With these tools Neville approaches the issue of time. He holds that each temporal mode, past, present, and future, has its essential features that characterize its "timeliness." However, no mode of time can be what it is without conditional features from the other modes. Temporality, as opposed to timeliness, is the harmony of all the modes in their essential and conditional features, a harmony that constitutes time's flow. Neville is concerned here to maintain the difference between past, present, and future and to avoid the assumption that one temporal mode is paradigmatic for all the others. Without recognizing the otherness between the temporal modes, it is impossible to accept the passage of time in its wholeness.

Very briefly stated, the timeliness of the past, its essential feature, is its objective everlastingness. It is "finished, actualized, and fixed."[21] The essential features of the present are spontaneous creativity, change, and actualization. The essential features of the future have to do with pure normative form and value.[22] While each set of essential features constitutes the timeliness of each temporal mode, none of the modes is real with only its essential features, for each is a harmony of essential and conditional features. Thus Neville holds that although essential features are what make each mode timely, contributing its unique element to temporal passage, they are not by themselves temporal. "But then, they are not by themselves."[23] They are an integration of essential and conditional features. That time flows is understood in terms of the mutual conditioning of the temporal modes. The flow of time is the actualizing of possibilities and the putting into the past of that actuality. This adds to the previous past. The actualizing changes the future possibilities so that no other actualization could be exactly like the one that flowed. And the immediacy of the present vanishes as soon as it is accomplished.[24]

While the temporality of each mode of time—past, present, and future—provides one form of conditional togetherness for the three kinds of temporality, this is inadequate to provide a togetherness of the different essential natures of past, present, and future.[25] Taking the present as an example, Neville details that the essential dynamism of the present neglects the everlasting fixity of the past. The temporality of the present unifies the three temporalities as inherited past and future potentials for present action. This does justice to the essential dynamism of the present, to the conditional readiness of the past to influence the present, and to the conditional structures supplied by the future for possible actions. But it neglects the essential objective, everlasting fixity of the past, and also the past's achieved values, because it treats both only as potential for modification in the present's creative action. And it neglects the essential intrinsic normativeness of the future by transforming it into what merely satisfies the need to achieve determinateness, relative to past conditions, in the present moment.[26]

Continuing in analogous fashion, Neville shows each of the modes of temporality to be insufficient to unify the three into one temporality (or, concretely, time). Hence, that time which is the unity of the three kinds of temporality is "somehow simply a fitting together of those three," which is itself a-temporal or eternal.[27] Neville concludes that "we must indeed appeal to eternity to understand time. For there is a togetherness of the modes of time that is not a function of any of the kinds of temporality."[28] The essential features of time are together in eternity. The temporal modes "are not before or after one another, nor are they together in the same time, but in eternity. . . . It is clear the temporal modes themselves are not together temporally. Rather, it is their togetherness that allows for the temporal togetherness of things that are earlier, later, and contemporary with other things."[29]

The generality of the issue as developed above in relation to time is partially indicated by Neville in his assertion that the inability of each of the three modes of temporality to unify them into one temporality is an illustration of an "important characteristic" of the general problem of the one and the many. "Stated abstractly, if there are two things, each with essential and conditional features, each can include the other within itself by means of the other's conditional features; but by definition it cannot include the other's essential features, without making the other just a proper part of itself. Therefore, a solution to the problem of the one and the many cannot be reached from the standpoint of any one and the many alone."[30] As he puts the issue "most paradoxically," "There is a togetherness of a thing's youth, when its maturity is still undetermined, with its age when nearly everything is fixed. Temporal sequence is not the whole of the togetherness because the thing's determinate character is different at different stages in the sequence."[31] In short, there must be some kind of nontemporal or eternal togetherness.

The problem does indeed involve the general issue of the one and the many, and in the context of the focus of this second section of the paper, the discussion of this general issue translates into the problem of the relation of continuity and discreteness.

Neville's discussion is rich with insights concerning temporality in its various dimensions, adding an originality and depth to the ongoing discussion. His development of the distinction between conditional and essential features of past, present, and future, and the way in which this provides a unification of time in terms of its conditional features, brings the issue to a deeper level than is found in Whitehead's position. But, while Neville's philosophy is pervaded by a keen insight concerning the difficulty for Whiteheadian philosophy of bringing together disparate aspects of time, yet the need for "the-bringing-together-of" is never really questioned. And, if truncation is in any sense allowed, then an appeal to eternity may well be needed to provide the togetherness. But as long as the assumption remains that the arrow of time requires an everlastingly fixed, finished, dead past, then it would seem that the more one moves toward a dynamic present, the firmer must become the truncation of temporal modes. As Neville states, the modes are related to each other by the conditional features. But with respect to the conditional features, their essential features are mutually external.[32] It is this fundamental intuition of "the-bringing-together-of" that which is mutually external that ultimately structures Neville's philosophy and that harbors the depth of his Whiteheadian as opposed to pragmatic bent. The remainder of the paper will turn to this issue, but first it is important to clarify just what the issue at hand is and is not.

First, the issue does not involve any claim that Neville's appeal to eternity indicates some weakness in his position on time. Within the framework of his theological interests such an appeal does not reflect the weakness of a position that must call on eternity to solve a philosophic puzzle, but instead the strength of a position that develops from the start with an intent to both draw upon and point to the need for eternity— now redefined in accordance with his radically processive approach. Nor does the fact that the pragmatists do not make this move to eternity point in itself to the issue at hand, for if one so desired, such a move could be made from a framework that is fundamentally pragmatic in its leanings—again with some process reinterpretation of eternity. Rather, the point of the discussion as regards the turn to eternity will be twofold: first, to show just how Neville's need for this eternal unification reveals his Whiteheadian distance from pragmatism concerning the general issue of the relation of continuity and discreteness; second, to question whether the move to an eternal togetherness closes this distance or reintroduces it at a "higher" or eternal level.

It may be objected that the above analysis of Neville's understanding of time fails to heed Neville's warning that "distinguishing and connecting" should not be understood in an old-fashioned substantialist way, as if the three temporal modes were three independent substances with some connections. Rather, they are three harmonies, each of which requires for its own being the conditional features derived from the others that, when harmonized with its essential timeliness, make the modes temporal.[33] However, the entire conception of harmony as developed by Neville is itself based on the model of the "coming-together-of." This can best be seen by focusing on his understanding of time from a slightly different direction.

This basic intuition of "the-coming-together-of" is evidenced again in Neville's understanding of the flow of time as composed of temporal atoms. As he states, "There is a least unit of time in a thing's temporal flow."[34] An atomic, indivisible unit of time for Neville is of course not pointlike, but rather is an indivisible extension or temporal dimension. Moreover, he stresses that the flow of time is smooth: "At no time is there a break between the finish of one emerging present and the beginning of the next; at the next time there is already a new emergent becoming. At no time is there a transitional bump from one present to the next."[35] In this way, "the flow of time is continuous."[36]

This "arising" of continuity from the putting together of atomic units in Neville's position can be seen again in his claim that "whereas present moments of actualization have an internal integrity and 'droplike' character, the actuality of the past has integrated these into larger structured elements. The past of a person is not the set of individual decision points but the history of deeds and accumulated character of the individual in context."[37] Once again, there is an integration of atomic units into continuities, into habits that pervade the various processes of a temporal universe and that ultimately manifest themselves as interpretive habits. This point can be further clarified by turning to Neville's discussion of things in the world and their nature as harmonies. The richness of the world at a level of metaphysical abstractness has two dimensions:[38] Ontologically, "to be determinate is to be a harmony of essential and conditional features created *ex nihilo* by an indeterminate ground."[39] This gives rise to the cosmological dimension of the world as a process of subprocesses, for since essential and conditional features are themselves determinate, "they too are harmonies, and so down and around, infinitely."[40] In this way, things are infinitely "associated" ontologically and also infinitely deep or dense harmonies—infinite in their component units.[41] Thus, just as time is ultimately composed of atomic building blocks, things in time are understood in terms of harmonies of infinite atomic components or units.

Thus, also, time is the conjunction of past, present, and future,[42] and though these are eternally together, they are together in the relationship of conjoined parts.[43] The intuition of "the-coming-together-of" pervades and in large part defines Neville's philosophic stance.

But continuity as it functions in pragmatic philosophy gains its key role because continuity is precisely the absence of ultimate parts in what is divisible. The putting together of discrete units of any type can yield only a pseudocontinuum, a contiguity of parts as opposed to a continuity. For pragmatism, the key intuition concerning temporality and the habit-takings that partake of temporal features is that of "emerging elements within" continuity rather than the "coming-together-of" discretes. Continuity is primary, and interacting portions of a processive concrete universe yield the emergence of quasi discretes, be it present, past, and future, or persisting "individuals."

Thus, Peirce holds that the present relates to the past through a series of real infinitesimals[44] that can in no way be understood in terms of an indefinite succession of discretes but rather as a continuous flow.[45] An infinitesimal is not an ultimate ontological unit because it is not a discrete segment. Peirce does allow for a certain temporal independence to infinitesimal durations of time but this is a functional independence; they represent the beginnings of spontaneity in the present, though in serving the function of providing these beginnings they are in fact infinitesimal intervals that are inherently continuous.[46] And as Peirce stresses, such continuities, though infinitesimal in duration, are nonetheless entirely unlimited; there is an absence of boundedness.[47] This absence of boundedness is incorporated in James's agreement with Peirce in the context of noting the importance of infinitesimals as the basis for creative novelty. As he states, the mathematical notion of an infinitesimal contains, "in truth, the whole paradox of the same and yet the nascent other, of an identity that won't keep except so far as it keeps failing."[48] The whole conception of atomic units as well as sequences of units is an abstraction, for the movement from one interval to another is not a movement over discrete units but a spreading out of a continuous process of becoming other.

Pragmatism, like Neville, recognizes that the flow of time cannot be a simple continuum, but rather requires "breaks." The pragmatic answer, however, is not to turn to atomic units but rather, as Mead summarizes the perspective, there must be some break, not *of* continuity, but *within* continuity.[49] The continuity is the condition for the novelty, while the novelty reveals the continuity through the oncoming adjustment that accommodates the novel, rendering it continuous with what came before. Time moves as a whole and with depth, and in the ongoing adjustments that accommodate the novelty of the ever-emerging present, time adjusts throughout.

Neville holds that process philosophers and pragmatists agree about the way in which the present "now" cuts between a determined past and a partially indeterminate future,[50] but this is precisely a key issue between pragmatic and Whiteheadian-style process philosophies. This difference can be seen by viewing their contrasting characterizations of the present "now." For Neville, the events that constitute the present do not occur through time but at a time, for their succession provides the building blocks of time. Moreover, because for Neville "that from which change takes place is the finished past," which is everlastingly fixed, it can be part of the present, not as an early part of the present but only as a logical "before."[51] As Neville encapsulates, "there is no temporal passage in the present";[52] the creative coming-to-be that characterizes the present is not itself temporal. In opposition to this, and because of its understanding of the primacy of continuity and the holistic nature of temporal movement, temporality pervades the present for pragmatism; hence Peirce can claim that "the present is half past and half to come."[53] While for Neville, earlier and later do not overlap in time, "although they are times with some dimension and with dates," James refers to the relation as one of interfusion.[54]

Within the pragmatic position the past is allowed its full integrity, though its integrity is not that of absolute fixity and finality; rather, while it is obdurate in that certain happenings have occurred, there is a certain amount of "loose play"[55] because of the pervasive role of continuity and the indeterminacy this involves.[56] From the pragmatic perspective, there is nothing absolutely finished, fixed, and final except the events of actualization, but the event as a metaphysically discrete determinate individual, as a moment of temporal/ontological atomicity, is an idealized abstraction from a history and process of becoming other. What it would be as such it cannot be because of its radically temporal nature. This involves an understanding of the discreteness of actuality as an idealized abstraction rather than as an ultimate ontological building block. From the pragmatic perspective, it can be said that the assertion of temporal/ontological atoms as discrete building blocks of time and the universe in general is itself an instance of the fallacy of misplaced concreteness.

In the ongoing "spreading out" or diffusion of continuities, the actualizations involved are themselves continuities that, as becoming other, are not fully determinate and, as actual, are constituted by present dynamic tendencies as possibilities and potentialities for bringing about further eventful results. Potentialities and possibilities alike can best be understood as concrete dynamic tendencies of reality toward actualizations of varying types under varying types of circumstances, and the difference between them is their relevance to the contexts within which they presently function. What this indicates is that 'concrete', for pragmatism, does not mean fully determinate. No slab of processive concreteness is fully determinate. The indeterminacy and continuity of concrete reality go hand in hand. Rather, reality is concrete in the sense that it is, as James so well expresses, the "living, moving, active thickness of the real,"[57] the thick ontological density of "the causal dynamic relatedness of activity and history."[58]

For pragmatism, the vagueness of the world is a function of the concrete continuities that pervade it. The law of noncontradiction does not hold of reality in its total concreteness, for, as James expresses this, "place yourself at the interior thickness of the doing, and you see that in its concreteness it has the potential for breaking into the most contradictory characterizations."[59] Or, as Peirce states the same point, reality is a continuum that "swims in indeterminacy,"[60] and the indeterminacy or vagueness of reality as involving continuity is what makes the laws of noncontradiction and excluded middle only imperfectly applicable.[61] All of reality in its concreteness harbors an element of vagueness because of the continuity and indeterminacy that pervades reality and its temporal dimensions. This of course lies in radical opposition to Neville's understanding of concreteness as the fully determinate,[62] with vagueness a function of the infinitude of possible harmonies among an infinitude of atomic units.

The pragmatic way of grounding the directionality of time, the arrow of time, does not call upon the conceptual tools of fixity and atomicity. Rather, the indeterminacy and adjustments incorporated in the temporal spread of the present provide an immediate experience of change or temporal movement, a direct sense of change given in the spreading out of the present and, with it, a sense of the movement of dynamic tendencies toward the future. While the pragmatic understanding of temporality renders impossible not only a fully determinate present or future, but also a fully determinate past, yet it provides for a thickness and directional movement to time within nature that is directly experienced in the temporal flow of the passing present. Indeed, human dispositional tendencies or habits, as continuities providing a readiness to respond to an oncoming future via emerging activities and to adjust throughout to novel directions arising from the creative interactions of the present, are concrete ontological activities that, in their ongoing functioning, provide a direct sense of the directional flow of dynamic tendencies as possibilities and potentialities and, in this way, provide our primordial sense of the arrow of time. The dynamics of interpretive activity, which are part and parcel of the concrete dynamics of human habits, do not dictate to the pragmatic understanding of time, but rather the pragmatic rethinking of the relation of continuity and discreteness provides for its understanding of the temporal dimensions of the universe in general and human interpretive activity in particular.

For Neville, then, time is tied to the succession of ontological/temporal atoms and the absolute fixity of the past to which they give rise, offering a quasi continuity of discrete units. For pragmatic process, time itself is a continuous spreading out in which quasi discretes, which are themselves continuous processes, emerge in the passing present through the interaction of dynamic tendencies constitutive of the ongoing temporal/ontological advance. The directional spreading out of these concrete, dynamic continuities in an ongoing process of activity or interaction provides at once a direct sense of temporal passage and an efficaciousness of the present to which both past and future adjust, each in its own manner. In this way, their differing intuitions of time are inseparably interwoven with differing understandings of the interrelations of discreteness and continuity, actuality and potentiality, concreteness and indeterminacy.

Both Neville and pragmatism attempt to account for a resisting, thick, ontologically dense processive universe characterized by both persistence and change, continuity and discreteness, lawfulness and spontaneity. They each recognize the importance of the embeddedness of interpretation in general in an ontologically vague universe if one is to avoid the extremes of modernism and postmodernism alike. Neville's understanding of the richness and holistic nature of experience and interpretation seems, like pragmatism, to better fit the paradigm of "emerging elements within," rather than the "coming-together-of." Yet it is precisely these divergent paradigms operative in their respective understandings of the processive dynamics of the universe that ultimately split Neville and pragmatism apart.

While these divergent paradigms hold the key to unraveling the differences between Neville and pragmatism, these differences are far overshadowed by the strong spirit of pragmatism that pervades Neville's work, and his creative and sensitive appropriation of pragmatic themes in his deeply penetrating analyses of metaphysical system, interpretation, value, culture, and concrete human existence offer a fertile field for the ongoing enrichment of the pragmatic tradition in American philosophy. Moreover, the many similarities and underlying differences between Neville and pragmatism provide an opportunity for an ongoing and deepened constructive dialogue about fundamental issues of philosophy, a dialogue that has its roots in Neville's unique, creative intertwining of the Whiteheadian and pragmatic traditions.

NOTES

1. *Recovery of the Measure*, p. 49.
2. Neville makes a distinction between modernity and modernism. Modernity encompasses the European Renaissance in the sixteenth century to

the present. Modernism refers to a specific cultural movement of the late nineteenth and early twentieth centuries, and postmodernism is the attempt to identify, totalize, and reject this modernism. Modernity is distinguished from the preceding scholastic period by its insistence on learning through an engagement with nature, and the pragmatists and Whitehead are thus late philosophers of modernity, building on and correcting the tradition, but they are not modernists. See *The Highroad around Modernism*, especially pp. 5ff. and 50ff.

3. *The Highroad around Modernism*, p. 129.

4. *Eternity and Time's Flow*, p. 9.

5. *The Highroad around Modernism*, p. 125ff.

6. Some would say that the distinction between meaningfulness and truth corresponds to the distinction between interpretive and descriptive.

7. *Recovery of the Measure*, p. 15.

8. *Recovery of the Measure*, passim; see especially pp. 322–25 for a brief summary of the position he has been developing throughout.

9. *Eternity and Time's Flow*, pp. 9–11.

10. This term of course is taken from William James.

11. *The Highroad around Modernism*, pp. 214–15.

12. Ibid., p. 104.

13. Ibid., pp. 214–15.

14. Ibid.

15. *Recovery of the Measure*, pp. 50–52.

16. Ibid., pp. 50–51.

17. Ibid.

18. Ibid.

19. The following features can best be found encapsulated in *Eternity and Time's Flow*, p. 71ff.

20. The Axiological dimension of metaphysics, so crucial for Neville's position, is the intuition of harmony. The exploration of this dimension, however, lies well beyond the scope of this paper.

21. *Eternity and Time's Flow*, p. 80.

22. Neville rejects Whitehead's use of God in understanding the reality of forms, holding instead to the ontological parity of actuality and form.

23. *Eternity and Time's Flow*, p. 92.

24. *Recovery of the Measure*, p. 181.

25. Ibid.

26. Ibid., p. 180.

27. *Eternity and Time's Flow*, p. 181.

28. *Recovery of the Measure*, p. 181.

29. *Eternity and Time's Flow*, pp. 110–11.

30. *Recovery of the Measure*, p. 181.

31. Ibid.

32. *Eternity and Time's Flow*, pp. 112–13.

33. Ibid., p. 109.

34. *Eternity and Time's Flow*, p. 96.

35. Ibid., p. 105.

36. Ibid.

37. Ibid., p. 101.

38. The following is a gross oversimplification of Neville's position here, but one that I think does not distort it and is adequate for the point being made.

39. *Highroad around Modernism*, p. 265.

40. Ibid.

41. Ibid., p. 266.

42. *Eternity and Time's Flow*, p. 92.

43. Ibid.

44. Charles Peirce, *Collected Papers*, vols. 1–6, ed. Charles Hartshorne and Paul Weiss (Cambridge: Belknap Press of Harvard University, 1931–35); vols. 7 and 8, ed. Arthur Burks (Cambridge: Harvard University Press, 1958), 6:109.

45. Ibid., p. 111.

46. Ibid., pp. 86–87.

47. Ibid., p. 138.

48. *A Pluralistic Universe*, The Works of William James, ed. Frederick Burkhardt (Cambridge: Harvard University Press, 1977), p. 154.

49. *The Philosophy of the Present*, ed. Arthur Murphy (La Salle, Ill.: Open Court, 1959), pp. 114–16; "The Nature of the Past," *Selected Writings*, ed. Andrew Reck (New York: Bobbs-Merrill, 1964), p. 350.

50. *Recovery of the Measure*, p. 179.

51. *Eternity and Time's Flow*, p. 98.

52. Ibid., p. 92.

53. Peirce, *Collected Papers*, 6.126.

54. James, *A Pluralistic Universe*, p. 153.

55. This is in no way to say that the ontological reality of the past is dependent upon our interpretation of it. See Neville's criticism of pragmatism's understanding of the past, in *Recovery of the Measure*, pp. 50–51. Our changing interpretations of the past are one thing; the ontological nature of the past is quite another thing. For a fuller discussion of a pragmatic understanding of the nature of the past, which can be mentioned here only briefly, see my *Speculative Pragmatism* (Amherst: University of Massachusetts Press, 1986); paperback edition (Peru, Ill.: Open Court, 1990), chapter 6.

56. The relation of continuity and indeterminacy will be discussed below.

57. James, *A Pluralistic Universe*, p. 116.

58. Ibid., p. 122.

59. Ibid., p. 117. This "breaking into" is to be understood not as a breaking up into parts but as an emergence into novel traits.

60. Peirce, *Collected Papers*, 1.171–72.

61. Peirce asserts that the general is that to which the law of the excluded middle does not apply, while the vague is that to which the principle of noncontradiction does not apply (5.448). He then explicitly identifies continuity with generality (8.279; MS 137, pp. 7–12). And, for Peirce, whatever is general or continuous is to some degree vague. Thus, neither the law of noncontradiction nor the law of excluded middle is perfectly applicable to the continuous.

62. See *Eternity and Time's Flow*, p. 101, for a concise statement of this point.

CHAPTER 5

Ethics, Metaphysics, and the Use of Comparative Cultural Traditions

George R. Lucas Jr.

In a number of major works, from *The Cosmology of Freedom* (1974) and *The Puritan Smile* (1987) to *The Highroad around Modernism* (1992) and *Normative Cultures* (1995), Robert Neville has demonstrated that his broader interests in speculative metaphysics hold a very practical moral and political focus. I propose in this essay to examine the main features of Neville's moral and political philosophy, paying attention to the diverse, multicultural sources of his views. My sense is that the multiculturalism (particularly the deference to Confucian traditions), while commendable and interesting, is not essential to the development of any of the substantive moral positions, although those positions do follow consistently from Neville's metaphysics. What the appeals to non-Western sources do demonstrate is the universal relevance to which several of Neville's moral positions can justifiably lay claim. Despite the apparent grounding of his moral philosophy in pluralism and claims of cultural difference, his work in the end militates against moral relativism and popular notions of cultural incommensurability.[1] In addition, while tracing the sustained evolution of his views on freedom, opportunity, individuality, community, voluntarism and participatory democracy, creativity and value, suffering, guilt, and social justice over the past thirty years, I will endeavor to show that Neville challenges the prevailing terms of moral debate between traditional liberals and conservatives, and in the process rekindles the old philosophical quarrel between "ancients" and post-Enlightenment "moderns."

ETHICS AND THE EVOLUTION OF NEVILLE'S THOUGHT

Neville's major scholarly contributions are customarily subsumed under three broad categories. Like his mentor, Paul Weiss, he has first and foremost remained a champion of the importance of metaphysics and speculative philosophical inquiry during a period when prevailing philosophical fashion strongly discouraged such projects. In pursuing this comprehensive vision of the philosophical vocation, he reveals his indebtedness to the writings of Alfred North Whitehead, C. S. Peirce, and John Dewey in particular. Secondly, and unlike these predecessors, Neville has championed the importance of comparative cultural philosophies, arguing that, in the late twentieth century, there is no longer any acceptable excuse for responsible Western intellectuals to remain ignorant of, or uninfluenced by, the classical philosophical and religious writings of East and South Asian cultures. Neville has himself been influenced particularly by his studies of Taoism and Confucianism, and has published important studies of the Confucian scholar-official Wang Yang-ming.[2] Thirdly, Neville has made important contributions to Christian and to comparative (interreligious) theology—contributions that have increased in frequency and substance following his appointment as dean of the School of Theology at Boston University, and that were formally recognized by his election as president of the prestigious American Academy of Religion in 1992. By contrast, of the many volumes of work he has authored and edited, only one book, *The Puritan Smile*, could properly be said to be devoted to ethics and moral philosophy specifically. The subtitle of this work, *A Look toward Moral Reflection*, suggests moreover that the attempt is more of a nonsystematic sketch of a range of moral positions or political stances than a carefully worked-out moral theory.

There are good reasons, however, to cultivate a hermeneutic of suspicion with respect to these sorts of neat and tidy classifications by scholars and historians. Such classifications may unintentionally reveal much more information through what is omitted than through what they choose to include. The philosophers influencing Neville's speculative metaphysical interests—for example, Whitehead, Peirce, and Weiss in particular—make no sharp distinctions in their own thought between what properly belongs to the realm of philosophy and what belongs to religion and theology.[3] This is a good part of the reason why (at least until quite recently) their thought has been relegated to the margins of philosophy. Indeed, it is a large part of the argument in Neville's *Highroad around Modernism* that these main figures of American pragmatism and process philosophy do not get caught up in the modernist's disciplinary division of knowledge and intellectual labor. Hence they are not tarnished by postmodernist critiques of the failures of modernism, and indeed provide an alternative, more comprehensive resource for the recovery of philosophy and of culture in the aftermath of the demise of modernism.

Likewise, the non-Western traditions that Neville frequently invokes do not make the disciplinary "turf" distinctions between what counts as philosophy or as "something else" so sharply as we tend to do since the European Enlightenment. Once again, this may account for the tendency among "serious" philosophers to patronize or downplay the legitimacy of these traditions as authentic and reliable resources for contemporary philosophical reflection. Most importantly, within both of these *Ursprungen* of Neville's own thought it is customary to view *praxis* as the aim of theory and to see public philosophy and civic responsibility as the goal and the outgrowth of the life of scholarship. If this is correct, it should be unnecessary, even redundant, to devote specific attention to ethics as if this were one more distinct discipline in the culture of disciplines. One would instead anticipate that moral and political issues should constitute pervasive and omnipresent themes in a systematic philosopher's work.

This is precisely what we find to be the case with Neville's own thought. One of Neville's earliest essays, published more than thirty-five years ago, is a work of metaphysics, published in a leading journal of metaphysics, that argues against the then-popular Sartrean-existentialist amorality of "aesthetic style." Instead, Neville there argued that it is one important task of religion to reconcile, prioritize, and harmonize the competition among ideal ends and conflicting responsibilities that themselves stem from the many and varied roles that go into constituting a single, unitary human existence.[4] Even in this early work, we can discern what will become the hallmark of Neville's systematic and inclusive stance: philosophy, metaphysics, theology, religion, ethics—all are conceived early on as *res publica*, the "public thing" of Cicero, Seneca, and Cato. *Soldier, Sage, and Saint* (1978), a work whose origins lie early in Neville's career, reflects this theme of integrated public philosophy. Many others of Neville's early works are specific pieces on ethical topics—psychosurgery, behavioral control, involuntary sterilization, drug usage—stemming from his association with the Hastings Center.[5] His first major book, *The Cosmology of Freedom*,[6] dealt with the problem of freedom both as a metaphysical and a moral and political issue, concluding with an effort to bring metaphysical discussions of action theory and free choice to bear on the opportunities and necessities for participation in localized centers of free, creative public activity that comprise a true participatory (localized) democracy. With the advantage of hindsight, we would now immediately recognize and celebrate that work as a contribution to communitarian ethics, well before the works of Robert Bellah or Charles Taylor had served to familiarize the public with this alternative to modern liberal political theory. The dedication of the first edition of that work, moreover, indicated the extent to which the moral and philosophical positions of its author were forged in the crucible of genuine human experience. The studies of Wang Yang-ming were devoted to the problem of striking the balance between scholarship and civic responsibility. And the entire second half of *The Highroad around Modernism* is devoted to the politics of postmodernity, including diagnoses of how to circumvent the destructive debates arising in the social sciences that have spilled over with such corrosive effect into our public life: political correctness, "free" speech and speech codes, the politics of ethnicity, gender, group (as opposed to individual) rights, and *différance*.

Over fifteen years ago I published a lengthy review article of work in the field of process metaphysics and singled out Neville's contributions even then as having already constituted a sustained, consistent, and highly original development of that philosophical tradition with a decidedly moral and political slant.[7] Looking back from the perspective of the present, it is nothing short of amazing to see the consistency, as well as the development, of Neville's views on these matters. His unique metaphysics of "discursive individuals," representing his own synthesis of Peirce, Whitehead, and Weiss, was first clearly articulated in *The Cosmology of Freedom*. It does not appear to me that he has wavered significantly from that fundamental ontological stance. He continues to portray individuality as a construction out of conditional (shared, community) and essential (unique, private) features. This construction of individuality and a realm of privacy and uniqueness is, in turn, portrayed as an achievement of value, as a unique harmony of these essential and conditional features. This ontology of individuality, which reverses the modernist logical priority of individual over community, owes much to Plato's *Philebus*, wherein the Good is described as a "mixture." This metaphysical stance is frequently reviewed in Neville's subsequent work, where he puts the fundamental ontology to wider and wider use. It is his attempt to develop a specific and comprehensive vision of moral philosophy in *The Puritan Smile*, based upon this metaphysics, to which I now wish to turn.

NEVILLE'S CHALLENGE TO MODERNISM

I have suggested that "modernism" in moral philosophy consists in privileging the notion of individuality over community, and in presupposing

moreover that society is in some sense an artificial construct out of logically and ontologically prior individuals. The modern view of morality
might also be characterized, following Stanley Rosen's suggestion, as
one of two sharply contrasting conceptions of the foundation of reason
itself. Kant, Rosen argues, framed the modernist conception of reason
during the Enlightenment as grounded in spontaneity, as an expression
of, or perhaps identical with, the freedom of the individual.[8] The
Enlightenment's conception of a moral agent, accordingly, is one who is
seeking to exercise his freedom and realize his individual desires through
the use of his reason. For the ancients, by contrast, reason is that faculty
that enables moral agents, who are fundamentally social and political
beings, to seek the Good.

One might propose yet a third distinction between the ancients and
the moderns, based upon a differing conception of the metaphysical status of past and future. Modernism emphasizes the reality and priority of
the future as a causal determinate within the present, tending (as in Heidegger or Marx or Nietzsche) to instrumentalize the present for the sake
of the future,[9] whereas the ancient view of morality stresses the present
as outgrowth, product, and most importantly, a continuation of the
past. Classical liberalism, from Aristotle to Hume, tends to stress this
continuity with, and power of the past as the foundation of social life,
whereas modern liberalism, from Enlightenment thinkers through
Marx, to Dewey, Heidegger, and beyond, tends to support a philosophy
of social engineering that discounts the value of the past and emphasizes
the infinite possibilities that human reason and freedom provide for creating or constructing a future social order whose blueprint can be more
or less "made to order" or tailored to meet exact social needs or to fulfill well-defined political objectives.

Conventional wisdom dictates that the modern view emerges most
clearly in the mechanism and metaphysical atomism underlying the
social contract theory of Thomas Hobbes. More recent and careful
scholarship suggests that modernism "begins" at least a century before
Hobbes, and is born in Reformation debates concerning natural law,
duty, and civic virtue, and in the skeptical writings of Montaigne concerning the origins of legitimate moral authority (if religion is dis-
counted) and the proper exercise of moral agency (when fear of divine
retribution no longer is an effective or believable sanction).[10] What is
beyond dispute is that the modern conception of morality that results
from these discussions rests, as in Hobbes, upon the fundamental notion
of discrete, disassociated, atomic individuals who exist prior to any
social convention or custom, and who subsequently contract together to
establish social institutions of law and justice, for the sake of fulfilling
essentially private motivations of self-interest. Despite the many varia-

tions of morality that occur from that time to this, including the utilitarian attack on contractual notions of justice in the eighteenth and nineteenth centuries, and the resurgence of contractarian theories in our own century, this one unquestioned presupposition has remained central to modernity: the atomic individual, whose rationality consists in the exercise of his or her individual liberty, and whose subsequent, voluntary, and in an important sense, optional deliberations and contractual arrangements give rise to all subsequent notions of rights, justice, responsibility, and value.

The point in describing and contextualizing the terms of modern moral debate is to demonstrate that Neville's work does not fit neatly within that context. In *The Puritan Smile*, for example, he marshals the traditions of Confucianism and Puritanism to criticize some of the shortcomings of the modernist liberal hegemony. The *Cosmology of Freedom*, however, is concerned with the nature of freedom and individuality, and gives the future an almost eerily preeminent status in determining the present. The earlier work intends, from the author's stance as a Whiteheadian or neo-Whiteheadian process philosopher, to develop a notion of individuality that will answer the objections of Weiss, Dewey, and Edward Pols against Whitehead, that process philosophy itself cannot provide an adequate account of enduring human identity and moral agency. Unlike Whiteheadian "actual entities," the being of Neville's "discursive individuals" extends temporally backward into a shared past as the source of their present self-constitution, but also extends temporally forward into unique alternative futures as their source of free individual creativity. The experience of our subjectivity, Neville claims, is the experience of an ongoing and persistent dialogue between our settled past and our real but still indeterminate future. Present experience is the unification and constant readjustment of selfhood and intentional agency in light of this ongoing dialogue and dialectic between past and future, and the differing perspectives on what is common in the past—as well as on what the indeterminate future can contribute essentially to the present moment of experience—is what differentiates one individual from another, makes each a source of unique value, and makes free intentional agency possible.

In *The Puritan Smile*, Neville draws on this earlier formulation of the metaphysics of personhood or selfhood. Individuals and their constitutive moral acts are described as "harmonies" of conditional and essential features, involving "contrasts" in particular patterns of relating such features as may result in finite objectifications of value. The alternative modes of actualization envisaged from the perspective of every present moment of experience provide (following Plato and Whitehead) the basis for discerning ideals, and for recognizing a normative obligation to actualize the "best possible" achievement of value from the perspective of each episode of present experience. All instances of actions, and of the discursive individuals whose being is constituted by these becomings or activities, thus objectify values or ideals of some sort. Hence, Neville follows John Dewey in holding that every description of a being or of its situation simultaneously enfolds a normative dimension: there are no clear dichotomies between "facts" and "values," or any sharp demarcation between what is and what *ought* to be. Moral obligation arises from, and is limited by, what is the case; but what is the case is always a finite realization of value brought about by consideration of what ought to be.

In *The Puritan Smile*, Neville credits the Puritans and their Asian counterparts the Confucians with recognizing this feature of individuality and moral agency. Theirs—and Neville's—is a kind of "field theory" approach to individuality, in which the individual is at least in part a unique localization of common (conditional, shared) features of the community or society. Interconnectedness and interdependence—the public realm—is the logically prior notion, whence individuality, privacy, and conceptions of individual rights must be artificially constructed through public convention as specific, contractual delimitations or boundary conditions on the underlying continuity of relatedness and common responsibility. This is a tortured way of claiming that, instead of encountering discrete individuals in a state of privacy and then *adding on* increments of public obligation by means of what Locke called the "tacit consent" of the individual, we find instead that we must begin with only relatively autonomous individuals immersed in a vast web or social matrix of public responsibilities, and gradually contract together to divide and delimit those responsibilities for the sake of efficiency, and to create artificial havens of "individual privacy" by common consent *whenever it serves the public interest to do so.*[11] I merely note in passing, however, that this insight is not unique to Puritans, Confucians, or to Neville: one finds a similar set of claims regarding the *a posteriori* nature of individuality, property, and rights in Rousseau's *On the Origins of Inequality*, reflected in Karl Marx's argument that the individual is, in reality, *Gattungswesen*, a "species-being."

According to liberal democratic theory, whenever I fail to find an individual or institution to whom authority and responsibility for a certain situation has been contracted, I must conclude that *no one* is responsible, and that I and others are free to choose whether or not to accept such responsibility. This is the extent of the public sector in the minimalist state of Locke, Mill, or of libertarians like Robert Nozick. For Neville, by contrast, whenever such a delimiting or proxy, delegated-as-responsible individual or institution cannot be found, then everyone is responsible for the situation, until we can contract together on how to divide or delegate that responsibility. No one automatically gets to secede into a realm of privacy, or to argue from some alleged "private sphere" that "this issue is not my affair and not my concern." Neville writes:

> [A]ny public obligation is the responsibility of all individuals in the situation to which the obligation obtains. Being responsible for the public situation's good is one of the crucial elements of having identity in that situation. For, one's identity consists in being conditioned by the situation with the achieved, excluded, and potential values in its description. Since everyone in the situation is responsible for its social obligation, everyone occupies a public position. There is no natural private station one might occupy that fails to have personal responsibility for all the situation's social obligations. If one has a private station exempt from certain responsibilities for social obligations, that is because the public is so structured as to provide that exempt private station.[12]

There is little doubt that Neville has thus reversed the accepted definitions of privacy and publicity. What might be argued, however, is that he has done so simply to advance the most familiar and threadbare sociological thesis of victimization and "liberal" responsibility: no individual agent is ever to blame for anything; instead, "we are *all* responsible." From this position, no clear lines of duty, obligation, or liability can be assessed. What Neville (it seems to me) has actually done is something quite different, as the appeal to Confucian and Puritan moral ideals illustrates. He has, like Hegel, attempted to call attention to the fundamental but hidden incoherence in the aforementioned modernist conception of the fundamental constitution of civil society.

Specifically: if individuals are the Cartesian simples out of which "society" and "community" are artificially constructed, and if individuality and privacy are the primary givens in the "state of nature," then pivotally important notions for morality such as interdependence and public responsibility or duty—the hallmarks of Aristotle's and Cicero's moral stance, as well as that articulated by Socrates in the *Crito*—have to be defined after the fact and constantly defended as binding upon those logically and ontologically prior individuals. In addition, and as a direct consequence of this problem, social or public obligations must inevitably seem an optional and perhaps intrusive burden to such libertarian individuals. Kant, in his well-known "fourth example" of "imperfect duties" to (unspecified) others in the *Grundlegung*, gives an excellent illustration of how this defense must be enjoined. Such duties are imperfect because the nature of the obligatory activity cannot be prescribed (in contrast to the earlier examples of so-called "perfect" duties to self and others, such as refraining from suicide or from deceit), and the duties are owed to "unspecified" others rather than to specific, concrete agents. Simply put, even if there is a duty of beneficence, then I am still free both to choose to whom I will be beneficent (the homeless in my local town, or the victims of famine in Somalia, for example), and what I will do to fulfill that duty (volunteer to work in a soup kitchen, or make a charitable contribution to an international famine relief organization). Kant gives credence to the libertarian view, wondering if we might all be better off if each person minded his or her own business, but argues that this libertarian maxim, while perfectly coherent, is inconsistent with other maxims that finite beings must simultaneously will—reflecting, for example, the necessary facts of reliance on assistance from one another in order for each of us to fulfill his or her own aims and goals. This is a noble and valiant attempt of a thoroughgoing Enlightenment modernist to defeat and defuse some of the more destructive, isolationist moral and political tendencies that otherwise follow consistently from the metaphysical underpinnings of modernist social thought.

It is also possible, however, to defeat these tendencies by challenging directly the metaphysical views on which they are based, as well as by marshaling the moral resources of cultures that never participated in forming or holding such views. So, as Confucius, the Puritans, Hegel, Aristotle, and now Neville all seem to agree, the metaphysical assumptions of modernity do not provide coherent foundations for understanding equally fundamental moral entities like family, community, or the state.

I hasten to correct the impression, however, that Neville intends to advance the examples of Confucians or Puritans as embodying some sort of esoteric moral doctrines that are somehow superior in every respect to modern (as opposed to classical) liberalism. Neville is certainly not intending to play the role of a self-styled prophet, demanding that this lost and morally loose generation redeem itself by returning to the lost heritage of its Puritan forefathers, for example. Indeed, Neville is as critical of the deficiencies of Confucianism and of early American Puritan thought as he is of the conceptual shortcomings and moral conundrums of modern liberalism. Both Confucians and Puritans, he writes, strike all but the most nostalgic as stern, sometimes cruel, and too often given to what he describes as an impulse to totalism (an excess of which he also accuses Hegel),[13] and especially prone to "humorless, interfering, restrictive authority."[14] What both of these older moral traditions lack, Neville argues, is a sense of irony: the self-reflecting, self-effacing ability to see the limitations of their own projects, their own virtues and especially to be cognizant of their own peculiar vices. Serious and morally sober peoples seldom sense that they have any limitations, shortcomings, or vices—or rather, that these flaws lurk in the very ideals toward which they strive. To see this would be to cease to take one's self or one's tradition quite so seriously—an impossibility for the serious-minded (as Umberto Eco so masterfully illustrates).[15] Puritans and Confucian moralists were earnest and serious, but (according to Neville) moral irony requires "both engagement and the distance symbolized by humor that puts its own project (and its own earnestness) in infinite perspective." Irony is the attitude "that binds together in contrast both the insider's passion to bless an order and the outsider's recognition of its arbitrariness and cosmic vanity."[16]

Neither is Neville dismissive of the values and contributions of the modern liberal perspective in morals and politics. He celebrates the commitments of liberalism to freedom, equality, and toleration, as well as its defense of justice and rights, and its opposition to all forms of tyranny. What our modern perspective incorporates, however, is not the requisite irony or humility, but a cynical cognizance of its own limitations. This very sense of the modernists's finitude and limitedness, our penchant for wallowing in individual psychological *Angst* and social alienation, our patronizing toleration of moral excess in the name of moral relativism, and most of all, our public *disengagement* in the name of each individual's inalienable right to privacy: these are the contemporary moral failings of modernism for which the examples of both Puritans and Confucians provide an antidote. It is their shared sense of covenant, of community, of purpose, and thus of self-transcending responsibility for the well-being of each and all who fell within their sphere of concern that we moderns must learn to recognize and acquire. Neville writes:

> Confucians might be pompous and authoritarian, but they are never cynical or alienated. . . . Public service is not something added onto private life but rather is the essence of personal life.[17]

The earlier cultural institutions of the Puritans and Confucians lacked the antidotes for the social ills they generated. Thus those institutions perished, and ought not to be exhumed simply for their own sake, out of either a misguided antiquarianism or a superficial fascination with the unfamiliar, the alien, or "the Other." Still, in America, as in the modern People's Republic of China, the ghosts of these older moral traditions haunt the margins of the polyglot, pluralistic cultures that supplanted them, and their presence as a forgotten resource, Neville argues, might serve as a useful corrective to what self-styled postmodernists often lament as the shortcomings of modernism. We might, in a spirit of Socratic inquiry (and irony) seek to temper our stubborn focus on individual rights, anti-authoritarianism, free choice, and privacy with an increased emphasis on our responsibilities within a covenant community that was the hallmark of Puritan virtue. We might permit our laissez-faire political cynicism to be challenged with the now defunct and forgotten ideal of the scholar-official (or statesman), that Confucian ideal of moral responsibility within a community in which the public and private sectors could not be so neatly severed as in the culture of liberal democracy.

Neville illustrates the significance of these views in a dramatic and moving dialogue between a young physician and her medical-school mentor concerning death and treatment of the dying—certainly issues at the forefront of contemporary moral debate. Weaving together differing cultural understandings of personal identity, desire, responsible selfhood, and temporal finitude, Neville dramatically illustrates the role that such (often tacit) understandings play in our conscious responses to the plight of dying patients, friends, or family members. He highlights in conclusion the irony of the dependence of an authentic achievement of a subjective sense of individual "self" on the inevitable facts of temporal passage, perishing, and loss, and suggests cultural resources outside of our own for making more satisfactory peace with this subjective dilemma. "The adventure of life is the creation of one's self," the student argues. "Freedom is knowing who you are and acting in character. . . . Life's fulfillment is possessing an identity of your own making . . . [while] the struggle for relative autonomy is still the heart of freedom." Yet, her teacher answers, "Nothing of value lasts. Most things can't even be repeated very often, since the changing environment loses tolerance for them. But this just means that things of human value, including individual human lives, must be seized and enjoyed in their own moments . . . in their own time of flourishing, because after that they can only be remembered. . . . If one's self-understanding employs [a] concept of self [as] the agent who is no thing and possesses no world, death is not fearful." That self, the teacher argues, is the conscious enjoyer of subjective experiences whose outcome it bequeaths to the rest of the world. It is not a kind of "fixed substance" that "possesses" such experiences and so "loses" these possessions through death. Rather, in death and the dissolution of the body, there is simply "nothing more there to be enjoyed."[18]

ON THE VALUES OF NEVILLE'S PROJECT

It should be clear that Neville passionately believes in the Deweyan project of making philosophy speak to public issues. He argues persuasively for the necessity and the urgency of this "task of developing a continuity running from metaphysics through political, legal, social, and cultural theory, to applied moral case studies, and back again."[19] He accuses more conventional moral philosophers in the analytic tradition of a kind of "moral nominalism" in which so-called "applied philosophy" is sensitive to cases and historical particulars, as in contemporary medical ethics, but profoundly mistaken "in its supposition that the moral character of general conditions, tendencies, and institutions can be reduced to consequences *for* particulars."[20] Thus, throughout his work in ethics, one is led through a series of difficult but clearly argued metaphysical and historical reflections upon the roots of our own political culture before turning to the probing analyses of specific practical issues like the limits of authority, the public definition of privacy, the objectified values encouraged by freedoms like the freedom of expression, and conflicting notions of individual responsibility. His broad position on this range of problems addressed in his many writings reduces in part to the observation that these crises of liberalism and modernism upon which he wishes us to focus attention do not stem from any lack of concern, or from the absence of focused, case-study analysis of the sort comprising the bulk of moral philosophy in the contemporary era. Rather, these dilemmas—abortion rights, care of the terminally ill, substance use and abuse, hate speech, and the politics of race and gender—fester as insoluably as they seem to do owing largely to an absence of the kind of systematic metaphysical, cultural, and historical inquiry that case studies alone cannot provide. This, however, is precisely the kind or "style" of philosophical reflection that has been, until quite recently, sharply criticized and discouraged by the philosophical mainstream. And it is precisely this kind or "style" of philosophical reflection that Neville's body of work over the past thirty-five years endeavors to provide.

That having been said, it is not clear, even to one appreciative of the value of this systematic project, that it is possible to have at once all the philosophical and moral positions that Neville sometimes seeks to incorporate. Dewey, perhaps even more than Whitehead or Weiss, stands behind Neville's project of public philosophy. Yet Dewey is about as thoroughgoing a modernist "social engineer" as one could imagine: surely no philosopher in this culture has been more imbued with the Enlightenment's sense of rationalism and "can-do" optimism that thoughtful reflection and considered, rational action will inevitably serve to alleviate human suffering and find a cure for most of society's ills. The dash of Socratic irony that Neville occasionally recommends, perhaps seasoned with the Taoist doctrine of *wu-wei*, however, is that philosophy may not, after all, even be a proper public pursuit, let alone a source of antidotes for the world's political ills. And even if one stubbornly and resolutely maintains that philosophy can, does, and must have such a function in society, I have already suggested above that the humorous side of Neville's ironic turn is itself difficult to reconcile with moral seriousness of purpose.

In quite another vein, Neville is unquestionably correct to champion a greater intercultural awareness of the resources that non-Western traditions offer, whether for metaphysics or for moral philosophy. Cultural illiteracy is certainly not a commendable virtue. One of the crises of modernity that Neville does not cite, however, is that the incessant temptation to deny or denigrate the past for the sake of the future leads to cultural illiteracy of many forms. It is not so much that Westerners in general or American citizens in particular are blind to the contributions of other cultures, as that they know little about the sources of their own. I have suggested above, for example, that one need not learn only from Confucius or Cotton Mather the deficiencies of the atomistic, individualistic perspective of modern social contract theory. Rousseau decries the emphasis upon individualism; the tradition of classical liberalism from Aristotle through St. Thomas to Hegel and the Hume of the English histories of "common life" all celebrate the transcendence of *polis* and *koinonia*; Alasdair MacIntyre's examination of the practices of Greek, Benedictine, and even rural English communities in previous centuries uncovers similar community virtues that temper the modernist emphasis on individualism, hedonism, pursuit of private self-interest, and cynicism. It is certainly not that I object to learning such lessons from the principal figures and classical writings of other cultures—one ought, rather, to take one's valuable lessons wherever one finds them. It is only that one need not venture outside one's own culture to do so, and the danger of doing the unnecessary might be the tendency to romanticize a superficial or facile understanding of some new, exotic doctrine that might, in the end, not underwrite anything like the values ascribed to it.[21] But this is merely to argue that, for the purposes of this essay, the emphasis on multiculturalism is a separate and nonessential issue.

What is essential to recognize is that, while Neville struggles to accommodate to the positive values of modernity and laissez-faire liberal democracy, his views suggest a rather strong critique of the coherence and moral viability of that perspective. I have argued elsewhere that, in the end, Whitehead quietly abandoned his earlier commitment to the modern liberal consensus and retreated to a more intellectually conservative and cautious position, reminiscent of the ancients.[22] It seems to me that Neville, not to mention the traditions (both East and West) that he cites in support of his views, represents a similar rejection of modernity's foundations—moral, political, and metaphysical. That is a perspective that is even less intelligible to most listeners or readers than is the focus on metaphysics. But that is also to argue, as Socrates knew and as Wittgenstein eventually discovered, that philosophy is not suited for everybody—and perhaps least of all for "professional" philosophers.

NOTES

1. Neville's presidential address for the Eighth International Conference on Chinese Philosophy in Beijing in 1993 suggests my point, in emphasizing what he terms the "portability" of insights concerning social responsibility, friendship, and family life that are not specific to East Asian culture. See "Confucianism as World Philosophy," *Journal of Chinese Philosophy* 21.1 (March 1994): 5–25.

2. See, for example: "The Scholar-Official as a Model for Ethics," *Journal of Chinese Philosophy* 13 (June 1986): 185–201; "Wang Yang-ming and John Dewey on the Ontological Question," *Journal of Chinese Philosophy* 12 (September 1985): 283–95; and "Wang Yang-ming's 'Inquiry on the Great Learning'," *Process Studies* 7 (Winter 1977): 217–37.

3. Paul Weiss does, however, make an important distinction between knowledge of God (which he sees to be the business of philosophy) and ritual practice (the province of religion); cf. Robert Cummings Neville, "Paul Weiss's Theology," in *The Philosophy of Paul Weiss*, ed. Lewis E. Hahn, The Library of Living Philosophers, vol. 23 (LaSalle, Ill.: Open Court, 1995), pp. 389–414.

4. "Man's Ends," *Review of Metaphysics* 16 (Spring 1962): 26–44.

5. See, for example: "The State's Intervention in Individuals' Drug Use," in *Feeling Good and Doing Better*, ed. Thomas H. Murray (Clifton, N.J.: Humana Press, 1985), 65–82; "Sterilization of the Retarded: In Whose Interest?" *Hastings Center Report* 8 (June 1978): 33–37; "The Limits of Freedom and the Technologies of Behavior Control," *Human Context* 4 (Autumn 1972): 433–46; "Blood Money: Should a Rich Nation Buy Plasma from the Poor," *Hastings Center Report* 2 (December 1972): 8–10; "Gene Therapy and the Ethics of Genetic Therapeutics," *Proceedings of the New York Academy of Science* (1975); and *Operating on the Mind: The Psychosurgery Conflict*, ed. Willard Gaylin, Joel Meister, and Robert Cummings Neville (New York: Basic Books, 1975).

6. This judgment of significance is mine, rather than Neville's, who holds that his first major book, and in many ways his best, was the earlier *God the Creator* (Chicago: University of Chicago Press, 1968). *The Cosmology of Freedom* was first published by Yale University Press in 1974. It is worth noting that the significance of both works has been recognized through their having recently been re-issued by the State University of New York Press (in 1992 and 1995, respectively).

7. "Outside the Camp: Recent Work on Whitehead's Philosophy, Part I," *Transactions of the C. S. Peirce Society* 21.1 (1985): 49–75. (Part II of this study was published in vol. 21, no. 3, 327–82.)

8. E.g., as in *Hermeneutics as Politics* (Oxford: Oxford University Press, 1987), pp. 8, 15, 24–27. This thesis about the distinction between ancient and modernist/postmodernist conceptions of reason is endemic to *The Ancients and the Moderns* (New Haven, Conn.: Yale University Press, 1989), and in *The Quarrel between Philosophy and Poetry* (New York: Routledge, 1988), esp. chapter 2.

9. Cf. George L. Kline's distinctions on this point in "'Present,' 'Past,' and 'Future' as Categoreal Terms, and the Fallacy of the Actual Future," *The Review of Metaphysics* 40 (December 1986): 215–35.

10. See, for example, Jerome B. Schneewind, *Moral Philosophy from Montaigne to Kant* (New York: Cambridge University Press, 1990), 1: 26–30.

11. Cf. *The Puritan Smile: A Look Toward Moral Reflection* (Albany: State University of New York Press, 1987), chapter 9.

12. *The Puritan Smile*, p. 59.

13. Cf. *The Highroad around Modernism* (Albany: State University of New York Press, 1992), chap. 5.

14. *The Puritan Smile*, p. 41.

15. Irony and humor are the enemy of moral seriousness, according to Eco's character, Brother Jorge, who has secreted the only extant copy of book 2 of Aristotle's *Poetics* in his monastery and engaged in murder and intrigue to prevent this discussion of humor from being discovered and thereby corrupting the faithful: see Umberto Eco, *The Name of the Rose*, trans. William Weaver (New York: Harcourt Brace Jovanovich, 1983).

16. *The Puritan Smile*, pp. 12, 42.

17. Ibid., pp. 33–34.

18. Ibid., chap. 11.

19. Ibid., p. ix.

20. Ibid., p. 7.

21. In a moving essay, Arthur Danto (who is certainly not opposed to intercultural philosophical contacts) writes about the odd experiment of rejecting one's own cultural past and seeking "new values" and new inspirations in an alien setting, citing the examples of Van Gogh and Gauguin, who, he writes "repudiated the entirety of their own artistic pasts and sought influences elsewhere, in Japan, or Egypt, or Polynesia—the art of which was (in Gauguin's view) finally more 'cerebral,' or, as Picasso said, more 'reasonable,' than that with which it had spontaneously been contrasted." Particularly in Gauguin's case, the innocence or purity that he sought was not to be found in his new locale in Tahiti; rather, it was a cultural influence of his own making that he constructed there, oblivious to the actual features of the cultural setting he had chosen. Cf. "The Shape of Artistic Pasts," in *Philosophical Imagination and Cultural Memory*, ed. Patricia Cook (Durham, N.C.: Duke University Press, 1993), p. 136.

22. "Whitehead and Wittgenstein: The Critique of Enlightenment and the Possibility of Metaphysics," *Ludwig Wittgenstein and the 20th Century British Tradition in Philosophy*, ed. Klaus Puhl and Jaakko Hintikka, "Proceedings of the 17th International Wittgenstein Congress, Kirchberg-am-Wechsel, Austria" (Vienna: Verlag Hölder-Pichler-Tempsky, 1995), pp. 122–37.

CHAPTER 6

On the Very Idea of Symbolic Meaning

Nancy K. Frankenberry

For the Greeks, the *symbolon* was a piece of pottery that was broken in two prior to someone's voyage. One of the pieces remained at the site of departure while the other was carried by the traveler. When he returned, the traveler's piece of pottery served as a sign of recognition and proof of his identity when it was rejoined with its complement. The word "symbol" referred to each of the two pieces individually, as well as to the act of putting the two pieces together.[1]

For us postmoderns, broken religious symbols are so many shards whose jagged edges trace the shape of the absent complement, itself another symbol. We study the shape and pattern of each jagged edge to find the direction or "sense" in which to hold the symbols so as to "read" their complement. We conjure an image of broken symbols as self-referential, referring only to other broken symbols and, when joined, able to form a seamless whole, rather than "fitting with" or "corresponding to" some (undescribed) reality. The meshing of our meanings is holistic, leaving no referential edges, and thus suggesting an alternative to conventional extensionalist semantics. The "meaning" of the broken religious symbols that litter the postmodern landscape cannot be equated with "reference."

For Robert Neville, broken symbols point not to more broken symbols but to an ultimate reference beyond all voyaging and all recognition of identity or difference. Like Paul Tillich's "broken myths," they conjure for Neville a "boundary," a borderline delineating the finite and infinite contrast. Rather than a holistic web, a radical abyss opens up here. Odysseus is pitched on perilous seas and voyages to foreign lands, but for Neville as for T. S. Eliot it appears that "the end of all our exploring is to arrive at the place from which we began and to know it for the first time." Neville's approach to symbols seeks to intuit the missing half, from the phenomenological features of the piece at hand. Interpretation is a matter of reading the seam, discerning meaning along the fissures of the break. In the final reconstruction, what religious symbols mean and what they refer to is always the same: a finite/infinite contrast.

Part classical in conception, part modern and cast in the context of a semiotics inspired by C. S. Peirce, Neville's development of a theory of reference, meaning, interpretation, and truth for religious symbols is complex, subtle, and many-layered. The difficulty I hope to identify in this essay is less with semiotics in general than with Neville's particular approach to the semantics of religious symbolism in *The Truth of Broken Symbols* (1996).[2] My focus is limited to that text, Neville's fourteenth book, because I believe it illuminates the core hypothesis central to all his writings perhaps better than his other volumes. It may also be the lens through which one can see more clearly the limitations of Neville's guiding hypothesis of creation *ex nihilo* as a species of the genus known in this volume as "finite/infinite contrasts."

FIVE EASY PIECES

I cannot hope to do justice to the complexity or the richness of Neville's treatment, only to identify the main elements of his theory that are important for understanding his approach to religious symbolism. In general, he holds to a correspondence view of truth, a representational view of knowledge, and a referential view of meaning, despite the heavy philosophical baggage these theories are known to carry.[3] "Reality is the measure" of the truth of religious symbols. Truth is defined ontologically as the carryover of value from the object interpreted into the experience of the interpreting individual or community. The interpretation is always positioned biologically, culturally, semiotically (240). In the causal theory of value that Neville has developed in many volumes, "value" roughly means the harmony an object has achieved in its own nature. Religious symbols are generically defined as including all of the following: "myths and religious narratives, theological ideas, particular notions such as karma or sin which are defined in one or more symbol systems, the symbol systems as such, religious acts such as liturgies or private meditations that move through and overlay various symbol systems, as well as architectural and artistic symbols with religious content, books, songs, devotional objects, and the like—anything that can be referred to a religious object and can bear a religious meaning" (xxii).

"Religious object," in turn, is Neville's broadest designation for a variety of other (intentionally vague) terms: the sacred, holy, divine, the transcendent, unconditioned, absolute, and so forth. Having already made certain normative theological judgments about the validity of religious symbols and what they purport to symbolize, Neville finesses the hard questions about how to define religion and what makes some symbols religious rather than not. This allows him to regard the "data" of such admittedly "mutually inconsistent" scholars of religion as Tylor, Frazer, Otto, van der Leeuw, and Eliade as indicative of commonalities that yield the conclusion that "probably the case is that *religion* roughly describes the collective human responses, individually and socially, to the divine as sacred or holy" (8). Reiterating the idea of religion-as-response, Neville offers a "provisional understanding of religion" as "the responses in rituals, spiritual practices, and representations to the holy or sacred and its bearing on life" (10).[4] Bluntly put, Neville believes that religious symbols can indeed symbolize something truly, and what they mean to symbolize is really there (14).

In the development of this position, five principal claims are worked out, exhibited, or introduced in *The Truth of Broken Symbols*. Simplified for the sake of economy and clarity, the argument runs as follows:

1. Nearly all religions take their objects to be infinite, in a variety of respects, and therefore beyond all literal characterization but still able to be symbolized by finite symbols or expressed through metaphor.

2. The primary referent of religious symbols is "finite/infinite contrasts," that is, something that transcends determinate identity, and the secondary referent is the interpreters' experience both individually and communally.

3. A religious object can *only* be referred to through symbols (31), most if not all religious symbols are metaphoric (117), and referents for any religious object that is in some respect infinite or unconditioned are irreducibly metaphorical.[5]

4. What makes symbols *religious* is that "the meaning involved is the relation of people to their very status relative to worldliness as such and what lies beyond that . . . on the infinite side of the world's finitude" (74).

5. Religious symbols of the infinite as well as abstract theological doctrines can be translated into statements involving metaphysical terms such as "the indeterminate source of all things determinate," which also refer to what is beyond all literal characterization but are still capable of symbolization by finite symbols.[6]

In the systematic development of these theses, Neville unfolds an inventory of the properties of symbols and the intricacies of a semiotic analysis of religious symbols, while leaving opaque the semantics of his analysis of religious symbolism. My summary therefore gives rise to three critical areas of difficulty that I will examine in the next sections: the conception of the religious object as infinite; the theory of meaning as reference; and symbolic meaning taken as a special *kind*.

THE WALKING GHOST OF TILLICH

The lingering influence of Paul Tillich's account of religious symbols, meaning, and truth has been traceable in Neville's previous writings, but it is impossible to mistake in *The Truth of Broken Symbols*. "Broken symbols" are to Robert Neville what "broken myths" were to Paul Tillich. Both refer to something that is regarded as "ultimate." Worried that even such symbols as the God of the theologians can be treated idolatrously, both posit a "God beyond the God of theism" that functions as the truly ultimate in each system. As Tillich thinks that being-itself is the "power" or "ground" that enables the be-ing of all things, so Neville thinks that the infinite is the indeterminate creative source that accounts for all determinateness. Neville's distinction between the primary referent and the secondary referent of symbols has an interesting parallel with Tillich's distinction between the objective and the subjective referents of symbols. Where Tillich wrote of the objective pole of faith in terms of "being-itself" and the subjective pole in terms of an individual's "ultimate concern," Neville distinguishes between a primary referent (finite/infinite contrasts) and secondary referents (individuals' existential context). Both sets of distinctions serve the purpose of trying to avoid the twin dangers of subjectivism (hence the objective pole or primary referent) and of idolatry (hence the role of Tillich's ultimate concern and Neville's secondary referent that anchor religious symbolism in something concrete and finite even while pointing in another direction to something infinite).

Both have employed a dialectic of affirmation and negation, of kataphatic and apophatic symbols, which can appear to be a device for deflecting philosophical criticism. Just as it is enormously hard to determine how or whether Tillich's principle of simultaneous affirmation and negation is intelligible as a method of predication to the divine, so too Neville slips with alarming ease from anthropomorphic affirmation on one page to agnostic negation on the next page.[7] This allows him to argue that religious symbols intend to point to the infinite, but are still capable of bearing finite forms, or that the infinite is not-like, but not so totally unlike that nothing can be said of it. Unlike Aquinas' *analogia entis*, which rested on the supposition of some natural resemblance between the finite and the infinite, Neville and Tillich hold to a radical discontinuity between finite and infinite. While Aquinas thought that without an ontological continuity there was no justification for the use of analogy or symbols, Neville thinks that we cannot know anything about the ultimate religious object except that it is creator of whatever determinate things there are. Negative theological qualifications are compatible with affirmative ones, and their joint assertion is apparently intelligible for Neville, a master dialectician. For less supple minds, however, his device of "distinguishing the respects" in which terms can be predicated may seem like being handed a card that says "see other side"—on both sides. With critics of anthropomorphism, Neville can point to the apophatic side of his theology, and with critics of agnosticism he can point to the kataphatic side, since both sides are always said to obtain.

Unfortunately, Neville's position appears to inherit some of the same difficulties that plagued Tillich's. First, in positing as the ultimate religious object that which is utterly indeterminate and unconditioned and beyond all characterization, Neville makes himself vulnerable to the charge that there is no way of distinguishing his infinite from sheer nothingness.[8] That it is no-thing, not a being, and nonfinite is precisely why Neville's infinite, like Tillich's being-itself, can only be engaged symbolically. Religious ultimacy for Neville and Tillich positively requires that we cannot speak of the primary religious object in literal terms. Neville even thinks that the one literal statement Tillich allowed—that God is being-itself—is really symbolic, not literal (129). But for the very reason that finite creatures are denied knowledge of "what lies on the infinite side of the world's finitude" (74), it would seem that we cannot determine whether symbolic language succeeds in talking *about* the religious object. To know that a symbol successfully refers, we would need to have a two-sided view, encompassing both the finite and infinite, which we lack. In light of this difficulty, there is considerable understatement in Neville's acknowledgment that "the interesting problems of truth in religious symbols have to do with the peculiar, not-wholly-finite character of their referents" (33).

Second, this theory is too permissive. If the religious object is, according to Neville's hypothesis, the source of everything there is (as the creating of all determinate things), then all sorts of symbolic predicates can be applied to it. There is no control over the possible symbolic representations without knowing some terms that define the religious object literally. This definition could then serve as a criterion for excluding and including various symbolic statements. But to do so would again require knowing the religious object in a nonsymbolic sense and this is ruled out in Neville's system. The infinite side of a finite/infinite contrast cannot be a particular object, not even for thought, much less for observation. It is utterly devoid of content. Therefore, we cannot have knowledge of it in any way that would permit us to characterize it as "compassionate," for example, rather than as "indifferent." Why not then attribute a coincidence of opposites to the ultimate religious object? Since everything determinate owes its existence to the indeterminate creative act, it would seem that everything determinate could serve equally well as a symbol of this particular religious object. Destructiveness would be just as apt as creativeness, or cruelty as much as lovingkindness, evil as well as good. "Christ is nailed to the cross and the fairies dance" (Whitehead).

Third, this theory assumes a *relation* between the infinite and the finite as creator to created. But how is this relation to be understood? The role of the religious object as "creator" in Neville's system is not meant in a literal sense. In what sense then? In a symbolic sense? But this symbolic meaning would have to be grounded in yet another relation. How then is that relation to be understood? Symbolically? But somewhere the symbolic meanings must stop, otherwise we have an infinite regression. This symbolic meaning explains this symbolic meaning, which explains this symbolic meaning which . . . . Somewhere the symbolic meanings must stop and be grounded in some statement that is nonsymbolic.

I am arguing that for symbolic meanings to work as religious meanings, some direct, nonsymbolic statement about the religious object must be made, or we can never determine what the symbolic meanings *mean*, which symbols are appropriate, and which ones are not appropriate. Even more, we must have the "literal" in order to make sense out of "symbol." A symbolic *use* of language is parasitic on an understanding of literal *meaning* defined in terms of truth-conditions. I am not arguing, however, that it is important to determine that to which symbolic meanings *refer*, or whether they do in fact refer. For unlike Neville, I am not espousing a theory of meaning as reference; I would prefer to leave open the possibility that key religious symbols may have meaning but no reference.

MEANING WITHOUT REFERENCE

Of the various theories of meaning in terms of use, of mental structures, of unconscious processes, and so forth, Neville's is a referential account of meaning, and untenable for several reasons.[9] First, when different words are used to refer to one and the same referent, it is not the case that they have the *same meaning*. Thus, "cat," "my cat," and "Fido" all refer to the same animal in the sentence "The cat on my lap is my cat, Fido," but the words do not all have the same meaning. Second, a word may alter its referent without altering its meaning. For example, the word "cat" means the same whether it refers to "my cat" or to "your cat." Third, and most important for work in religious studies, not all words refer, and those that do not are not thereby meaningless. Perhaps key religious terms have meaning but no reference in the same way as words such as "and" or "if" or "the present king of Hong Kong."

Neville's argument about reference unfolds in three stages, seeking to show, first, the religious character of imagination; second, how imagination works to "engage" experience with its objects; and third, the reference of religious symbols as finite/infinite contrasts. Although the first two steps are full of assumptions that need careful inspection, it is only the third step that concerns me here. By making a strong claim for transcendent reference and for there being an ultimate religious object and for its being so located, Neville avoids the reductionistic pitfalls of other interpreters, only to stumble into a ditch of another sort. Rather than endorse a "hermeneutics of suspicion" that would interpret religious beliefs as nonliteral and symbolic of sociopolitical, economic, or psychic structures of one kind or another into which they can be decoded, Neville maintains that they symbolize the transcendent, that is, the sacred, the divine, the ultimate, of which his indeterminate creative source of all things determinate is one variant of finite/infinite contrasts.[10] In this way he bestows an autonomous and irreducible character on religious symbols, saving them from hijacking by other disciplines, but at the price of endowing symbols with a dubious referent that is, as we shall see, incomprehensible. The question then arises as to how finite symbols can *mean* any such contrast as between finite and infinite. For if one holds that (1) meaning is reference; and (2) the primary reference of religious symbols of all kinds is, at least in part, to the infinite, the abyss, the great nothingness whose only character is to be the source of other things, then one cannot escape the conclusion that (3) therefore, the *meaning* of religious symbols in their primary sense is unsayable. If it is unsayable, it is also unknowable. If it is unknowable, it is unknown even *symbolically*.

In the final analysis, transcendence, in Neville's system, amounts to the fact that no literal characterization of the religious object can be given. Hence, all language about the infinite is necessarily symbolic. Pansymbolism, however, invites questions about inconsistency or self-refutation. Is the claim that all language about the infinite is symbolic language itself symbolic? If everything said about the primary religious object can become a symbol, that would imply that nothing could be interpreted literally. No meaning would be determinate in any way at all. If everything is a symbol, then nothing can be taken literally; interpreters would be in a position of having to decode everything. But they could not decode anything, for the methods used for decoding would all be symbolic, and thus in need of decoding also. To avoid this outcome, one need only accept the dependence of the very idea of symbolic meaning upon knowing the literal meaning of the words, and repudiate the idea of symbolic meaning as constituting a difference in *kind*.

There are further difficulties to consider. According to Neville's hypothesis, the finite/infinite contrast is that to which all religious language and symbolism is intentionally referred. However, far from solving the semantic problem, this theory compounds it. Rather than establishing the truth of broken symbols, all that Neville has shown is their "intentional reference" on the part of those speakers who are theologically inclined. But "intentional reference" does not automatically produce "existing referent" any more than, in a Wittgensteinian context, "actual use" amounts to "proper use."

The dilemma that Neville's theology confronts is this: either a translation can be made of symbolic language, or it cannot. If it is translatable, then it is possible to say what it "literally means" for it would have a syntax and semantics even if it is still puzzling that such a meaning was coded as a symbolic message in the first place. If a translation can be made, a symbolic language would have to have a syntax and semantics or else no translation would be possible. On the other hand, if it is not translatable, because the symbolic meaning is held to exceed the literal meaning, then the theologian is obligated to explain just what this "extra meaning" is, and how she is in a position to know it is different from any translation or paraphrase. Theologians have had a dismal record with the second horn of this dilemma, and understandably so: in this case we are no longer talking about meaning at all. On the other hand, any success theology enjoys with the first horn usually creates the added difficulty that once one grasps the non-mythological or nonsymbolic meaning and can perform the translation into metaphysical terms such as Neville's, the "power" of the symbols is quite broken, but in a sense different from Neville's notion of "broken" and much more similar to the outcome of successful psychoanalysis: once one sees through one's various rationalizations, they no longer work.[11]

The final problem is that language about the infinite, according to Neville, can be translated in terms of metaphysical statements about the indeterminate source. But his hypothesis of an indeterminate source holds that it is uncharacterizable except in terms of its created determinations, which would have to include each and every determinate creature. This then pushes the problem of translation back one step—the metaphysical statements are as much in need of translation as the initial statements about the infinite they were to translate. If no translation can ever hope to eliminate the metaphor and no statement about an indeterminate source can be nonsymbolic, then the ontological interpretations of theological statements must be recognized as themselves symbolic. But the replacement of one symbol by another symbol still leaves us imprisoned within a web of symbols. The translation of *S* into *S'* if both are symbolic statements, gives us no nonsymbolic statement about the infinite.

Neville is of course aware of these problems. His arguments in favor of the apophatic path boil down to two principal reasons for employing the notion of an infinite/indeterminate source: (1) it provides a reference for religious language, and (2) it is the only hypothesis that provides an answer to the question, why is there something and not nothing?

However, if symbolic meaning can in fact be translated into literal meaning, there would seem to be little reason to use symbolic language, except perhaps to highlight or italicize or call attention to what we already know. In that case, we can wonder why we would need the first of the two main functions that finite/infinite contrasts provide in Neville's system. Since we can know the religious object only through symbols, and since the truth of these broken symbols can in no way be judged in terms of their correspondence to this metaphysical referent, but only in terms of human experiences and transformations, why do we require the metaphysical reference at all? Could we not have the same meaning without reference?

One could also question the need for the other major function of the infinite/indeterminate source in Neville's system as an answer to the question, why is there something and not nothing? The alternative would be to acknowledge an awareness that one might not have existed and of the inevitability of one's death, all triggering an experience of contingency, and prompting one to question why there is something when conceivably there might have been nothing—*without* acknowledging the pressure to supply a metaphysical explanation. This is to admit that there are in principle things we do not understand about the universe and never will. Why there is something rather than nothing is inherently inexplicable.[12]

A NICE DERANGEMENT

A final difficulty in Neville's study of symbolic meaning and truth in religion arises with the presumption that there is another *kind* of meaning over and above, and in addition to, literal meaning in terms of truth-conditions. Whether it is called "symbolic meaning" or "religious meaning," or "metaphorical sense," it is presumed to be a special, hidden meaning that needs to be interpreted or a code that needs to be decoded.

Theologians and anthropologists alike have long presumed it their intellectual duty to probe behind or beneath the literal meaning of words in order to understand a symbolic or metaphorical meaning. Different tribes call for different scribes. Neville, for example, thinks that there are "mythopoeic people" and "post-mythopoeic people," and the symbols of both "refer to reality as like how it is" (39). In addition to the assumption that symbols and myths "refer to reality" and "say what reality is like in certain respects," the hard part of this formulation is understanding what is involved in "thinking mythically" and why people would "think mythically" or symbolically in the first place. Neville does not suppose mythic thinking always recognizes that it is a symbol for something else. In contrast, post-mythopoeic peoples, according to Neville, think that the symbolic representations of religion "are only metaphorical, but we have no better images than our best ones" (73). "Religious thinkers," on the other hand, "for thousands of years have known that the gods they symbolize are not finite as symbolized, really and truly" (xvi). It is interesting to note the assurance with which Neville maintains that *inquiring minds* have always known the gods to be symbols. With this, Neville the theologian joins with the anthropologist John Beattie, who flatly declares that if the natives would only "think deeply" enough about their rituals they would see them as symbolic.[13] Other historians of the study of religion are not so sure. Jonathan Z. Smith reminds us that it was a rare figure during the Enlightenment who would recognize that the religion of both the "primitive" and the "ancient" was never allegorical or symbolic. Hans Penner points out that Beattie and other symbolists, well aware that their informants do not authorize a nonliteral reading, wind up denying that the natives know what they are doing; they also overlook the salient detail that "the beliefs are mistaken" if taken as hypothetico-deductive or instrumental.[14]

Why do theological interpretations of religious systems so easily assume the symbolic-expressive method of interpretation? After all, when it comes to explaining something like kinship systems, for example, explanation can be sought in empirical infrastructures and their social and economic relations. However, when it comes to explaining the gods, goddesses, spirits, angels, demons, and heavenly realms that populate religious literature, no such reference is plausible. Therefore, theologians, historians of religion, anthropologists, and a wide variety of other scholars have assumed that the language of religion is not to be taken literally but rather symbolically. The method of interpreting religion in terms of symbolic forms then leads to the investigation of hidden meanings, indirectly expressed in symbolic representations. For Durkheim, the "real" meaning turned out to be symbolic representation of society; for Marx, it was consolation and legitimation; for Freud, infantile illusion. For Robert Neville, a metaphysical conception is the real meaning of all religious symbols in their primary reference, not social, political, or natural structures, not mental classifications or moral concerns. Rather, religious symbols mean the transcendent, the infinite.

Those of us trained in theology and philosophy of religion are perhaps too quick to treat religious symbols as though we were archaeologists, digging among the documents of an unknown language attempting to decipher them. We think that what is given is "something" that "has" a definite meaning content that an interpreter must grasp if she is to get the message. We treat symbols as though they are vehicles that "carry" meaning, like cargo on a freight train, or a virus in a computer program. We may have become so inured to this method of thinking that we have been innoculated against certain questions in the field. Questions that are likely to seem obtuse to many liberal theologians nevertheless remain obstinate to other scholars of religion. A vast amount of intellectual labor has gone into the study of symbolic systems that have been assumed to harbor hidden meanings and encoded messages that need to be cracked. A language has been assumed to exist, from which the code is constituted and then decoded. But what is that language? And why is there notorious disagreement about its meaning?

In religious studies, the principal problem with the assumption of hidden meanings or uncracked codes has been the difficulty of explaining (1) why people invest such time and effort in a form of coded communication rather than more direct expressions; and (2) how it is that most believers remain ignorant of the real meaning, all the while participating in symbolic systems whose meaning is hidden from them and which they do not (on this assumption) comprehend.

More than twenty years ago anthropologist Dan Sperber presented a persuasive critique of traditional semiotic approaches to symbolism, highlighting this twofold explanatory difficulty.[15] Approaches to semantics concerned with arriving at appropriate interpretations by decoding the symbolic material fail for several reasons, according to Sperber. First, symbols are so multivalent that it is impossible to pair them with their interpretations. The underlying code is not essentially the same for all, and there is too much variability of symbolic material and of individual appropriation of it to permit construing it in terms of a code. Second, symbol systems fail to supply their own algorithm for assigning interpretations to symbols on any systematic basis, they never wear their

meanings on their sleeves, and attempts at their interpretation only produce additional layers of symbolic material rather than elucidation of
the original layers, thus extending the problem but not solving it. Third,
religious actors typically do not worry about the correct exegesis of symbols but will engage in symbolic activities, like the Dorze of Ethiopia,
without any interpretative schemes for them at all. The standard semiotic approach would cast doubt on the rationality of the participants,
committing what Robin Horton has called "the cardinal interpretative
sin of flouting the actor's point of view."[16]

Flouting the actor's point of view is seldom considered a problem in
theology and philosophy of religion. This is curious, as it leads to some
odd classifications of folk and distributions of literal versus symbolic
meaning among them. Distinguishing, for example, among a given religion's founders, its fundamentalists, and its *cognoscenti*, are we to imagine that Buddha, Confucius, Muhammed, Moses, and Jesus understood
their utterances literally, that Jerry Falwell understands Christian symbols literally, and that Robert Neville interprets the *same* meaning in the
broken symbols of an abstract metaphysical system? Do ordinary religious folk understand the meaning of eucharistic symbols as Neville
does, complete with a cannibilistic layer? If not, and if religious folk do
not or cannot explain what the eucharistic symbols "mean," what sense
does it make to say that the eucharist serves as a *symbol* for them? Can
I say that Mt. Meru is a symbol for me if I cannot explain or understand
what I take it to be a symbol of? Alternatively, if "creation *ex nihilo*"
can function as a symbol for me only if I can explain what "creation *ex
nihilo*" symbolizes, and if I am a religious actor unread in philosophy
and theology and cannot explain what, on Neville's account, "creation
ex nihilo" symbolizes, must it not be the case that for me "creation *ex
nihilo*" does not function as a symbol of the ontological context of
mutual relevance by virtue of the fact that it creates things with their
essential and nonessential features together? If this is not its symbolic
meaning for me, then it seems unlikely that "creation *ex nihilo*" could
ever symbolize for the religious community, unless they undertake the
study of metaphysics, what Neville regards as the meaning of this symbol. I am trying to bring to light an implicit contradiction between two
different assertions: (1) For religious actors, X can function as a symbol
of Y; and (2) religious actors are unable to specify what X symbolizes.
Neville's position, unless I am mistaken, seems to affirm both (1) and (2)
without showing how it is possible for both to be true.

One way to read Neville's exegesis of nine levels of meaning of the
eucharist in chapter 3 is as illustrating Sperber's criticism that the interpretation of symbols produces only extra layers of symbolic material
rather than clarification of the original layers.[17] Theologians supply

illustrations of symbolic interpretations and generate extensional interpretants, but no systematic basis for assigning particular interpretations
to particular symbols is ever provided. At the same time, no keys to
cracking the codes are contained within the symbol system itself. If only
symbol systems would wear their meanings on their sleeves we could
better "read off" their surfaces (or from their "depths," *pace* Tillich) the
"proper" or "correct" or "adequate" interpretations. Lacking both self-
evidence and an algorithm for assigning or ascertaining "meanings,"
symbolic forms are themselves mute, ingloriously at the mercy of theologians' hermeneutical manipulations to make them yield up their lay-
ered look.

According to Sperber, particular symbols have *no* meanings to
decode, and we should not therefore be surprised that most natives
employ meaningless symbol systems uncomprehendingly. Convincing as
Sperber's critique is, it would be premature to accept his pessimistic conclusion, that symbolism proves intractable to all of the usual standards
and methods for the semantic analysis of natural language.[18] If Sperber's
verdict is one extreme (symbols do not *mean* at all) then the usual theological reading (symbols mean the transcendent) is equally disappoint-
ing. Until recently, the history of efforts to develop a semantic theory of
symbolic meaning has seemed to offer few promising directions.

THE DREAMWORK OF LANGUAGE

Far from having no theoretical alternatives but to lapse into a kind of
semantic eliminativism or to adopt a form of theological cryptology, the
current study of religion is opening in new directions from which we can
expect important results. Among the range of methods available for
semantic analysis generally, a compelling case can be made for holism.
Common to versions of holism is the claim that meaning is located, not
in isolated elements that enter into symbolic materials, but only in the
way those elements are unified. The primary bearers of meaning are systems, rather than particular symbols that have meaning only in relation
to their place in the whole. If the question arises as to what the overall
system refers to, the answer can only be "to itself." Scholars across a
wide variety of disciplines using holistic analysis in semantics have
demonstrated that the elimination of reference does not imply that sym-
bolic-cultural systems and religious systems in particular have no *meaning* at all.[19] Even if traditional (i.e., empiricist) techniques for the semantic analysis of natural language in terms of reference and truth have not
proved productive in the treatment of symbolic systems, it is becoming
clear that holistic strategies, akin to what Donald Davidson means by

"the holism of the mental," are able to purchase "meaning" without "reference."[20]

Davidson's holism, truth-conditional semantics, and "anomalous monism" should be welcome resources for Robert Neville and others interested in theoretical problems in the study of religion.[21] In an influential essay on metaphor,[22] Davidson has inveighed against the notion that there is a special, second, coded, or hidden meaning needing to be interpreted over and above, and in addition to, literal meaning. He has argued that the distinction between literal and figurative meaning can be abolished along with the dogmas of empiricism that constructed a distinction between analytic and synthetic statements, and between conceptual scheme and empirical content. Metaphors, on Davidson's view, are a certain *use* we have for literal meaning, similar to such other verbal activities as irony, sarcasm, or promising. Metaphorical or symbolic *use* of language, however, does not imply that a distinctive metaphorical or symbolic *meaning* exists.

Much of Neville's account in *The Truth of Broken Symbols* can be read as a prolonged examination of the many *uses* of religious symbols in theological, practical, and devotional contexts, together with the more troubling treatment of symbolic meaning as a different *kind*. I am afraid that the latter leads straight to the confusion Davidson sees in the theory of metaphor promoted by I. A. Richards and Max Black: "on the one hand, the usual view wants to hold that a metaphor does something no plain prose can possibly do and, on the other hand, it wants to explain what a metaphor does by appealing to a cognitive content—just the sort of thing plain prose is designed to express" (261). With the idea of metaphorical or symbolic meaning, we are pulled in two directions at once, as though both alongside of and yet somehow beyond literal meaning, there is something distinctive in kind, in which "the message may be considered more exotic, profound, or cunningly garbed" (246). On the one hand, it is thought to have cognitive content and to convey truth or falsehood much as plainer language does, and on the other hand, we are not able to explain it in literal terms. Symbolists and proponents of metaphorical meaning must deny the possibility of paraphrase, but, as Davidson demonstrates, the only way they can *say* what the metaphorical meaning *is* is by paraphrasing it, in which case they make it literal, thus denying it is metaphorical after all. The paraphrase may remain not fully satisfactory as a translation, but nevertheless we will be able to formulate one for any metaphor we can identify as such. In that case, a better reason for maintaining that metaphors are not paraphrasable, according to Davidson, is because a metaphor does not *say* anything different from its literal meaning. What makes an utterance a metaphor is not a matter of saying something ineffable, or saying anything at all. "Metaphors mean what the words, in the most literal interpretation, mean, and nothing more" (245).

On this view, the important point about symbols and metaphors, whether in religious systems or elsewhere, is that they express in unlimited ways what it is they call to our attention. We can paraphrase them in various ways, but this ought not fool us into thinking that we should be able to harness all the various paraphrases we can come up with under a central cognitive content, something called "symbolic meaning," that inevitably eludes our complete grasp. To give the meaning of a symbol or metaphor is the same as giving the meaning of any other use of language, that is, by pairing sentences with truth-conditions. All there is to give of the meaning of *any* sentence is given in the pairing of it with truth-conditions. This is not to assign any special privilege to literality but only to deny that there is a special *kind* of meaning called "symbolic" as distinct from the literal meaning of a sentence, something that could lead to the paradoxical result that the *same* sentence can be said to be literally false, yet symbolically true.

Religious symbols and metaphors may make us see one thing as another, or the same thing in a brand new light, and thus cause us to alter our belief about it, as when, in John Wisdom's classic paper on "Gods," one woman says to another who is trying on a hat: "My dear, it's the Taj Mahal." The meaning is literally false, but the novel usage prompts insight. Like Wittgenstein's duck-rabbit example, this "dawning of an aspect" induces a "seeing-as" experience. Is that insight propositional in character? Davidson, for one, thinks not. "What we notice or see is not, in general, propositional in character" (263).

By rejecting the idea of a cognitive content that is antecedent to the metaphor or symbol in the form of a knowable but unstated likeness, we can think of the likeness as what a metaphor *produces*, indistinguishable from the endless literal paraphrases of it that interpreters provide. What I am calling paraphrase is, then, the condition for what metaphors mean, so that to interpret a metaphor is to start with various alternative expressions or competing candidates, none of them pointing to some more originary meaning that could reconcile them all. Orthodoxy and heresy alike are out of the question.

Still, not all paraphrases are created equal, a fact that has implications for the work of religious critics. If "the legitimate function of so-called paraphrase is to make the lazy or ignorant reader have a vision like that of the skilled critic" (264), then Neville's is a religiously inspired vision surely worth having. As the different essays in this very volume indicate, there can be multiple interpretations of his texts, because there is no reason to say one rules out others. Each author has made what he or she can of Neville's texts; and these differ. But no relativism follows from this truism. If several of the authors in this volume, or readers of it, try to compare our interpretations of Neville's texts we can do so only to the extent that we have or can establish a broad basis of agreement. If what we share provides a common standard of truth and objectivity, difference of opinion makes sense. Relativism about standards would require what there cannot be, a position beyond all standards. If the argument I have been presenting has merit, the vision of even so skilled a critic, philosopher, and theologian as Robert Neville does not and could not carry us beyond the holistic, infinitely ramifying and interlocking character of linguistic meaning, belief, and action that alone provide us with a measure of reality.

NOTES

1. See Esther Rashkin, *Family Secrets and the Psychoanalysis of Narrative* (Princeton, N.J.: Princeton University Press, 1992), p. 38.

2. *The Truth of Broken Symbols* (Albany: State University of New York Press, 1996). Hereafter *TBS*. Page references are cited within the text.

3. *TBS* 36–47, 66; and for truth see esp. chap. 7. For critiques of the correspondence theory of truth and representational views of knowledge, see Donald Davidson, "The Structure and Content of Truth," *The Journal of Philosophy* 87.6 (1990): 279–328; Donald Davidson, "Reality without Reference"; "Radical Interpretation"; and "On the Very Idea of Conceptual Meaning," in *Inquiries into Truth and Interpretation* (Oxford: Clarendon Press, 1984); Donald Davidson, "A Nice Derangement of Epitaphs," in *Truth and Interpretation: Perspectives on the Philosophy of Donald Davidson*, ed. LePore (Oxford: Basil Blackwell, 1986), pp. 433–46; and Donald Davidson, "The Myth of the Subjective," in *Relativism: Interpretation and Confrontation*, ed. Michael Krausz (Notre Dame: University of Notre Dame Press, 1989), pp. 159–72. In the last source, Davidson sums up much of what separates his starting point from Neville's by saying: "Beliefs are true or false, but they represent nothing. It is good to be rid of representations, and with them the correspondence theory of truth, for it is thinking that there are representations that engenders thoughts of relativism" (165–66).

4. This manner of speaking appears to presuppose what needs to be explained. One wishes Neville had only written that religion is "the responses in rituals, spiritual practices, and representations to *what practitioners take to be* holy or sacred."

5. Cf. Robert Neville, *Normative Cultures* (Albany: State University of New York Press, 1995) p. 103.

6. Cf. "Religious symbols are those whose primary reference, direct or indirect, is to a finite/infinite contrast, that is, at least partly to the divine or the infinite" (*TBS* 65). "Religious symbols mean to refer to the divine as located in finite/infinite contrasts" (*TBS* 104).

7. Or sometimes on the very same page. See the mildly facetious but indicative conclusion as to cigars in heaven on page 271.

8. Indeed it is characteristic of Neville's entire *oeuvre* to insist that the ontological ground has no character in itself, except the created character of being the creator of this world.

9. Neville is not only committed to a reference theory of meaning in connection with religious symbols, but also to a realist or correspondence theory of truth, as his ontological definition and causal account of truth make evident, especially in his *Recovery of the Measure*. Unfortunately, space does not allow me to do justice to this topic here.

10. The claim that *all* religious symbols refer to the divine as located in finite/infinite contrasts would startle scholars of Theravada Buddhism. Neville writes: "There may be symbols everyone would agree are religious that do not fit this understanding at all; perhaps those associated with Theravada Buddhism are a case in point" (104). I would modify this by two crucial words to say that there *are* symbols everyone would agree are religious that do not fit this understanding at all; and those associated with Theravada Buddhism are *precisely* a case in point. See, e.g., W. Rahula, *What the Buddha Taught*.

11. On this topic, see *TBS* 197–98, where Neville questions just such a conclusion. The burden of his argument in chapter 5 leads to the troubling claim that religious symbols can be "existentially true" in the context of practical devotional life even though they are known to be heuristic fictions. This equivocal use of "true" appears to mean something like "passionately believed," "authentic," "sincere," or "spiritually transformative."

12. Although it is too complicated a problem to analyze here, I cannot help but wonder if there is a contradiction between appealing to creation *ex nihilo* as the explanation for the existence of all determinate things and simultaneously contending that creation *ex nihilo* is essentially mysterious in itself. An explanation, in order to explain a range of data, cannot be more opaque and mysterious than the explanans.

13. John Beattie, "Ritual and Social Change," *Man* 1 (1966): 69–70.

14. See J. Z. Smith, *To Take Place* (Chicago: University of Chicago Press, 1987), pp. 101–2; and Hans H. Penner, *Impasse and Resolution: A Critique of the Study of Religion* (New York, Bern: Peter Lang Publishing, 1989), pp. 70–71.

15. Sperber, *Rethinking Symbolism* (Cambridge: Cambridge University Press, 1975), esp. chap. 2.

16. Robin Horton, "Tradition and Modernity Revisited." Of course, Horton's own way of drawing an analogy between the Kalabari gods and water spirits and "Western" theoretical entities commits the same sin. The Kalabari regard the gods and water spirits as real objects, with undoubted existence, hardly theoretical, whereas Horton claims they are analogous to theoretical objects.

17. Sperber, *Rethinking Symbolism*, p. 50. Neville, *TBS*, chap. 3.

18. See ibid., chap. 1; and Sperber, *On Anthropological Knowledge* (Cambridge: Cambridge University Press, 1983) pp. 72, 83–84. Historian of religion Hans Penner criticizes Sperber's verdict on the "meaninglessness" of symbols as mistakenly based on a theory of meaning derived from logical positivism.

19. See, for example, E. Thomas Lawson and Robert N. McCauley, *Rethinking Religion: Connecting Cognition and Culture* (Cambridge: Cambridge University Press, 1990).

20. See, for example, Donald Davidson, "The Inscrutibility of Reference," in *Inquiries,* pp. 227–41 and "Reality without Reference," ibid., pp. 215–25. The holism of the mental implicates not only beliefs but also wishes, hopes, desires, emotions, and fears.

21. For an excellent account, see Hans H. Penner, "Why Does Semantics Matter to the Study of Religion?" *Method & Theory in the Study of Religion* 7.3 (1995): 221–49. I am indebted to Penner for stimulating conversations on these matters over many years.

22. Donald Davidson, "What Metaphors Mean," in *Inquiries,* pp. 245–64. Provocative and decisive as this essay is, it is hardly a complete account. Cf. also "Communication and Convention," pp. 265–80.

CHAPTER 7

Neville's Self in Time and Eternity

J. Harley Chapman

The purpose of this essay is to lay out Robert Neville's notion of the self, at least in its main outlines, and to suggest some modifications, at least in accent and emphasis. Though Neville wrote an early book *Soldier, Sage, Saint* (1978) on the models of spiritual perfection, drawing on Plato's image of the tripartite soul, and though he has addressed a number of issues that deal profoundly with the ethics, metaphysics, and theology of human experience and behavior, one will not find a more-or-less scientific treatise on selfhood (as in Aristotle's *De Anima*) or an absorbed exploration and meditation on selfhood (as in Augustine's "I wish to know only God and the soul" or in Descartes' self-reflexive search of the *cogito*) or a puzzled or haunted search for an elusive "I" (as in Hume's *Treatise*) or a dramatic portrayal of the self's becoming (as in Hegel's *Phenomenology*). Nonetheless, Neville has a discernible notion of the self, though not fully worked out as such, at least to this point; and it is to this task of elaboration that we now turn.

A WAY INTO THE ISSUE: "A TASTE OF DEATH"

As a way into what will be seen to be the paradoxical nature of selfhood in Neville's writings, I suggest a probing look at his dialogue "A Taste of Death," which he includes as the final chapter in his book *The Puritan Smile*.[1] Modeled somewhat on the ironic-Socratic dialogues of Plato but linked rhetorically even more closely to the Upanishadic conversations of a god and a human, the dialogue features two characters: Dr. Thomas, pathologist-turned-medical-school-dean, and a Miss Nonscivi, a brilliant fourth-year medical school student. She challenges him to

111

explain death. Convinced of the infinite value of human personality and describing herself as an enlightened secularist and existentialist, she is horrified of death as existential annihilation, an absurd and tragic destruction of the self as the subjective experiencer of the world with its image of itself that allows for the organizing of that world. She does not warm up to the view of Dr. Thomas that death is an aspect of the natural process, natural as birth, and that having mistakenly separated personal identity from the natural and social process we have made death into "an ultimate discontinuity" (*PS* 208). With death, Dr. Thomas admits, there is a poignant loss of the subjective enjoyment of the natural process; and with the loss of the subjective enjoyment, which operates only in the present, moment by moment, there is a loss of intensity and thus a lowered value. But all valuable things are vulnerable, fragile, and finite, personal life included. The falling-cherry-blossoms view of death does not capture for Miss Nonscivi either the sense of the reputed infinite value of personality, a sacredness that is even transferred to the body of that personality, or the abject fear that so often attends death.

Both Dr. Thomas and Miss Nonscivi see death as holy: she, as a holy dread as the self faces its existential annihilation; he, as a holy loss as the subjective moments of life perpetually perish. Holiness for the one is revealed in the contrast of the self's being and not-being; for the other, in its being the kind of particular thing it is—limited, ephemeral, but valuable.

Dr. Thomas clarifies his position over against the concerns of Miss Nonscivi by distinguishing two senses of the self, one good and one bad. The "bad" understanding of self sees it as an entity composed of certain features and distancing itself from other features of reality that do not belong to it. This is a narcissistic self, defining its world relative to the roles things play in relation to it, especially regarding its loves and hates, that is, relative to its self-image. This is a self as an enduring entity, an "ego." The "good" understanding of self sees itself as a subjective agent of enjoyment whose identity emerges from the resources given to it for its acting, from the things it creates, and from the resulting responsibilities. Having no self-image based on how its actions feed back upon itself and thus creating an entity of oneself, it can see clearly, create freshly and effectively, and give unselfishly. Such a self is a free self, unfearful; death has no hold over it.

This dialogue nicely raises many of the issues of selfhood—identity, value, temporality, finitude, death, holiness, freedom, subjectivity, and substantiality—and indicates, primarily through the character of Dr. Thomas, the direction in which Neville's own systematic reflections will move. It is clear that Neville intends and works out some variant of a process notion of selfhood (he mentions Whitehead approvingly), which will be addressed in the next section of this essay. It is probably the case that Neville did not intend that Miss Nonscivi's largely existentialist view, with substantialist overtones, gently refuted in the dialogue by Dr. Thomas, would be an element in the transformed process view of selfhood, to be developed below. The unacknowledged assumption in my interpretation (and one which is beyond elaboration and defense at this point) is that the existentialist concern with the sacredness of existence, with holy dread, with the terrifying possibility of annihilation, and with its implied shock of nonbeing (which no process theory seems able to grasp) bespeaks a profound ontological intuition, its somewhat overwrought rhetoric notwithstanding. Profoundly engaged existentialists, whether or not they would acknowledge it, are singed by the fire of eternity. Neville, as will be later shown, enfolds this insight into his transformed process view.

THREE COSMOLOGICAL MODELS OF SELFHOOD: PROCESS, SUBSTANCE, AND AXIOLOGICAL

As indicated in the previous section, Neville espouses some variant of a process view of selfhood, yet his own final position is different enough to warrant its own separate designation as axiological. To position his own unique contribution, I wish to lay out three main types of cosmological models of the self, which models are rooted in different metaphysical cosmologies: (1) self as personally ordered society of actual occasions (as in the process tradition, represented by Alfred North Whitehead); (2) self as substance (the Aristotelian tradition, represented by Paul Weiss); (3) and self as discursive individual (Neville's own variant of the axiological cosmological tradition that includes Plato and Chinese thinkers, among others).

The Process Model of Selfhood

Acknowledging a dynamic and pluralistic universe, Whitehead posited units of experience or "occasions" that successively incorporate the past units of experience, now become objectified. This incorporation of the past into the present, the prehension of the given data to form a new unit of becoming, is the means by which novelty becomes ingredient in the universe and the cosmos advances. "Creativity" is the principle of this novelty and, along with "many" and "one," belongs to the category of the Ultimate.[2] Each occasion or unit of becoming is a creative synthesizing of the many received into a new one. Additionally, the concatenation of the units of experiencing in such a way as to form a serially ordered group or society make up the enduring objects of common experience.

Whitehead's implied view of selfhood (he acknowledged that his own philosophy of organism had yet to account adequately for the "inescapable fact" of personal unity)[3] can only be a series of successive moments of experience possessing a common thread, that is, the reiteration of a common feature. Both William James and David Hume and not a few Buddhists have struggled with something like this as an alternative to the traditional substance view of selfhood, in which personal identity over time is accounted for by means of a substratum underlying the various modifications of consciousness. Several contemporary scholars sympathetic to the virtues of process thought have offered criticisms and struggled with various proposals to ground personal identity, freedom, and moral agency in basically an atomistic event-cosmology.[4]

The Substance Model of Selfhood

One of the earliest, and in some ways one of the most trenchant, criticisms of Whitehead's position was put forth by the eminent metaphysician Paul Weiss, who argued that an event theory such as Whitehead's accounts for neither identity over time nor responsible action. Again and again in his writings Weiss demands that philosophy be able to account for what Everyman/woman upon reflection knows to be true: that they possess an irreducible core, a unique center of action, expression, domination, integration, and reference; that they are sensitive to values and are responsible.[5] None of these features can be separated out as an event-slice or temporary state of the body-mind or considered a part of the whole. Weiss takes his stand in what he takes to be the deliverances of common sense, which suggest a substantive view of the self.

One set of meanings of the self for Weiss clusters around the fact that the human being is a concrete entity, an actuality, a substance, a spatiotemporal unit having both an inside (privacy) and an outside (publicity). Along with other actualities in nature, the human being continues in such a way that it can be reidentified (i.e., it is the same at t_2 that it was at t_1), that it can act on its environment and resist collapse, that it can integrate its aspects and features. Weiss is careful to maintain that the actuality persisting through time is not just a string of events internally related and instantiating the same pattern. Rather, the actuality acts efficaciously to produce, through a temporal sequence subsequent to its own initiating activity, the desired effect.

A second set of meanings clusters around the notion of the self as sensitive to values, particularly ethical ones; the self through its actions is responsible and inevitably guilty. These are characteristics not of one's body nor of one's mind but of one's self. These qualities set the self off as peculiarly human; animals have psyches, but not selves. The self can respond to the universal Good and not simply the local or tribal values. And, finally, the self is both represented by and epitomized by the "I."[6]

What emerges in these schematic and compressed statements is a view of the self rooted in commonsense awareness, able to organize the energies of the body and to manipulate objects in a spatiotemporal environment, and to act for ends normed by the Good. This is the self as substantive agent, goal-directed, vigorous, and responsible.

The Axiological Model of Selfhood: Discursive Individuality

Having dialectically engaged the thought of both Whitehead and Weiss, Neville is ready to propose his own axiological theory of selfhood: enduring personal identity exemplifying discursive individuality. From Whitehead he has taken the notions of causation as prehension, the rooting of the self in the processes of nature, decision as a mark of reality and the accounting for the subjective reality of a thing (the reality a thing has for itself), and the nondiscursive individual as momentary with its attendant perishing.[7] From Weiss he has taken the distinction between essential and nonessential features (modified as essential and conditional features) and the concern that moral agency requires an identity over time. Neville has come to disagree with Whitehead largely over the issue of temporality; he has long argued with Weiss over substance philosophy. He believes neither has worked out a satisfactory theory of value, hampering any adequate treatment of selfhood. Here Neville has elaborated an axiological cosmology and within that cosmology a theory of discursive individuality in which persons are individuals with temporally developing harmonies.[8]

Put simply, to be anything at all, to be a determinate something, is to be a harmony of essential and conditional features. This means that everything is related by means of its conditional features to at least one other thing and that it possesses by means of its essential features its ownmost, unique reality. Lacking the former, the thing could not relate to or connect with its world; lacking the latter, the thing would be nothing other than the (not its) world. The two sets of features are integrated or harmonized; they hang together. The sheer fitting together of these features is called a contrast, in Whitehead's terminology.[9] The essential features of a unit of becoming order the conditional features into a harmonized whole, producing a value both for itself and for all others that will prehend it. To be anything at all is to be an achievement of value and thus to be valuable. Value therefore is ingredient in everything. Each developing thing aims at value and must avail itself of the relevant normative measures to distinguish better and worse ways of putting all the elements together. Each thing attempts the richest contrast possible in the context of its arising—subjectively, the richest enjoyment and intensity; objectively, the greatest synthesis of simplicity and complexity among the constitutive elements. Each thing therefore is normed, valuable, and productive of value.

It might be objected that concern with axiology is interesting perhaps but beside the point with regard to issues of personal identity, which might be understood as a matter of form: whatever the self is, it might be argued, it is simply the reiteration of a form or set of common characteristics over time, the unity in the diverse moments being a formal one. Neville will argue against that because personal identity or selfhood is a temporally developing or discursive affair, requiring the *harmony* of past, present, and future: one never has a personal identity only in a given moment. What makes Neville's view unique is not that a present moment has an inheritance from the past and a set of possible consequences for the future but that it receives *essential* features from its own past and from its future as well as the spontaneous features of the moment. Whereas Whitehead, lacking the metaphysical distinction between essential and conditional features, had no clear way of distinguishing the whole of the inherited past (conditional features for the actual occasion) from one's own past (the promise I made last month that *essentially* binds me in the present) and the whole array of future possibilities from those to which one is essentially related (as the future date when the promissory note must be paid), Neville carves out a notion of personal identity as the togetherness of moments the essential features of which—past, present, and future—harmonize. Whereas Weiss, employing the metaphysical distinction between essential and nonessential features, cannot handle adequately the togetherness of the temporal modes or the way in which the essential features are norms binding the temporal moments of life, Neville can root personal identity in the normativity at each moment of a temporally thick existence as the togetherness of the modes. A discursive individual has a developing identity that, moment by moment, is constituted by the togetherness of the essential features of past, present, and future occasions. Again, a discursive individual is the unique stream of occasions—past, present, and future—the essential features of which are normative for the present. Though shifting moment by moment subjectivity extends throughout the whole of the life and not simply in the present moment of actualization since subjectivity is embodied in the essential features of past and future moments as well as the present.

At this juncture it is important to emphasize that the subjectivity of the whole of the temporal stream constituting a life is a matter of the harmonic togetherness of essential features of past, present, and future but that the togetherness is not temporal. Something more is required: eternity. We turn now to a consideration of the eternal dimension of selfhood.

THE SELF IN TIME AND ETERNITY

Though by no means unique in his understanding of the temporal nature of selfhood, Neville is unique in the process, substance, and axiological traditions considered in claiming that selfhood cannot be understood except as involving and embodying eternity. Following Peter Manchester, Neville claims that "time and eternity make one topic, not two."[10] Consequently, any serious treatment of temporality *eo ipso* requires the treatment of eternity. This is, of course, difficult to argue in modern culture since the two have been "put asunder" with the disastrous result that time has been overvalued and eternity has been forgotten, modern science having little to offer for understanding it (*ETF* 20–21).

There are at least three areas of human concern that provide an entree into eternity: religious experience, theological reflection, and the moral aspects of personal identity. The focus will be upon the last-mentioned, partly because this concern is closer to general secular experience and partly because the current discussion of selfhood is set in the context of both temporality and personal moral identity.

A human self is temporally thick, which means not only that personal identity requires a past and a future but also that one's identity at a given moment requires elements from both the past and the future: one's identity is spread out over past, present, and future. Neville lays out three levels of claims that must be distinguished and clarified (*ETF* 48–49). First, the present requires for its own being and meaning the past and the future, and that in a real way, not just as projected backwards and forwards. Second, the past and the future are not real in the way that the present is real but real according to their own modes: as settled, nonacting factuality and as normative possibility. Third, one's personal identity, temporal as it is, is not just identity at a time but equally an identity in eternity, as one eternally is the youth of promise, the mature adult of heavy responsibilities, and the senior with limited options and a largely fixed identity.

As indicated earlier, personal identity or selfhood is the weaving together of past conditions, future possibilities, and present decisions. But for Neville, and as an improvement on Whitehead, it is not all the past moments or future ones that are relevant to the identity of the self; only some past occasions, not all, are essentially connected with the present and have to be integrated so that the character of the identity continues, and only some future moments, not all, will be constitutive of the self then, related now to the present.

How are the past and the future present in the present? It has been claimed that the past is ingredient in the present as data setting the conditions for deciding and the future is ingredient in the present as normative possibilities, but it must be more radically urged that the past and future must contribute to the present in their temporal wholeness; that is, each past or future moment must be seen as sometimes future, sometimes present, and sometimes past and not simply as past or as future relative to the present moment. As Neville puts it: "The past and the future moments are not exactly *present* in the present [emphasis his]; that is, they are not temporally present. Yet the present cannot be temporally present in that the temporally different past and future moments being what they are. . . . There is thus a togetherness of past, present, and future moments, each in its temporally wholeness, that is not mere temporal togetherness" (*ETF* 97).

This is undoubtedly paradoxical but is an essential part of the moral identity of a self. Neville illustrates this with the situation of a bank robber on trial. Let us suppose that today (August 1, 1997) the accused is standing trial for a robbery committed a month prior (July 1, 1997). If the accused is to be judged guilty now as charged he must have committed the crime then; that is, he must have as part of his identity today that he is the one who actually committed the crime a month before— he was presently robbing the bank then (July 1, 1997). Furthermore, to be responsible for the crime now he must have been capable of not committing the crime on June 30; he could have done otherwise, and the future possibility of his not doing so on June 30 is part of his present identity. Yet again, the man standing trial on August 1 is a man who has been guilty for a month. Thus, a part of his identity on August 1 is that committing the crime on July 1 was first a future possibility, then a present action, and finally a settled fact. If only the present were real, as some are inclined to assert, none of the aforementioned aspects could be constitutive of the present and thus there would be no basis for his being on trial. Neville concludes; "The temporal past . . . is eternally present in the present moment of the trial" (*ETF* 58).

Let us assume that the accused is judged guilty and is sentenced to three years in prison for the crime. Let us further assume that the intent of the punishment is the satisfaction of the demands of justice and not primarily the reform, education, or healing of the guilty nor the deterrence of other possible offenders. Thus the future date of August 1, 2000 as future, present, and past would have importance for the robber's present identity. Thus now and for the intervening three years the future release date is the date on which justice would be done, assuming the sentence is carried out. When that date is present (August 1, 2000) the prisoner will change from one who owes a debt to society to one who has paid that debt, and on August 2, 2000, justice will have been restored and the completing of the sentence is the past condition for the prisoner's restoration to society and its privileges. Thus the temporal future as future, present, and past is eternally present in the present date of the sentencing. The past and future in all their temporal modes could not be temporally present in the present. Yet they are essentially together—how so? They are together in the context of eternity. The identity of a self is thus temporal *and* eternal.

We began this section with the thesis that "time and eternity make one topic, not two" (*ETF* 20) and have attempted to show how eternity is implicated in the togetherness of the modes of time, as even secular moral experience shows. This by no means is all that needs to be said, nor is it all that Neville has said on this exceedingly complex topic. The phenomenology of moral experience reveals that time flows, a profound and ultimately baffling metaphor, but an insight hinted at in the passage from possibility to decision to settled fact, from the shifting of the present from date to date. But time can be understood as flowing only as it is contained within the ultimate ontological context of eternity, another thesis in Neville's metaphysics of time and eternity. Eternity is not static but is the dynamic context for temporal change. This context is best understood according to a theory of divine creation. Finally, personal identity, selfhood *sub specie aeternitatis*, is eternal as well as temporal and participates in the divine life. These fundamental theses provide the grounds not only for moral experience but also for religious life and theological speculation as well. Beyond this bare acknowledgment, the limitations of space and the intricacy of the subject do not allow us to go. (The argument for the above is summarized in *ETF* 12–14.)

THE THEORY SPECIFIED: INDIVIDUATION

Neville has sketched out a speculative and highly abstract notion of the self, particularly in his claim that personal identity or selfhood is eternal as well as temporal and participates in the divine life. Wisely he knows that highly abstract and logically vague notions have to be specified before they are of much use to men and women conducting the business of living. Here and there he has suggested ways that the metaphysical claim might be specified, thus making possible some probation of the claim. His most systematic attempts at specification cluster around ethics, theology, and spiritual development. As already mentioned, Neville produced a sustained treatment of the models of spiritual perfection in his early *Soldier, Sage, Saint* (1978). Arguably his most succinct attempt of specification of his claim about selfhood is in his comparative treatment of the theme of individuation in Confucianism and Christianity. Generally, he understands the theme to be spiritual development, a life of spiritual progress in which one becomes ever more individual, ever more related in concrete ways to one's environment, and ever more translucent in the manifestation of divine things.[11] More specifically, he understands individuation to refer to "that element in cultivation or education by virtue of which a person develops fulfilled concrete relations with the particular circumstances of life" (*BMG* 127). Two implications of this characterization should be noted: (1) as *cultivation*, individuation or becoming a self, or more of a self, is a matter of effort over time in conjunction with forces, powers, and energies not directly under one's control; and (2) individuation is a *relational* process requiring attentive openness to specificity—to these "concrete" relations, to those "particular" circumstances. Selfhood is thus an achievement through specific interactions with life's particularities, the outcome of which is not fully controllable, predictable, or assured; a mystery remains.

Neville illustrates this understanding with reference to both Christianity and Confucianism. With regard to the former, individuation occurs through covenant fidelity, which entails the acknowledgment of personhood as social and not simply natural; as involving the contract of the society of which one is a part with a covenant-initiating being; and as requiring maintenance through performance of covenant-obliging duties (*BMG* 130). Just as there is no story if there are not characters who through their involvements with other characters learn things, grow, fulfill their duties, achieve goals, and realize some destiny or other—in short, develop and refine a character structure over time—just so there is no individuation unless persons are storylike things, having a narrative structure with its Jamesian flights and perchings, its tensions and releases, its conflicts and resolutions, its juxtapositions and pacings, its moods and meanderings, and its epiphanic moments. On this model the identity of the self approximates an autobiographical narrative; one works out one's identity, episode by episode, scene by scene, vis-à-vis God and others (*BMG* 132).

With regard to Confucianism, individuation cannot be the covenant fidelity to a covenant-maker and to the duties, tasks, and responsibilities enjoined upon the covenant-partner. Nor can it be the concern for the life story enacted in the larger context of the narrative of one's family, community, society, and cosmos. Rather, individuation is the progressive perfection of a core in its relation to the larger environment through physical, psychological, and social structures. As Neville puts it: "A person, for the Confucians, is always a substance functioning in a context" (*BMG* 133). The substance or core is the ability to appreciate the values of things and to respond appropriately. This cannot be done properly if the structures through which the substance functions are opaque. Individuation therefore is the constant clarification and refinement of the structures relative to the plurality of things in the environment so that harmony, equilibrium, or attunement prevails. On this model the social structures are not so many roadblocks to the self's fulfillment but rather the means through which the self becomes itself. The perfection of the semiotic codes, social patterns, and ritual propriety is the stuff of individuation.

That Neville is committed to the importance of the theme of individuation as the becoming of the self over time is evident in his pairing up of Christianity and Confucianism against all forms of gnosticism in which the self is perfected by withdrawing from its environmental demands and prescinding from its history. Both are "incarnational" in the sense of seeing fundamental value as being manifested in the circumstances of life; both understand life on the Path as a progressive exhibition of holiness, though of course divinity is variously interpreted. Further, Neville believes each is a needed corrective to the other and together, purified, they provide a more adequate view of individuation; each self has an obligation for the way his or her narrative uniqueness contributes to the whole of society, and the perfection of each requires the perfection of the social order.

Neville has given a strong and in many ways persuasive characterization of selfhood and its specification in the process of individuation: discursive individuality, in itself a most vague and abstract notion, needs for its own probation something like individuation as the spiritual development of the self through the interaction with the particularities of life's circumstances; theory has to come down somewhere. Further, he finds that two major traditional Paths, singly and together, can be generalized and interpreted fruitfully as individuation, as spiritual perfection, thus giving dialectical legitimacy to the theory.

CHALLENGE: SELF AS SOUL

By way of challenge I wish to encourage Neville to open up his notion of self, which is largely self as spirit, with its primary accent on the mind and the will, on thinking, doing, striving, and achieving, to include more significantly self as soul with its emphasis on the heart and its loves, on the erotic, the affectional, and the imaginal. This distinction is suggested by the work of the archetypal psychologists, especially James Hillman, and in phenomenological psychology, especially in the work of Edward Casey.[12] As a kind of rough-and-ready way of distinguishing important matters in grasping human reality, I suggest understanding spirit as that dimension or orientation of the self as it drives toward abstraction, up and away from the earth, the body, and the concrete; as it aims high and shoots far; pursues vigorously its ends, striving for perfection; hot, dry, solar, stereotypically masculine in tone, seeking, climbing, dominating by word and gesture, commanding obedience, serious, never resting. By contrast, soul is that dimension or orientation of the self as it seeks the concrete, moving inward and downward, as it loves water and earth; cool, dark, stereotypically feminine, lunar; mulling, stewing, imagining, circumambulating, linking and relating, fascinated by birthings, decayings, and dyings; playful, impure, loving imperfection and wholeness.

I contend that any theory that primarily proffers an unrelieved self as spirit, dismissive of self as soul, is a serious distortion of human reality and a personal and cultural danger. Every thinker needs to ponder the distinction, find appropriate ways of balancing the two, avoid the attraction of one-sidedness, and heed the danger of thinking away the concrete, the circuitous, and the chaotic. It is not that there is no place in Neville's thought for the concerns indicated by the distinction. He has written extensively on the role of imagination in thinking, on symbolization in the arts, religion, and culture in general. He has elaborated the model of the saint with her or his loves, desires, and passions. Nevertheless, the desires are to be perfected and the heart to be purified, which goals belong to the spirit. Furthermore, imagination as a species of thinking, while in itself unconcerned with truth, tends to be seen *for the sake of* the other species of thinking—interpreting, theorizing, and taking responsibility. What emerges is a strong agential sense in Neville's theorizing: the self as knower and doer; the self as sense-maker; the self as pursuer of the good, always aiming at perfection either Platonic or Wesleyan. But suppose things are not quite like that nor should they be. Suppose that in addition to doing work, spiritual or otherwise, the self as soul simply delights in a relationship, enjoys the joke, thrills to the aria, finds satisfaction in putting the pieces together just that way, relishes the gossip, lives with the dark secret, relives the bitter experience, ponders its own ambiguity, and anticipates its own ending. Somehow these experiences of the complexity, the beauty, the depth, and the intensity of things have to be included in the life of the self and in the stories it tells itself.

Now Neville knows all this so my challenge is somewhere between a tease and a seriously intended suggestion. He might open up his thought and language soulfully in at least the following ways. First of all, he might exploit distinctions he has already made, namely in his description of the three modes of present experience: action, enjoyment, and engagement (*ETF* 50–54). The first and the third accord well with self as spirit; the second and third fit nicely with some aspects of the notion of the soul as I am using it. For him, enjoyment connotes pleasure, suffering, quality, harmony, immediacy, and ecstasy; engagement implies being-with, interaction, and relationship. Sustained meditation on how these aspects are inwardly felt, expressed, and lived with in the vast manifold of human experience would enrich Neville's notion of selfhood.

Second, Neville might venture forth more boldly in his use of "soul," which he rarely uses except in the context of the religious life.[13] He is right to point out the controversial history of the term in Western theology and the limited parallels to other traditions, but he would surely be right to persevere, even in a modest way, in his use of "soul." The term has a wider application than to the explicitly religious dimension of life, and something important is lost from discourse—and experience—when the term is either voided or avoided. It must be admitted that the use of "soul" can be awkward and in some cases hardly politically correct. But one wonders what the greater offense is. The self as it appreciates, responds to, and enhances the values ingredient in experience is soul.

Third, the individuation process of self-becoming does not, indeed cannot, proceed without the intense involvement of soul. The heart and its loves—eros, desire, delight, passionate longing—are awakened, stimulated, and enhanced by the emergence into conscious awareness of images and symbols. The self as soul is always imagining, and the psychic activity of humans from the most immediate of practical concerns to the loftiest of speculations is laced with images and fantasies that lure, contextualize, orient, focus, and refresh. For Neville, imagination, "the elementary capacity to experience things with images," is religious, whether or not there is any reference to God or the divine (*TBS* 47). This is especially and explicitly the case when images, always experienced contextually, perspectivally, and as value-laden, are taken as world-constructing, setting the very boundary conditions for the appearance of the world. One characterization if not definition of religion is that it is that "cultural enterprise that shepherds the symbols of the boundary conditions" (*TBS* 55). I hesitate to make too tight an argument linking soul and religion (broadly or narrowly conceived) through a middle term imagination (either as activity or as product). Yet there is a clear configuration in which these three terms illuminate, link, and enhance the worth of each other. If this claim can be made good, then the self in its becoming requires soul, which is imaginative, and thus religious. Serious engagement with religion, either in its more public and historical form or in its private and ad hoc fashion is always achieved through its imagery and stimulates the soul. Imagination pulls self as soul into religious openness and involvement.

Robert Neville, master dialectician, has given us a highly original treatment of the self, improving in significant ways upon some of the best speculative thinking of the twentieth century. His inclusion of eternity as essential both to time and to the identity of the self is nothing if not brilliant and will materially shape the discussion of these issues in the future. The challenge to his treatment of the self will be to include more centrally its soulful aspects.

NOTES

1. Robert Cummings Neville, *The Puritan Smile: A Look Toward Moral Reflection* (Albany: State University of New York Press, 1987). "A Taste of Death" comprises chapter 11 of this work, hereafter abbreviated as *PS*.

2. Alfred North Whitehead, *Process and Reality: An Essay in Cosmology*, corrected by David Ray Griffin and Donald W. Sherburne (New York: The Free Press, 1978), p. 21.

3. Alfred North Whitehead, *Adventure of Ideas* (New York: Macmillan, 1933), pp. 188–89.

4. George R. Lucas Jr., *The Rehabilitation of Whitehead* (Albany: State University of New York Press, 1989), chapter 18.

5. Paul Weiss, *Nature and Man* (Carbondale: Southern Illinois University Press, 1965), pp. 252–62.

6. Paul Weiss, *Privacy* (Carbondale: Southern Illinois University Press, 1983), pp. 185–218.

7. Robert Cummings Neville, *The Highroad around Modernism* (Albany: State University of New York Press, 1992), p. 98.

8. Robert Cummings Neville, *The Cosmology of Freedom* (New Haven: Yale University Press, 1994), p. 94.

9. Whitehead, *Process and Reality*, p. 22.

10. Peter Manchester, quoted in Robert Cummings Neville, *Eternity and Time's Flow* (Albany: State University of New York Press, 1993), p. 20, hereafter designated as *ETF*.

11. Robert Cummings Neville, *Behind the Masks of God: An Essay toward Comparative Theology* (Albany: State University of New York Press, 1991), p. 138, hereafter designated as *BMG*.

12. See especially James Hillman, "Peaks and Vales: The Soul/Spirit Distinction as Basis for the Difference Between Psychotherapy and Spiritual Discipline," in *On the Way to Self-Knowledge*, ed. J. Needleman and D. Lewis (New York: Knopf, 1976), pp. 114–47. See also his *Re-Visioning Psychology* (New York: Harper & Row, 1975). Edward S. Casey, influenced by the archetypal psychology of Hillman and others, has written *Spirit and Soul: Essays in Philosophical Psychology* (Dallas: Spring Publications, 1991).

13. Robert Cummings Neville, *The Truth of Broken Symbols* (Albany: State University of New York Press, 1996), p. 153 and passim, hereafter designated as *TBS*.

PART III

Metaphysical Questions

CHAPTER 8

Neville's 'Naturalism' and the Location of God

Robert S. Corrington

The main concern of this paper will be to come to grips with how Neville envisions the transcendence and immanence of God vis-à-vis the normative and formal properties of the world, as they obtain essentially and conditionally. This is directly related to his Schleiermacher-like sense that every determinate thing in the world (and there are no non-determinate things) is absolutely or sheerly dependent on the creator. To be determinate is to be the locus of identity and otherness within a system of infinite reciprocities and negations.[1] Primary among the 'things' of the world is temporality. To grasp the fullness of the creator it will be necessary to analyze the relationship of ontological mutuality between the flow of time and eternity. At the heart of all of these analyses will be the delineation of the utter centrality, for Neville, of the reality of *creatio ex nihilo* as the ground principle, or perhaps pre-principle, that guarantees the full incarnationality of God as Logos within a world that is fully determinate and closed, yet allows for finite freedom (a position that Neville refers to as neo-Calvinism). This ontological ground creates the world in a unique sense and is held to be the case regardless of the status of the cosmological theory of the Big Bang, or any possible alternative, in astrophysics. That is, ontological creation is different in kind from any event that could be delineated by scientific inquiry, which, by definition, deals with cosmological creation.

It might help us to gauge the radicality of Neville's concept of ontological creation if we remember that it is similar to the shock of the ontological difference in Heidegger. That is, there is an abyss of difference between indeterminate being-itself and any being thing that takes on essential and conditional determinate traits. Actually, for Neville there are three terms in the fundamental structure of his system. There is indeterminate being-itself and the opposite extreme of determinate being. Connecting them is the creative act of God that brings determination to the divine precisely in the act of creating the world.

> The creator makes itself creator when and as it creates; in order to do this, it must be independent, in itself, of the products it creates and even of its own role of being creator. The role of the creator is the nature the creator has in virtue of its connection with the created determinations. (GC 72)

> My own alternative [to the process view] is that God is creator of everything determinate, creator of things actual as well as of things possible. Apart from the relative nature the divinity gives itself as creator in creating the world, God is utterly transcendent.[2]

God becomes determinate in a relative way, that is, as relevant to the world, by and through the eternal act of creation. But God as being-itself, that is, as living on the nether side of the ontological difference, is transcendent of any analogy or determinate comparison that could bring God into human purview. The God that we actually encounter in the world is the God that lives as the third term straddling the ontological difference between indetermination and determination. Put most succinctly, "being-itself is essentially indeterminate and conditionally determinate" (GC 41).

It should be noted here that the world does not give determination to God, contra the process view, but that God gives itself determination in a strictly relative way so as to remain in eternal relevance to the determinate orders of creation. Neville's God is an extremely large God, if we may use Bernard Loomer's language, and cannot be confined in any analogical structure that would bind the divine to finite proportionality (GC 18–19). There is nothing similar to the consequent nature of God that gains ontological weight with each objectively immortal occasion as physically prehended. Nor is God an "as-if" construct or a neopragmatic symbol, but is sheer being-itself transcendent of analogical bridges. Even the God of Aquinas seems rather tame and domestic when placed against Neville's indeterminate ground and abyss. And the process God, especially in its now-faded glory, looks like a straight put-up job when projected onto the traitless ground of being-itself. The primordial dimension of God seems too static and determined by internal contrasts, while the consequent dimension is like an omnivorous cousin that eats one out of house and home. If nothing else can be said, Neville's indeterminate ground cannot get any bigger because of what the world does, it is already and always that than which nothing greater can be conceived.

In order to grasp the full richness and scope of Neville's philosophical theology it will be necessary to address several connected themes
that cumulatively show us the location of God vis-à-vis his quasi-process
understanding of creation or nature. These themes are the transcendence
of God, the presence or immanence of God, the nature of eternity, and
the structure of the things of the world. Insofar as Neville considers himself to be a naturalist, and in this we will give him the benefit of the
doubt, his conception of nature will be probed to see how it might frame
his understanding of God. By way of a proleptic hint of our conclusion,
we may find that his God is too big and his nature is too small, and that
he wants things from the indeterminate ground, *qua* self-determining,
that simply might not be available.

We have noted Neville's extreme version of the ontological difference between Being and a being. However, he prefers to speak of being-
itself rather than Being by way of emphasizing the utter independence of
the primal ground and its position prior to the divide between Being and
nonbeing. God transcends the world in the sense that God cannot be
reached by any conceptual or analogical bridge that starts from any
order of creation. As noted above, God or being-itself has no traits and
cannot be predicated in any way. For Neville, only the mystic has something like direct access to the indeterminate God. Like Tillich's God
beyond the God of theism, Neville's God has no internal contrasts and
cannot be in dialogue with itself. This dimension of God, God in essential indifference, has no providential reality. Indeed, Neville marks a distinct departure from so many twentieth-century Protestants, for example, Moltmann and Pannenberg, who see the *not yet (noch nicht sein)* as
a fundamental trait of the divine life.[3] The indeterminate Ground, hardly
unruly for Neville, can only be arrived at by contrast to the determinate
things of creation that fully participate in God, but that are separated
from being itself by an abyss. While Neville is convinced that we can
make a series of forceful arguments for the necessity of the ontological
one, as a unifying principle that is not part of the many as a kind of
superunity *within* the world, it does not follow that we can enter into
the inner life of the indeterminate God.

This position should remind us of the mature Schleiermacher who
has been labeled a pietistic agnostic on the God question. For Schleiermacher, of course, the delineation of the features of self-consciousness in
its three grades, animal/immediate, middle level, and religious/higher
level, gives us indirect access to God through the primacy of the feeling
of absolute or sheer dependence. While Neville would be friendly to
aspects of this account, he prefers to work in the other direction via a
cluster of interrelated arguments that refuse to privilege the human starting point. At the heart of these arguments is the sense that creation could

only be what it is because of an eternal creative act that transcends creation. Yet it does not follow that we can say why God created the world, or why the world is unified in the way that it is (*GC* 71). Neville is quite clear that Leibniz's theodicy is in error. That is, it makes no sense to see some kind of divine mind prior to creation making decisions as to which essential perfections will be granted existence in such a way as to maximize the amount of realized perfection in the world.[4] Neville's God has no mind, and entertains no possible universes prior to the act of creation. Hence we must endure the utter mystery of why the world is as it is. There are no sufficient reasons linking a divine decision with creation.

What lies beyond the sphere of sufficient reasons, so carefully developed by seventeenth-century thinkers? Shifting to more theological language, Neville emphasizes the radical novelty of creation and its grace-filled heart. The essential and indeterminate God becomes the creator through an eternal act of self-constitution:

> God as source creates the world, having no determinate need to do so but strictly and purely out of divine self-constituting grace. The universe is wholly dependent for its existence as a set of determinate things on God as source. That God is source is itself a function of the world's being created.[5]

The primal and gracious act of creation is asymmetrical in the sense that the created cannot in turn act on the creator. The process account, it will be remembered, is a symmetrical one in that the subjective aims and prehensive fields of actual occasions can add to and modify the divine life through their death and simultaneous objective immortality. Hartshorne's God can indeed be surprised and transformed in a way that Neville's cannot.

God, in becoming conditionally determinate through the eternal act of creation that creates space, time, and the world, overcomes its utter transcendence. The world that the now-relational God creates is a closed one. By this Neville does not mean that it is a bound but expanding totality in the sense of contemporary astrophysics, although this may be the case on the cosmological level, but that it consists of the 'sum' of all determinate things (*TP* 30). The bridge between the power of God the creator and the created orders is through the economic trinity. Here Neville works out of the classical distinction between the immanent trinity, namely, the trinity *an sich*, and the economic trinity seen as the time-embracing unfolding of God's glory within creation. He privileges the economic trinity precisely because his own conception of the indeterminate ground would make it profoundly difficult to probe into the immanent trinity prior to its self-determination under the conditions of temporality and finitude.

Using traditional language, he sees God the Father as the source of everything determinate, God the Son as the product or end point of the creative act, while the Spirit is the creative activity itself (*TP* 39). The economic trinity, the "how" of the indeterminate ground as it becomes determinate, moves to overcome the utter transcendence of God. The creating God, as opposed to the creator prior to creation, is immanent within all of the orders of the world. Like Tillich, Neville has a strong sacramental sense of the incarnation, namely, that it is manifest in forms of divinization or epiphanies of power that directly participate in the conditional God. In some passages that might shock Barthians, Neville insists that the human process can enter into the power of God and take on some of its divine power (e.g., *TP* 18–19). While we can rest assured that Neville knows what the Protestant Principle is for, he also wants to free the self from its alienation from God by his categorial sense that direct participation in creative activity is indeed part of the way of grace, as most clearly actualized in the Covenant (*TP* 52).

The paradox here is that Neville has an extreme sense of divine transcendence combined with an equally extreme sense of divine immanence. His interest in world religions has its source, so I would argue, in this deep sensitivity to the innumerable ways that the triune God can appear within the world and the human process. Like Pannenberg, Neville insists that God is robustly self-revealing in the history of religions. His theory of revelation works in consort with his ontology to show that what had been meant by revelation, as the presentation of group-specific information, can best be seen as a special kind of learning that is less bound to antecedent "messages," which are often little more than demonic missives from the gods of space.[6]

The dialectical tension between God's essential transcendence and conditional immanence does not, however, bifurcate God into two disconnected dimensions that can only speak to each other across an abyss of nonbeing (a concept that has already been ruled out). In some mysterious sense, the indeterminate ground "chose" in a non-necessary and nonemanating way to create both itself as determined and the closed world of determinate things. We have absolutely no access with any of our philosophical tools to the inner logic of this nonchosen choice. We simply live in the continuing power of its ongoing effects. All of our spatial and temporal pictures of this event of creation shatter on the rock of the ontological difference between being-itself and the things of the world. But there is a very striking sense in which we are left with more than enough semiotic material that can serve as signs of God's radical immanence. Like Bonaventura, Neville can see the "footprints of God" within creation and can follow those footprints back to the invisible sign maker that never creates an order without leaving its traces in its product.

Perhaps the most dramatic footprints of the creator are found in the elusive momenta of time and time's flow. One of the most basic connecting links between creation and the created is that between time's flow and eternity. Neville has taken very great pains to develop a theory of eternity that does full justice to our own experience of time. He reworks his understanding of eternity in the context of a philosophical environment that privileges the present and has a subsidiary tendency to spatialize time as if it could be bound and contained in discrete packets. To understand eternity it is also necessary to give equal ontological standing to all three modes of time and to despatialize our understanding of any or all of these modes.

The analysis of eternity and time also opens up the basic ontology of things, insofar as each determinate thing is what it is vis-à-vis the mode of time in which it obtains. Here we begin to get a glimpse of Neville's quasi-process form of naturalism. I call it a "quasi-process" form because of the centrality of such notions as decision, spontaneous creativity, actualization, objective everlastingness, and pure nonnative form. While Neville will of course deny that these terms denote or imply an anthropomorphic structure, we shall see that they do serve to give an honorific and zoösemiotic (even anthroposemiotic) stamp to the delineation of the fundamental traits of the orders of the world. While he has gone beyond the mythology of the actual occasion, thereby refusing to reduce the things of the world to some kind of primal atomic whatness, he still clings to notions that can only blunt the generic sweep of a naturalism that wishes to honor the utter complexity of the world's traits, many of which obtain in utter semiotic darkness.

The first thing to note is that time is created, that is, it is not an emergent product, perhaps from spatial extension, and that its creation is rooted in the eternal. Thus the ultimate source of time and time's flow is in the indeterminate ground. "God is the living dynamism of the eternal act creating time's flow."[7] It is interesting that Neville brings in rather dynamic language at this point to indicate the living connection between eternity and the three modes of time known to the human process. He also prefers to talk of "time's flow" rather than the moments of time so as to stress the gathering and sustaining power of eternity that continually erases any ultimate atomicity or epochal quality for the moments of time.

Philosophical and theological perspectives often unwittingly privilege one mode of time, thus putting the other two into a kind of ontological eclipse. Earlier we noted that Neville's indeterminate being-itself does not have the features of many of the more recent eschatological Gods, who groan through creation, read in politically correct terms, toward an ultimate theophany on the nether side of *chronos*. At the other extreme are those perspectives driven by the myth of origin that make antecedent orders numinous per se. Tillich, more forcefully than anyone else, has brilliantly deconstructed these powers of "blood and soil" and shown that they must be chastened by the God of time. Of course, he ends up privileging the future in this move, thereby blunting the efficacy of his framework. There is a sense in which the process view of epochal time privileges the present, insofar as the only living realities are those that are in the infinitesimal moment of becoming in which the past ingresses according to the lure of the future.

A further problem with the process reading of epochal time and ingression is that it cannot allow for genuine otherness or discontinuity within the finite orders of the world. The self is the world from the perspective of a subjective form. Neville makes a bold move at this point to rescue a strong sense of difference or otherness for the orders of time so that they are not reduced to a common set of traits or gathered into the power of an omnivorous subjective form. Above we noted some of the differentia for the three modes of time in their essential constitution. The present is characterized by decision and spontaneous creativity. This is, of course, a strongly flavored process account. The past is essentially the fixed reality of objective everlastingness, not, however, as preserved in some alleged consequent nature of God but in the eternity that cannot be consequent to anything within the determinate orders of the world. The past is "the fixed achievements of the universe, all structurally ordered and determinate with respect to one another and each embodying an actualized value" (*TP* 68–69). The future is essentially a kind of normative reality, the locus of value. Interestingly, Neville rejects anything like a static primordial mind in which compossible forms would reside, and affirms a kind of Peircean "would be" or conditional. His formulation is precise: "Form is what would integrate a plurality, real or subjunctive" (*ETF* 102).

The three modes of time are both distinct from each other, and deeply relevant to each other. Neville, as always, wants to avoid any static or container analogies that would compartmentalize time. The differentia among the modes are related to their essential and conditional ways of being, rather than to some kind of locatedness that has fixed boundaries. The way of being for the modes of time in consort is to flow together in a kind of "ontological context of mutual relevance" (*ETF* 109). But the foundation for this relevance is not through ingression of the past and responsiveness to the divine lure in the future. Rather, it is through a direct and total participation in eternity: "Eternity is the condition for and inclusion of time's flow" (*ETF* 112).

Looking more directly at eternity, if such language is not too guilty of hubris, we can rule out some misguided conceptions that have plagued generic level analysis. For Neville, eternity cannot be (1) static form, (2) the *totum simul* (a position he sees embodied in Augustine and Hartshorne), (3) a total determinate fact, (4) normative goodness, or (5) an Aristotelian unmoved mover. For one thing, the future is still open in the sense that it is the dimension of the "would be," thus ruling out (1), (3) (which privileges the past), and (5). Number (4) is ruled out on the grounds that eternity is the measure of form and thus the reality that empowers and sustains form from outside of itself, shades of Plato's *Euthyphro*. Number (2) is ruled out because the concept of the divine mind grasping all reality at once privileges the present and makes genuine future novelty impossible.

It is crucial that time's flow be understood from the perspective of eternity. That is, one cannot separate human time from eternity as they entail each other in any sustained analysis of the *way* of God and God's created world. The mutual relevance of the three modes of time to each other is made possible by the presence of eternity: "[T]he only thing that could constitute an ontological context of mutual relevance is an eternal divine creative act and . . . the eternal dynamism of time's flow constitutes what we should mean by the life of God" (*ETF* 113). Hence God approaches us with a special power and intimacy in the flow of time that we learn to experience when we overcome the idolatry of any one mode of time. The past is ontologically different from the present and future, and the same applies to the other two modes. Difference is preserved while identity is secured through the flow of time that participates in eternity. Put in stronger terms, eternity is as close to us as our own breath. Eternity and the flow of time are grace-filled even if things in time often suffer blindly and have no sense of their whence and whither.

Neville's conception of the future is particularly fascinating because it represents an alternative to the process view while still using some of the more basic process categories. The future is tied to form and different forms entail different values. "It is the forms in things that make the difference in value" (*ETF* 89). Yet we must always ask: just where are the forms? Whitehead would have us believe that they are resident in the primordial mind of God, waiting to be sent out as tantalizing lures to hungry actual occasions. Neville, a reconstructed process thinker and Platonist, prefers to let the future have its own distinctive features. Hence, forms are not mental quasi actualizations in a divine mind, but realities awaiting actualization via the other modes of time. "Far better to say that form is the essential feature of the future and that determinate forms are the ways the future is made determinate by concrete actualities in the past and by the shifting decisions of present moments" (*ETF* 89). Actualities and decisions work together to render certain forms actual to the things of the world. These forms are located in a kind of cosmic "would be" that is not a form-bank so much as a potential for actualization. By putting form in this special ontological niche, Neville preserves a more genuine sense of novelty than Whitehead for whom all eternal entities are already attained.

The function of form, as the locus of value, is to sustain the togetherness of things. The relation between form and the future prepares the way for an analysis of things in their essential and conditional reality. By looking at the determinate things in the closed world of time we can gain access to the most basic "where" of God vis-à-vis nature, understood here as creation or *nature natured*. It is at this point that many of Neville's most creative categorial elaborations come home to roost. We have noted that a fundamental distinction in his system is that between the essential aspect of a thing and its conditional aspect. Creation is constituted by the "sum" of all determinate things that each share in some mixture of essence and conditionality. Each and every thing is determinate in some, but not all respects. "That a thing is determinate does not mean it is wholly determinate: the future is not wholly determinate, for instance, although it is what it is at least by being future to something in its past" (*TP* 30). Hence anything occupying a time process will have some of its future open to it, even though this opening may be infinitesimally small in a given case. A Peircean would even say that the laws of nature are themselves only partially determinate and that they could take on new habits in the future as they are punctuated by firstness and secondness.

Thus we should be clear that the word "determinateness" in no way denotes or connotes a closed deterministic system for Neville, although my suspicion is that his universe is a little less rambunctious than Hartshorne's on this issue. Be that as it may, each and every thing (and the word "thing" is used as an extremely generic placeholder for the differentia of the world) has an essential core and a deep relational or conditioned dimension. Neville is very much aware of the issue of identity over time and faults the process epochal view for failing to give a depth structure to the human character and the other things of the world.[8] Instead of little epochal pulses that hand the torch of identity down the line, he prefers to see each thing as having an essential core that endures per se and that helps to order the conditional features by and through which the thing takes on relations and relata. More precisely, normative form relates to essential features to sustain identity. "[T]he continuity, the irreducible unity of a life, the subjectivity of the whole, is a matter of the normative side of the forms, of essential features" (*CF* 50–51). He refers to his perspective on things as an "axiological pluralism," where the focus is on the role normative form plays in the ultimate constitution of the things of the world.

Even more important is his sense that things are not relational in a totalistic sense. For a process thinker, any given actual occasion will positively or negatively prehend all noncontemporary occasions, thus entering into what could be called an absolute web of robust internal relations. Neville's naturalism comes to the fore when he denies that such relational totalities exist. A given thing will have "multiple effective locations,"[9] but these locations will not belong to some kind of superfield that envelops all subaltern realities. Arguing against Weiss's view that space-time fields are antecedent to their 'occupants,' Neville insists that fields are themselves products or functions of harmonies, and harmonies are subject to change over time. Therefore the cosmos cannot be a totality that is in some sense prior to all things. No thing will be related to all other things. There are genuine ontological breaks in the world that cannot be filled in, especially by an idealistic system that refuses to grasp the utter power of secondness within continua.

Thus a thing, the constituent of creation *(nature natured)*, will sustain itself against decay by having intrinsic and essential features. Its conditional features will, of course, be subject to spoliation or augmentation as environing conditions change. As we have just seen, the concept of "harmony" now makes its entrance as the togetherness of the essential and the conditional features of the thing. Neville rejects the atomistic view that would confine harmony to the essential features alone (a position defended in Wittgenstein's *Tractatus)*, and wants us to understand it as a strong bridge connecting the essential and the conditional. The concept of harmony is, of course, one found in process perspectives, and has a decided aesthetic cast. The harmony of any given thing does not come to it from outside, but is its own structure of togetherness. We gain access to it by a kind of aesthetic intuition. We are cautioned, however, not to assume that the word "harmony" always denotes a stability or a peaceful process of regular change. Harmonies can be profoundly displeasing and need not reflect anything congenial to human aspiration or desire. In this sense, the concept of harmony is morally neutral.

Neville accepts Whitehead's general cosmological view that harmony brings a multiplicity into a unity; namely, "that the reality of the event for itself is the processive becoming of the unity" (*CG* 8). But the internal creativity of any event/thing is deeply related to the ontological creativity of God. Remember, that for Neville the process tradition has erred in separating creativity, as some kind of ultimate ground, from God. In particular, this muddies the relation between God and the world by making divine presence almost a secondary reality. He sees an intimate relationship between self-becoming in time's flow and the continuing power of ontological creativity. Put in theological terms, it is as if the creation is actually the same event as the act of sustaining the world. If Tillich can identify creation as the Fall into finitude, I suppose Neville is allowed to see the creative power of the indeterminate ground as continually present in the things/events of the world. Again, his sense of utter transcendence is richly balanced by his sense of the radical immanence of eternal creativity in the movement of self-forming events toward harmony and unity.

Things/events are thus in formation in the present, responsive to that which obtains everlastingly in the past, and open to prospects of transformation in the future. While Neville is hardly a thinker of the groaning *not yet,* he does understand that self-formation requires an intimate relation between God and the future. However, this relation is one of divine otherness in which God remains deeply elusive to our present desires and inquiries. In a particularly striking passage that I quote at some length, he lays out the correlation of human or thingly temporality and divine eternity:

> From our limited standpoint, where the future is still open and at which point the eternal actual resolution of our future connection does not exist, the future of God's address to us is "other." The character God will take in response to our needs and to our deserts remains alien to us in the present, however real it is in eternity. From the standpoint of the present, God's creation in the future is really other: this issue is not one of our ignorance. Even God does not *now* know what the future holds because God is never only *now*. For ourselves, who truly are temporal, existing now with a future still future, the future and God's special presence as redemptive or condemnatory, helpful or negligent, merciful or punitive, remains other. (*ETF* 211–12)

Insofar as prehuman orders are also to some extent self-choosing, this categorial framework can be applied across the board. What is interesting is that our temporality is clearly blind to its own whence and whither, and can only see God, *qua* future, as an alien otherness that may or may not be punitive or helpful, and so forth. Yet I don't see Neville as affirming a kind of Hartshornian blindness on the part of *God*, insofar as God truly lives in and as eternity. It takes a great stretching of mind to understand the seeming paradox between God's blindness in the *now*, which is, of course, a misconception on our part, and God's omniscience in eternity. In structural terms I would say that there is no room for a *not yet being* in eternity, while there can be an energizing otherness/future for finite and perspectival orders.

Things/events are self-forming creatures of time and eternity that combine essential and conditional features, participate in the primal creative act that is still with us, harmonize from within their diverse traits, contain form *qua* value, and occasionally show forth the glory of the creator in their sacramental splendor. Nature, which is "constituted" by these things, is the measure within which things can form themselves the way that they do. Neville rejects anything like some superorder of nature that would measure each and every thing in some kind of pre-scient way. Rather, the measure of nature comes from the orders them-selves as they participate in each other and in the divine creative ground. From the human perspective, our own interpretive acts are validated insofar as they bind themselves to a measure that is extrahuman, "Inter-pretation is a special kind of participation in the natural world by natu-ral beings" (*RM* 5). In a quasi-process form of naturalism it follows that other beings beside the human interpret, and that they too must partic-ipate in environing conditions that can provide a powerful goad to hermeneutic success, since the cost of interpretive failure could be death.

Now that we have arrived at the concept of nature that is implied in Neville's concepts of the divine and the divine's creation, we can begin the far more difficult task of appraisal and critique. I have devoted a great deal of energy to the task of exposition because of the painfully reiterated experience that philosophers rarely take the time and care to *truly* understand each other. In a perspective as rich and powerful as Neville's, it is imperative that the basic categories be delineated with sensitivity and care. Whether I have succeeded in this remains to be seen, but my hope is that at least the rudimentary topology of this landscape has been charted by the preceding reflections.

Neville's arguments against the process account are compelling in the main. But my own rejection of the process perspective comes from a sense that the world is fundamentally a sad place and that naturalism, not quasi-process naturalism, is the one perspective that has the courage to be sad in an informed way. From this it follows that I don't think that Neville has enough ontological sadness to be a true naturalist, certainly not of the ecstatic variety that must face the utter indifference of the ground to anything that issues from it, even while honoring the self-transforming energies that do obtain in the innumerable orders of *nature natured.* While this evocation of ontological sadness may not sound like an *argument,* and I hesitate to place it before an interlocutor who is a master of rigorous argumentation, it does emerge out of a per-spective that is to some extent an articulation of what this ground feel-ing has uncovered. For me, the fruitful interchange between thinkers involves an exhibition and articulation of what they each *see* as well as the underlying strategies that may support the infrastructure that corre-sponds to their vision. After all, any significant philosophical frame-work is overdetermined as to antecedents and no one argumentative trail or strategy can exhaust the richness, and occasional internal con-tradictions, of the nurturing streams.

On the other hand, I don't want to end up with a kind of morphological comparison in which you are asked to pick the metaphysical flavor that is most appealing. Therefore, something like arguments will make their appearance in our remaining reflections, remembering that all such strategies are at the service of a vision that has deep unconscious roots and motivations. It is one thing to say that one is ontologically sad, it is another to say why. My hope is that you will share this sadness by the end of our reflections. and that you will know the reasons why this must be so.

Following our wayward trail, then, I wish to focus on three distinct issues. The first is the nature of the things of the world as articulated in a quasi-process account versus a semiotic one rooted in ecstatic naturalism. The second is with the nature of the indifferent ground and its relation, or lack thereof, to unity. The third is with the twin concepts of nature and God as they refract each other through different prisms. The primal feeling-tone of ecstatic naturalism will weave itself in and around the categorial elaborations, bringing us to the boundary where ontological sadness envelops but remains open to a kind of naturalist *jouissance,* understood as the eros that is the true meaning of agape.

We have seen how Neville still uses mentalistic language to describe the trajectory of given things within time's flow. Things decide, are spontaneous, shape a harmony that unites essential and conditional traits, and embody value. Neville gives great weight to the concept of value in his system. Even truth, and the search for validation, is related to the disclosure of value: "If reality is the achievement of value, then truth must say what that value is; and if this is so, then saying what properties a thing has contributes to truth telling only insofar as the bearing of properties is tied to the achieved value" (*RM* 68). And, of course, form is never far away: "[V]alue is the implicit contribution of form" (*RM* 161). Like John Cobb, Neville envisions the world as the locus of increments of value, all participating in nature itself. It should be pointed out that Neville does stress participation as a key ingredient in his naturalism and theory of interpretation. Signs, values, objects, and selves all participate in an infinitely complex nature that is enveloping, at least in a secondary sense vis-à-vis the creator.

What are we to make of concepts like "harmony" and "value"? Are they innocent descriptors within an otherwise healthy metaphysical system, or are they really Trojan horses of an antinaturalist perspective that still clings to honorific language? Neville has stated more than once that he rejects the process understanding of a dipolar God, while affirming a process understanding of the things of the world. However, as noted, he goes beyond the windowed monads of Whitehead toward a more judicious macro or meso account of the orders of the world. Of even greater importance is his stated rejection of panpsychism for what he calls pan-naturalism that allows for different levels of reality, some of which are indeed material and opaque to any form of mentality. The process account in its classical form, that is, before it is reconstructed by Neville, privileges the present experience of the actual occasion. Neville wants to speak of what he calls "discursive actualities" that are "enduring" and "temporally thick." The concept of the "discursive actuality" covers most of the discriminanda of experience. Neville refers to a human being as a "discursive individual." In either case, the important point is that the things of the world are equally embodied in all three modes of time, even though each mode will prevail in a different way.

In rejecting panpsychism, does Neville escape the net of idealism that wishes to mentalize the world? Is his axiological pluralism the real Trojan horse because it smuggles in normative structures where we should remain on the level of description? To put the question differently, does Neville conflate honorific with descriptive language, precisely because his creator God is immanent within things somehow supporting value in an otherwise cold and entropic universe? Could he talk at all about things as "discursive actualities" without God and eternity propping them up against what might still be called absolute nonbeing? The answer seems to be no. And I might make an even stronger claim. If eternity and God are present within creation in the way that Neville intends, can he really outflank panpsychism in his categorial delineation of things?

The issue of value in the ontology of things is a sticky one. On the one hand, Neville is to be commended for his unrelenting efforts to deprivilege the anthropocentric starting point. While I think that his quasi-process form of naturalism fails in this task, it fails less dreadfully than almost all of the alternatives. On the other hand, Neville seems to fall prey to a kind of cosmic mythology that wants things to be far more meaningful and structurally loaded with positivity than they can possibly be. I have in mind his idea that there is "an infinitely dense achievement of value presented in each component" (*RM* 155). This is a principle of plenitude that might make even Leibniz blush. Neville is a very subtle Plato scholar and knows what happened to Plato when he made his Forms (assuming that they "exist" at all) into normative structures; namely, "Plato had a profound insight in associating the Good with form" (*RM* 154). Plato's later dialogues, however, show his awakening to this problem, as well as his awareness of the need to counter Aristotle's analysis of fourfold causation. Neville, of course, wants harmony to be in and through things, rather than functioning as an outside principle that somehow hovers in an indeterminate way before instantiation in particulars.

It is not just a problem of terminology, although I doubt that *merely* terminological problems exist on this level of reflection, but a sense that the terms chosen, especially those that have a process pedigree, subtly extrude a kind of semiconscious mental aura onto the things of the world. The Trojan horse comes into the naturalist settlement and begins to leak, not Greek soldiers, but brightly shining values and harmonies that gather around things that are otherwise opaque or semiotically dense. I have stated that the quasi-process form of naturalism is in tension with a semiotic understanding of the orders of *nature natured*. This is an especially ticklish point because Neville and I both have deep roots in Peirce's semiotics, as opposed to the minor and glottocentric tradition of Saussure, where roots can hardly even be said to exist. Yet I suspect that Neville and I do very different things with the Peirce we inherit, and that his crypto-idealism surfaces at this point.

Put in Peircean terms, a framework on the semiosis of things can, but need not, stress one of Peirce's three primal categories: firstness, which is a kind of swirling and indeterminate "could be"; secondness, which is brute diadicity without intelligibility; or thirdness, which for Neville would be normative form and value as related to harmony, that is, a potentially determinate "would be." Quasi-process naturalism will stress thirdness, its own rhetoric not withstanding, while ecstatic naturalism understands that the depth mystery of nature and "its" things lies in firstness. Of course, it goes without saying that to be a discriminandum at all is to embody all three categories, even if in a degenerate form. Firstness has no degenerate case since it does not admit of comparisons.

My sense is that Peirce remained profoundly ambivalent about the relation between God and the three categories.[10] Is God an emergent and developmental force that is self-clothing in thirdness, or is God the material maternal[11] that is mysteriously tied to the heterogeneous momenta of nature? This ambivalence about the locatedness of the divine is directly relevant to the way things are envisioned. A quasi-process reading of Peirce and of God and God's creation will privilege thirdness, almost in spite of itself, thereby bringing the lucidity of concrete reasonableness to the things of the world. Neville's being-itself is, of course, prior to thirdness. But his God the creator as self-determining in the eternal act of creation, clothes itself in the Logos structures that bring an ultimate intelligibility to nature and things. For Neville, thirdness *qua* Logos, involves pattern, components, actuality, and value (*TP* 30). Logos is God's character as expressed in each thing. This character is intelligible and available to semiotic scrutiny. Divine footprints are, by definition, examples of thirdness. Of course, one can fall directly under one and experience divine secondness, much like Job.

Hence, for Neville, God's character, as loving creator, appears within the semiotic structures of things. Philosophical theology is the description and appraisal of semiotic thirds as they manifest themselves within religious experience. The first and fourth aspect of Logos come to the fore: namely, pattern and value. But what happens if semiosis moves in the opposite direction, toward the ground of absolute indifference that has no obligation to any of its offspring? Thirdness does not collapse in secondness, nor does firstness pull the world back into the material maternal. Something far less dramatic happens, even though this movement will transform thirdness and make it translucent to something that always hovers around its edges.

For the ecstatic naturalist, semiosis consists of a series of reminders of the ejective ground that lies trembling within the heart of each thing. Any thing within the domain of *nature natured* will be the potential locus of signs and interpretants.[12] We can feel the dyadic pressure of things, and we can gauge their intelligibility (Logos as pattern and value). But we must also develop something darkly analogous to Neville's aesthetic intuition. This special night vision, if you will, is a kind of melancholy tinged eros that hungers to return to the ejective, but non-nurturing ground. Firstness is that "within" each thing that pulls it back to the origin that has no semiotic density, nor any possible relation to Logos or thirdness, however defined.

Things interact and open out thirdness. Yet they also contain traces of the elusive primal otherness that made them possible in the first place. For the human process, the most basic around feeling is that of loss, experienced in each and every form of suffering that punctuates life. Signs become transparent to this loss when the sign-using organism sees that elusive space between the sign and its object, between the sign and its interpretant, and between the interpretant and its inheritor. In this ontologically unique space of betweenness, there is something like an open draft or pull toward the unconscious of nature. Signs struggle toward lucidity and toward consciousness, yet their betweenness structures all point in the opposite direction, toward the far more pervasive unconscious of nature, an unconscious in which even gods and goddesses disappear, perhaps even the God of Western monotheism.

The unconscious heart of signs and their corollary things is not simply to be equated with entropy, which is, of course, a cosmological notion. The image is not so much disorder and loss of heat in a closed system as it is the haunting presence/absence of an ejective ground and abyss that has absolutely no teleology, no thirdness, no agape, and no ultimate plan for the human process. Things harbor a place where the prepositional ground can enter into and alter positionality, thereby making thirdness vibrate to a deeper melody of loss. This breakthrough of *nature naturing* is far from being a harmony, or a value, or a form that could somehow constitute a divinely supported unity of the thing.

In a fundamental sense, things are "on their own" against the churning night of the unconscious of nature.

Signs and sign systems live in a nature that has more semiotic fecundity than it has semiotic space. Spoliation and loss permeate the orders of *nature natured,* leaving each and every foundling of *nature naturing* without a positive ontological creative ground. Unities exist within the manifest orders of the world, but there is no creative ground that somehow supports or even "wants" unities. Unities are in and among finite orders or not at all. We have seen that Neville envisions the indeterminate ground as the ultimate source of the one that can permeate the many. The one, in his sense, is, by definition, a unity within things and for the closed world as a whole, although this latter sense is tempered by the awareness that this unity is not some kind of bound order or container, a heteronomous Logos, if you will.

Thus Neville envisions a unity that is emergent from the ground *as* that ground gives itself the Logos that can be manifest in the flow of time. From my perspective, unity is an ideal within the fragmented orders of *nature natured* and has absolutely no relation to the heterogenous ground of *nature naturing.* I confess to being one of those thinkers of the groaning *not yet being,* but I try to confine these groans to emergent interpretants and spiritual pulsations within the orders of the world. Each thing of the world is a foundling, cast out of the dark garden of *nature naturing,* carried forward by signs and interpretants into the promiscuous orders of *nature natured,* and, where mental, caught in the painful dialectic of melancholy longing for the lost object and the hope for erotic transfiguration in the *not yet.* Now, as we conclude our reflections. we must ask: Where is God in all of this?

We should now have a fairly clear picture of what Neville means by God, even though we need to be mystics to become permeable to the "way" of being-itself. How does an ecstatic naturalist see God? Neville, of course, thinks that I have it wrong. In a recent review of my second book he states that my first and second divine dimensions, that is, God as fragmented origin and God as fragmented goal within the innumerable orders of the world, are "merely spooky and secularly moral, respectively."[13] I certainly don't want to foist a "spooky" God on the world, as we have enough frightening ephemera as it is. Nor do I want to pawn off a kind of secular moralist who tells us how to clean up our corrupt social orders. As to my fourth divine dimension, where God is self-overcoming in the face of the almost mocking unconscious of nature *(nature naturing* or the Encompassing), and my third divine dimension, where God is sheerly relevant to all of the orders of *nature natured,* Neville sees only a novel but weak gnosticism in which the ancient and nasty gnostic God is replaced by one that is "politically correct."[14] Why not, he asks, just worship *nature naturing* and "eliminate middling gods?"[15] Why not? Because they are there as complex products of an "eternally" ejective nature that spawns the numinous and its carrier, for reasons that will forever remain beyond our ken.

It is at this point that I can make my final observation, one that is clearly adumbrated in Neville's critique. Quasi-process naturalism has generated a picture of nature that is too small and too tied to a creative ground that seems to privilege human traits. The nature that is delineated is too small and too ready to enter into semiotic lucidity. The God that creates/sustains this wonderful world is so large as to become thin and spooky in its own right. Nature shrinks, God grows, things hum to the tune of the loving Logos, and the human process knows that there is a fitting home, if not here and now. at least in the embrace of eternity that weaves itself in and through time's flow, although the weaving, of course, does not take place *in* time.[16]

In ecstatic naturalism nature is understood to be both the indeterminate unconscious of *nature naturing* and the impossibly complex and fragmented domain of *nature natured*. God is an emergent product of the unconscious of nature while also being located within the orders of the world in reasonably specifiable ways. Yet God is not processive in the romantic sense of Whitehead and Hartshorne, but in a far more fitful way in which the divine can be at war with itself. Thus the epiphanies of power of the first divine dimension (God as fragmented origin) can be in tension with the lure toward justice in the second divine dimension (God as fragmented goal). The first two dimensions of God are thus fully orders within the world. The third dimension is somewhat akin to Neville's sustaining aspect of God with the strong proviso that God is absolutely indifferent to the orders of the world in this mode of sheer relevance (that is, God cannot alter a single trait of the world).

For an ecstatic naturalist, God is encountered in those erotic moments in which the melancholy lure of the lost object is briefly overcome by the encompassing presence of the *not yet*. Nature per se is absolutely indifferent to its most semiotically complex product (in our small corner of the galaxy), but there is a presence/absence *within* nature that has traits that are unique among all of the other orders of the world. We are all expelled from the garden of *nature naturing,* an ontologically unique garden without a gardener. Once we are ejected, we can never return. But we can become permeable to the movements of the divine and reconfigure the lost object just as God must do again and again. Ontological sadness can never be fully erased, as there is genuine loss and tragedy in the world, but we can enter into an erotic momentum that lives on the edges of ecstatically transfiguring orders that in turn lead us into the rich ambiguities of the divine life, not just our own.

NOTES

1. Robert Neville, *God the Creator: On the Transcendence and Presence of God* (Chicago: University of Chicago Press, 1968), p. 49. Reprinted with new preface by the State University of New York Press in 1992. Hereafter cited as GC.

2. Robert Neville, *Creativity and God: A Challenge to Process Theology* (New York: Seabury Press, 1980), p. 8. Reprinted with a new preface by the State University of New York Press in 1995. Hereafter cited as CG.

3. Thus Pannenberg can say, "Creation and eschatology belong together because it is only in the eschatological consummation that the destiny of the creature, especially the human creature, will come to fulfillment. . . . Nevertheless, creatures that are awakened to 'independence (i.e., living creatures) open themselves to the future as the dimension from which alone their existence can achieve content and fulfillment." *Systematic Theology*, vol. 2, trans. Geoffrey W. Bromiley (Grand Rapids, Mich.: William B. Eerdmans, 1994), p. 139.

4. Leibniz gives a clear statement of his view of essence and perfection in his 1697 essay, *On the Ultimate Origination of Things*. He states, "all possibles, that is, everything that expresses essence or possible reality, strive with equal right for existence in proportion to the amount of essence or reality or the degree of perfection they contain, for perfection is nothing but the amount of essence." Taken from G. W. *Leibniz: Philosophical Essays*, ed. and trans. Roger Ariew and Daniel Garber (Indianapolis: Hackett, 1989).

5. Robert Neville, *A Theology Primer* (Albany: State University of New York Press, 1991), pp. 40–41. Hereafter cited as TP.

6. Paul Tillich, *Die Sozialistische Entscheidung* (Potsdam: Alfred Protte, 1933). English translation by Franklin Sherman, *The Socialist Decision* (New York: Harper & Row, 1977).

7. Robert Neville, *Eternity and Time's Flow* (Albany: State University of New York Press, 1993), p. 13. Hereafter cited as ETF.

8. Cf. Robert Neville, *The Cosmology of Freedom* (New Haven: Yale University Press, 1974), pp. 40–51. Hereafter cited as CF.

9. Robert Neville, *Recovery of the Measure: Interpretation and Nature* (Albany: State University of New York Press, 1989), p. 148. Hereafter cited as RM.

10. Robert S. Corrington, *An Introduction to C. S. Peirce: Philosopher, Semiotician, and Ecstatic Naturalist* (Lanham, Md.: Rowman & Littlefield, 1993).

11. Robert S. Corrington, "Nature's God and the Return of the Material Maternal," *The American Journal of Semiotics* 10.1–2 (1993): 115–32.

12. Within the Peirce community there is a continuing debate as to whether or not interpretants (signs emerging from previous and less interpreted signs) require some entertaining mind in order to exist. Peirce's texts fail to give a definitive answer. For the pansemiotician, all orders can generate signs, and many, whether funded by mind or not, can create or sustain interpretants. From the perspective of my own ecstatic naturalism, it makes the most sense to see just how far "down" we can envision interpretants, perhaps erring on the side of ontological generosity.

13. Robert Neville, Review of Robert S. Corrington's *Nature and Spirit: An Essay in Ecstatic Naturalism*, *International Philosophical Quarterly* 34, issue no. 136 (December 1994): 505.

14. Ibid.

15. Ibid.

16. In terms of our home in eternity we are told that, "God is the mansion's perfect host" (Robert Neville, *The Truth of Broken Symbols* [Albany: State University of New York Press, 1996], p. 271). We are even assured that there will be cigars in heaven, that, if not Cuban, will at least be worthy of our divinized taste buds.

CHAPTER 9

Being, Nonbeing,
and Creation Ex Nihilo

Carl G. Vaught

This essay is a stage in a family dispute that has been unfolding gradually for more than thirty years. The philosopher whose work we are celebrating in this volume and the author of this paper have been discussing the problems of being, nonbeing, and creation *ex nihilo* since graduate school, where we studied with many of the same teachers and thought about many of the same problems. This accounts, in part, for the broad background of philosophical agreement between us, where each of us embraces a version of what might be called "the Augustinian tradition." This context of agreement is important, for basic philosophical issues are so intractable that progress can never be made with any of them if we must defend every claim we make against an indefinite multiplicity of objections.

Neville and I agree that the concept of creation *ex nihilo* is intelligible; that Being and God are identical; that God creates the world from nothing; and that nonbeing is not simply the negation of something positive, but the absolute contrast term that makes creation *ex nihilo* possible. Where we disagree about these issues is the focus of this paper, which will develop in three stages. First, I will summarize Neville's account of the relations among being, nonbeing, and creation *ex nihilo* as he has expressed it in a variety of public contexts.[1] Then I will point to difficulties about his view that have troubled me for many years, and that continue to do so. Finally, having confined myself in the past to only one article about the issues in question,[2] I will outline what I believe to be a viable philosophical alternative to Neville's position. In doing so, I hope to participate in the first and the third features of family disagreements, which have often been regarded as the deepest, the most bitter, and the most productive kind of confrontation.

147

I

Neville has developed his views about being, nonbeing, and creation *ex nihilo* in three radically different but complementary contexts. In *God the Creator* (*GC*) he explains and defends his position systematically; in *Behind the Masks of God* he argues that his position can serve as the foundation for comparative theology; and in *A Theology Primer* he shows how his views can be schematized to the context of Christian theology (*GC* xxi). Though *God the Creator* is Neville's earliest book, I will take my bearings from this complex dialectical context; for after three decades, I still regard it as the most profound book he has ever written. However, the other two books are important, not simply because they expand systematic philosophy in comparative and traditional directions, but because they reveal tensions in Neville's position that strike at the heart of its philosophical integrity.

I will point to these tensions as the argument develops, but will refrain from exploiting them except as illustrations of philosophical objections that will be developed independently. It should go without saying that the rhetorical strategies appropriate to systematic philosophy, comparative theology, and traditional Christianity should differ in ways that reflect differences in the audiences to which they are addressed. I will not encroach on this rhetorical freedom, but will confine myself to the ways it illustrates important systematic difficulties in the philosophical position it expresses.

The fundamental thesis of *God the Creator* can be stated in the following way: (1) God creates the world *ex nihilo*; (2) In the act of creation, God creates everything determinate, including his[3] own character as the creator of everything else; (3) God as he is in himself is absolutely indeterminate; and (4) The ontological contrast term for God is the determinations of being rather than absolute nonbeing, where God is to be identified with Being–itself. Each part of this thesis deserves detailed elaboration, but since Neville himself has supplied it (*GC* 1–119), I will confine myself to two expository paths. First, I will point out the philosophical advantages of Neville's position in contrast with the ones he rejects. Then, I will consider the systematic structure of his fundamental thesis, focusing on his commitment to the univocity of being (*GC* 18–21, 138–42), his rejection of *analogia entis* (*GC* 17–19, 140), his defense of cosmogony as more fundamental than cosmology (*GC* 126–36, 148–67), and his use of constitutive dialectic as a way of securing himself against challenges from Kantian and post–Kantian critical philosophy (*GC* 123, 136, 143, 147–67).

One of the most important features of Neville's fundamental thesis is that it establishes an indissoluble link between philosophy and theology. In claiming that Being and God are identical, and that the contrast term for God is the determinations of being, the fundamental concept of philosophy and the most important concept of theology are brought into a positive relation with one another and are placed over against fideistic theological positions that try to locate themselves beyond the reach of philosophical criticism (*GC* xiii). The second philosophical advantage of Neville's thesis is that it provides a provocative solution to the philosophical problem of the one and the many. In maintaining that God in his aseity is absolutely indeterminate, Neville claims that God can be the one for the many without becoming a one of many that requires a further principle of unity—a problem that he believes cannot be solved if God in himself is determinate (*GC* 47–60). The third and most theologically important virtue of Neville's position is that it attempts to preserve the transcendence and the immanence of God simultaneously. If God creates the world *ex nihilo*, he not only transcends it infinitely, but is also immanent within it, since every determination of being is a terminus of God's creative act (*GC* 1). Finally, if we accept Neville's view that God creates everything determinate, including his own character as the creator of everything else, the resulting "concept" of God can become a vehicle for comparing different interpretations of God and for interpreting religious experience. The determinations of being that God creates can become symbols for God without exhausting God's infinite richness; and when these symbols are compared with one another, they can be used as alternative ways of interpreting the significance of the determinate dimensions of religious experience (*BMG* 1–50).

The systematic structure of Neville's position can be understood only if we appreciate the force of his commitment to the univocity of being. Neville argues that unless being is univocal, there can be no common context in which determinate beings can both be and be together. If being-itself is to be the ontological one for the many determinations of being, both it and they must "be" in the same sense; otherwise, there would be no context in which Being could bind the many beings it creates into a unity. On the other hand, the univocity of being required for the solution of the problem of the one and the many cannot be determinate, for then it would require a further context in which it could be unified with the other determinations with which it would stand in determinate contrast (*GC* 55–60). This means that being is not a determinate property that all beings have in common (*GC* 22–24); that it is not the most perfect being to which they must be subordinated (*GC* 24–28); that it is not self-structuring power (*GC* 28–35); and that it is not determinate in a fashion that transcends determination by negation (*GC* 35–40). In all these cases, being would not only be univocal, but also determinate; and it would follow from this that a different univocal and radically indeterminate context would be required to solve the problem of the one and the many. Neville's commitment to the univocity of being not only gives him a common context within which to solve the problem of the one and the many, but also commits him to the view that being must be radically indeterminate if we are to avoid an infinite regress in trying to resolve the problem in question.

The only viable alternative to the univocity of being that does not destroy the common context we need for solving the problem of the one and the many is the classical doctrine of *analogia entis*. This view takes two forms, one of which is less radical than the other, but both of which Neville rejects (*GC* 16–21). According to the first, the analogy of being is an analogy of proportion, where we know the meaning of two of its terms and try to find the third to which these others are referred. In this case, either we do not know the determinate distance between the first two terms and the third, causing the analogy to collapse, or we know the determinate distance, committing us to the univocity of being as the common context that binds the finite and the infinite together. Neville suggests that in the first instance, the analogy of being collapses into equivocity; and he claims that in the second, it presupposes the univocity of being it was intended to displace (*GC* 16–21). The second form of *analogia entis* is the analogy of proper proportionality, where two terms that pertain to finite beings are said to stand in a relation that is *similar* to the relation between two terms that characterize Being itself. However, this means that we do not know the determinate distance between beings and Being, where this implies that the analogy of proportionality rests on an equivocation. If we claim to know the determinate distance after all, the *similarity* between the two relations presupposes a common term to which they both can be referred, where the common term presupposes univocity. Again, Neville claims that the analogy of being fails as an alternative to univocity, either because it collapses into equivocity, or because it presupposes the univocity it purports to transcend (*GC* 16–21).

In the form in which he develops it, Neville's defense of the doctrine of creation *ex nihilo* not only commits him to the univocity of being and to the rejection of *analogia entis*, but also to the view that *cosmogony* is more fundamental than *cosmology*. *Cosmology* is the attempt to discover the fundamental categories presupposed by all the determinations of being, just insofar as they are determinate, where this implies that the cosmologist is concerned with the logos of being and with the relation between the logos and the beings structured by it. By contrast, *cosmogony* is the attempt to explain why there is something rather than nothing, where not only the determinations of being, but also the logos in virtue of which these beings are determinate require an explanation.

In the case of cosmology, we presuppose the determinations of being and attempt to discover the intelligible structure that permits them to display the determinations they do. In the case of cosmogony, we shift our attention from the question of the meaning of being to the question of the being of beings, where Neville suggests that the answer to this second question is more fundamental than the answer to the first (*GC* 126–36, 148–67). His answer to this question is that God is identical with Being-itself; that Being-itself is radically indeterminate; that Being creates the determinations of being; and that Being creates the logos to which the cosmologist looks in answering the question of the meaning of being.

The final crucial feature of Neville's position is its commitment to constitutive dialectic and its use of what he claims is a harmless version of analogy to supplement the conclusions it enables him to reach. Constitutive dialectic differs from its methodological counterpart by attempting to demonstrate that reality itself is dialectical and that we can solve the problem of the one and the many, answer the fundamental question of cosmogony, and articulate a doctrine of creation *ex nihilo* only by moving through a set of reflective stages in which the terms we use undergo systematic transformation until they are finally able to express the truth we seek (*GC* 147–67).

Neville claims that in reflection of this kind, we presuppose the univocity of being, use analogies to move from one level of being to another, and that when we have reached "the unconditioned condition of all conditions," we first detach it, and then speak about it univocally with the only language that survives as we move from one dialectical stage to another. In this way, dialectical reflection proves to be more than a methodological device for reaching the truth and becomes instead a way of pointing to the intelligible structures we must traverse in moving from the determinations of being to the conclusion that Being-itself is the indeterminate ground of all determinations, including its own (*GC* 147–67).

Constitutive dialectic begins with the univocity of being, moves from stage to stage by using analogical discourse, and concludes by making univocal claims about the indeterminate ground that makes the act of creation possible. Unlike *analogia entis*, constitutive dialectic subordinates analogy to univocity, beginning with univocal claims about the meaning of being and ending with univocal statements about the way the determinations of being presuppose creation *ex nihilo* (*GC* 147–67). In section II, we shall consider difficulties that arise in Neville's commitment to the univocity of being, his solution to the problem of the one and the many, his rejection of the analogy of being, and his commitment to constitutive dialectic; and in section III, we will suggest an alternative to Neville's position that places figurative discourse at the center of the relation between God and the world and at the heart of the conceptions of being, nonbeing, and creation *ex nihilo*.

II

The most frequent objections to Neville's fundamental thesis can be stated in the following way: first, though the production of an artifact and the generation of a genetic successor are intelligible, creation *ex nihilo*, which bears a superficial analogy to them, is not (*GC* 108–9); second, if there is a creator, he must be finite, since he works with antecedent materials and is as much conditioned by them as they are conditioned by him (*GC* 78). These two objections are expressions of the view that God is finite; and Neville responds to them from both religious and reflective points of view.

From the standpoint of religion, Neville suggests that a finite God is not worthy of worship, but can at best be an object of respect or veneration; and from this same standpoint, he appeals to Schleiermacher's claim that our most fundamental experience of God issues in a feeling of absolute dependence. When these two points are taken together, they point beyond the finite God of personalism or of process philosophy to what Tillich and others have called "the ground of being." To be religiously significant, this ground must stand outside the created order altogether, unconditioned in his aseity by the finite beings he creates (*GC* 176, 190–202).

From the standpoint of philosophy, Neville argues that though the analogy between creation *ex nihilo* and production or generation is superficial, we can understand this concept dialectically by grasping the need for an explanation of the world that is cosmogonic rather than cosmological. Cosmological explanations answer questions about why the world has the nature it does, while cosmogonic explanations answer the question about *why there is something rather than nothing* (*GC* 126–36, 148–67). If we appreciate both kinds of question, and make the dialectical transitions required to move from one to the other, creation *ex nihilo* will not only be intelligible, but will also enable us to understand the sense in which God is conditioned by the world, and the sense in which he is not conditioned at all. As the creator of the world, God is conditioned by it and is finite in what Whitehead has called his "consequent nature." However, in his aseity, God stands outside the world, is prior to the distinction between something and nothing, has no antecedent material that stands in contrast with him, and creates the finite order with which he stands in determinate contrast because he also creates his own character as the creator of all the determinations of being.

I am sympathetic with both of these replies; for I share Neville's views that God creates the world *ex nihilo*, that only a God of this kind is worthy of worship, that the ontological question cosmogony attempts to answer is important, and that creation *ex nihilo* is an intelligible conception. However, there are other more serious difficulties with Neville's defense of his thesis about the transcendence and the presence of God that must be considered against this broad backdrop of philosophical and theological agreement. These objections to his fundamental thesis are not issues that Neville has never considered; for one of the distinguishing marks of his ontology is the way in which it turns back upon itself, moving dialectically from one possible objection to the next until the position it is attempting to establish is secured.

Like the Plato of the Divided Line, Neville not only moves up the ontological ladder; but having caught a glimpse of the Good beyond being, he moves back down, drawing the ontological consequences of God's creative relation to the world. Along the way, he attempts to deal with every conceivable objection; and he is remarkably successful in leaving nothing out of account. Indeed, as one of his teachers noted many years ago, the dissertation that was the philosophical ancestor of *God the Creator* is one of the longest and most sustained dialectical arguments in the history of philosophy. What I intend to do in raising the following objections is not to take Neville by surprise, but to allow the cumulative effects of serious difficulties with his version of creation *ex nihilo* to point to an alternative version of it to be adumbrated in section III.

The first difficulty with Neville's fundamental thesis is that being and absolute nonbeing collapse into one another, where God as he is in himself is indistinguishable from nothing at all. Neville maintains that God in his aseity is absolutely indeterminate, creating not only the world, but also his own character as the creator of it. He also argues that the determinations of being have absolute nonbeing as their contrast term and that being-itself is the common ontological context in which this contrast obtains. This asymmetrical arrangement of ontological categories suggests that being-itself is prior to the contrast between determinate beings and absolute nonbeing; that as it is in itself, being has no contrast term; and that being is the indeterminate source out of which all the determinations of being emerge (*GC* 25–28, 88–93). Since these determinations of being include not only finite entities, but also the principles of intelligibility in virtue of which they are distinct from one another, creation *ex nihilo* involves the displacement of absolute nonbeing with determinate beings, and with the intelligible logos that makes nonbeing impossible from a logical point of view (*GC* 88–89).

In *God the Creator*, Neville suggests that absolute nonbeing is "empty," that God as absolutely indeterminate is "full," and that the determinations of being emerge from what I would call the "creative intersection" of being and nonbeing in the act of creation *ex nihilo* (*GC* 61–64). The problem with these suggestions, and with the asymmetrical ontological framework they presuppose, is that we have no ontological ground for distinguishing the indeterminacy of Being from the emptiness of absolute nonbeing. Given creation *ex nihilo*, it seems that we can draw this distinction by claiming that the fullness of being in its indeterminacy creates determinations of being, where otherwise, there would be the absolute emptiness of nothing at all. However, this distinction cannot be sustained; for if the indeterminacy of being does not stand in contrast with absolute nonbeing, there is nothing to prevent being and nothingness from collapsing into one another. It might seem that creation *ex nihilo* prevents the coalescence of being and nothing, where creation presupposes the fullness of being and displaces the emptiness of the absolute *nihil* with the determinations of being. Yet if the distinction between the fullness of being and the emptiness of nonbeing is logically dependent on the act of creation as Neville suggests, there is no antecedent distinction between being and nothing that permits us to say that one rather than the other is the ground of being.

In *Behind the Masks of God*, where his rhetorical purpose is comparative rather than systematic or traditionally Christian, Neville admits this, arguing that one of the advantages of his doctrine of creation is that it identifies God as he is in himself with absolute emptiness (*BMG* 89–98). Whether this identification of the indeterminateness of God with the emptiness of absolute nonbeing is a fatal difficulty remains to be seen. However, we must emphasize once more that instead of saying that God creates the world *ex nihilo*, Neville could have said just as well that the world comes into existence from absolute nonbeing, which is unintelligible from the standpoint of the created logos, and is prior to intelligibility as the absolute *nihil* from which the determinations of being spring.

The second difficulty with Neville's fundamental thesis is that given creation *ex nihilo*, God collapses into the act of creation itself. As Neville formulates the point, the act of creation has three dimensions—the created product, the power that brings this product into existence, and the source out of which this power and product emerge. The power of creation is the middle term between the world, on the one hand, and God the creator on the other. Yet since the power of creation not only produces finite beings, but also the principles of intelligibility and God's own character as creator, it is difficult to escape the conclusion that the source, the power, and the product of creation *ex nihilo* are abstractable aspects of creation itself. In *Behind the Masks of God*, Neville acknowledges this, speaking not primarily about God the creator, but about God as the process of creating, where the source, the act, and the product of creation are determinations of being that arise out of the process of creation itself (*BMG* 21, 38, 74, 89–98). The connection between this second difficulty and the first is that we must not only conclude that the absolute *nihil* is the unintelligible ground out of which creation *ex nihilo* arises, but that the act of creation holds its determinate source, its product, and itself together as abstractable aspects of itself.

The third difficulty with Neville's fundamental thesis is that it collapses what is usually called the "immanent Trinity" into its economic surrogate. When Neville claims that God not only creates the world but also generates his own character as the creator of it, it follows immediately that the three persons of the Trinity are not aspects of the "primordial nature" of God but are created products in an ontological continuum that depends upon the process of creation itself.[4] As he implies in *A Theology Primer*, the eternal logos and the historical Jesus are not distinct by *nature*, but distinct in *function*, where to say that Jesus is the incarnated logos is to say that he functions as the logos in an unsurpassable way (*TP*, 44–48, 141–50). The reason Neville shifts from nature to function in this traditional context, and the reason he claims in the new preface to the second edition of *God the Creator* that salvation history must be subordinated to the philosophy of nature (*GC* xvii–xviii), is his conviction that *the whole of nature, including the determinations of being that make beings intelligible*, is created. From this perspective, it makes no sense to claim that God in himself has a nature that could be incarnated in an historical personage or to suggest that the Trinity is to be identified with the nature of God prior to the creation of the world. Thus, Neville concludes that since the Trinity is one of the determinations of being that emerges in creation, the best way to distinguish it from whatever else there is, is to say that it is the theological expression of the created transcendental principles that define the meaning of intelligibility itself (*TP*, 46–48).

The final difficulty with Neville's fundamental thesis is that constitutive dialectic presupposes and collapses into *analogia entis*. When he claims that cosmogony involves a different kind of explanation from cosmology, and that in order to pursue it, we must ask *why* beings are rather than *what* they are, Neville presupposes the analogy of being as a way of binding these two kinds of explanation together. As Aquinas puts the point in defending himself against the kind of argument Neville presents in the first chapter of *God the Creator*, the analogical unity of cause and effect transcends the difference of "genus" between the finite

and the infinite, where an analogical unity is presupposed in our statement of the distinction between the two kinds of explanation Neville
wants his readers to appreciate.[5] Neville himself calls our attention to
this Thomistic response to the problems he raises, but dismisses it by
claiming that the unity needed to understand the unity of cause and
effect is the unity of the genus (*GC* 21). However, this not only begs the
question against Aquinas, but also leaves Neville without a ground for
claiming that his readers can understand his own distinction between
cosmogony and cosmology *ab initio*.

The distinction between cosmology and cosmogony rests upon the
irreducible similarity between two "kinds" of cause, where this similarity is the analogical ground Neville's project presupposes and on the
basis of which it unfolds. Constitutive dialectic collapses into *analogia
entis* because it presupposes analogy at the beginning of the inquiry, and
it collapses into *analogia entis* in the end because a new univocal meaning of causality can be detached from the dialectical argument only as
an abstraction from a prior analogical understanding of causality itself.
In the final section of this essay, I will sketch a theory of creation *ex
nihilo* that acknowledges and defends the priority of the analogy of
being, avoids the difficulties raised by Neville's fundamental thesis, and
recommends itself as an alternative way of relating philosophy and theology, solving the problem of the one and the many, binding the immanence and the transcendence of God together, and serving as a vehicle
for engaging in the task of comparative theology.

III

As I understand the term, "creation *ex nihilo*" means that God creates
everything other than himself out of absolute nonbeing, where the creator and the product are not only different in "kind," but also different
in the senses in which they are what they are. The difference in kind is
reflected in the contrast between the finite and the infinite, and the difference in the senses of being is reflected in the contrast between the conditioned and the "unconditioned." The quotation marks in this initial
formulation are not merely stylistic devices, but are ways of indicating
that a version of the analogy of being is at work in the statement of the
thesis I am presenting. The analogy in question is a strong one in the
sense that the univocity of being is not presupposed as a common context of ontological comparison, but it is weaker than the *analogia entis*
of traditional Thomism in the sense that our knowledge of God does not
rest entirely on an inference from the finite to the infinite. I agree with
Tillich and with Neville that in meeting God we are not encountering a

stranger, but are overcoming estrangement; but I differ from them in holding that an adequate conception of analogy is the presupposition for any viable transition from estrangement to fulfillment.

The doctrine of analogy I defend is relevant to both cosmogony and cosmology, and within the context of a doctrine of creation *ex nihilo*, it presupposes radical distinctions among three ontological "domains." First, there is God as he is in himself; second, there is the world that he brings into existence; and third, there is the creative relation between God and the world in virtue of which the finite order comes into existence from absolute nonbeing. God as he is in himself is not absolutely indeterminate, but displays a "metaphorical" interplay among the structure of being, the power of being, and the mystery of being that can never be delimited by either structural or dynamic articulation. Without the structure of being, God would not be intelligible; without the power of being, God would neither be nor be able to create anything other than himself; and without the mystery of being, God would simply be the highest being in an ontological continuum more fundamental than himself.

The world God creates from nothing also displays the structure, the power, and the mystery of being; for every finite entity is intelligible in contrast with others, expresses the power to be and the power to develop, and has an indeterminate dimension in virtue of which it is able to unfold in unexpected and unpredictable directions.[6] In addition, the act of creation that brings the world into existence reflects the power, the structure, and the mystery of God, where the power of Being brings something into existence from the absolute *nihil*, where the structure of Being expresses itself in an act of creation that can be distinguished from other kinds of relation between God and the world, and where the mystery of Being expresses the freedom with which God creates what is other than himself in an utterly gratuitous act.

One way to elaborate this ontological, cosmogonic, and cosmological picture of God, the world, and creation *ex nihilo* is to suggest that both God and the world are boundless "metaphors" *in the real order*, and that they are connected, not only by the act of creation, but also by the analogy among three levels of mystery, power, and structure that bind them together and hold them apart.[7] The mystery, the power, and the structure of being are analogical terms because they mean different but related things at all three levels, and it is crucial to notice that these three analogical levels must be understood together before we can hold them apart in analogical self-separation. However, this does not mean that we begin with the univocity of being, that these three terms have a univocal meaning at the outset, and that we reach new levels of univocal meaning by engaging in dialectical reflection that proves to be constitutive of its own dialectical content. Rather, it means that mystery, power, and logos are analogical concepts from the outset; that they apply to three regions that are first understood together and only later understood apart from one another; and that both univocity and equivocity are abstract degenerations of analogy rather than the ontological and semantical superstructure upon which the analogy of being depends.

Three consequences follow immediately from this analogical approach to the doctrine of creation *ex nihilo*. First, figurative discourse is neither an ornamental addition to a univocal concept of being, nor a supplement to constitutive dialectic that allows us to detach a new univocal meaning of creation from an original univocal meaning of causality in the more familiar sense of the term (GC 136, 138–39, 141, 146). Rather, figurative discourse, and the analogical relation between God and the world as unbounded "metaphors" are irreducible conditions for an adequate conception of creation *ex nihilo*. Second, the cosmogony we defend is not separated from cosmology as it is on Neville's view, but contains cosmology as a constituent element. This follows from the fact that God as he is in himself is not absolutely indeterminate, but displays a "metaphorical interplay" among mystery, power, and structure that not only makes God the ground of being, but also makes God the structure of being as well.[8] Finally, rejecting Neville's claim that God as he is in himself is absolutely indeterminate allows us to avoid the conclusion that being-itself collapses into absolute nonbeing. At least one way to make sense of the distinction Neville draws in *God the Creator* between the fullness of Being and the emptiness of absolute nonbeing (GC 88–93) is to abandon the claim that God as he is in himself is indeterminate, replacing it with the view that both Being and God are identical with the mystery, the power, and the structure of being.

Before I turn to a defense of my own version of creation *ex nihilo*, and before I point to some of its philosophical advantages, let me mention three additional features of the ontological position I have outlined. First, the source, the product, and the act of creation should not be understood as abstractable aspects of the act of creation. Since God as he is in himself is a "metaphorical" interplay among mystery, power, and structure, and since both the world and the act of creation involve these same concepts in different but related senses, God, the world, and the act of creation are radically distinct levels of being in an adequate ontology, cosmogony, and cosmology. Second, it is both possible and important for us to distinguish between the immanent and the economic Trinity, where God as he is in himself displays an immanent trinitarian structure, and where only the economic Trinity is a product of the act of creation. If we do not make this distinction, the trinitarian personae are reduced to products of the act of creation, where they differ in degree, but not in kind, from the other determinations of being God has created. Finally, the kind of analogy our view of creation presupposes is not subordinated to constitutive dialectic and to a new univocal meaning of creation to which it gives us access, but is presupposed as the ground of dialectical reflection itself. If this were not so, we could never understand the concept of creation sufficiently well to draw a distinction between the task of cosmology and the different but related task of cosmogonic explanation.

The best way to offer a defense of the view I have adumbrated here is to point to some of its implications for the relation between philosophy and theology, the problem of the one and the many, the immanence and the transcendence of God, and the task of comparative theology. With respect to the first of these issues, philosophy and theology are intertwined inexplicably because it is plausible to claim that Being and God are identical. The mystery, the power, and the structure of Being-itself, and the mystery, the power, and the structure of God as he is in himself are the same, where the fundamental dimensions of Being and the fundamental dimensions of the immanent Trinity can be correlated with one another. On Neville's view, Being and God are the same because both are radically indeterminate as they are in themselves. By contrast, on the view I am defending, they are identical because both display a "metaphorical" interplay among mystery, power, and structure as constituent elements.

In categorical terms, God the Father correlates with the mystery of Being, God the Son with the structure of Being, and God the Spirit with the power of Being. Yet in descriptive terms that permit the Father, the Son, and the Spirit to be aspects of a distinctive Christian theology rather than correlates of an ontological theory, the Father is the concatenation of mystery and power, the Son the concatenation of mystery and structure, and the Spirit the concatenation of power and structure. At the categorical level, ontology and theology are convertible terms; but at the descriptive level, a distinctively Christian theology can be framed by combining the relevant categories in ways that are appropriate to the specifically Christian context of interpretation in which they appear.

The problem of the one and the many is the most difficult issue to cope with in defending a doctrine of creation *ex nihilo*, and Neville was wise beyond his years in choosing this problem as the touchstone by which the adequacy of his ontology ought to be measured. If there is only one problem of the one and the many, it is difficult to see how it can be solved without claiming that the one in itself is radically indeterminate in contrast with the determinations of being. If the one is determinate, it would seem to be one determination among others; and if this is so, it would require a one different from itself to unify the determinate one with the determinate many with which it stands in determinate contrast. However, my own position is that there is not simply one problem of the one and the many, but three at least, and that the solution to the problem at one level is both the same and different from its solution at the other two.

This view can be elaborated in the following way. First, the world taken by itself is both a one and a many and requires a solution at the horizontal level without invoking an ontological level beyond itself. Second, God as he is in himself is both a one and a many; and this problem must be solved at the vertical level independently of the solution of the corresponding problem as it pertains to the world. Finally, the relation between God and the world involves a problem of the one and the many that can be solved only by the act of creation *ex nihilo*, where this problem and the solution to it are important, but must not be used to circumscribe the other versions of the problem that arise in distinctive ways at the other two levels.

My insistence that there are three problems of the one and the many is not simply a way of saying that the problem arises in three contexts. Rather, I am making the stronger claim that the problem has a different but related structure as it arises in relation to God, to the world, and to the creative nexus that binds them together. This claim is a reflection of my earlier commitment to a doctrine of analogy that is related to but different from the Thomistic doctrine of *analogia entis*, where the solution to the threefold problem of the one and the many to which this doctrine points emerges from it in four stages. First, the one for the many beings in the created world is the *de facto* unity they enjoy simply because they exist. At this first level, to answer the question, "Why is there something rather than nothing?" is simply to claim *that* the world *is*, however mysterious this fact may be. Most philosophers who stand outside the rationalistic tradition are content to accept an answer of this kind without moving beyond it to the other two levels where analogous questions arise. Second, the one for the world understood as a product of God's creative act is the act of creation itself, where creation is the cosmogonic explanation for the world, not only in its essence, but also in its existence. At this second level, the answer to the question, "Why is there something rather than nothing?" is simply that God made the world that way, though we are unable to understand why he made it as it is, or even why he made it at all. Neville's theory of creation *ex nihilo* is a detailed articulation and defense of a position of this kind. Third, the one for God as he is in himself is the interplay among mystery, power, and structure as the *self-referential* structure, power, and mystery of itself, where the "metaphorical" spiraling in the internal life of God allows God to be the one for himself as a many, and a many for himself as a one.[9] At this third level, the answer to the question, "Why is there something rather than nothing?" is that God is, where the Being of God is displayed in the unending spiral of Being to which the experience of religious mystics in every epoch has attempted to point. Finally, my own view embraces all three levels at once, where three solutions to the problem of the one and many emerge simultaneously. These solutions are then related to one another by analogy, which is a way of binding God, the world, and creation *ex nihilo* together while also holding them apart.

Against the background of the problem of the one and the many, an additional problem is posed by the task of connecting the immanence and the transcendence of God. Neville claims that his view of creation is superior to its rivals because it enables him to say that God both transcends the world in the most radical way and that God is also immanent within it by being closer to creatures than they are to themselves. On Neville's view, God as he is in himself is utterly transcendent because God is absolutely indeterminate; and God is completely immanent because everything determinate is the terminus of God's creative act (*GC* 1). By contrast, God is transcendent on my view because he is a "metaphorical" interplay of mystery, power, and structure "prior" to the creation of the world and is a one for a many in a sense appropriate to God's existence as he is in himself. On the other hand, God is immanent in the world because having chosen to create it as an imagistic reflection of his own nature, the world as a de facto one for a many is also a many for the one act of creation that enables it to be at a deeper level of ontological dependence.

If we begin with the analogy of being, we can move back and forth among God, the world, and the relation between them by acknowledging the mystery, the power, and the structure present in them all in different, but related senses of these analogical expressions. The power of the world is its capacity to develop and to resist encroachment; its structure is the collection of specific determinations in virtue of which it is one possible world rather than another; and its mystery is its existence as a de facto unity in contrast with other possibilities. The power of the act of creation is the efficacious choice of one possible world rather than another; the structure of the act of creation is the reason for choosing the actual world rather than another possible world; and the mystery of the act is the fact that we can never give this reason from a finite point of view. Finally, the power of God in his aseity is the power to be; the structure of God is the set of principles that define the meaning of intelligibility; and the mystery of God is the unending spiral of self-reference that logos and power display with reference to one another and with reference to themselves. I repeat: if we begin with the analogy of being, we can embrace God, the world, and the relation between them as three ontological levels that can be bound together and held apart simultaneously. When they are bound together, God is immanent in the world and in the act of creation as analogical images of himself. When they are held apart, God transcends the world as the "metaphorical" interplay of mystery, power, and structure as they are in themselves.

The final advantage of my account of being, nonbeing, and creation *ex nihilo* is that it can serve as a vehicle for undertaking the task of comparative theology. If Being and God are identical, and if this identity involves an interplay of mystery, power, and structure, alternative theological positions can be compared in two ways. First, they can be understood as distinctively different ways of concatenating these three elements, where their similarities and differences are reflected in the ways in which they offer variations on these common themes. Second, they can be understood as ways of trying to get along with one or two of these categories as fundamental concepts, generating a typology of theological alternatives that stand over against one another and that can be compared both descriptively and from a normative point of view.

Since I am claiming that both Being and God involve a "metaphorical" interplay of mystery, power, and structure, the kind of comparative theology I recommend is both descriptive and normative at once. If a theological alternative offers a variation of this interplay, it can be appraised as descriptively sound and judged normatively on the basis of its way of articulating the interplay in question. By contrast, if a theological position leaves out of account any of the elements of mystery, power, and structure, it can be judged defective just to the extent that it fails to measure up to the richness of the philosophical framework to which I am calling your attention.

In the final analysis, I am claiming that Neville's account of being, nonbeing, and creation *ex nihilo* is an inadequate version of the position I have been defending because it subordinates the power and the logos of being to the mystery of being as the absolutely indeterminate ground of all the determinations of being. Yet since I am addressing him directly in this essay, and am concerned only incidently about what others may think about the differences between us, I intend this paper more as a compliment than a critique of the position it calls into question. I could not have developed the view I have sketched out here without the conversations I have enjoyed with Neville for so many years; and I can only hope that this friendly quarrel can be advanced by what he says in response to the position I have taken.

NOTES

1. For the purposes of this essay, the three most important contexts are Robert Cummings Neville, *God the Creator: On the Transcendence and Presence of God*, 2nd ed. (Albany: State University of New York Press, 1992); *Behind the Masks of God: An Essay toward Comparative Theology* (Albany: State University of New York Press, 1991); and *A Theology Primer* (Albany: State University of New York Press, 1991). Subsequent references to these books appear in the body of the text, using the following abbreviations: *GC*, *BMG*, and *TP*. In this essay, I capitalize Being where Being and God are regarded as identical and use the lower case letter in all other cases.

2. Carl G. Vaught, "Being and God," in *Essays in Metaphysics*, ed. Carl G. Vaught (University Park, Pa.: The Pennsylvania State University Press, 1970), pp. 213–33.

3. [While we acknowledge the need to avoid exclusively masculine language with respect to God, we have let stand Neville's own exclusively masculine language of his 1968 *God the Creator*. Vaught is working with Neville's idiom; therefore we will let stand his own exclusively masculine references to God.—*Eds.*]

4. Neville's clearest formulation of his views about the relation between these two forms of the doctrine of the Trinity is developed in *The Tao and the Daimon* (Albany: State University of New York Press, 1982), pp. 69–91.

5. Thomas Aquinas, *Summa Theologiae*, Pt. I, Q. 13, a. 5.

6. I have developed this view in "The Quest for Wholeness and Its Crucial Metaphor and Analogy: The Place of Places," *Ultimate Reality and Meaning* 7 (1984): 156–65.

7. I have developed this point in more general terms in "Metaphor, Analogy, and the Nature of Truth," in *New Essays in Metaphysics*, ed. Robert Cummings Neville (Albany: State University of New York Press, 1986), pp. 217–36.

8. For a discussion of the self-reflexive interplay of mystery, power, and logos, see "Being and God," *Essays in Metaphysics*, pp. 213–33 and Carl G. Vaught, "Faith and Philosophy," *The Monist* 75 (1992): 321–40.

9. Ibid.

CHAPTER 10

Creation and Concrescence

Lewis S. Ford

Whitehead and Neville have proposed two of the most distinctive theories of creation in the twentieth century, both in terms of what it means to bring actualities into being, and in terms of funding the relationship between God and the world in its widest perspective. In some ways, however, these theories are diametrically opposed. Whitehead rejects *creatio ex nihilo,* which is the cornerstone of Neville's endeavor.

Concrescence, the act of actualization, is the hallmark of Whitehead's philosophy. It is derived from the Late Latin *con + crescere,* "to grow together." A concrescence is a drawing together of many strands to achieve a concrete actuality. Neville in effect regards the core activity of concrescence to be divinely created. Process theists deny that, seeing each to be self-created. The divine provision of initial aim is an essential factor, but it is one factor among many to be integrated together by the occasion itself. Whether concrescence is divinely created or self-created is the central issue to be examined.

Neville argues that the primary distinguishing characteristic of process theology is its refusal to identify God and creativity. Creativity is the core activity of concrescence, generalized for all instances of concrescence. This is only another way of stating the issue, for if creativity were wholly identified with God, there could be no other instances of creativity. This would eliminate all finite instances of self-creation. Yet the presence of other acts of creation need not mean that God cannot be a particular form of creativity.

Neville's relation to process thought is complex. His first book, *God the Creator* (1968) uses the idiom of Paul Weiss, but in his second book, *The Cosmology of Freedom* (1974), he adopted Whitehead's philosophy for much of his account of cosmology. This flexibility is possible, because Neville's ontology (i.e., the philosophy of the act of creation) is compatible with any cosmology (i.e., the philosophy of the world—of all that is created), if it is the case that God can create any philosophical structure whatever.[1] Hence Whitehead's cosmology can be selected on its general excellence, and still fit with Neville's overarching ontology. To be sure, some adjustments must be made in detail to insure the fit, but the resulting cosmology is still recognizably Whiteheadian.

While the use of process terms is most explicit in *The Cosmology of Freedom*, later works have deepened his appropriation of its conceptuality, as in *The Reconstruction of Thinking* (1981).[2] Superficially, Neville's system looks like a version of process philosophy in which traditional theism has replaced process theism. This is not accurate, because classical or traditional theism assumes God to be immutable, with or without the world, while Neville conceives whatever determinateness God has to result from the act of creation. God is transformed by creating the world, in much the way Whitehead conceives God to be transformed by the primordial envisagement. In this respect Neville's theism is profoundly process oriented, away from classical theism.

Neville's immersion in process cosmology, coupled with his own distinctive theism, gives him a privileged vantage point from which to criticize process theology. In *Creativity and God* (1980),[3] he augmented several occasional essays to mount a significant critique. Since I am closer to his outlook than most process theists, I concur with some of his criticisms. I am closer because I accept two distinctive features of his approach: (1) there must be an aboriginal nontemporal determination of first principles; and (2) the creativity for each occasion comes from God. Nevertheless there are sufficient other qualifications needed that keep me squarely on the process side of the fence. The primary issue will be: does God create the spontaneous features of each occasion, or does the occasion create itself by actualizing the creativity it receives from God?

NONTEMPORAL DETERMINATION
AND THE ONTOLOGICAL PRINCIPLE

Let us consider the first point. Process theists typically resist Neville's appeal to creation *ex nihilo*. The usual views of creation presuppose a totally unacceptable conception of divine omnipotence, and Whitehead's requirement that every actuality have antecedents seems to exclude any absolute beginning to the world.[4] (To be sure, Neville's use of creation really prescinds from the question whether the world had a temporal beginning or not.) Basic principles are seen as requiring no creation.

Yet is this really in accordance with Whitehead's ontological principle? Consider this formulation of the principle:

[T]he reasons for things are always to be found in the composite nature of definite actual entities—in the nature of God for reasons of the highest absoluteness, and in the nature of definite temporal actual entities for reasons which refer to a particular environment. (*PR* 19)[5]

Charles Hartshorne takes these principles to be analytically *a priori* true, regarding any alternatives to be strictly inconceivable. The necessary is simply that which is common to all possibilities, and needs no further explanation. Only that which can be decided between need be explained, and decision presupposes alternatives that can be selected among in decision.

Moreover, a primordial decision such as I once espoused is impossible.[6] How could any multiplicity of eternal objects antedate the nontemporal divine synthesis? Whitehead asserts that God's "conceptual actuality at once exemplifies and establishes the categoreal conditions" (*PR* 344), yet how is this possible? For the divine concrescence cannot exemplify the principles that are first established as a result of that concrescence (so *CG* 12).[7] For these reasons David Griffin recommends that we exclude the metaphysical principles from the scope of the ontological principle. Neville observes that such a restricted ontological principle is really a cosmological principle.

Neville paraphrases the ontological principle as requiring "that any complex state of affairs calls for an account by reference to the decisive actions that determine it" (*CG* 138).[8] This has been branded inaccurate, and so it is to some of Whitehead's formulations. The one usually regarded as most definitive has "every condition to which the process of becoming conforms in any particular instance" (*PR* 24) for "any complex state of affairs." Yet Whitehead does not seem to have one precise formulation in mind, but is constantly striving to articulate it in ever richer ways.[9] Furthermore, Whitehead admonishes us that "there is no justification for checking generalization at any particular stage" (*PR* 16).

Neville may not state Whitehead's principle exactly as the master stated it, but the more important question is whether he has been able to generalize it in suitable ways. Our quest is not for the actual, but for the ideal form.

First of all, the principle should apply to the divine instance. It may well be that the metaphysically necessary is common to all possibility and hence itself without alternative. Only if decision among alternatives is the only way anything can come to be can we exclude these principles from the scope of the ontological principle. Neville, however, speaks more precisely of nontemporal determination. Determination presupposes only that which is less determinate, not any determinate alternatives. Since even metaphysical principles are determinate, even if without alternative, they can be determined.

Whitehead's category of the ultimate calls for the creative unification of the many into one (*PR* 21f). How can this be squared with determination? The many may be individually determinate, but as a multiplicity they are indeterminate. This understanding of determination is peculiarly temporal, for it allows every being to be determinate in itself, yet opens the present at every moment to continue the process of determination. The many become one is a dynamic, temporal understanding of the movement from the indeterminate to the determinate. Yet it resists application to the nontemporal that cannot presuppose a preexistent many. I propose that we generalize the category of the ultimate such that it can apply to the nontemporal as well as the temporal. This can be accomplished by casting it in the form of a conditional: "if there is a many, then it is to be creatively made one."

If so, then Whitehead's formulation of the ontological principle, although it expresses an extremely pervasive form (applying to all temporal acts), is still a particular meaning of determination. It can be generalized. So generalized, the category of the ultimate is the obverse of the ideal ontological principle. "Whatever is determinate requires determination" (or is to be explained in terms of its act of determination) has as its obverse: "every indeterminacy is rendered determinate by an act of creativity."[10]

This does not necessarily mean a divine voluntarism at the ultimate level. Whitehead warned against this:

> Metaphysics requires that the relationships of God to the World should lie beyond the accidents of will, and that they be founded upon the necessities of the nature of God and the nature of the World. (*AI* 168)[11]

These relationships are not arbitrary, subject to temporal decisions. Nor can they be determined by a being whose essential nature is already determined. Yet these necessities relative to the nature of God and the world may well be determined not by any decision but by a nontemporal act of determination.

Metaphysical principles can be explained as common to all possibilities, and hence brook no possible alternatives. This explains their necessary nature. Even so, that does not explain how they came to be, if they came to be. The generalized category of the ultimate and the ideal ontological principle imply that there is nothing that did not come to be. If nothing were to "exist," there would be no metaphysical principles. They cannot exist apart from actualities. Moreover, it is possible to explain their origination by means of a timeless act of determination.

The strength of Neville's theory of creation lies in its abstractness. Whatever is in any wise determinate, such as the metaphysical principles, requires determination. Since that from which they are determined is comparatively more indeterminate, they must be created *ex nihilo,* and this act of creation determines God as the creator of these principles. I believe Whitehead sought something like this in asserting that God both establishes and exemplifies the categoreal conditions (*PR* 344), but his notion of a primordial decision amidst many eternal objects prevented him from realizing it fully. Creation in the form of nontemporal determination facilitates this conclusion. The ideal ontological principle cries out for its fulfillment in Neville's central idea.

Neville originally argued that every set of first principles needed to be grounded in some transcendent unity.[12] Since Whitehead's set are interdependent, they already have unity, and do not need any such grounding. More recently, however, as in *A Theology Primer,* Neville has generalized his argument in terms of determination.[13] This form of the argument can be more convincing to those of a process persuasion, for it can be connected to two central features of Whitehead's thought: the ontological principle and the category of the ultimate, suitably revised, to be sure.

While nontemporal determination nicely explains the determinateness of the metaphysical principles, can Neville appropriately extend his argument to the contingencies of the world? I contend not. Using resources drawn from Whitehead's philosophy, I shall argue that this requires finite, temporal acts of self-creation, and that God's creative act should be conceived as itself an act of self-creation.

THE LIMITS OF NONTEMPORAL DETERMINATION

Traditionally creation has been an opaque notion. Biblically it has made rough sense as maker of heaven and earth. In the course of Western theism's interaction with science, however, theology has tended to exclude time and causation from the notion of creation. This has rendered the notion nearly vacuous. It has been crowded out of the world processes, signifying only its putative beginnings or underlying basis. The concept of nontemporal determination does clarify matters, while retaining the traditional assumption of divine nontemporality.

There are meanings of creation, however, that are not required by nontemporal determination, which we shall address in a final section. There are also meanings of determination not required by creation. That determinateness requires determination does not require that all determination be nontemporal. One temporal form of determination is efficient causation, for example, which hardly qualifies as creation.

Another form is self-determination or freedom. Neville would say that freedom is created,[14] itself the result of divine determination. Whitehead conceives it as an act of self-creation. In the many becoming one in each concrescence, beyond all the factors ingredient in the occasion "there always remains the final reaction of the self-creative unity" determining how that many becomes one (*PR* 47). Since without that self-determination the many simply remain many, and do not become a being (a unity), the self-determination is the ultimate means by which it is created or brought into being. Thus for Whitehead freedom is essentially self-creation.

Not only is there self-creation, but there is only self-creation. There is room only for one or the other, for only one act ultimately brings a being into being. Traditionally, God creates by bringing an actuality into being that then can act. As Whitehead conceives it, the occasion in its act of becoming synthesizes together all other factors, including the divine input, to bring about a new being. Were God to create the occasion at the outset, it would already be, and there could be no self-creation to bring about its being at the end. This is a radical theory, inverting our understanding of being and becoming, for now being is seen as derived from becoming. Self-creation is my way of understanding Whitehead's theory of concrescence. He avoided the term 'creation' throughout his writings (cf. *AI* 236), because he thought of it as other-creation, which he opposed, as entailing determinism within an event-theory.

Yet he does use the notion of 'self-creation' on occasion. It first emerges in *Religion in the Making*:[15] "there are not two actual entities, the creativity and the creature. There is only one entity which is the self-creating creature" (*RM* 102). He uses the concept several times in *Process and Reality,* such as in describing the subjective aim as "this subject itself determining its own self-creation as one creature" (*PR* 69).[16]

Classical theories of creation conceive an immutable Creator creating that which is other to God, which includes not only the abstract metaphysical principles, but also the entire concrete contingent world. Moreover, the act of creation does not modify the Creator in the slightest. Neville trades on this traditional notion to the extent that God creates the contingent world, although this may not be strictly warranted by the concept of nontemporal determination.

If we limit ourselves solely to the nontemporal, then we may say that nontemporal determination is self-determination. Unlike in classical theism, God is transformed through the act of creation, for apart from nontemporal determination, God is conceived as wholly indeterminate.[17] Insofar as God is now determinate, God has been rendered so by this act of creation. While Neville need not agree that God exemplifies the metaphysical principles, still all that is necessary with respect to the divine being is the result of nontemporal determination. This is the supreme instance of self-creation.

To be sure God also creates the world, but in so doing God creates self as the creator of this world. God is not only creator, but the creator of this particular world with its particular contingent history, as contrasted to any other world God might have created.[18]

If creation were other-creation, then what is created need not be homogenous with the creator. God could create both the necessary and the contingent. If creation is self-creation, however, then we can insist upon homogeneity. If it creates itself, what is created must have the same character as the creator. Thus necessary activity produces the necessary, and contingent self-creation could produce the contingent. Since nontemporal determination produces atemporal necessity, this can be put in temporal terms. If God determines God's self nontemporally, what is created must be nontemporal. What is temporal, then, must be created temporally.

Then there would be many acts of creation besides God. This is counter to Neville's initial formulation of his central thesis. Instead of arguing that every determinateness needs an agency of determination, he argued that every multiplicity required some agency unifying it.[19] If so, there could ultimately only be one single act of creation, which Neville identifies with the one nontemporal determination. For there could not be a multiplicity of creative acts, if these acts are also created by another. The same act cannot both be created by another and be self-created. Creation is that which brings something into being. If it is brought into being by another, then it already has being (and unity). Any attempt to attain any further being would be futile.

It is for this reason that Whitehead's occasions (in their concrete contingency) are not finally created by God, but are self-created, for this is the only way to preserve temporal creation. His occasions (as concrescences) are not beings engaged in acting, as substantialist theory would have it, but acts of becoming creating, or processes of unification attaining new unities.

I have interpreted Neville's nontemporal determination in terms of self-creation, which limits the scope of his principle severely. Instead of creating the entire world, God only creates self and the metaphysical principles that characterize God and whatever world might exist. All else is contingent, requiring contingent self-creation. Neville, however, would well not recognize this interpretation, relying on traditional notions of other-creation. Thus it will be necessary to criticize the notion of other-creation as incoherent in the very technical sense that Whitehead gave to this term, as "the arbitrary disconnection of first principles" (PR 6).

INDEPENDENCE AND INTERDEPENDENCE

Clearly, this is a very special sense of 'incoherence'. Cartesian dualism, whereby mind and matter are conceived in complete disjunction from one another, is Whitehead's example of incoherence. Ordinarily, if someone is incoherent, we think that he is making no sense at all. Descartes, however, makes very good sense, even though the elements of his system are basically disconnected. Whitehead means 'cohere' in the root sense: "to stick together." Dualisms fail, he argues, because the basic principles fail to stick together.

Principles stick together (cohere) in terms of dependence. One principle can be derived from the other, or cannot exist or be what it is apart from the other. Two principles are interdependent if each is dependent on the other. For example, an actuality would be characterless without its characters, but the characters could not exist except when characterizing actualities. Whitehead considers such triads as creativity, many, and one (PR 21f.), or God, creativity, and creatures (PR 225) in terms of interdependence.[20]

Like wooden struts fashioned in the form of triangles, interdependent principles have stability, a metaphysical stability to be absolutely invariant throughout all time. They constitute a very tight unity. Thus Neville's earlier formulation of his thesis, namely that every multiplicity, including a multiplicity of principles, required unity in terms of a creator, was unpersuasive.[21] Interdependence provides that unity. But interdependent principles are determinate, and require determination.

The opposites of dualistic independence and interdependence, however, do not exhaust the alternatives. There is also a one-sided dependence, where one principle or actuality is dependent on the other, but not vice versa. That term is independent in the relation. If it is independent in all relations, then it is absolutely independent.

God in classical theism is conceived to be absolutely independent, at least with respect to the contingent world. This preserves and protects God's complete immutability. The creation of the world is an act creating that which is other than God, and which does not affect the nature or being or experience of God in any case. The world depends absolutely on God's creative act, but God is not dependent on the world in any respect.

This means that creation is a wholly extrinsic act. It is wholly gratuitous. For many theists this means an act of pure grace, but pure gratuity is also arbitrariness. No reason can be given why there should be any creation.

Provided there are in fact real relations of dependence that connect the world to God and God to the world, classical theism makes a virtue of incoherence, understood as "the arbitrary disconnection of first principles." Reason, in one of its many forms, is the discernment of necessary connections. The failure to discern relations that are really there is arbitrary, for it is a failure of reason.

The value of rationalism, however, need not mean that we go to the opposite extreme, and posit more relations than are really there. Thus much British Hegelianism opted for complete internal relatedness, whereby the nature of the future was inextricably bound up with the character of the past, and vice versa. Then the future was as determinate as the past, or the past was as interdeterminate as the future. Hegel promoted the passion for internal relations, but did not allow it to eliminate time in this fashion.

Let us consider two examples of one-way dependence:

1. In classification theory, the species is dependent upon the genus, but not vice versa. The species (and the individuals under it) must exemplify the features of the genus, for otherwise they cannot belong to that genus, but the abstract character of the genus need not indicate the sort of differences the species could harbor.

2. The present is causally dependent upon its past. A present occasion is initially constituted out of its prehensions of past actualities. But those past actualities, being fully determinate in themselves, are not affected by whatever happens subsequently. The past is absolutely immutable. Charles Hartshorne in particular has analyzed the nature of such prehension as "asymmetrical internal relations" as a solution to the problem of internal relatedness.[22]

This one-sided dependence of the present on the past enables the present and the past to be modally different, the past as determinate, the present as indeterminate in process of determination. If they were symmetrically internally related, either the present would acquire the determinateness of the past, or the past the indeterminateness of the present. The modal differentiation would be lost. Freedom also depends upon the present's not being completely determined by the past.

In general, however, interdependence can be discerned on a more general plane. Usually the modes of dependence are different in interdependence. In the one-way dependence of genus and species, both terms are forms. On this general level forms characterize actualities, but are dependent on concrete actualities for their existence. Present prehending is dependent on the past for its content, while the past is dependent upon its appropriation by the present for its effectiveness.[23]

With these distinctions in hand, we can return to the question of Neville and creation. His proposal has freed itself from the traditional assumption of divine immutability and its fantasy of God as existing before the world came into being. This was based on the assumption of God's complete necessity and the world's complete contingency, the assumption that God's perfection means that the existence of the world cannot enrich God in any way. (We shall argue later for interdependence: for God, necessity is primary, contingency derived from the world, whereas for the world, contingency is primary, and necessity is derived from God.) For Neville, creation is at least the self-creation of God, rendering God as determinate as God becomes.

Although his theory is not based on immutability, Neville endorses the same absolute independence of God from the world as does classical theism. The world utterly depends upon God for its existence, but God does not depend upon the world in any way. This is most evident in his distinction between ontology, the philosophical account of the creative act, and cosmology, the corresponding account of what is so created. Cosmological alternatives are possible with the same ontology. "Since the character of the world is empirically given, however, God could have created a different kind of world, one with no time, for instance, or no continuity of order" (SSS 108).[24] Thus cosmology depends on ontology, but ontology is independent of cosmology.

The independence of ontology enables Neville to persist in traditional distinctions. Thus he can distinguish between creation as a nontemporal act between God and the world, and causation which is a temporal exchange between inner-worldly actualities. This separation of causation from creation blocks further inquiry, just when the identification of creation with (nontemporal) determination would have facilitated it by drawing the parallels between divine nontemporal determination and causal as creaturely temporal determination.

Whitehead's greater rationalism, on the other hand, always seeks to discern relations of interdependence, which makes it possible to connect creation with causation in terms of determination. The integration or concrescence of the prehensions of all influences, including the divine, is his way of explaining temporal determination as self-creation, which can then be correlated with divine creation as nontemporal determination.

To be sure, we could stipulate that the only meaning of creation permitted is nontemporal determination. Then all temporal or contingent determination is simply cosmological causation. In that case, however, divine creation is radically equivocal, if it pertains to the contingent order at all. On the nontemporal level, divine creation is determinative, but on the contingent level creation simply sustains in being whatever is determined otherwise.

That creation means determination, and determination needs some determining agency may well be Neville's greatest insight. That which is exists as determinate. Whatever ultimately determines it creates it. Should that be abandoned by settling for a notion of creation with respect to the contingent world as merely providing its being without thereby determining it?[25]

On Neville's view God is not dependent on the world in any way. Since for him the world derives its existence from God, there must be other-creation in addition to divine self-creation. The world's dependence is a one-way dependence, and lacks the full coherence of interdependence, assuming that it is proper to discern interdependence here. (For Whitehead there is interdependence: the world depends on God for its necessary structure and purpose, God depends on the world for the contingent content of divine experience.)

NECESSITY AND CONTINGENCY

Put most generally, the relation of God and the world concerns the connection between necessity and contingency. I propose this principle: the contingent is dependent upon the necessary for its basic character, but the necessary depends upon the contingent for its concrete actuality.

Note that necessity is excessively abstract and barren, since it is that which is common to all things without exception. Only the contingent can be concrete, for every concrete thing is this rather than that. It exists, standing out from the penumbra of alternatives it might have been. The necessary is without alternative, so that its "existence" cannot contrast with anything. We can never encounter in the world any pure necessity. To exist it must be clothed with contingent concreteness.

This is the reason why the notion of nontemporal origination of the necessary always seems to be surrounded by a mythical penumbra of contingency. The nontemporal is the primordial, and the primordial is also thought to be some distant past event at the beginning of time. This sense of primordiality is difficult to shake even if time is conceived to be without beginning, and the nontemporal is strictly conceived to be independent of all temporality. In the end, such may not be possible. While the nontemporal may be independent of any particular temporal contingency, it may not be independent of all temporality.

If we find any pure necessity, it must be out of this world. Necessity without contingency is ascribed to God in classical theism to protect divine immutability. If God were contingent in any way, then there would be the possibility of realizing the alternative so excluded. Then God would be capable of change, becoming otherwise.

On the other hand, if we drop the requirement of immutability, there need be no pure necessity. All necessity would depend on concrete actuality from which it could be abstracted.[26] Thus to be actual, God must have contingency in the form of experience. This interdependence of necessity and contingency means that the world, in some sense, must always accompany God, for a necessary being must derive its contingency from that which is other than the divine.[27]

The abstractness of the necessary also applies to the nontemporal act of determination. To be sure, the necessary cannot be affected in its nature by the contingent. No contingent action can alter the necessary since it is what is under all circumstances. In that sense the necessary is absolutely independent, and this tempts us to suppose that its origination can also be independent of contingency. To be so, however, means that it must be capable of independent existence, and precisely that is problematic.

Also, it tempts us to believe that necessary can generate the contingent by creating that which is other than itself. Yet if solely derived from the necessary, could the contingent have sufficient independent status to exist by itself? Does it have the necessary ontological detachment? That which God could imagine has only an imaginary status within God, that is, no status other than God. Only that which would be surprising to God would be worth creating, and to be really novel it would need some basis outside God. To be truly a world, the world needs to be ontologically detached from God.[28] Other-creation cannot achieve this.

Classical theism proposes to do just that. If God is immutable, the same with or without the world, possessed of all perfections, including the perfect power of omnipotence, God can create the world, and must, since the world does exist. Yet just how that creation takes place remains unexplained.

Neville's nontemporal determination clarifies the notion of creation further. It is genuinely illuminating with respect to necessary principles. Can it be extended further to the contingent? Here there is a fundamental determination to be made. There are three alternatives with respect to necessity and contingency: pure necessity, necessity with contingency, or pure contingency. These are not determinate alternatives prior to the act of nontemporal determination, for there can only be indeterminacy apart from the act. Yet they are alternative results of the act, ways in which the nontemporal determination could be determined.

Pure contingency is basically chaos, but it could possibly evolve an order through repetition and habit. All order would be historically emergent, independent of any nontemporal determination. God's role in such a world becomes problematic, although not impossible, since divine valuation of possibility could still be a feature. Yet could God's own existence be contingent?

Pure necessity could be the outcome of divine determination. In many ways this might seem to be its natural outcome. Yet if all contingency is excluded nontemporally, it is difficult to see how it could be introduced at some later time. Nontemporal determinations are for keeps. Only temporal determinations could be reversed at some later time. In classical theism God apart from any world is deemed capable of nontemporally introducing contingency with the creation of the world. Classical omnipotence is held capable of overcoming all obstacles, but just how it can do so remains profoundly obscure.

We have two "possible" alternatives, pure necessity and necessity with contingency, but any "decision" between them must be nontemporal. For temporality presupposes contingency. Only if what is could be otherwise can there be any distinction between what was and what will be. Moreover, once contingency is established, decisions can be made between prior alternatives. The determination that there be temporality at all, even though it involves alternatives of a sort, cannot itself be temporal, for it creates the possibility of temporality.

If our world exhibits both necessity and contingency, it must be nontemporally determined as both. To guarantee metaphysical stability, each must be dependent on the other: the contingent derives its basic order from the necessary, while the necessary exists only as concretely actualized by the contingent. If God determines the necessary nontemporally, there is necessarily room for temporal determination as well. Temporal determination presupposes alternate possibilities and past multiplicities to be ordered contingently, since they could have been ordered differently. The independence of temporal determination from the divine nontemporal determination ensures the ontological detachment required for the existence of a world that is not God.

SELF-CREATION

Temporal determination is contingent self-creation. The world can be conceived as constituted by many successive temporal acts of self-creation. Each contingent act derives its necessary structure and purpose from God. In that sense God contributes to its self-creation, but it must be recognized that creation must be ultimately ascribed to that single agency that brings about the unity or being of the actuality. It cannot both be other-created and self-created.

Self-creation creates the unity of the self from multiplicity received. It is not *ex nihilo*. It is creative because it fashions for itself a new unity; the antecedent multiplicity is quite indeterminate as to its synthesis. Finite self-creation derives its necessary structure from God, but God derives the many that is integrated within the divine experience from the world. Nontemporal determination is conceived by Neville as independent of the world, which is created thereby. Yet since the nontemporal determination can only be abstract, it should be conceived as the most abstract dimension of God's ongoing temporal determination of divine experience.

In this sense God exemplifies the metaphysical principles, or better, the transcendental conditions governing divine experiencing. Yet in another sense these principles are being nontemporally determined, since their author is ultimately God, according to the ontological principle. Nontemporal determination is that aspect of temporal determination that remains when abstracted from all contingent temporality. Its nontemporal character, however, ensures that these necessary principles will be the same in every instance. Temporal determination would be needed to introduce variation.

Neville invokes the model of other-creation to explain freedom.[29] This follows from larger considerations: God nontemporally creates the entire world and all that is within it. If there is human freedom, as Neville affirms, it must be created. He adroitly avoids determinism in the form that God has already predetermined the outcome of every "free" act. Rather the free action of the individual determining the outcome coincides with God's nontemporal determination. (How God's determination of a succession of acts remains nevertheless nontemporal is unclear.)

In contrast Whitehead understands human freedom to represent the most intense form of self-creation. God does contribute to the determination of the occasion, but the contribution is only partial, and does not complete the determination. It is brought about by successive determinings, first God's, then the occasion's.

Since the occasion's self-creation is ontologically detached as an independent act of existence, the occasion's determination of itself is ultimately distinct from God's determining. It must first be prehended to form part of the divine experience. The occasion determines the initial character of divine experience, to be sure, but this conformation is both natural and harmless, since the experiencing subject determines how what is initially received should be integrated into an intelligible whole.

On Neville's theory, however, since God does not predetermine the creature, there is still the question of God's knowledge of the world. Basically God knows through creating, by means of divine activity, not by experiencing or prehending the world's determinate acts. Yet to truly know, there must be a conformation between the knower and what is known. This question of conformation prescinds from problems of temporality and nontemporality so evident in questions of determinism.

Which conforms to which? If the finite agent conforms to the divine determination, its freedom becomes quite problematic. On the other hand, if God conforms to the free determinations of the creatures, then God loses any core of personal identity and action. God is dispersed into the many determinations of free beings. This makes sense only by conceiving God as an impersonal generalized creativity and by reconceiving creation as that which sustains whatever happens in being.

On the prehensive view, in which God experiences the world the way finite actualities do, there are some things that cannot be prehended. Only determinate being, not the becoming of determination, is prehensible. This distinction is essential from realism as contrasted to idealism. The brute facticity of what is out there can be maintained only if it is rigorously distinguished from what is in here. Classical empiricism, with its substantialist assumptions, distinguished between the reality and its copy or representation. The notion of an eternal object or atemporal characteristic that is the same both out there and in here overcomes the skepticism inherent in the copy theory, but then the distinction has to be maintained between the concrete actuality out there and the form abstracted from it.[30] The distinction between the imprehensible act of determination (the concrescence) and the prehensible (or objectifiable) determinateness enables Whitehead to argue that the concrete being as such is experienced.

The essential privacy of the creative act is protected, as is the truth of relativity physics that contemporaries cannot prehend one another. Neville charges: "God cannot know us as we are in our hearts, where that means the subjective immediacy of our own concrescence" (*CG* 141). Yet just as God cannot know the future, God cannot know the brief fleeting moment of the present.[31] Both are too indeterminate to be known. If they were knowable, there could be no further determination to achieve.

Neville's theory of creative determination basically applies to two sorts of determinate entities: metaphysical principles and actualities. This is ill adapted to self-creation, both in the sense of self-reflexive acts of creation, and to the creation of subjective features. By subjective features I have in mind primarily those transcendental conditions that make experience and actualization possible.[32] I conceive nontemporal determination, within a process context, as the creation of God's transcendental conditions. Kant argued that the use of transcendental conditions without empirical content is empty, and I extend the argument to God: God requires contingent actuality in order to give content to the divine experience. The divine transcendental conditions are the means whereby God gives unity and intelligibility to this experience, and values the situations confronting new occasions.

Finite occasions receive their transcendental conditions from God.[33]

Otherwise they would have no means for prehending anything. Besides this necessity received from God, they need other contingent actualities for the content of their experience, and for the multiplicity they unify, thereby actualizing themselves.

ETERNAL CREATION

We have shown that, from the process perspective at least, there is the nontemporal determination of metaphysical principles, but nothing else. Yet Neville not only affirms the creation of the world, but of freedom and time. In *Eternity and Time's Flow*,[34] he argues that there cannot be any adequate temporal togetherness of the temporal modes, and therefore they must have an eternal togetherness transcending time. Both claims can be questioned. Why could there not be a final multiplicity? Here Neville is relying on his former assumption that every multiplicity must be unified by a transcendent power rather than on his more recent assumption that everything determinate requires determination.

For the temporal modes are unified insofar as they are interdependent. The past depends on the present as that which brings it into being. The present depends on the past for its content and upon the (active) future for its aim. The future depends upon the past for its experience, and provides the present with its power and aim.[35]

For our present purposes, however, we must recognize that if there is an eternal creation transcending time that accounts not only for time but for the togetherness of the temporal modes, eternal creation must be much more than strict 'nontemporal determination'.[36] Both terms of this designation are seriously ambiguous:

1. 'Nontemporal', by itself, simply excludes the temporal. The non-temporal can be less than time as the total absence of time, time-lessness. Or it can be that which is more than time, transcending time. Used in a Greek context, the eternal meant that which was timeless. In a Hebraic context, it meant that which was endless time, the everlasting. Modern concepts of the eternal either endorse time-lessness or attempt to combine the fullness of everlastingness with the absence of temporal modality.

   In any case, 'nontemporal determination' in a process perspective means timeless determination along the lines of the primordial envisagement of the eternal objects Whitehead proposes. Let us call this 'timeless determination'. On this interpretation, Neville's call for the timeless determination of metaphysical principles makes excellent sense.

On the other hand, Neville may well mean by the nontemporal the eternal, stipulating this to mean that which is more than time as its ultimate source.

2. 'Determination' may mean rendering an entity fully determinate. In this sense the metaphysical principles are determined. For Whitehead, an actual entity is not fully determined until all indeterminacy in its constitution has been resolved in the final unity. Its concrescence becomes in the present, to be a determined unity in the past. Other theories, however, may have a looser understanding of determination as that which confers the unity of being upon an actuality. In other words, it would be possible for an actuality first to be, then to act. If so, it can be determined to be, even though indeterminate with respect to its own action. Since an actuality can be created with its freedom, it seems that Neville would adopt this latter approach. Let us stipulate this as 'creation'.

Thus 'nontemporal determination' may mean either 'timeless determination' or 'eternal creation'. 'Timeless determination' is included within the meaning of 'eternal creation', but not vice versa. Let us concentrate upon the excess of intended meaning inherent in 'eternal creation'.

I say "intended meaning" advisedly, for I am not certain that any clear meaning can be attached to creation beyond timeless determination. Creation is a time-honored traditional notion of Western theism, but it is not for its clarity that it is celebrated. Already as early as the Hebrew Bible its mystery and human inaccessibility has been explored (Job 38–41). Reconceiving it as a nontemporal activity under Greek philosophical influence did not increase its intelligibility, and since then it has suffered the death of a thousand qualifications by being exempted from all forms of finite causation and self-creation.

If eternal creation is supposed to mean something in excess of timeless determination, what could this additional meaning be? Consider the possibility that freedom could be created. Created freedom seems to have meaning, whereas determined freedom is self-contradictory. One could stipulate that creation means only divine determination, and that there is also both causal determination and self-determination. If so, then God only partially determines those actualities, including the conditions for freedom.

We prefer an understanding of 'creation' as that which brings actuality to being. Then the difference between Whitehead and Neville would be whether being requires complete determination or not. For Neville divine creation could be partially determinative and still bring actualities into being. For Whitehead complete determination requires some self-determination as well as causal determination. If there can be no being apart from complete determination,[37] then creation requires self-creation as well as divine creation.

Another meaning in excess of timeless determination must be given to the eternal creation of the temporal modes. If they have no temporal togetherness, Neville claims that their togetherness must be eternally created by a source that far exceeds temporality. If there is no togetherness in terms of interdependence, how can we understand what its created togetherness should be? What can we say about its creative source, other than that it is supposed to be?[38]

Now even with respect to the timeless determination of metaphysical principles we have been skirting on the fringes of intelligibility. Is it necessary to hold that *every* determinateness requires determination? Many believe that the necessary needs no determination, and hence are unwilling to make that move. I have argued that process thinkers ought to look for a source of determination for the necessary as required by a perfected version of Whitehead's ontological principle. This pushes intelligibility one step further than many are willing to go.

We should appeal to timeless determination, let alone eternal creation, only when it is necessary to do so. It is not necessary in the case of contingent determinateness, because it can be adequately accounted for in terms of contingent determinations, either by past actualities or by present self-determination. Intelligible explanation should be tailored to its subject-matter. Unnecessary explanation quickly becomes unintelligible.

In appealing to eternal creation as appealing to something exceeding time, Neville can at most indicate that there is such a thing, but he cannot make out what it is, except in terms of its products. To do even this Neville must assume not only that every determinateness requires determination, but that such determination is primarily nontemporal.

We have endorsed the nontemporal determination of metaphysical principles. This determination is complete: although they may be further specified and applied, there is no way these absolutely universal principles applying to all events can be modified.[39] Nor is there any reality other than a cosmic actuality that could be the agency of their determination. Thus we are warranted in appealing to divine nontemporal determination in this case.

Neville may well understand this in terms of eternal creation. I believe this excess of creative power to be unnecessary, for timeless determination is sufficient for the task. Moreover, any excess of creative power does not seem to be very intelligible. Intelligibility requires that we affirm both sides of the ontological principle: "the reasons for things are always to be found in the composite nature of definite actual entities—in the nature of God for reasons of the highest absoluteness, and in the nature of definite temporal actual entities for reasons which refer to a particular environment" (*PR* 19).

SUMMARY

Neville's central claim, that there is a nontemporal determination of the necessary features of reality, must be affirmed from a process perspective, because it embodies an idealized version of the ontological principle. At the same time, however, it must be severely limited as applying only to the necessary. Only what is invariant in all circumstances need be nontemporally determined. That which could vary, including even the most general physical constants of our cosmic epoch, should be temporally determined. If God only nontemporally determines, there must be scope for contingent determination outside God. This requires self-creation as the basis for the ontological detachment of the world from God.

Thus instead of a necessary God creating a contingent world, there are a multiplicity of self-creative acts, a divine act determining the necessary, and worldly acts determining the contingent. The world depends upon God for its necessary structure and aim, while God depends upon the world for the particular contents of divine contingent experience.

Neville's 'eternal creation' may have intended meanings transcending this bare notion of 'timeless determination', but we find these both unintelligible and unnecessary.

NOTES

1. Thus, for example, Neville writes: "On the *cosmological* level, God has the character of creating a world described by a particular cosmological system. Since the character of the world is empirically given, however, God could have created a different kind of world, one with no time, for instance, or no continuity of order. Whereas God's metaphysical character in principle is supposed to be *a priori* valid for any determinate world, his cosmological character is related to the specific world which he in fact created." *Soldier Sage Saint* (New York: Fordham University Press, 1978), p. 108. Hereafter, *SSS*.

2. Albany: State University of New York Press, 1981. This is not evident in most parts of the book, but the cosmological parts, which form its backbone, are implicitly based on Whitehead's philosophy: pp. 154–59, 193–210, 246–53.

3. *Creativity and God: A Challenge to Process Theology* (New York: Seabury, 1980; 2nd ed., 1995). Hereafter, *CG*.

4. See my essay on "An Alternative to Creatio ex Nihilo," *Religious Studies* 19.2 (June 1983): 205–13.

5. A. N. Whitehead, *Process and Reality*, corrected edition (New York: Free Press, 1978), p. 19. Hereafter, *PR*.

6. In "The Non-Temporality of Whitehead's God," *International Philosophical Quarterly* 13.3 (September 1973): 347–76.

7. For reasons given below, I believe the notion of a primordial decision between many eternal objects must be replaced by the notion of a nontemporal determination, for it presupposes only indeterminacy, not prior alternatives. But "conceptual actuality" is ambiguous. It may mean either the divine concrescence of conceptual feeling, or the resultant primordial satisfaction. If Whitehead means both meanings, there is no contradiction, for the divine concrescence establishes the conditions that the primordial satisfaction then exemplifies. In nontemporality there is no temporal succession here.

8. So also *CG* 13: "anything complex is the result of decision."

9. See my "Perfecting the Ontological Principle," in *Metaphysics as Foundation: Essays in Honor of Ivor Leclerc,* ed. Paul A. Bogaard and Gordon Treash (New York: State University of New York Press, 1993), pp. 122–49.

10. Thus creativity becomes the ultimate explanation why actuality constitutes the only reasons. See William J. Garland, "The Ultimacy of Creativity," in *Explorations in Whitehead's Philosophy,* ed. Lewis S. Ford and George L. Kline (Fordham University Press, 1983), pp. 212–38. Hereafter, *EWP*.

11. *Adventures of Ideas* (New York: The Free Press, 1967), p. 168. Hereafter, *AI*. This particular paragraph is important for the discussion of interdependence, a topic I shall introduce shortly.

12. "Whitehead on the One and the Many," *EWP* 257–71. As editor of a special issue of *The Southern Journal of Philosophy* 7.4 (Winter 1969–70), I asked Neville to adapt his general critique in *God the Creator* to process philosophy. Neville made the most creative revision I have experienced in my many years as editor of 950 manuscripts over the years. I returned the original version with about sixteen substantive objections. He sent back an entirely new essay, meeting all these objections, and yet maintaining his basic thesis. I then published it, and we reprinted it in *EWP*. It took me several years to find any difficulties with it. In a preliminary way, these are expressed in "Neville on the One and the Many," *Southern Journal of Philosophy* 10.1 (Spring 1972): 79–84, but more extensively, in "Neville's Interpretation of Creativity," *EWP* 272–79.

13. An interdependent set, although possessing unity, still requires determination if it is the case that every determination requires determination.

14. For a contrary view, see my essay, "Can Freedom Be Created?" *Horizons* 4.2 (Fall 1977): 183–88.

15. First published in 1926, *RM* has been reprinted, according to the original pagination, by Fordham University Press, 1996, with an extensive glossary.

16. See also *PR* 25, 47, 85, 289.

17. Absolute indeterminateness has been rejected on the grounds that it is simply nothing, citing the ancient rule, "ex nihilo nihil fit." That must be so in the absence of any external or internal creative power bringing out further determination. Yet form must come from either form or formlessness. If it comes from form, there must be some class of basic forms that generate all others. Whitehead adopts this alternative, but I find reason to question the uncreated-

ness of eternal objects. If form comes from formlessness, a determining power is sufficient. In the one case of novel forms, there may be a proper sense to creation *ex nihilo*. See "Contrasting Conceptions of Creation," *Review of Metaphysics* 45.1 (September 1991): 89–109.

18. Cf. the last sentence of *SSS* 108 quoted above.

19. See, e.g. *God the Creator* or "Whitehead on the One and the Many," (*EWP* 257–71).

20. Whitehead seeks such interdependence everywhere: "What metaphysics requires is a solution exhibiting the plurality of individuals as consistent with the unity of the Universe, and a solution which exhibits the World as requiring its union with God, and God as requiring his union with the World" (*AI* 168).

21. See my essay on "Neville's Interpretation of Creativity," in *Explorations in Whitehead's Philosophy*, ed. Lewis S. Ford and George L. Kline (Fordham University Press, 1983), pp. 272–79.

22. See "Whitehead's Revolutionary Concept of Prehension," *International Philosophical Quarterly* 19.3 (September 1979): 253–63.

23. Causation, by vesting all activity in the cause, exemplifies one-way dependence. The effect is totally dependent on the cause. Prehension is Whitehead's interdependent counterpart to causation.

24. See note 1.

25. There is, however, much to be said for the Thomistic tradition of the communication of *esse*. Transposed into a process context, however, *esse* can be thought to pertain to the power of determination rather than (as for Thomas) to the specific concrete act whereby an actuality comes into being. This concrete act is self-creation; but *esse* can be thought as the power whereby self-creation is possible. I conceive this power to be derived from God, but that requires a modification of Whitehead's philosophy beyond the scope of this essay. See "Creativity in a Future Key," in *New Essays in Metaphysics,* ed. Robert Cummings Neville (Albany: State University of New York Press, 1986), pp. 179–98. Hereafter, *NEM*.

26. Analogously, Aristotle's moderate realism could be rendered more consistent if form were only actual if united with matter. He affirms a pure necessity without contingency by excepting the divine as pure form.

27. Since he implicitly rejects this interdependence, Neville can allow *creatio ex nihilo* to have its traditional meaning as implying the absolute beginning of time. Yet the traditional notion of God existing in supreme perfection before the world began is abandoned, since God without creation is utterly indeterminate. Neville's nontemporal determination may mean that the world has a beginning, but it is also compatible with the claim that the world is without any beginning.

28. This argument for ontological detachment was made years ago by Paul Weiss in class.

29. Here see particularly, *SSS*, chapter 5.

30. This is essentially the theory of Whitehead's *Science and the Modern World* (New York: Macmillan, 1926). Hereafter, *SMW*.

31. The most complex moment of human experience is estimated to be

about 1/20th of a second, while simpler subhuman occasions may be considerably briefer.

32. Kant coined the term "transcendental" to refer to the conditions making experience and knowing possible. But since concrescence means both experience (inwardly) and actualization (outwardly), I am extending the concept to apply to actualization as well.

33. This reception must be in some other way than by prehension. Since Whitehead considered prehension to be the only way an occasion received anything, his philosophy must be modified on this point. See my essay on "Creativity in a Future Key," *NEM* 179–98.

34. Albany: State University of New York Press, 1993. Hereafter, *ETF.*

35. The interdependence of the temporal modes is more fully explored in my essay on "The Modes of Actuality," *The Modern Schoolman* 67.4 (May 1990): 275–83.

36. I shall be using Neville's sense of the 'eternal' throughout this discussion. It is emphatically *not* the sense Whitehead ascribes to the 'eternal objects', which could more properly be designated as 'timeless' or 'atemporal objects', or as 'zeitlose Gegenstände', as the German translation has it.

37. Complete determination unifying all past influences, because an actuality is indeterminate with respect to its unification with other actualities for subsequent occasions. In this way Whitehead escapes the determinism of complete internal relatedness proposed by one interpretation of absolute idealism.

38. This begins to sound a lot like Paul Tillich, whose divine being-itself was literally that which is not a being but the source of all being. All other statements about God could only be made symbolically. We know how they do not apply, but not clearly how they do apply. *Systematic Theology,* vol. 1 (Chicago: University of Chicago Press, 1951). For my critique, see "Tillich and Thomas: The Analogy of Being," *Journal of Religion* 46.2 (April 1966): 229–45, and "Tillich's One Non-Symbolic Statement: A Propos of a Recent Study by William Rowe," *Journal of the American Academy of Religion* 38.2 (June 1970): 176–82.

39. If they were temporally capable of modification, they could not apply to *all* events, since they would not apply to those events prior to the modification.

PART IV

Theological Problems

CHAPTER 11

Knowing the Mystery of God: Neville and Apophatic Theology

Delwin Brown

INTRODUCTION

The task of the academic theologian, in my view, is to evaluate and reconstruct the dominant religious symbols of a people in order to address the needs of the day. What in fact constitutes the needs of the day, how they should be addressed, and whether or not particular reconstructions adequately address these needs are issues to be discussed in communities of contemporary discourse, simultaneous with a consideration of the criteria of these discussions. The criteria of adjudication, in other words, are always those defensible and defended in the present. But presents have pasts, and my own view is that the constructions to be assessed, as distinct from the process of their assessment, are most likely to be effective if they are *re*-constructions—if, in the case of religions, they are reformulations of the inherited galaxy of religious symbols and practices. What precisely is inherited for a given people and whether their inheritance remains strong enough to count for much among them are empirical questions, questions so complex they perhaps can never be answered with finality. But any such empirical judgment, about what is or is not the dominating symbol system of a people, gains some credibility when it is conjoined with a theory that explains how the empirical claims being made might in fact be consistent with other things we think we know.

One empirical claim underlying this essay is the judgment that the biblical symbolic complex, in its Christian and Jewish redactions, remains dominant in North America, which is the place where I work as a theologian. That, therefore, is the symbolic complex I seek to recon-

struct in light of the needs of the day. I have sought, elsewhere, to complement this empirical judgment with a theoretical proposal that
explains how this might be the case, despite the markedly different
expectations we once held deriving in particular from twentieth-century
secularization theory. My alternative theory—a theory of tradition I
have called "constructive historicism"[1]—can be described negatively as
a rejection of the bee-and-nectar view of human historicity. I do not
think humans, viewed in general, can draw adequate symbolic nourish-
ment by flitting from flower to flower, drawing rather indiscriminately
from the fruit of one tradition, then another, and another, and so on.
Neither, however, do I think humans are nourished from only one
flower, so the contrary of the analogy does not describe my view either.
Nor do I deny that some individuals—whether perspicacious or just culturally alienated, we need not decide—can and do reconstruct meanings
by drawing quite equitably from varied, alternative traditions. But cultures, I think, do not construct meanings in this way. They are dominated by particular galaxies of meanings, and they proceed most effectively by integrating novelty, whether alien or domestic, into the
reconstruction of their dominant inheritance, whatever that happens to
be. The foregoing explains why, in our culture, I am inclined to work
quite intentionally with the inherited symbols of Christianity. It is
through the reconstruction of these symbols, I believe, that one is most
likely to be able to deal with the pressing needs of our culture.

HUMAN ARROGANCE AND THE MYSTERY OF GOD

The category of the Christian inheritance that interests me in this essay
is the persistent Christian affirmation of the mystery of God. I shall
argue that Robert Neville's system provides the basis for an especially
clear and consistent articulation of that theological affirmation. But I
shall also contend for the pragmatic utility of the affirmation of the mystery of God, and hence a Nevillean foundation for that affirmation, in
relation to what I take to be one of our culture's more pernicious problems. This is the problem of idolatry, to use a religious term, or in secular parlance, it is the absolutizing of belief with its attendant attitudes
and actions—arrogance, intolerance, oppression, and the varied forms
of the destruction of the other that are so rampant today. The problem
that I speak of, in other words, is the evil of absolute truth.

The myth of absolute truth perhaps came to power because it had a
valid function in social evolution. At least we may speculate that once
upon a time the notion of absoluteness was a valuable, maybe even
indispensable, means of introducing useful forms of order into the flux

of social and natural chaos. To emerging humans nature was fickle, whimsical, capricious, and wanton in its ways. Humans, themselves nature's progeny, may not have been less so except insofar as the needs of survival gradually required the creation of tenuous systems of social order to protect against the caprice of the environment. But how to ground such order? Surely not in the observable world as such, the wantonness of which was the problem in the first place. The social order could only be grounded in an unseen, but not unknowable, realm of transcendent order, some infallible foundation of things on the basis of which proposed human orders could then be validated. Structures of order erected to fend off absolute destruction required absolute justification—some such logic as this may have been the evolutionary origin of the notion of absolute truth.

Today, however, the absolutes of our culture have turned on us like lapdogs gone mad. Our absolutes are killing us, or more precisely with them we are killing each other. Whether as a fearful reaction to the advance of pluralism with its threats, or the advent of technology with its powers, or the breakup of dependable economic structures with its insecurities, or a combination of these or other things, our culture is now driven by the dogma of infallibilism. I believe this dogma is made possible by the myth of absolute truth and, hence, this myth is now a serious threat to our society.

I also assume that the myth of absolute truth in the West is rooted to an important extent in the dominant religious view of God. Both Judaism and Christianity, twin heirs to the religion of Israel, have consistently affirmed the mystery of God—"No one has seen God," "God's ways are not our ways," and so forth. But, especially in Christianity, this apophatic note has been overwhelmed by a kataphatic chord in most versions of the Christian vision, that is, the doctrine of the incarnation— "He who has seen me has seen the Father." The will of the mysterious God is revealed in Jesus Christ. Thus, in dominant forms of Christianity, the doctrine of the mystery of God has lost its power to negate human claims to absoluteness. True, absoluteness is attributed to God alone, but the additional claim that portions of this mystery have been unveiled extends an absoluteness by proxy to anyone who believes he or she has received this divine knowledge. Moreover, the doctrine of the mystery of God, thus tamed, has been retained to shield kataphasis from rational critique, for challenges to the claim that the absolute will of God has been revealed in a particular place to a particular people are dismissed, when all else fails, by appeal to the remaining margin of divine mystery. This or that challenge cannot be answered, it is said, not because it is unanswerable but because the response lies in that portion of the divine that remains inscrutable. The doctrine of the mystery of

God, thus, has yielded to the doctrine of God's disclosure, and in the process it has become the grounds for, and defender of, the human pretense to absoluteness, not its corrosive critic.

Against this strain dominant in Christian theology, however, there has persisted an alternative assertion, the apophatic claim that God, and thus God's will, is not knowable. The apophatic impulse, in Christian history, is rooted in what is commonly referred to as the prophetic tradition of the Hebrew Bible, according to which God's ways are never to be assimilated to human images, actions, or ideas.[2] This impulse never gained dominance, but it continued to assert itself through claims that God simply is (Exodus 3:14), that God is incomparable (Isaiah 40:18), that God is unknowable (Job 36:26), and so forth. The christologies of the New Testament did not necessarily abrogate the apophatic approach to God, at least insofar as they intended simply to claim that Jesus is "the way, the truth, and the life" (John 14:6), but the identity language (equating Jesus and God) to which they became vulnerable in Christian interpretation seriously threatened the insight that God is mystery. Thus Jesus became *God's* way, truth, and life, knowable by all, to which no others could compare and in relation to which no others could be justified.

It is somewhat surprising, therefore, that the apophatic insight persisted at all in Christian history. But it did—albeit, again, as one subdued theme in considerable tension with other elements of the tradition. Augustine said, "If you have understood, then this is not God."[3] Anselm declared, "Therefore, O Lord, . . . thou art a being greater than can be conceived."[4] And Aquinas insisted, "we cannot know what God is, only what God is not."[5] Each theologian—and the many others, ancient and modern, who have voiced similar conclusions about our knowledge of God—goes on to compromise the apophatic insight, and to do so quite obviously. This is illustrated by one contemporary theologian who writes: "Revelation . . . does not and cannot dissolve the mystery of God. In its light we see ever more clearly the incomprehensibility of God [and then she adds] as . . . free and liberating love."[6] Not that theologians have necessarily been oblivious to their apparently contradictory practice. David Burrell, in fact, says that explaining how it is possible to know the unknowable God is the "quintessential theological task."[7] The strategies for doing so are numerous: claims both that "we know" and "we are unable to know" can be maintained simultaneously, it is said, because they belong to different levels of discourse or apply to different aspects of deity, or because their tension denotes something distinctive about humans or God or our relationship, or, indeed, because their very contradictoriness is itself proper to the mystery of God.[8] As subtle as these strategies may be, however, they all qualify the unknowability of

God, not simply in the valid sense that if God were totally unknowable then even that assertion about God would be impossible, but also in the sense that the mystery of God is, in the final analysis, substantively circumscribed. Some positive knowledge of God is salvaged, some knowledge about or from which we can deduce God's will, to which we can then appeal to justify and elevate our ideas, our ways of life, our agendas and projects and programs against all other merely human points of view. In short, the apophatic vision is abandoned and the basis for the human pretense to absoluteness is reinserted into the Christian theological framework. The impulse to kill, whoever or whatever we wish and in whatever way, can once again be grounded in God's will.

Robert Neville's understanding of God as creation *ex nihilo*, when it is consistently developed, provides a systematic framework for recovering, clarifying and, most important, for *protecting* the apophatic Christian tradition against compromise, and it allows the integration of this tradition into a viable contemporary Christian vision. That will be my argument.

NEVILLE'S CONCEPT OF GOD THE CREATOR

Neville's view of God as creator seems to have developed in conversation with the process theism of Whitehead and Hartshorne. They and their theological interpreters constructed a view of God as the supreme persuasive power for good in the cosmic process. The Whiteheadian God is in many respects profoundly appealing to modern religious sensibilities. "The fellow sufferer who understands," "the poet of the world's becoming," "the lure toward higher and richer forms of life"— these and other apt characterizations of the process God reflect at once the ethical, teleological, and existential components of Western and particularly Christian spirituality. The points at which the process God differs from that of classical Christianity have not necessarily hindered its religious availability. For example, the process God is not omnipotent or omniscient in anything like the traditional senses of these terms, but these differences are an advantage because they legitimate religiously the senses of contingency and even tragedy that so strongly mark the modern spirit and, of course, they at least set to one side the problem of theodicy that has dogged classical theism throughout its history. These theological innovations, then, make sense in an era of dizzying change and massive destruction.

Neville, however, has been a persistent critic of this process theism even while sharing with those whom he criticizes an appreciation of the Whiteheadian process cosmology. Indeed, Neville is a process thinker of the first importance, and if "theology" can be extended to the entire domain of religious reflection he is as much a process theologian as anyone around. But for Neville himself "theology" is more narrowly and traditionally conceived as disciplined talk about God and it is the Whiteheadian process theology, in this restricted sense, that Neville finds wanting. His criticisms are several, not all of which, in my judgment, are compelling.

Neville argues, for example, that in the Whiteheadian view of God, at least as adumbrated by Hartshorne, the tragedy of tragedy is diminished because "nothing really perishes from God's memory; the world is fundamentally cumulative and lasting. . . . Tragedy can only be the short-run view."[9] If this is intended as a reading of Whitehead, I think it is wrong. For Whitehead the *fullness* of God's prehension of the world, that is, the preservation of everything in God's consequent nature, is not a metaphysical necessity; the claim that God saves all is based on a hopeful "rendering of the facts."[10] Moreover, it is a rendering that Whitehead himself seemed not altogether able to share. Whitehead's affirmation that God loses nothing "that can be saved"[11] makes little sense unless it is being assumed that there are some things even God cannot redeem. But even so, the preservation of everything in God would not in itself mitigate tragedy. If, that is, tragedy is viewed as value that "might have been, and was not,"[12] the fact that God remembers this loss everlastingly does not eliminate it; rather it gives to tragedy a cosmic permanence.[13] There is, of course, the passage in which Whitehead speaks of God weaving feelings derived from the world on to God's conceptual feelings in such a way as to give the loss of value ingredient in those physical feelings a broader and presumably more positive context.[14] But such a vision by no means entails the erasure of all such loss, and among Whiteheadians only Marjorie Suchocki, so far as I know, makes the claim that this conceptual weaving in the divine life somehow means the "end of evil."[15] In sum, a Whiteheadian God need not diminish the tragedy of tragedy, and the most plausible interpretation of Whitehead, in my reading, is that the world is tragic and so is his God.

Neville also criticizes Whitehead for the inability of his God to prehend actual entities in their concrescence and, by extension, for this God's inability to prehend us in our subjective becoming. Neville's claim is quite true, but of debateable importance. The issue is complicated because on Whitehead's view of an actual entity there is nothing to know "part way" through concrescence. The subjectivity of an actual occasion is nothing at all, until it achieves satisfaction and hence is objective. But this paradoxical view of concrescence is not what Neville challenges. He objects that the interiority of the becoming occasion, however that is to be construed, is not prehended by God. "God can not know people in the subjective immediacy of their heart," Neville says.[16] Whether not being totally exposed to God constitutes a religious defect is something that might be questioned, but admittedly there are traditions of piety in which that kind of divine-human immediacy is important. It is odd, however, that Neville himself would launch this complaint, for two reasons. First, this is the same critic who in another context accuses the Whiteheadian God of being "a smother-mother."[17] Now, however, Neville is objecting because there is an area of the personal life into which, for an infinitesimally small moment, God cannot intrude. But, secondly, those who are likely to dismiss the Whiteheadian God because he cannot prehend them in their subjectivity will not be more satisfied by a Nevillean God who cannot prehend at all. A grocer who does not sell produce should not criticize a competitor for not selling bananas! In any case, I doubt if the crucial religious issue is the timing of God's knowledge of us, or, for that matter the timing of our knowledge of God.[18] What is religiously important, I suspect, is the character of our knowledge of God, and on this Neville's view is quite interesting, as we shall see.

Robert Neville's most compelling argument against the Whiteheadians is both metaphysical and religious in character. It is his observation, first, that a strictly Whiteheadian theism has no answer to the ontological question—Why is there something rather than nothing?—and, second, that Whiteheadian theism cannot accommodate the widespread religious predilection to somehow associate divinity with the fundamental ground of things. For Whitehead, the metaphysical ultimate is Creativity, with its everlasting process of ones and manys. Whitehead's God is a creature of Creativity. The problem with this formulation is twofold: First, Creativity in Whitehead's scheme is a cosmological process that itself begs for explanation. Why is there an everlasting creative process and not no process at all? Second, Whitehead's God—that in the nature of things that makes for right[19]—accounts for only a part of the religious vision. What is it that makes for a universe at all, within which the right can be sought? Whitehead cannot answer that question.

There are those who think the ontological question need not be answered because the world does not require an explanation. Neville's reply to them is his extensive analysis of the nature of explanation.[20] In many respects Neville's dialogue with his interlocutors on this point is reminiscent of the classic debate between Bertrand Russell and Father Frederick Copleston.[21] At the end of Copleston's lengthy account of the correct, that is, ontological, interpretation of Aquinas' "argument" for a First Cause, Russell remained totally unimpressed. The world is the sum total of all particular things, Russell says in effect, and once one realizes that each particular thing in the world has an explanation it is quite absurd to ask for yet another explanation of these particulars when they are combined because to explain each is to explain them all. To Russell, however, Neville would have replied that the ontological question is not about the "why" of one particular thing or of all particular things together. It is: Why are there particulars at all? What accounts for particularity?

Yet in a rather winsome passage Neville acknowledges that the importance of the ontological question may have much to do with one's fundamental temperament.[22] But temperament, he quickly adds, is not simply an individualistic predisposition; temperament is deeply rooted in the structures of social myth and symbol. The temperament that seeks fundamental or ontological explanations is pervasive enough in human cultures that it should not be summarily dismissed. How it is to be regarded may in the end depend on whether it can be given a clear and coherent explication. Neville's doctrine of creation *ex nihilo* is his effort to provide a clear and coherent account of, and response to, the ontological question.

The religious antecedent of Neville's concept of creation *ex nihilo* is the logic behind the insights of works like the Book of Job and concepts like that of the Logos. Whether or not Job provides a satisfying answer to the theodicy question, its insistence that God's creating is entirely "disanalogous" with human creating is, Neville says, "perhaps the first clear instance of a distinction between ontological and cosmological senses of causation."[23] But if Job uses this distinction to terminate questions about God, Neville uses it to redirect them. And the same ontological/cosmological distinction, put to the same use by Neville, is implicit in the concept of the Logos, through whom all things are created—all things, including the cosmic process of creativity.

Neville's way of clarifying the distinction between ontological and cosmological hinges on another: a distinction between the determinate and the indeterminate. The world is the sum total of things that are determinate.[24] The determinate is not to be equated with the actual as distinguished from the possible. Possibilities, too, are determinate; they are particular possibilities. The world, put another way, is the totality of actual and possible particulars. The ontological question is a question about the explanation of particularity and thus of all particular or determinate things. That which accounts for all determinate things whatsoever cannot be one more determinate thing, hence it must be indeterminate. That is the answer to the ontological question. Neville's term for the indeterminate is creation *ex nihilo* or ontological creativity.

The move from "indeterminateness" to "creation *ex nihilo*" might appear to be an unwarranted inference. How is the indeterminate as such to be equated with the, in some odd sense, determinate ontological process of producing or creating a world? The answer, I think, is that precisely as determinateness is in any particular case necessarily the exclusion of alternative forms of determinateness, so indeterminateness is the exclusion of nothing and thus is the potential for all particulars. Hence indeterminateness necessarily excludes the exclusion of being the potential for all particulars. Thus the character of being "the creating of" all particulars or determinate things is necessarily included as a potential within the indeterminate. The "indeterminate," in other words, is not quite so baldly indeterminate after all—it is the potential for creating particulars that excludes, therefore, the absence of that potential. And if there are determinate things, as evidently there are, then the indeterminate is actually, as well as potentially, the creating of particulars. And if it is, that creation of determinate things is a creation out of the indeterminate, thus out of no thing, thus *ex nihilo*.

Hence about the indeterminate or creation *ex nihilo* one can say nothing. Or more correctly, one can say nothing more. This is important because the indescribability of creation *ex nihilo* is not absolute. About it one can say two things. First, it is the ground, source, or explanation of all things determinate. Second, nothing more about it can be said. The second point is as important as the first. The "mysteriousness" of the indeterminate is not subject to circumvention. We know enough about it to know that claims to know more about it are necessarily false. That would include claims of believers that by some special person or event some additional aspect of the ultimate ground of things has been disclosed. It would also include claims of philosophers and theologians that by some methodological distinction some further talk about God has been permitted. All such claims are false, and false necessarily. Whatever else is said about the indeterminate, other than that it is the explanation of things about which nothing more can be said, is at best misdirected, a claim about something else. If anything at all, it is a claim about the world, not about creation *ex nihilo*.

CHALLENGING AND CHANGING NEVILLE

The stringent apophaticism I have been describing exceeds Neville's own view, for Neville wants to allow talk about God insofar as such talk derives from the nature of the world. Hence, for example, he says that "the divine character is only as good as experience shows it to be as creator of just this world."[25] Or again:

> If the world is the sort of thing a rational agent would create, the creating can be ascribed to a creator who is a rational agent. . . . [I]n all

instances of filling in the character of the divine from the character of
the created world, the creator has no characteristics except those deriving from the world.[26]

Within the framework of Neville's system, however, the only character of the creator to be derived from the world is the character of creating, and that aspect of the divine character is derived from the *fact* that
there is a world, not from anything about the world's contingent nature
or character. This is the case, first, because if creation *ex nihilo* is indeterminate then it is simply indeterminate, and therefore nothing else
determinate can be said about it (e.g., that it is or is not good). But, secondly, there is no basis for supposing that the character of the ontological creator, even if it could be spoken of as having a character, is
reflected in the creation. This is so because (*a*) even in cosmological cre-
atings we can think of good effects that imply nothing about the character of the cause, (*b*) even if on the cosmological plane we could always
infer the quality of a cause from its effect, we have no basis for knowing whether that inference is appropriate at the ontological level, and
(*c*) there is certainly no basis for assuming that we could ascribe intentionality or "agentiality" to indeterminateness as such, whatever it
might produce. Indeed, the very term "creator," while legitimate enough
in itself, might be taken to suggest a subject, an agent, an intender, etc.,
none of which can properly be ascribed to Neville's creation *ex nihilo*.
Neville's God is a not a creator in the sense of being an intentional or
agential subject. In Neville's system, God is "creating *ex nihilo*."

Thus we must also challenge the propriety of Neville's specific way
of speaking about God in trinitarian terms. In doing so Neville distinguishes "God as source of everything determinate, God as the product
or end point of the creative act, and God as the creative activity itself"[27]
or, more succinctly, he distinguishes the "world created, the source of
creation, and the activity itself."[28] But Neville has given us no reason for
distinguishing the source of creation and the activity of ontological creation. The activity is itself the source; the source is an activity. Further,
because the created world is determinate and God is indeterminate,
there is no reason to call the world one of the "identifiable features" of
creation *ex nihilo* except in the very loose and not always informative
sense that every effect is a "feature" of its cause. The interpretations of
the world embodied in different religious and cultural traditions are
important and tell us something about these religions even as they tell
their adherents something about the created world, but they provide no
basis for inferences about the creator.

Neville's doctrine of God would be more adequate if the apophaticism implicit within it were consistently developed. God is the cause,

ground, source, or explanation of all things determinate. Nothing more can be said about God. The mystery of God the creator cannot be lessened by the witness of believers or the reason of philosophers and theologians. The ways of Neville's God are beyond our ways; we do not know this God except as the creating of all that is. Our ignorance is not the function of some epistemological inability that might eventually be overcome, some moral flaw that might be cured, or some strategic failure to look in the right direction or listen in the right way. We can say nothing of God the creator except that God is the source and ground of all things determinate, actual and potential, now and forevermore. That, I believe, is the consistent Nevillean view of God. His theology, properly developed, is an apophatic theology.

When speaking of creation *ex nihilo* Neville sometimes appears to dismiss its religious and practical relevance. Recently, for example, he wrote that "the conception of creation *ex nihilo* . . . has little religious power, little force as a symbol conveying the divine to engagement with human life."[29] Earlier, to be sure, he had insisted that nothing short of the ground . . . of the whole of things is supreme enough to be worshipped"[30] and he has often associated poetry, mystic insight and the work of "profound thinkers" with the contemplation of ontological creativity.[31] But, even in these statements, Neville seems to mean that creation *ex nihilo* acquires its religious worth and importance only insofar as it is conceptually amplified in the additional claims about divinity made by the various religious traditions.

On this I believe Neville is seriously mistaken. Religions differ, of course, and I pretend to make no claim about all religions. But I do think a strong case can be made for the relevance of creation *ex nihilo* to many religions and many forms of religious expression.

First, as Neville notes, there is the prominence of an intellectual interest in ontological origins in many, many cultures and traditions. Why *is* there something and not nothing? Even the analyst who thinks the question can be dismissed as nonsense or a category mistake should find some significance in the fact that the question arises and keeps arising, in many places and many forms. Whether or not the question is philosophically admissible, it is relatively pervasive and usually associated with whatever in a given context is taken to be religion. Far from having little religious force, then, reflection on the ontological question may be at the center of many forms of religion.

Second, the specific answer that Neville and others give to the ontological question connects directly with the experience of contingency, dependence, and mysterious givenness that is frequently associated with religious moods, attitudes, and life forms. Some people not only think about ontological origins, they also *feel* themselves and the world about them to be inexplicable, mysterious. Schleiermacher showed how this feeling, which he called "the feeling of absolute dependence," might be thought central to religion. Neville's view of God is a way to make sense of this experience in theistic terms.

Third, there is the persistence of something we call mysticism. However it is to be characterized, typologized, and even psychologized, people do claim to have modes of awareness or apprehending that do not match our ordinary forms of consciously knowing and analyzing things. Whether or not these phenomena are evidence of anything at all other than that people have them, and whether or not they exclusively have to do with religion, some religious people do have these experiences and they are central to their understanding of their religiousness. More importantly, they are often characterized as being ineffable, or having the ineffable as their object. This is important because if there were an indeterminateness such as Neville postulates, and if it were in some manner or other experienceable, the only thing one could say about what is experienced is that nothing can be said about it, that it is the experience of mystery, the ineffable. Neville's concept of creation *ex nihilo* provides a positive interpretive context for this kind of religious experience and this kind of religious claim.

Fourth, Neville's concept of creation *ex nihilo* is a compelling philosophical framework for understanding and conceptually grounding the apophatic tradition of Christian theology, described above. To this point in Christian history the apophatic perspective has largely been a demand of the pious and an expedient of the apologist. Hence it has been abandoned or compromised whenever the needs of the pious or the apologist have changed. Neville's analysis, consistently developed, shows that *if* one enters the territory demarcated by the ontological question, and *if* one associates whatever is found there with divinity, and *if* what one finds there is the ground of all determinateness, then, necessarily, nothing can be said about it except that it is the creative source of all that is and that nothing else can be said about it. The relevance of Neville's view to a historic form of Christian theology is, of course, another form of religious relevance.

Finally, as indicated at the outset, I believe Neville's doctrine of creation *ex nihilo* is religiously relevant because it is a theistic means of undermining every form of absolutism based on some version of the belief in the knowable nature or will of deity. Religions are fallible interpretations of humans, the world, and human life in the world. An apophatic theology, properly developed and consistently maintained, is a way of affirming deity, the importance of deity, and the persistent claim to a sense of deity in human experience—in short, it is a decidedly religious standpoint that, however, by its very nature thwarts any attempt to use deity to deny the fallibility of our interpretations, to elevate some interpretations above others as a matter of privilege, and to employ those so privileged as weapons of destruction. Religious interpretations, however "religion" is to be construed, are human interpretations of the world. None can claim a basis in the divine. The divine is not known to us, except as the ground of all things whom we cannot capture for our causes. Any standpoint, especially any religious standpoint, that can oppose the destructive potential of absolutes has enormous relevance for religion, society, and culture.

CONCLUSION

Obviously, what religions are concerned about extends well beyond God, well beyond ontological creativity. Religions deal with how the world is and how humans are to understand themselves and to live within the world. The myriad ways these and related concerns are adumbrated and addressed—in feeling, ritual, morality, institutions, and thought—constitute the depth and richness of religions. From the standpoint of an apophatic theology, these are not grounded in, nor are they elliptical or implicit forms of, claims about God. They are claims about the world God creates, made by humans who are a part of that creation. They have the same type of grounds, with the same need for warrants, and the same variety of eccentric formulations and distinctive traits as other claims about the world, whether religious or not.

Specifically Christian interpretations about the world are interpretations of the world grounded in the dynamic and porous traditions of Christian reflection, piety, and practice. And, of course, they may take many forms. To take only some contemporary examples, Christians may hold that the world is so created as to be influenced by "tender elements" that "slowly and quietly operate by love,"[32] or that "inherent in the nature of things . . . is a character of permanent rightness,"[33] or that the cosmic process gives evidence of a serendipity within "persuading [it] to aim at fineness beyond the faded level of surrounding fact,"[34] or that there might be an even larger reach of subjectivity than our own that in some sense understands our sufferings[35] and values our achievements.[36] Such claims about the created process, however, are just that—human claims about the character of the natural and human world grounded in God, not claims about God. They speak out of specific historical circumstances about that in history with which we might align our efforts and to which we might devote our energies, not about absolutes we are entitled to worship. The apophatic Christian theologian will be attentive to these and any other Christian ideas of the world in the context of their concrete communal practices, asking about their warrants, their coherence with the rest of what we think we know, and their potential for good and ill. Therefore, an apophatic theology will be a historicism, a naturalism and humanism, and a pragmatism.

The Christian apophatic theologian, however, could also contribute to the heritage of Christian trinitarian reflection, even if in a nontraditional but quite interesting way. The three elements of such a theology might be *the creating* that is the source and ground of the world, *the disclosing* that is taken to be the key to the character of the world, and *the confirming* that is taken to be the varied and always somewhat evanescent support for one interpretation of the world rather than another. The parallel with traditional Christian talk about the God who creates, the Christ who reveals, and the Spirit who confirms and nurtures is obvious. But, an apophatic christology is a claim about the key to the *world's* structure or logos, that is, the way created things are to be understood, and an apophatic pneumatology is a claim about the dynamics of the *world* as they are immediately experienced, dynamics that confirm the adherent and sustain him or her in this way of living. Christian claims about the disclosing and the confirming, about the world, stand in principle on a par with all other comprehensive interpretations of the world, no more free of fallibility and no more exempt from scrutiny than are they.[37]

From the apophatic standpoint all Christian claims about Christ and Spirit, about the disclosing and confirming, are ways of speaking about the world, not its source. They are attempts to understand the creation in which we live and how we should live within it. They are not claims about God the creating, for God is mystery.

NOTES

1. Delwin Brown, *Boundaries of Our Habitations: Tradition and Theological Construction* (Albany: State University of New York Press, 1994). For other current elaborations of theological historicism, see especially William D. Dean, *History Making History: The New Historicism in American Religious Thought* (Albany: State University of New York Press, 1988); Linell E. Cady, *Religion, Theology and American Public Life* (Albany: State University of New York Press, 1993); and, most recently and comprehensively, Sheila Greeve Davaney, *Pragmatic Historicism: Reconstructing the Theological Task* (forthcoming).

2. David L. Petersen has argued that this is much too restrictive a portrayal of the Hebrew prophets, their views, and their roles, in D. Petersen, ed., *Prophecy in Israel: Search for an Identity* (Philadelphia: Fortress Press, 1987).

3. Augustine, *Sermon 52*, section 16.

4. Anselm, *Proslogium*, chapter xv.

5. Thomas Aquinas, *Summa Theologiae*, Ia, question 3, preface.

6. Elizabeth Johnson, *She Who Is: The Mystery of God in Feminist Theological Discourse* (New York: Crossroad Publishing, 1992), p. 105.

7. David B. Burrell, *Knowing the Unknowable God: Ibn-Sina, Maimonides, Aquinas* (Notre Dame: University of Notre Dame Press, 1986), p. 2.

8. For discussions of the apophatic tradition in Christian theology, see especially David Burrell, *Knowing the Unknowable God* (Notre Dame: University of Notre Dame Press, 1986); William J. Hill, *Knowing the Unknown God* (New York: Philosophical Library, 1971) and *The Three-Personed God* (Washington, D.C.: Catholic University of America Press, 1982), esp. part III; Joseph C. McLelland, *God the Anonymous: A Study in Alexandrian Philosophical Theology* (Philadelphia: The Patristic Foundation, 1976); and Karl Rahner, "The Concept of Mystery in Catholic Theology," in *Theological Investigations*, vol. 4 (New York: Crossroad Publishing, 1980–92), pp. 36–73.

9. Robert Neville, *Creativity and God: A Challenge to Process Theology* (New York: Seabury Press, 1980), p. 68.

10. Alfred North Whitehead, *Process and Reality* (New York: Macmillan, 1929), p. 521.

11. Whitehead, *Process and Reality*, p. 525.

12. Alfred North Whitehead, *Adventures of Ideas* (New York: Macmillan, 1933), p. 369.

13. cf. Whitehead, *Adventures of Ideas*, p. 368.

14. Whitehead, *Process and Reality*, p. 525.

15. Marjorie Suchocki, *The End of Evil: Process Eschatology in Historical Perspective* (Albany: State University of New York Press, 1988).

16. Neville, *Creativity and God*, p. 17.

17. Ibid., p. 9.

18. Ibid., p. 17f.

19. Alfred North Whitehead, *Religion in the Making* (New York: Macmillan, 1926), p. 61.

20. See Robert Neville, *Behind the Masks of God: An Essay Toward Comparative Theology* (Albany: State University of New York Press, 1991), pp. 96–98, and *A Theology Primer* (Albany: State University of New York Press, 1991), p. 34f.

21. See John Hick, ed., *The Existence of God* (New York: Macmillan, 1964), pp. 167–91.

22. Neville, *Behind the Masks of God*, p. 98.

23. Neville, *A Theology Primer*, p. 29.

24. Ibid., p. 30.

25. Neville, *Creativity and God*, p. 12.

26. Neville, *A Theology Primer*, p. 29; cf. *Behind the Masks of God*, p. 2.

27. Neville, *A Theology Primer*, p. 39.

28. Neville, *Behind the Masks of God*, p. 13; cf. p. 21.

29. Neville, *A Theology Primer*, p. 29f; cf. p. 32.

30. Neville, *Creativity and God*, p. 14.

31. See, e.g., Neville, *A Theology Primer*, pp. 16, 21f, 26.

32. Whitehead, *Process and Reality*, p. 520.

33. Whitehead, *Religion in the Making*, p. 61.

34. Whitehead, *Adventures of Ideas*, p. 368.

35. Whitehead, *Process and Reality*, p. 532.

36. Whitehead, *Adventures of Ideas*, pp. 353, 367.

37. Curiously, as in the dominant Western Christian trinity, the disclosing or second element proceeds from the creating or the first element, and the confirming or third element proceeds from both the creating and the disclosing, for that which is taken to be a potential confirmation derives from that which is taken to be the clue to things and both, of course, derive from the creating itself.

CHAPTER 12

Neville's Theology:
A Feminist and Process Dialogue

Marjorie Hewitt Suchocki

To read *A Theology Primer*[1] puts one in mind of Thomas Aquinas and his reasons for writing the *Summa Theologica*. The Angelic Doctor had the task of teaching introductory theology to beginning students. Despairing of the difficulties his students had as they attempted to grapple with the *Sentences* and other respectable theological writings of the day, Thomas decided to take matters into his own hands. He designed and wrote a simple, introductory text to ease his students into the study of theology, thus bringing the great *Summa Theologica* into existence. But the judgment of seminarians through the past eight hundred years is that the *Summa* is less than an easy introduction, creating opportunities for numerous theologians since Thomas to write introductions to his introductory text.

Robert Neville has not yet been dubbed an "Angelic Doctor," but surely his own introductory text rivals the great Doctor's as a call for an introduction to his introduction to theology. Neville bases his treatment of major doctrines of the Christian church in a subtle metaphysics that must itself be thoroughly understood in order to grasp the import of his doctrinal developments. Others writing for this volume will explore the intricacies of Neville's metaphysics; my task in this essay is to probe his theology from the perspective of a feminist and process point of view. But in order to do so I must sketch out at least those aspects of his metaphysics that are given in the first chapters of *A Theology Primer*, since these are essential to every aspect of his theology, and provide the necessary basis upon which feminist and process questions may be raised. Through this questioning I hope to find myself in the happy position, like the commentators and questioners of that angelic doctor of old, of clarifying or highlighting Neville's important contribution to theology in our own time.

THE METAPHYSICS: ONTOLOGY/COSMOLOGY

Neville argues that the continuing importance of metaphysics for theology rests in the necessity of developing a theory of God that is coherent with one's theories about the universe in general. That is, given a "closed system" of the universe, religious symbols of the divine can only make sense if there is ground within the universe for positing a referentiality to the symbols. Otherwise, the arbitrariness of God jars the coherence of religious belief. And so Neville follows his own injunction by beginning introductory theology with exploration of the role of God within the closed system of the universe as we know it.

Determinateness is the key to Neville's understanding of the world, and therefore of God insofar as God is creator of the world (universe). The one universal quality of everything existent is that it is in fact determinate. It is this, and not that; it has these characteristics, by virtue of which it is itself and no other. There is no existent reality that is not determinate. Determinateness is therefore a universal character of existence per se, and thus the "measure" that defines the "all" of things as "universe."

Determinateness, upon analysis, consists in a harmony of essential (ontological) and conditional (cosmological) features.[2] Neville's treatment of these features is much like Alfred North Whitehead's treatment of abstractions in *Science and the Modern World*. That is, for Whitehead each possibility is what it is both in relation to itself, and in relation to all other things. The relation to itself is "essential," but by virtue of being itself it also relates to all other things in graded hierarchies of importance, and this is the "conditional" nature of every possibility. In Neville's analysis, the "redness" of the color red is its essential feature, and that which puts it in distinctive relationship to other colors, to the class of colors, and—or so he could have added—in relation to all other abstract possibilities. In principle, there is nothing to which the color red could not connect in either positive or negative fashion. The coherent togetherness of both essential and conditional features as aspects of the one determinate reality is what Neville terms "harmony."[3]

The importance of this notion of determinateness cannot be overemphasized in Neville's system. It is the means by which he establishes the referentiality of God, and hence the metaphysical as well as psychological importance of all references to the divine. Because of determinateness, the notion of God cannot be reduced solely to psychological states of the human mind or to social constructions projected as part of the organizing structure of human community. The caveat, however, is that God is not only the ground of determinateness, but *also* embodies determinateness, so that God is a harmony of essential and conditional features. Insofar as God is conditional, God is determined by other determinate realities, which is to say that the divine is conditioned by the world. Further, any knowledge of the divine must be in and through this conditioned determinacy added to God through relation to the world.

Determinateness allows the referentiality of God in this fashion: To be determinate is to be conditioned by otherness; hence all determinate things must find their causes at least partially in otherness. This refers to those "things" we call "laws of nature" as well as to the "this" and "that" of the physical world. Consequently, existence per se requires referentiality. But what referentiality makes "laws of nature" what they are? For these are more than abstract descriptions of the way of things, they are principles that themselves require a cause beyond simple referentiality to their instantiations. Neville's move is to argue that the only reasonable explanation is that they came into being as a result of "*creatio ex nihilo*," that they can only be accounted for by the positing of a divine reality sufficient to bring them into existence. Further, the conditioned nature of things depends on their essential givenness, which cannot itself be accounted for through conditionedness. The possibility for the togetherness of essential-conditioned existences must lie outside of their givenness to each other; it rests within their joint emergence through the creative activity of God. Thus the determinateness of the reality we know is itself an argument for the referentiality of God as creator *ex nihilo*. I will leave it to the Kantians among us to raise questions concerning this revival of the cosmological argument; I turn instead to a second feature of Neville's determinacy that deeply frames his theology: the Logos structure of reality.

Logos follows from Neville's description of the triadic structure of the divine. God as determinate must logically be source (which cannot yet be considered determinate), terminus of the creative act (since such creation defines God), and creative activity (or the dynamism that allows the source/terminus relation).[4] Clearly, this will provide Neville with an opening for a unique development of the trinity, but his major theological focus is on the second of the triadic terms: God as the terminus of the creative act, or Logos. This is his basis for a doctrine of incarnation, which in turn becomes the determination of God in history that allows us a basis for revelatory knowledge of God, and through this knowledge, the emergence of creation as covenant. Apart from Logos, God would be absolutely unknowable, for God can only be known by God's effects. And those effects are Logos.

The metaphysical structure of the Logos is all-important for Neville's theology of sin and redemption. Logos, as the determination that is the creation, is necessarily fourfold: form, components to be formed, their actual mixture, and value as the cause of their mixture.[5] This fourfold structure creates the interrelatedness of that which exists. As such, it also grounds the interpretation of existence as "covenant," and covenant, in turn, provides the definition of sin as failing to live according to the covenant. Neville works numerologically with the threefold structure of creation, the fourfold structure of Logos, and the fivefold structure of covenant. But just as "logos" is contained within the triadic structure of creation, even so covenant is contained within the quadratic structure of Logos. The fifth element that turns Logos into covenant is love, that which binds the disparate aspects of Logos together within creation. Covenant presupposes both Logos and creation.

Covenant provides identity in relation to God, presumably through the very act of being created by God. Neville wishes to move from an individualistic reading of this relation, and so asserts that our identity in relation to God is that God has created many, and therefore we relate not only to God, but also to all that God has created. By virtue of originating from a single creator, we are in relation to one another.

Traditionally the concept of "father" has been used to convey this sense, given the analogy that all children of the same parent are siblings, related to one another through genetic and contextual identity. Presumably informed by feminist sensibilities, Neville does not use the construct of "father," but it's not clear that stemming from a common *creatio ex nihilo* is sufficient to establish relational identity. If each creature is *ex nihilo*, the connection between creatures would seem to be arbitrary rather than obvious. In a process view, the interrelational dependence follows from internal relations established through prehension, and Neville could also draw on this through the "components" aspect of Logos. Instead, he seems to establish the necessity for mutual relations among one another to the created essence of each individual by God, with one's identity as creature-among-creatures established in the very essence of the individual. Further, God as the terminus of each created act is also participant in each created act, so that through this pervasiveness of the divine a common link is established among creatures. Covenant lifts this linking to the forefront as essential to one's identity.[6]

With the threefold structure of creation, the fourfold structure of Logos, and the fivefold structure of covenant, we have completed this sketch of Neville's metaphysics as required for interface with his actual theology. To that we now turn, first with a feminist critique, and second to theological questions raised from the point of view of process theology.

A FEMINIST CRITIQUE

Early in the *Primer*, Neville writes, "At the present time, I believe, no other systematic theology attempts to reconstitute Christian categories so as to incorporate major feminist concerns as thoroughly as the *Primer's.*"[7] This is a curious claim, to which exceptions abound. At least four important precedents are well known. One of the earliest works in feminist theology is Mary Daly's 1973 *Beyond God the Father*,[8] in which she systematically addresses each major theme of Christian doctrine. Her work is both highly critical and constructive. She deconstructs each doctrine according to its patriarchal bias, and reconstructs the doctrine according to feminist and—at that time in her journey—Christian sensitivities. Feminists surely claim this book as a groundbreaking systematic treatment of Christian doctrine that takes feminist concerns eminently into account. Why does Neville not do so?

The next explicitly systematic treatment of Christian doctrine from a feminist perspective was (I blush to remind him) my own 1982 *God-Christ-Church*.[9] This is a systematic process theology written by a feminist, and has some strong claims to thoroughness in incorporating major feminist concerns. Like Neville's work, my own depends heavily upon a description of the metaphysical structure of existence. My reinterpretion of Christian doctrine is fashioned through a grid created by the blending of process thought, the Christian historical/biblical tradition, and feminist theology. What is Neville's criteria, that this book does not qualify as a systematic theology incorporating feminist concerns?

Rosemary Radford Ruether's *Sexism and God-Talk*[10] followed soon in 1983. While Ruether's work modestly claims to be "toward" a feminist theology, just as surely as Neville she treats the various subject matters of Christian theology. Her work is systematic insofar as she strives for an inner coherence among these doctrines, and insofar as she uses the same guiding principles (feminist experience and a "prophetic principle" she claims as central to the Christian biblical and historical tradition) to develop each doctrine. Neville uses her work, but claims she does not have a "systematic structure, although [her] orientation is systematic."[11] He does not clarify the distinction between a systematic structure and a systematic orientation, but evidently it is sufficient to disqualify this feminist theology from vying with his own in taking feminist concerns into account.

Sallie McFague has written a series of four books that systematically explore a reconstruction of Christian theology through the rubric of guiding metaphors, the most significant of which is "the world as God's body."[12] The focus of her work is on the relation between God and the world, with an ever-present testing of the theology's implications and effects on our relationships with each other and with our environing earth. She treats doctrines of God, human nature, freedom, Christology, and ecclesiology throughout the series. Feminist concerns are explicitly woven into all four books. Is it because the doctrines are not dealt with *seriatum* in one book that she fails of Neville's criteria?

Given the above as a minimal survey of books in systematic theology written by feminists, it is surely curious that Neville overlooks—and thus disqualifies—theologies written by women as properly meeting the criterion of incorporating major feminist concerns. Those very concerns, however, suggest that one can systematically develop theology in ways that do not necessarily depend upon a metaphysics—and may in fact be highly critical of such dependency. But this does not render such theologies nonsystematic; rather, the system within which the theology is developed may well depend upon the coherence given to existence through multifaceted ethical principles drawn from the root assumption that existence is relationally interdependent. Insofar as these principles are systematically applied to the redevelopment of doctrine, with attention to the inner coherence that connects the doctrines, the resulting theology legitimately lays claim to being systematic. On this basis, many feminist theologies systematically explore a variety of ways to express Christian faith; this needs to be taken into account by Neville as he judges his own work relative to feminist concerns.

It may be that Neville's discounting of the systematic nature of feminist works leads him into a rather egregious misappropriation of feminist concerns in his development of the Logos. The fourfold structure of the Logos is, as mentioned above, "form, components to be formed, their actual mixture, and value as the cause of their mixture."[13] Neville identifies "form" with religious expressions of a male Sky God who is the source of moral and social order, righteousness, and judgment. At this point Neville seems to be speaking descriptively rather than prescriptively; he is describing androcentric expressions of God. However, his grounding of such descriptions in the "form" aspect of the Logos gives these expressions a legitimacy that Neville does not seek to deny.

Predictably, the second element of the Logos—components to be formed—becomes the female "Mother Nature" or the "Earth Mother." "She" represents fertility and the powers of nature; she is chaotic and amoral, and is that which the Sky God must control through the imposition of order. Happily, Neville does not identify this feminine component of the Logos with evil—nor could he, since for him it is an expression of God. Nor does he place a negative value on chaos. But his naming of chaos as feminine, combined with his naming of social and moral order as masculine, perpetuates the stereotype that to be male is to be ordered, rational, and righteous, whereas to be female is to be chaotic, subrational (intuitive?), and—with an allusion to Whitehead—a little oblivious as to morals. Since the masculine principle by definition rules over the feminine principle (even though the mystery of the feminine eludes all attempts for full control), is it not socially acceptable then that men are to rule women—to "civilize" women, if you will, insofar as their chaotic and amoral characters make this possible? Such stereotyping has worked against the interests of women for millennia. One can easily recognize that human existence in this world involves form, moral and social order, and the environing, intricate, and often chaotic-appearing elements of the nonhuman world. But there is every reason to disassociate this recognition from the age-old tendency to personify one as masculine and the other as feminine. Why must these qualities be gendered? Why perpetuate the stereotypes that have wreaked such harm on women?

While feminist concerns do raise a serious and deep critique of Western attitudes and actions toward nature (McFague in particular insists upon the transformation of Christianity toward ecological consciousness and action), feminists do not make a primary distinction between "male" and "female" on the basis of women's supposed closer affinity with nature.[14] To do so is to perpetuate negative stereotypes that assign rationality, morality, and social order to men (who are therefore presumably more capable of running society) and their negative opposite to women (who are therefore presumably most suited to the nurturing activities of the home). The irony of the stereotype is that the one invariable theme in all feminist work is the call toward the creation of a more just social order. If this is identified symbolically as a "masculine" trait, we have the absurdity that all feminists are therefore "masculine." As to the "Mother Earth" nomenclature for nonhuman nature, Nancy Frankenberry has put the issue most succinctly: "The earth is not your mother."[15]

Neville could learn of another feminist way of dealing with so-called male and so-called female aspects of God through Rosemary Radford Ruether's *Gaia and God*, published a year later than *A Theology Primer*.[16] Ruether, like Neville, takes account of the stereotypical association of the male with order and the female with nature, but she conflates the two in a "coincidence of opposites," and de-genders them in the process. Thus the ability to associate men with ordering and women with being ordered is totally undercut in her treatment.

It is interesting to see the further implications of Neville's identification of earth/nature as feminine in his treatment of the covenant and its breaking, which is sin. The covenant is the transliteration of the fourfold structure of the Logos into five moral qualities required of us as creatures. The form/male/sky-god equation yields righteousness as a covenantal virtue; the components/female/earth-mother equation yields piety as a covenantal virtue. Piety is the honoring of the powers of nature, whether or not they are organized to serve the human good.[17] The other moral requirements of covenant, in keeping with its Logos structure, are the "faith to embrace the actuality of circumstances," which correlates with the actual mixture of things, and "hope" as the process of "finding our center in the cosmos and relative to God," which correlates with value.[18] The fifth component is not a separate virtue, but is rather the integrative virtue of "love," binding all the elements together, even in their disparity. Thus the Logos structure of existence involves all creation (insofar as applicable) in the moral structure of the covenant, which is righteousness, piety, faith, hope, and love.

The equation of the second element of the Logos (and covenant) with the female has unfortunate ramifications in Neville's development of sin. Sin becomes the breaking of the covenant. Note that the covenant need not be "given" at any historical moment; it is simply woven into the structure of existence as a requirement for how we should live. When we do not live that way, we have broken the covenant, which is to say that we have violated the very structures that call us into existence. This is, by definition, a corruption of our nature. It leads to the opposite of the covenantal qualities: unrighteousness, impiety, faithlessness, despair. The breaking of any component of the covenant is at the same time the violation of love, which otherwise holds the disparate elements together in harmony.

Given the peculiar equation of the female with the second component of the Logos and covenant, it is instructive to examine impiety—the violation of piety—in light of feminist concerns. Neville notes that "the feminine dimension of religion focuses on the components of things organized below the level of the human moral orders, at the level of component. Of course the components have their own order, and the feminine is related to the order of nature untamed, or perhaps tameable. Furthermore, the feminine is associated with the nexuses and connections that make possible the explicit orders of the moral and political scale, the connections of family and domesticity."[19] The sin of impiety, then, tends toward a passivity in failure to honor these feminine aspects. It also has an active component, to be examined below, but the passive dominates. In the masculine form of sin, however, the active dominates. This is the objective harm done to neighbors, institutions, and nature.[20] It is at heart the rejection of God's covenant and therefore the corruption of one's very nature, which is constituted in and through this covenant. Again, we are in the realm of stereotypical masculine and feminine qualities relative to sin.[21]

By definition, the masculine presents a clear delineation of right and wrong relative to neighbor and institutions, but it encounters an ambiguity relative to harm done to nature. This is due to the "feminine" character of nature, which is defined as deeper than the masculine moral order (hence its "amoral" quality as defined above), and as inevitably entailing conflicting values. Hence the "feminine" is irreducible to matters of right moral order.[22] There is in the feminine, then, not only a certain amorality, but also that which defies morality. Is it such a short step from this to equating the feminine—and women?—with evil and sin in a more primordial way than is the case with men? Relative to the masculine, the feminine stands in negative opposition, whereas the masculine relative to the feminine stands in a righteous ordering position.[23] The problem is not Neville's delineation of the ambiguities necessarily involved in human existence, but his identification of the root of these ambiguities, amoralities, and immoralities as feminine. Had he truly taken feminist concerns into account in his theology, he could not have fallen into this error.

But thus far we have only identified the inherent opposition to morality that Neville identifies with the feminine. In one sense, this is a passive breaking of the covenant, since it is a natural opposition to righteousness. But impiety can also have an active form. Impiety is both subjective and objective: subjectively, it is a failure to appreciate the value of things in themselves; objectively, it is the acting on this failure through direct "abuse, neglect, or subordination to moral concerns of the things perceived as components of our world."[24] We can become so preoccupied with justice and morality that we fail to value the naturalness and inherent value of things, or the wholeness of the created order. We fail to recognize the divine presence that permeates creation. We are impious.

But why is this particularly related to the feminine? Women are feminine. Do women as a class fail to appreciate the value of things—or, in its more positive covenantal form, do women more particularly than men appreciate the value of things? Are women inclined to subordinate nature to justice and morality? Or, when men do this, are they somehow succumbing to a distortion of the feminine? In his effort to give equal place to women and men, Neville has caricatured both unnecessarily. A fine analysis of existence as covenant falls prey to the weakness of stereotypes all too pervasive in religious traditions, to the detriment of women and men. In his treatment of faith, hope, and love, Neville kicks away the masculine/feminine stereotypes and deals with these virtues simply as human qualities built into the structure of existence which, when violated, lead to a corruption of that structure. I suggest that righteousness and piety and their negative corollaries likewise would benefit enormously if the stereotypical link to masculine and feminine were severed, letting the analysis stand as a description of the human situation, applying equally to men and women.

Principles are neither male nor female—only people and other animals that perpetuate themselves by sexual reproduction are. "Masculine" and "feminine" should be confined to actual descriptions of actual men and women, with "masculine" defined by any and every man, and "feminine" defined by any and every woman. Let the words be no more than adjectival forms of real men and real women, ejected forever from arbitrary assignation to things or principles that are neither male nor female, but which, once gendered, constrict men and women into straitened conformity with their preestablished givens. This is a feminist concern: would that it were "incorporated thoroughly" into Neville's systematic theology.

A PROCESS QUESTION: ESCHATOLOGY?

Neville directly addresses all of the major doctrines of Christian theology but one: eschatology. The omission is interesting, particularly given the care with which he develops the ontological structure of existence. Given ontology, one should be able to deal with the question of eschatology, whether positively or negatively. Process theologians apply their metaphysics to the question of eschatology, albeit in a variety of ways.[25] The point, however, is not uniformity of interpretation, but the power of metaphysics to project that which is not yet a part of experience.[26] Can Neville's ontology yield an eschatology?

Eschatology, of course, has two foci: justice within the human community within the confines of history, and redress beyond the human community within the life of God. Neville surely speaks to justice within the human community as the goal of the covenant, but he is silent about the more traditional aspect of eschatology, the life of the world within God. If eschatology were simply a way of sliding out of life's ambiguities and tragedies through a "pie-in-the-sky-bye-and-bye" phenomenon, then this form of eschatology would hardly be worth addressing within contemporary theology. But insofar as any theology must deal with the effects of evil, and insofar as theology recognizes that for many persons and causes evil is the last word in history, then every theology must at least address the question of redress or reconciliation beyond that offered by history. The way of addressing the issue may indeed be to argue that the issue is unresolvable within the data of history or the assumptions of theology—but to leave the issue unaddressed is to leave theology incomplete. Neville accepts the tragedy of history, and develops a notion of the relation of history to eternity—but he fails to apply this notion to the issue of eschatology. Why?

The seeds of eschatology are contained in Neville's intriguing section within his trinitarian chapter, "Time and Eternity."[27] His argument has some analogies with "big bang" theories in contemporary physics:

In answer to the question of where the big bang occurred, the answer is "here," because all spaces, times, and conditions are preestablished by the phenomena entailed within that initially posited explosion. The universe as now constituted *is* the "Big Bang"; hence all points are the "where" of that event. Neville argues similarly that eternity contains all time. A thing in time is created in and through its relation to the past and the future. The present of each event is its union of past data and future possibilities within the peculiarity that it constitutes as itself. This is standard "actual entity" fare to a process theologian. But time is itself a condition that conditions. Whether as past, present, or future, time is a determinate reality in all its infinite manifestations. As determinate, it has its source within the indeterminacy of God—eternity. God is thus the ground of all time, without being temporal. But God as terminus of creation, God as determinate, is determinate in and through that which is created. Thus God is source of time, but also recipient of all time. In this sense, God as determinate is so because time qualifies God, even while God is eternal. All times—and the events that constitute time—are "in" God.

Theoretically, this provides a basis for developing the "more than" to historical life demanded by traditional eschatologies, for if all times qualify God, and are "in" God, then one is given leave to discuss what this "in-ness" means. In Neville's system, it could be read to mean no more than the abstraction of what it says: Everything in some sense defines God the creator, and by so saying one has said no more than that something happens in history. Eschatology would then be no more than a tautology. Could Neville go beyond this, and say that in the infinite mystery of God it is possible that there is a "more" to history that offers succor to the tragedies of history? While his system could allow him to state this in principle, it can allow him to go no further. For if the ultimate qualification of God as creator is that God is indeterminate, then this indeterminacy cannot admit the determinacy of relativity to shape God's essence. It is as with the color red that Neville uses as an illustration in discussing conditioned and essential features of reality: red is the essence of the color, that without which it would not be, but all one can say of this essence is the effect of its relation to the varieties of things that are distinct from red. The essence itself is unspeakable, an irreducible datum about which nothing further can be essentially said. Even so, if God is Creator ex Nihilo, ultimate source and therefore ultimate indeterminacy, to posit an effect of creation within this reality is not possible, for it would qualify the unqualifiable. So Neville cannot develop an eschatology that goes beyond history.

His most concrete discussion of eschatology comes not in the body of the book, but in the introduction through his poignant account of

Gwendolyn, the infant daughter of Bob and Beth Neville. He speaks about her baptism within a particular faith community, of the surrounding care and comfort provided by that community when Gwendolyn died at four months of age. This contemporary community mediated the whole church, past and future, in its own compassionate presence to the Neville family. It mediated the past through its embodiment of its history; it mediated the future through its anticipation of generations to come. Thus the community, ministering to the grieving parents, is the embodiment in time of a community that spans time. In this sense, the community participates in eternity.

Also, of course, the community as determinate is one of the effects of the determinacy of God as the enlivening presence in all things. And since God as source is eternity, God's own eternity is present in and to the little child, however brief her life. Eternity, as the ground of time, encompasses time, and is manifest in time. Therefore, the child is embraced by eternity both historically, through the community that itself embodies time past and time future in its presentness, and through God, the ever-present determiner within all things. But by definition one cannot enter the mystery of God beyond the determinacy of creation. One must therefore leave eschatology within the wonder of that mystery.

For those who rest easier within a world in which terrible evils have the last word in the lives of all too many, perhaps this is enough. Perhaps one must leave a Nevillean universe and enter a Whiteheadian one in order to reach some coherent vision of God as the reconciler of all things, as the one who, just as surely as did that community manifesting God's own eternity, touches with living fingertips the tears of those torn by too much sorrow. The difference, of course, is that a process metaphysics applies the actual entity model in reversal to God, positing an eternal primordial nature of possibility and an everlasting consequent nature through reception of the world. The world, entering into that infinite time, participates in its own transformation as God integrates it within the everlasting, everliving concretization of the primordial nature. Neville's God disappears in the mystery of divinity; one can posit no such transformation of the world within God's eternity/everlastingness. Perhaps. Neville, who is so close to process theology in so very many respects, may yet venture closer with his image of eternity.

If God the creator does in fact choose to create (an undeniable concomitant given the universe!) why is it not possible that the determinacy received by God in and through creation should not also enter into the heart—or, in Neville's terminology, essence—of who God is? What if God's indeterminacy, which Neville claims must be highly dynamic, is indeterminate on the order of what we now call chaos theory rather than indeterminate per se? For Neville, the problem is akin to that of infinite regress—if God is at all determinate within the essence of the divine nature, then God stands within the order of causation and needs an indeterminate explanation from some deeper divinity.

But chaos theory within the world suggests that what we have called chaos, or that which is without any form of order whatsoever, is rather to be understood as an order of such complexity that it defies our comprehension. In other words, what appears to be indeterminate is in fact determinate. Neville would argue that appearances to the contrary, he knew chaos was determinate all along, since it is something rather than nothing. But the point might yet be pushed. God is the source of infinite mystery, if totally indeterminate, for we cannot "say" such a God. But in principle, if this God is, then this God has an essence—that without which God would not be God. For Neville, this essence is "indeterminacy." In Whiteheadian terminology, this "essence" would be God's primordial nature—that source of infinite possibility, ordered in infinitely variable permutations of divine harmony. Possibility is indeterminate relative to its instantiation. Why can we not consider Neville's indeterminate God in a similar fashion? Indeed, Neville's closest characterization of essence is in his section that most closely parallels the chapter "Abstractions," which defines what Whitehead will eventually call the primordial nature of God. And what else can indeterminacy be, relative to a creator, than infinite possibility, not yet applicable to a world?

If God's indeterminate essence is akin to infinite possibility, then the determinacy God receives from the world—even from little Gwendolyn—is the actualization of possibility, which itself then becomes part of the determinacy of God. For Neville, this determinacy is embraced within God's eternity. Can this not mean that this determinacy is embraced within God as source? If so, why is it not possible to suggest that determinacy does not simply sit on the edges of God, like some clothing one happens to put on, but that the ever-newly-determinate world is integrated with its source, taking determinacy within God's eternity? Neville speaks of determinacy as a manifestation of eternity; it can be that, but if it is also a determiner of God's eternity, then it must have a return effect on God that takes it deep within God—as source. Or, God as terminus has a twofold end: the actuality of creation, and the actuality of creation's determining effect within God.

Neville's objection comes from his telling nonrelational description of essence. "Red" is "red" is "red," regardless of any relations. The essence of redness, then, is untouched by any determinacy. Likewise with the essence of God—it must remain forever untouched by those determinate edges; else it fails to be the indeterminate source. But if "red" as untouched by determinacy is merely the *possibility* of redness, then redness as actual is precisely *this* redness in relation to this setting. Its essential characteristic as actualized is also relational. But of course to make this move is to move into a Whiteheadian as opposed to a Nevillean universe, where only possibility is indeterminate. If Neville must maintain that the essence of all actuality is indeterminate, then he has no way of moving to a God who is redemptive beyond history.

Furthermore, to carry the speculative vision this far is to make room for the further suggestion that the God who is affected by determinacy must in some sense integrate this determinacy. Otherwise, Neville's own positing of the mutuality of God as source/terminus/creative act is violated, and we have a tritheistic modality for God. But if all determinacy is integrated within God, beyond its own constitution within the world, is there not room for eschatology? May one not hope for Gwendolyn's larger participation in God's full integration of the universe? May not the egregious evils of history meet their further resolution/reconciliation within the mystery of God? For in truth, to admit of a theistic universe without allowing for some redress of history's sorrows seems to me either arrogant or forlorn: arrogant, because the theologian has suffered relatively little in this world, and sees no need for a greater redress of evil than history offers; forlorn, because apart from God's further work with the world beyond its history, the cumulative tragedy of so much human history would seem unbearable.

I suggest, then, that while there are philosophical reasons for Neville's refusal to address eschatology within this *Primer*, he must revisit his speculative vision in light of the eschatological question. He has made the claim that his *Primer* comes from "a long historical process," and that "it is typical of Christian systematic theology from Thomas Aquinas . . . down to Paul Tillich."[28] That process and that typification require treatment of the traditional doctrine of eschatology as life beyond earthly history, even if only to announce the impossibility of dealing with such a question.

CONCLUSION

I have taken Neville to task on his claim to primacy in incorporating feminist concerns into his theology, goaded in part by his cavalier dismissal of feminists as having achieved this goal. For all that, I surely applaud his intention to be thoroughly adequate to feminist insight. With the lamentable and egregious exception of his "earth mother" stereotypes, he has achieved at least a nonsexist systematic theology.

With regard to my questions from a process point of view, I recognize and respect Neville's guarding of the mystery of God. My own process speculations are put forth as possibilities consistent within the process interpretation of the way of things; they relate to the "might be," and do not purport to be what "is." To develop eschatology relative to that which is beyond history is to extend a metaphor beyond its possibility of existential testing; it is an exercise of faith and hope within the confines of "if this . . . then possibly that." Thus to develop an eschatology is not to do violence to the mystery of God; it is to take that mystery with deep seriousness and gratitude as providing some ground to Christian hope both in and beyond history. But perhaps, in the nature of things, the different approaches of Neville and process thought provide a creative tension that preserves both poles in theology. "It could be this way" is countered by "we dare not say," and each offers a caution and correction to the other. I express my deep gratitude to Neville for his side of the tension, expressed so well in *A Theology Primer*.

NOTES

1. Robert Cummings Neville, *A Theology Primer* (New York: State University of New York Press, 1991). All references to Neville in this essay are from this text.

2. Ontology, Neville tells us, relates to the world as God's creation, whereas cosmology has to do with the specificities of that world (see pp. 30, 77, and 85, for example). The distinction between the two is not always clear, given the strong doctrine of creation employed by Neville. That is, God as creator of all that is determinate appears to be the creator of the specificities of the world as well as the creator of the ontological world as such. If God is thus the creator of all things, then isn't the cosmological absorbed into the ontological?

3. The analogies with Whitehead are striking, for Whitehead envisions all possibilities to exist in God's primordial harmony, so that the coherence of each possibility is harmonious in itself, and also a participant and contributor to God's harmony in the primordial nature. However, whereas for Whitehead these myriad possible relations exist as abstractions, Neville apparently wishes to relate them more concretely to actual existence in the world. Thus in Whitehead the conditional (possible) relations are as infinite as the realm of eternal objects, whereas for Neville the conditions are bounded by the actuality of circumstances. It appears that the distinction Whitehead makes between sheer possibilities and real possibilities, both of which are abstract, is transmuted by Neville into possible relations (abstract) and relations actually realized in history (concrete).

4. See Neville, p. 39 for the full discussion.

5. See ibid., p. 45. In Whiteheadian terms, this would be a description of the actual occasion: the form given through the initial aim, the components given through the data prehended from other actual occasions, the mixture which is the concrescence, and the value or satisfaction that is the teleological end of the occasion.

6. Neville's second aspect of covenant expands upon this essential identity of God-and-other relatedness by specifying natural and conventional components. One relates not only to God and other humans, but to the natural world of other animals. The conditional features of existence relate to the particularities of natural and social existence. The human community lives alongside the nonhuman, and that which defines the human as being in community is precisely the social condition of laws regulating interactive behavior.

7. Neville, p. xxiv.

8. Mary Daly, *Beyond God the Father: Toward a Philosophy of Women's Liberation* (Boston: Beacon Press, 1973; revised edition with "Original Reintroduction by the Author" published in 1985).

9. Marjorie Hewitt Suchocki, *God-Christ-Church: A Practical Guide to Process Theology* (New York: Crossroad, 1982).

10. Rosemary Radford Ruether, *Sexism and God-Talk: Toward a Feminist Theology* (San Francisco: Harper, 1983).

11. Neville, p. xviii.

12. McFague recognizes her dependence on Charles Hartshorne for this metaphor and its metaphysical connotations. The works in her series of four are *Metaphorical Theology* (1982), in which she develops her basic methodology, *Models of God* (1987), *The Body of God* (1993), and *Super, Natural Christians* (1997), all published by Fortress Press.

13. Neville, p. 45.

14. Early feminist books in the 1970s sometimes worked from the woman/nature correlation, usually to suggest that the rape of nature was concomitant to the rape of women. The arguments were made that new attitudes toward women would require new attitudes toward nature as well.

15. Nancy Frankenberry, "The Earth Is Not Our Mother: Ecological Responsibility and Feminist Theory," in *Religious Experience and Ecological Responsibility,* ed. Donald Crosby and C. D. Hardwick (New York: Peter Lang, 1996), pp. 23–50.

16. Rosemary Radford Ruether, *Gaia and God: An Ecofeminist Theology of Earth Healing* (San Francisco: Harper, 1992).

17. See Neville, p. 57.

18. Neville, pp. 57 and 58 respectively.

19. Neville, p. 67.

20. Neville, p. 65.

21. This matter has been dealt with extensively by feminists, beginning with Valerie Saiving Goldstein's groundbreaking 1963 article, "The Human Situation: A Feminine View," *Journal of Religion* 40 (April 1960): 100–112. Other formative works are Judith Plaskow's *Sex, Sin and Grace: Women's Experience and the Theologies of Reinhold Niebuhr and Paul Tillich* (New York: University Press of America, 1980), and Susan Nelson Dunfee, "The Sin of Hiding," *Soundings* 65.3 (Fall 1982): 316–27. While Neville purports to take feminine concerns thoroughly into account, he does not utilize any of these texts within the body of his work. Rather, he summarizes Goldstein's position in a footnote. The works by Plaskow and Dunfee are not mentioned.

22. Neville, p. 67.

23. One is reminded of Karl Barth's depiction of evil in male and female terms in his own theology, particularly *Dogmatics in Outline*, where evil is symbolized through three terms: moral evil, typified by the Jew; finite weakness, typified by woman; and finite ambiguity, typified by Pilate who was "righteous against his will." One grows sadly accustomed to the "whitewashing" of evil for the white, non-Semitic male relative to women and others outside that category.

24. Neville, p. 67.

25. Neville dismisses process theology's adequacy with the statement, "It is not yet clear that [process theology] serves to make sense of the needed array of symbols of the divine employed in religious life" (28). But Mary Daly has long taught feminists to ask the useful question of, "'clear' to whom?" when reading such assertions. My own experience of teaching in classrooms, churches, and various other contexts suggests that many persons do indeed find that process theology makes sense of the needed array of symbols of the divine employed in religious life. Many of these persons are women. Would that this were as clear to Neville as it is to them!

26. The most comprehensive work in process theology dealing with eschatology is my own *The End of Evil: Process Eschatology in Historical Context* (Albany: State University of New York Press, 1988). However, the topic is also dealt with in John B. Cobb, Jr. and David R. Griffin's *Process Theology: An Introductory Exposition* (Philadelphia: Westminster, 1976), in Lewis Ford's *The Lure of God* (Philadelphia: Fortress, 1981) and in a number of Charles Hartshorne's articles.

27. Neville, pp. 37–48.

28. Neville, p. xiii.

CHAPTER 13

Neville's Theology of Creation, Covenant, and Trinity

Hermann Deuser
(Translated by Ulrich Lincoln)

I. INTRODUCTION

Seen from the perspective of German Protestant theology at the end of this century, Robert Cummings Neville's *oeuvre* presents itself as a blend of traditions from both sides of the Atlantic in a way quite characteristic of these traditions. First of all, in terms of *philosophy of religion*, Neville, with his first book *God the Creator* (1968), ventures to outline a speculative theology that he himself at that time had not acknowledged as such, but had cautiously called a "philosophical book."[1] To do that was to presuppose, on the one hand, a certain philosophical training and debate that could well exist in mid-twentieth-century America, but not in Germany as dominated by Neo-Kantianism and Protestant existential philosophy and, on the other hand, a concept of theology that rather ignored fundamental problems of philosophy of religion and hence was in accordance with American traditions but would be absolutely foreign to Germany.[2]

In the second place, in terms of *theology*, and from the German perspective, Neville's work naturally and right from the beginning finds its place within the fields of theology of creation, of Protestant philosophy of religion, and of phenomenology of religion. However, the grounding of all of theology in a firm philosophical argument that even culminates in a cosmological argument for God's existence remains surprising and amazing.[3] Until recently such thinking would have been inconceivable within German Protestantism; and it is only in that respect that Neville's early self-restraint to call his speculative theory a theology would have been justified in retrospect—but for very different reasons: by virtue of the particular development of *American Philosophy* since Emerson and Peirce, and in productive dialogue with the sciences, speculative metaphysics in the form of cosmology was made possible in North America as early as in the second half of the nineteenth century[4] and was even intensified in this century by process philosophy (Whitehead, Hartshorne);[5] however, to the German Protestant tradition these cosmological cornerstones of Christian philosophy and creation theology had been almost entirely lost since the nineteenth century and its prevailing Kantian philosophy.[6] Therefore, to expel Neville's speculative philosophy of religion from theology would have been done on *theological* grounds in Germany, whereas in the American tradition the justification for that was *philosophical!* With regard to the first, because German theology no longer had any understanding, or not yet, of such cosmological arguments; with regard to the latter, because Neville the theologian could place his cosmology only within the family of philosophy, as it were (which would have been hardly imaginable at that time in Germany, as already stated).

Finally, another reason for this blending of perspectives is the fact that even until recently religiosity and religion were regarded quite differently on both sides of the Atlantic.[7] Toward the middle of this century, a productive awareness of different religions as well as the intentional openness, and sometimes biographical orientation, toward individual religiosity was alive and well within Neville's philosophical community, and in particular among his teachers at Yale University, Paul Weiss and John E. Smith. On the other hand, German philosophy and Protestant theology tended rather to ignore religiosity and regard it as private, or as something totally alien to reflection. To Peirce, Whitehead, and Hartshorne, it was natural to look at religious experience as a field to test their respective theory-making; hence, Neville as early as 1968 could write as a philosopher "On the Transcendence and Presence of God." But doing so with an explicit *theological* intention and application, as proven especially by part 3 of *God the Creator*, is something that clearly also goes beyond the American tradition, and that is the distinct *theological* self-identification of Neville's *philosophy of religion* in the German sense of this notion.

To put it briefly: This actual integration of speculative creation theory, elements of religious experience, and theological conceptualization renders Neville's work suggestive, instructive, and exemplary. The following critical analysis of this *oeuvre* from the years 1968–96 shall bring the first book, *God the Creator*, to the fore, but this is not to be taken as the interpreter's arbitrary choice. Rather, it is what follows from the theological interest in Neville's axiological thinking as based on creation theory. In this particular work it finds its comprehensive theoretical foundation, so the ideas of later works can be identified here *in nuce*; and vice versa, despite the broadening of argumentation and demonstration, those later ideas can always be traced back to the early approaches and discoveries, as the author himself does regularly in his references.

II. CREATION

1. The three concepts I have chosen for my subject by no means rank equal within Neville's theology. The philosophical and theological status of each of them is quite different, and so is their systematic function. However, I have chosen these particular three concepts because, owing to their clear-cut difference in status, they allow at best the critical examination of Neville's theology. For if there is anything by which the author of *God the Creator* can be characterized in general, it is that theological classification (which later was explicitly employed by him) as a Methodist in a Calvinistic tradition.[8] As an enthusiastic reader and critical interpreter, I may add that just by reading Neville's theology I learned on a fundamental and most excellent level that my very own tradition is represented precisely not by Calvin, Wesley, and Weiss (as I would like to arrange Neville's fathers here), but rather by Luther, Kierkegaard, and Peirce. It is the common ground and differences between these two traditions that make the task of the following analysis attractive, which however is conducted not for the sake of these traditions but to render the concepts of creation, covenant, and trinity more precise in terms of philosophy of religion and theology.

2. For Neville, the concept of *creation* has a unique and fundamental meaning, that is to say, metaphysics and ontology are grounded in a theology of creation argument, traditionally speaking, a cosmological proof of God's existence and which is also the foundation for all the following systematic theological unfolding. Prior to the analysis of this argument I shall demonstrate its particular rank by pointing out some possible alternatives. These alternatives emerge from the competing concepts of *covenant* and *trinity*.

Although knowledge of God is essentially grounded in creation for Calvin's theology,[9] Karl Barth alters the theology of creation approach, which is typical of theology's reaction to the modern triumph of science, by means of the reformed covenant theology;[10] his famous line reads "Covenant as the internal basis of creation."[11] Thus, creation (as a concept of theological doctrine) should strictly be denied any metaphysical or ontological priority. Neville, quite consciously, does not follow this theological solution. As a result, the concept of covenant enters the debate only when Neville discusses the public role and social effect of religiosity and churches (and their social responsibilities); in *God the Creator*, for example, the concept appears however not yet prominently, in the penultimate chapter *The Expression of the Religious Life*: "Brotherhood."[12]

For theological tradition, for example, for Augustine and Thomas Aquinas,[13] the concept of God usually includes the trinity as an obligatory fundamental that is also discussed philosophically. Neville does not deny this, but it is obvious that, compared with the function of creation as the dominating theological foundation, the trinity can hold but a secondary, explanatory position. The fundamental ontological difference between the creator and the created clearly precedes God's "conditional features" which can be described in trinitarian terms; in other words: the trinity has no ontological primacy.[14]

Therefore, relating the special position of Neville's philosophical theology to the history of Christian doctrines leads, not coincidently, to the early Christian cosmogonies, for instance to the speculative theology of Origen;[15] this is supported by Neville's preference for the notion of *cosmogony* over the modern scientific notion of *cosmology*.[16] This is by no means an anachronism, since this speculative approach is prompted and influenced by modern physics and cosmology associated with process philosophy. It is precisely these physics that demand a renewed doctrine of God on the basis of the notion of creation. Therefore, the twentieth century's renewed argument for God's existence, which does not ignore religiosity but essentially refers to it, is the cosmological argument, and the corresponding Christian speculative theory is supplied by the doctrine of creation tradition.

3. Neville's *cosmological argument for the creator god*[17] is carried out in three *propositiones*; here *propositiones* 2 and 3 merely develop the consequences regarding the presupposed determinations of the world of experience (69f.) and the determinations of the notion of the creator (70ff.). This means that *propositio* 1 presents the core of the argument including all its premises entailed in the previously given ontological distinctions. I will proceed by explaining the main moves of the argument of *propositio* 1 together with their respective premises.

(1) *"The determinations of being need a creator in order to be"* (65). The defense of this sentence begins with an analysis of the notions of "being/Being" and "determination." It had been argued previously that a solution to the classic ontological questions is possible if

(a) the concept of "being" is used univocally (16),

(b) this concept of "being" is identified with the "One" from the relation of the One and the Many (15),

(c) these two concepts of "being" and the "One" are identified with the onto-theological concept of "being-itself" as coined by Paul Tillich (21).

These premises taken into account, it is clear that for Neville the metaphysical question of *being as such* actually is also the principal problem of (creation-) *theology* ("being-itself") and *ontology* ("one/many"); its logical explication is carried out by means of relating *identity* and *difference*. Here Neville's system and terminology are as follows:

(d) Everything which *is* in one way or another must be determinable by both "identity" [essential features] and "difference" [conditional features] (45).[18]

(e) Therefore, the notion of "determination" presupposes the mutuality of the many (65), but at the same time it is not conceivable without its unifying function, since the "identity" of indivdual entities (as a condition for its mutuality with the others) would otherwise be denied.

(f) As the most general determination of being, the distinction of "determinateness" and "indeterminateness" must also be applied to "being," the "one," and "being-itself" (40ff.). However, in this case "being-itself" cannot but belong solely to the side of identity, whereas the world of things must represent the "many" in its mutual determinations; any other division would be self-contradictory, and this is precisely the whole argument!

(2) Neville answers the difficult question of how the mutually dependent determinations of the "Many" can amount to a unity by leaving nothing but an only relative unity on the level of the determinations, the so-called "de facto unity" (65) but not the ontologically required unity of the "One." That is to say, things determine each other (e.g., America is not Germany, and Germany is not China, etc.) so that the actual distinction and relative identity of the one in relation to the other make a unity on an only "factual" level, as it were; but this does not explain how a "genuine unity" (50) or a (creative) "One," which would be the ground for all distinctions, can be possible at all. Here Neville makes use of the Whiteheadian terminology of "contrast" (40, 45) and "harmony" (49, 66) in order to cast light both on the emergence of differences and the function of unity.[19]

The crucial point of the argument is reached when, on the basis of the unity just explained, one can say: "A *de facto* unity does not account for itself" (65). Here we are at the core of the cosmological argument *e contingentia mundi*,[20] which is convincing as long as three alternative explanations can be ruled out:

(a) *Too much* would be explained if the unity was an application of a general "principle"; since such a principle would again require an explanation (65), and introducing a principle as the ground for mutual determinations would deprive the actual plurality of determined things of its real distinctiveness and individuality, thus giving priority to a preceding idealistic concept.[21] Neville defends the integrity of the nondeducible individual things in their *actual* [de facto] interrelation.

(b) *Too little* would be explained if the unity were reduced to the extent that a "pluralistic ontology" (65) would always have the one provide determinations for the other but have no account for the identity as such.[22] Neville defends the aspect of "wholeness," for identity [essential features] is obviously invariably more than what can be made conceivable in determinations relative to others [conditional features].

(c) Finally, the unity could explain itself as "harmony." This is the most interesting, and probably the most current objection against the cosmological argument; autopoiesis and self-organization are seemingly most radical in rendering any external explanation unnecessary. Neville's answer to that is striking precisely in that he neither wants to explain too much nor too little. For him, "harmony" is nothing but that harmony itself, that is, it is not a theoretically conceivable, deducible, or producible "pattern" of "harmoniousness" (66). At this point Neville defends the actual immediacy of a simply given "harmony" just as Peirce does with his examples for the category of *Firstness* (we will come back to this in our discussion of the Trinity): "A harmony simply is what it is, that is, harmonious, and this gives no account why it is harmonious" (66).

(3) Thereby the proof of the cosmological argument is thus already established: If the determinateness of the things cannot be explained through itself, it must be from outside. At this point, however, a certain notion of *contingency* is presupposed that, as such, calls for an explanation. At this crucial point Neville, apparently deliberately, does not follow a notion of contingency as defined in terms of modal logic.[23] Instead, in his own argument he defines "ontological contingency" as "what does not account for itself," that is as "dependent on something else for its whole being and nature" (67). At first sight this looks like a circular theory, as if contingency were defined as dependency by means of which the argument would be over before the contingency would even have been employed! However, I believe the actual understanding could be as follows:

(a) An explanatory dependency of the total cosmos is attempted here, a dependency that does not leave out coincidental events, that is, events for which we cannot give any causal accounts. It is placed within the framework of the *ontological* question in which everything that *is* must be accounted for according to its determinations of *being*. Otherwise there would be a deficit, or a contradiciton within the notion of "being." Where identity and difference exist, where unity exists despite of and because of the plurality of determinations, the question for being-itself becomes fundamental to the describable coherent fabric of things.

(b) However, this given fabric of all things had proved incapable of accounting for itself and that is precisely how Neville defines contingency. Obviously, this is inspired by Scholastic traditions, namely, that things can be explained either *a se* or *ab alio*. An explanation *a se* for every being is ruled out, according to Neville's fundamental ontological distinction of essential and conditional features of every real determination. Therefore, this leaves only explanations *ab alio*, which are stated in three instances:

(α) There are causal grounds of explanation.

(β) There are coincidental events without causal explanation that are nevertheless included in the explanatory model of *ab alio*.

(γ) There is the ontologically self-contradictory case of those things or events that have no way of being at all and these are *impossible*, strictly speaking (67).

Thus, we are dealing with a specific concept of *contingency* that not only formally excludes necessity and includes possibility and actuality, but in an *ontologically* all-encompassing way defines every actuality—if not impossible—in its being actual as *contingent* and thus simultaneously as *ab alio*. One cannot step behind this understanding of *contingency* as *dependency*, insofar as it captures the meaning of determinateness, that is, of ontology in general (67): To distinguish something from something else presupposes "being," and such determination of the thing reveals its contingency or *ab alio*–determinateness; otherwise the ontological context of the question for being-itself would be broken, left, or answered in a self-contradictory way.

(4) The notion of "being" has inevitably become ambiguous: first, it means the total structure within which all real determinations are to be found and that makes it possible to conceive determinateness as such; second, it denotes the determinate being's individual participation in its form of unity. The second part of the first argument (*propositio* 1.b) merely consists of a conceptualization of the ontological signifi-

cance of the very difference between the given structure of being and the individual being as actually determined by this structure (67–69):

(a) It can be demonstrated, that mutual determinations function reciprocally because of the given fact of their interrelation. However, since this fact cannot be explained by again referring to the same mutuality, the notion of contingency now extends to the meaning of *contingent upon*: "The very possibility that one determination is conditioned by another means that both are contingent upon their togetherness. And this togetherness must be contingent upon some further thing, not a determination" (68).

(b) But if the contingency of all determinations and all determinatenesses cannot be explained by itself and its mutuality; and if (as demonstrated in *propositio* 1.a) for the sake of avoiding ontological self-contradiction an explanation is still required, then there remains but one, and therefore necessary, way. The world of the (determined) being must be explained by referring to something external; *theologically* speaking, it must be created: "Therefore, if any are [i.e., unity of togetherness], all must be created, that is, made to be . . . , what makes them be must be outside the realm of determinations and create them from nothing, that is, from no determination" (69).

(5) As the last and essential mark in Neville's cosmological argument, its *theological* implication, the strict *creatio ex nihilo* shall be emphasized.[24] Here again we have an ontological *and*, at the same time, theological argument, or we have an upshot from dealing with the question of determination (identity and difference): God the creator who as the being-itself is the ground for all determinations cannot be determined himself, that is, when the cosmological argument proceeds from everything determined to God as the ground of everything it also proceeds to the *indeterminate*. One can therefore conclude that the act of creating out of this indeterminate realm, as it were, is done from *nothing* (69).

(a) The notion of "nonbeing" is problematic insofar as it is ontologically absurd, with regard to the creation as a whole, that is, with regard to given and conceivable determinations (92). Within the context of the contingent being one can speak only of relative nonbeing,[25] but "absolute nonbeing," as a contradiction to the created determinations (114), is an impossible thought, since actual thinking is conditioned by determinateness.

(b) Yet, the realm of *indeterminateness* is burdened with *Nothing/nonbeing* insofar as solely from here determinateness can be created.

God's *transcendence* and *indeterminateness* are synonomous with *creatio ex nihilo*. As for ontology and theology, nothing determinate can be predicated of "being-itself" and of God's transcendence, but the *reality* of the creator-god must nonetheless be conceivable; this is an implication of the cosmological argument as it traces the contigent back to its ground.[26]

(c) But then, the crucial question with regard to this ontotheological conception is: How can *real indeterminateness* be understood as *creative* without permanent contradiction? A first answer to that is the *creatio ex nihilo*, since it realizes the indeterminateness for itself as an absolute act but also relative to the created as "absolute spontaneity" and "absolute novelty" (109).[27] That is to say, creativity is alien and not subject to the created determinations, measured by their nature, and yet it is found among the created!

(d) At the same time, it must be possible to mark the specific connection and contact between creator and created without asserting some determinations for the creator's side or some noncontingent facts for the side of the created, respectively. The *creatio ex nihilo* precisely marks the borderline between indeterminateness and determinateness; on the other hand, it must also be able to explain the interrelation between those two ontological elements. This again is achieved by means of the concept of *harmony*. The concept of harmony had already been introduced as denoting a factual unity without thereby being an intellectual principle or pattern disposable to humankind (independently of its creator).[28] The harmony of actual determinations and determinateness forces itself upon us just as it is; and again, its ground can be found only in the transcendent *indeterminateness*, or in the *creatio ex nihilo* (112). Theologically, with regard to the question of the creator-created interrelation this means "that harmony *is* at the heart of the connection of determinations of being with God" (112).

(e) However, talking about a point of contact remains a poor construction for it entails the whole meaning of creation; it is also dangerous, for nothing beside the fundamental difference of creator and created must be established. Neville wants to do equal justice to both sides: The connection between creator and created does not simply separate, but rather, productively and creatively, distinguishes nonbeing from being; this connection is "God's power" (104), the "creative ground" (114) of everything—and thus, as God's determination, it is relative to his creation.[29] But in the same argument it must be assured that no third "medium" (114) is established between God and the created: in a certain sense and from a human perspective, God's creative power *is* his creation, and he "determines" himself solely by this. As an act creation is real, but not subject to any created determination, and thereby remains *ex nihilo.*[30]

4. We can end our account and explanation of the basic ideas of the cosmological argument on the basis of *God the Creator* by pointing out some problems, which will later be referred to in connection with the systematic-theological concepts of *covenant* and *trinity.*

(1) In contrast to the cosmological argument[31] in its classic form, Neville's "speculative theory of being-itself" (61) is not about proving God's existence, nor is it about the notion of a necessary Supreme Being. In the context of the specific, while also universally valid, ontological question it is demonstrated that on the basis of contingent reality the fundamental connection of that reality with the transcendent and indeterminate "being-itself" must be comprehended. However, this also reveals a modal-logical argument as contained in the proof: The "necessary and actively effective ground"[32] of an ontological determination must be concluded from the actuality and possibility of that determination.

(2) Kant's two classic objections against the cosmological argument were that, *first*, there was an unwarranted leap from the infinite regress of causal relations to the qualitatively supreme cause;[33] and, *second*, that the just ostensible beginning with experience in reality was only to disguise the ontological argument,[34] that is to say, the cosmological argument also had to presuppose and apply the concept of a *necessary Supreme Being*. The ontological argument, however, finally fails (on the basis of Kant's theoretical philosophy) because an absolute concept would lose its object.[35] This criticism does not apply to Neville's speculative theory for the very reason that Kant's transcendental framework of conceptualizing cannot resound within American philosophy.[36] In other words, if Neville had to come up with an argument for (God's) existence, it would be the argument of *religious experience*, but it is absurd to look for a proof of experience, and here he is in agreement with Kant! Now it is understandable that Neville in a certain sense can accept the *ontological argument* (79). But he does that with the (theological) reservation that the "reality of the creator" precisely cannot be grasped under the contingent condition of human intelligence. This reveals the priority of *religious experience* that is capable of dealing productively with what philosophical theory must call "mystery" (73f., 93). If religiosity in principle is not excluded from speculative theory, and the latter is designed as experience-oriented as it was in Scholastic philosophy, then the arguments for God's existence have a totally different and

new status (compared with the modern debate about their relevance).[37]

(3) What is special about Neville's cosmological argument is that he does not infer a theoretically distinctive concept of God, but instead proves his transcendence as *indeterminateness*. Thereby religious experience is properly applied, and the limits of theoretical explication are conceded. What constitutes the quality of Neville's philosophical theology is not to give in at this point, neither theoretically nor practically, nor is it to divide these two realms of thought and experience into separate branches that then by virtue of this division would lose their critical relation; Neville's thought does not appear to accept the usual divisions at this crossroads so crucial to modernity.

(4) To this seemingly paradoxical solution,[38] the *creatio ex nihilo* is necessarily fundamental. At first sight, there appears to be a striking contradiction between the classic principle of the contingency argument *ex nihilo nihil fit* (which Neville also employs as a matter of course) and the notion of *creatio ex nihilo*.[39] To understand this not as a contradiction but as a necessary double perspective is Neville's essential discovery. The basic ontological scheme of the distinction of identity and difference (essential and conditional features) applies to all things and therefore also to God, but, of course, not in the same way (74ff.). The *indeterminateness* of God—or the ontological "One"—cannot have conditional features in the same way as all other things do; however, in the *relation* to his *creation*, apparently there exist the very phenomena that must be considered as "conditional features" (75). That means the clear distinction between creator and created leaves us, in negative terms, with the problem of how to conceive a "nothing" of determination within the concept of God although all determinations arise from here.[40] In positive terms, the *creatio ex nihilo*, from the perspective of being-itself, says nothing different from what the principle of *ex nihilo nihil fit* says in the perspective of the created.

This is the problem to be discussed in the following section: How is it possible to conceive God's *relationality* with regard to the created (as well as with regard to the concept of God) and yet, at the same time, to exclude all determinateness within God himself because of this very same ontology?[41]

III. COVENANT

1. Neville's fundamental ontological distinction of "essential and conditional features" is in accordance with the traditional metaphysical difference of viewing an entity with regard to its *being* (i.e., its identity, existence, and factuality [*quodditas*]) and with regard to its *determina-*

tion (i.e., in its difference toward the other, its essence or nature, its structure of properties [*quidditas*]).[42] As stated earlier, this leads, in the case of God's association with his creation, to the problem of God's *ex nihilo*–indeterminateness within himself as against his relational determination in his bonds with the created. Here the notion of *covenant* might provide a mediative function since it is precisely the covenantal bond that encompasses the relation of God and creation (of humankind).[43] In the dual perspective necessary for Neville's philosophical theology, the creation *ex nihilo* can be conceived together with its ontologically necessary comprehension by virtue of the principle of *ex nihilo nihil fit*; however, there would be no point in talking of a divine covenant *ex nihilo*. And indeed, Neville's actual theology of covenant[44] talks about an "ontological covenant,"[45] but this clearly has to be seen as merely denoting the relational side of the created, that is to say *covenant* is an "interpretive metaphor" for the sake of describing the *conditio humana*[46] in its contingency, dependence, and relationality between human beings, between humankind and nature, between humankind and God. Therefore, the covenant theology is always derived from creation theology and can be employed only from the ontologically *conditional* perspective; it cannot and must not say anything about God himself.[47]

2. Consequently, the meaning of *covenant* unfolds into the foundation of a modern social ontology, including the moral and institutional self-representations of the human race and its development.[48] The theological interpretation corresponds exactly to this function: justice, piety, faith, and hope extend the biblical-Christian tradition to the contemporary questions of religion, politics, and churches; and in contrast to the social ignorance of a quietistic individualism, Neville develops a vital and warranted theory of Christian social responsibility in world society dimensions.[49]

My theological question is not aimed against the intentions of this conception of a covenant-theological social ontology. Rather, it wants to draw attention to a different way of reasoning that is often regarded and underrated as a merely individualistic alternative: the doctrine of *imago Dei* as the foundation and description of the *conditio humana*.[50] But here we are not concerned with the question of which social theory may lay claim to greater persuasiveness, justification, and capability, the predominantly Lutheran or the Reformed tradition; rather, the question in the context of Neville's creation theology revolves around the already stated problem of the connection, contact, or relation between God the creator and the created. The covenant theology has no function *ex nihilo* if merely applied, as in Neville's conception, from the perspective of the created.[51] The *violated covenant* also serves as a meaningful descriptive structure of personal and social realities, but can not explain the God-relation itself with regard to its indeterminateness.[52]

3. The question raised thereby is a difficult one because Neville does not at all demand silence on the transcendence but rather demands a firm predication on the indeterminateness of transcendence.[53] In other words: What is, strictly speaking, the meaning the *ex nihilo*–indeterminateness holds for the *conditio humana*, if the search is not only about descriptive structures of the created but also about its (creational) relationship with the noncreated? Without unnoticedly and falsely being portrayed as a determination, the "intrinsic mysteriousness of being-itself" (98) needs a characteristic presence; otherwise the basic creational distinction of indeterminate transcendence and contingent determination of everything created is threatened by dualistic desintegration.

It is Kierkegaard's existential theology, as evolved from Lutheran tradition, sharpened on the theoretical level in the face of Christianity's modern crisis, and lived through in religious experience, that offers a respectable solution in terms of the *imago Dei* doctrine. And it is this very tradition of thought and experience that, contributing to the more Reformed tradition of covenant theology and social ontology, proves its capability in addressing a problem that genuinely arises in Neville's theology of the "Transcendence and Presence of God."[54]

4. The "point of contact," the relation between God and humankind, creator and created, would have to be described consistently by showing how the divine *ex nihilo*–indeterminateness also reveals itself within the created realm in precisely that way.[55] The place for this would be human conscience, as the inexplicit, still-undetermined experience of freedom, the "possibility of being able" that is experienced as the anxiety of "nothing" within hunch and dream,[56] as in Kierkegaard's analysis. At the heart of human personhood and its concept of freedom we would find the foundation of all sociality to be explained and to be existentially described by means of the characteristic (religious) priority of indeterminateness (of *anxiety*) with regard to the actual possibility of failure and success as part of the determinateness (of the contingent creature). Thus understanding a person as a relational structure[57] would correspond to the "paradox" (99) of the divine *transcendence* and *immanence* (94) so that, within the context of human experience, this experience would be found *indeterminately* referring to its ground, without being derived from or mastered by the determinateness of the created. This specific (existential) relationality *ex nihilo* recommends itself to the "speculative theory of being-itself" (61) without requiring a change in the program as a whole. But the task of how to think of the *nothing* would have been widened; that is, to declare absolute nonbeing impossible, as required by metaphysics and ontology,[58]

does not mean that there is no existential experience of *nothing*. That experience is part of the cosmological interplay of God's creation and the creature's contingency.

IV. TRINITY

1. This question of the relation between transcendence and immanence, between God's indeterminateness and his very determination as the creator of the created, has its classic place in the trinitarian doctrine. For it is God's outward determination [*ad extra*] that brings about God's self-relation as the creator, and this self-relation must not contradict the relation with the contingent created. As a first solution to that problem Neville employs an *asymmetry*[59] between both perspectives: the transcendent creator's independence of his creation must be maintained as well as his relation with the created, but this does not imply a dependence on the created (96). God's aseity or "in-itselfness" holds ontological priority; his relation with creation is an epistemic reality in the realm of the created (96). Does that mean that we can speak only of an *economic trinity* but not an *immanent trinity*, that is, a relation within God himself, as it were? Would not God then be inaccessible except for some "mystic experience" in some, that is, *indeterminate*, way (97)? Indeed, beyond stating the problem, *God the Creator* does not appear to attempt to formulate the relation between creator and created, transcendence and immanence in a way that would render the transition between the two ontological spheres conceivable. *God's self-constituting* (97) in the distinction of creator and created apparently is the limit of what can be said ontologically.

2. If we acknowledge Neville's aim to clearly distinguish between transcendent indeterminateness and contingent determinateness but also want to search for an understanding of the realization of this difference even within God's *self-constituting*, then again a form of indeterminateness would have to yield this mediative function. Neville's explanation (98ff.) at this point is limited (ontologically seen) solely to God's "conditional features"; however, these features are displayed in *trinitarian* terms:

(1) God "being the creator" (99),
(2) God with regard to "the created realm" (100),
(3) God's "power" (102) or "creative activity" (104).[60]

The crucial point here is whether God's "mystery" (76) is excluded from this trinitarian structure, whether this structure be understood distinctly as an *economic* trinity or whether as an *indeterminate* form of the *immanent* trinity. In the following I shall pursue the second interpretation.

3. In the act of creating the *creatio ex nihilo* definitely precludes any material or divine beside itself but does not preclude the creative new itself.[61] The "absolute new" and "absolute spontaneity" (109) are uniquely significant for the creational act.[62] Why not understand this act as granting the possibility of, and thereby as the ground for, describing an immanent trinity? Neville wants to differ here from Leibniz' concept of possibility (81) as well as from process theology with its cosmologically immanent structure of creativity, which is where the concept of God is anchored and derived from, now obviously as a secondary concept (108f.).[63] It is *this* concept of possibility (as a previously conceivable structure that then allows for comprehending God immanently) that must be challenged on the basis of God's *ex nihilo*–indeterminateness; but not to be challenged is a concept of possibility that would be characterized by its creative indeterminateness: as an *original potentiality* [*ursprüngliche Ermöglichung*][64] of contingent reality, where the *original potentiality* would be present within the created as "absolute spontaneity."[65] The creative is the *new*, and between this and the contingent conditions is no derivative relation but a *leap* (thus employing another category from Kierkegaard's *Concept of Anxiety*).[66] It is this independence that Neville wants to safeguard, and his notion of God's *self-constituting*[67] tries to do that, just as the trinitarian idea of the creative "power" (which is a necessary implication of this notion).

4. If in this sense *God's self-constituting* can be understood as an act where, in trinitarian terms, the original creative act, its object, and the creative power itself, are to be distinguished,[68] then no created determinations are falsely assumed for the divine transcendence; rather from the creative act itself its certainly hypothetical and fallible relational description as immanent trinity can be derived, which can claim for itself the same reality as the ontologically derived indeterminateness of transcendence. Its "power" is "immediate and eternal" (104), no already existing "potency" or "substance" (113), but the absolutely primary quality of a creative potentiality for everything else. This account is not distorted by saying that God himself is this very *first*[69] (of original potentiality), and as such he is this for a *second one*, for his object (the created and its reconciliation), and the necessary connection is, as a *third* element, the relation as such: the life-giving power of God's spirit; to say it with Neville: the *harmony* and *unity* in everything created (112), the *power* withstanding nonbeing (114), and the *creative ground* for the distinction of old and new (115). In this trinitarian concreteness God's aseity becomes the abundant fullness of the creative in its indeterminateness and determinateness. The vitality implied here literally provokes one to

speak of God as a *person* not only in the sense of the *economic* (264) but also in the sense of the *immanent* trinity.

Can this trinitarian interpretation do justice to Neville's theology of creation by understanding, on the basis of its fundamental distinctions, relationality as one of its crucial ontological problems? For this attempt, too, an insight from experience might be true: "The untidiness of this indirect approach is that there is always difficulty in showing that where philosophy has gotten us is where religion wanted us to get" (94).

NOTES

1. Robert Cummings Neville, *God the Creator: On the Transcendence and Presence of God*, republication (Albany: State University of New York Press, 1992); original edition, Chicago: University of Chicago Press, 1968, p. xxiv; cf. the preface of the new edition, p. xiii: "it is no longer true that the book is not theology."

2. That is the only way to understand Neville's remark, ibid., p. 119: "Although the speculative arguments given above should be the philosophic reasons for holding our theory, its religious consequences should not be lost on theologians."

3. Cf. Neville, *God the Creator*, chap. 3, section A.

4. Cf. H. Deuser, "Einleitung," in Charles Sanders Peirce, *Religionsphilosophische Schriften*, ed. H. Deuser, Philosophische Bibliothek, vol. 478 (Hamburg: Felix Meiner Verlag, 1995).

5. Cf. K. Röttgers, Art. *Prozeß II.*, HWP 7 (1989): 1558–62; I. U. Dalferth, Art. *Prozeßtheologie*, HWP 7 (1989): 1562–65; H. Husslik, Art. *Prozeßphilosophie*, EKL³ 3 (1992): 1360–63; M. Welker, Art. *Prozeßtheologie*, EKL³ 3 (1992): 1363–66.

6. Cf. H. Deuser: *Gott: Geist und Natur. Theologische Konsequenzen aus Charles S. Peirce's Religionsphilosophie* (Berlin/New York: W. de Gruyter [TBT 56], 1993), chaps. 1 and 2; cf. also "Hume's Pragmaticist Argument for the Reality of God," *The Journal of Speculative Philosophy* 9 (1995): 1–13.

7. For a specific determination of these notions, cf. Deuser, *Gott*, chap. 9.

8. Cf. Robert Cummings Neville, *Behind the Masks of God: An Essay toward Comparative Theology* (Albany: State University of New York Press, 1991), p. 163f.

9. Cf. *Institutio* I.5.6.

10. With regard to the history of doctrines, cf. J. F. G. Goeters, Art. *Föderaltheologie*, TRE 11 (1983): 246–52; A. I. C. Heron, Art. *Bund 3. Dogmatisch*, EKL³ 1 (1986): 570–72.

11. *Church Dogmatics*, 3.1: §41/3.

12. Neville, *God the Creator*, chap. 12, section F, p. 289; cf. the systematic account in Robert Cummings Neville, *A Theology Primer* (Albany: State University of New York Press, 1991), chap. 5: "The Human Condition: Covenant."

13. *Sancti Aurelii Augustini De Trinitate* Libri XV, ed. W. J. Mountain (Turnhout, 1968), CCSL, L/LA: *Aurelii Augustini Opera*, XVI.1.2; cf. the summarizing formulation of the "catholica fides" in book I.4.7. *Sancti Thomae*

Aquinatis Summa Theologiae, I, q. 27ff. In this same way, and directly within the context of the doctrines of creation and scripture, also *Iohannis Calvini Institutio* (1559), I.13.

14. Cf. the cautious use, structurally required, of trinitarian vocabulary in *God the Creator,* p. 98ff.; confirmed in the discussion of the concept of the person, ibid., p. 264. Also the textbooklike teaching on the Trinity in *A Theology Primer,* chap. 4: "God as Trinity," does not alter anything about this ontological groundwork: "In the asymmetry of the act of ontological creation, the source of the act is indeterminate" (ibid., p. 40).

15. *De principiis Libri IV/Vier Bücher von den Prinzipien,* ed. H. Görgemanns and H. Karpp, 3rd ed. (Darmstadt, 1992), cf. I.3.3 and I Praef. 4: "quod unus est deus, qui omnia creavit atque composuit, quique, cum nihil esset, esse fecit universa." Cf. also A. v. Harnack, *Dogmengeschichte* (1889/91), 8th ed. (Tübingen [UTB 1641], 1991), p. 146f.: "Der beherrschende Gegensatz [namely, in Origen's περὶ ἀρχῶν] ist Gott und das Geschaffene . . . / . . . Gott ist das *Eine,* welches dem *Vielen* gegenüber steht."

16. Cf. Neville, *God the Creator,* chap. 5. This usage does not occur anymore in later writings, and the speculative theory quite rightly claims the scientific notion of *cosmology;* but then it is differentiated between ontologically and speculatively abstract *metaphysics* and the world of determinations, i.e., cosmology. Cf. *A Theology Primer,* p. 30, and Robert Cummings Neville, *Eternity and Time's Flow* (Albany: State University of New York Press, 1993), p. 67f.

17. The analysis is primarily based on chap. 3, section A, from *God the Creator;* references from this volume will be marked by page number within the main text.

18. Cf. also Robert Cummings Neville, *Recovery of the Measure: Interpretation and Nature* (Albany: State University of New York Press, 1989), chap. 5. The chapter headlines here are dominated by the terminology of "identity" and "difference" without giving up on the old distinction of "essential" and "conditional features." The principal ontological categories are repeated in Robert Cummings Neville, *The Cosmology of Freedom* (New Haven: Yale University Press, 1974); reprinted in (Albany: State University of New York Press, 1996) under the chapter heading "The Cosmological Scheme," in the paragraph titled "Metaphysical Categories," cf. p. 30ff. More clearly than in *God the Creator,* here in 1974 "harmony" (besides "essential and conditional features") is counted among these categories (31f.), and the connection with A. N. Whitehead's cosmology is explicitly stated (36).

19. Cf. also in *Recovery of the Measure,* p. 108f.; it is also necessary to differentiate between mutual determination of things and integration of parts of a determination. Cf. *God the Creator,* p. 49f.

20. Cf. H.G. Hubbeling, *Einführung in die Religionsphilosophie* (Göttingen [UTB 1152], 1981), p. 88.

21. This dissociation from the idealistically explained, primarily spiritual reality of things by virtue of a "third term" is directed explicitly against F. H. Bradley, cf. *God the Creator,* p. 47n5 and p. 101f. Cf. also *Cosmology,* p. 32.

22. This argument is based on a detailed discussion with Paul Weiss; cf. *God the Creator,* pp. 55–59.

23. Cf. Hubbeling, ibid., p. 88: "Kontingent ist das, dessen Nichtexistenz wenigstens gedacht werden kann" [contingent is what at least can be conceived as not existent]. Cf. also H. Poser and H. Deuser, "Kontingenz," *TRE* 19 (1990): 544–59.

24. Therewith the analysis moves on to a text of great importance with regard to this notion: chap. 4, section B, cf. *God the Creator*, 106–16. Cf. also the short outline on *creatio ex nihilo* in Robert Cummings Neville, *The Tao and the Daimon: Segments of a Religious Inquiry* (Albany: State University of New York Press, 1982), pp. 132–35. Cf. also E. Wölfel, *Welt als Schöpfung. Zu den Fundamentalsätzen der christlichen Schöpfungslehre heute* (Munich: [Chr. Kaiser], 1981), pp. 24–34.

25. Cf. ibid., 114: "since by definition of non-being some determinate being is."

26. Up to chap. 3 Neville uses mainly and consciously the neutral form of "creation" and "being-itself" (grammatically, as the neuter and with reference to "it" in relative clauses), which cannot be done the same way in German. But with chap. 4 creation is interpreted by *God's* transcendence, cf. ibid., 111: "All determinations, because of this, must have a common source or creator, which we now call God."

27. This also is an idea that is close to Peirce, and which I will take up in the discussion of the trinity. Cf. also C. R. Hausman, *A Discourse on Novelty and Creation* (The Hague: Martinus Nijhoff, 1975).

28. See above, II.3(2)(c).

29. Neville, *God the Creator*, p. 114: "The creative power is a conditional feature God gives himself in the actual creating."

30. Ibid.: "The coming-to-be of the determinations is a novelty on the ontological scene. They come out of nothing, and there is no process with middle stages through which they are made. They are created through the power and the power is immediate."

31. Cf. John Clayton, "*Gottesbeweise II. Mittelalter, III. Systematisch/Religionsphilosophisch*," *TRE* 13 (1984): 724–84; here, 747–51.

32. Hubbeling, *Einführung*, 184–89; here, 187: "notwendiger, aktiv wirkender Grund."

33. Cf. I. Kant, *Kritik der reinen Vernunft*, A 605 (footnote).

34. Kant, ibid., A 607.

35. Cf. Kant, A 593: "ob ich alsdenn durch einen Begriff des Unbedingt-notwendigen noch etwas, oder vielleicht gar nichts denke."

36. Cf. Deuser, *Gott*, chap. 1; also "Charles S. Peirce's Contribution to Cosmology and Religion," *Religious Experience and Ecological Responsibility*, ed. D. A. Crosby and Charley D. Hardwick (New York: Peter Lang, 1996), pp. 159–72.

37. Cf. Neville, *God the Creator*, p. 64: "But the proof must not stand alone; it must be taken in the context of the whole speculative scheme that interprets it, and it must also be related to the appearance of God in religion." Quite obviously, this position is in accordance with I. U. Dalferth's interpretation of the arguments for God's existence, cf. especially: Fides quaerens intellectum, in Dalferth, *Gott. Philosophisch-theologische Denkversuche* (Tübingen: J. C. B.

Mohr [Paul Siebeck], 1992), pp. 51–94. This is supported by Neville's explicit interpretation of Anselm's *ontological argument* as "rule of thinking," and therefore exactly not as an abstract proof of God's existence (*God the Creator*, p. 194).

38. Neville tries in part 2 of *God the Creator* to develop a concept of dialectics that could correspond to this multitude of perspectives from theology, philosophy, and religious experience.

39. Cf. Hubbeling, *Einführung*, 92f.; cf. Neville's limitation of this principle with regard to the *creatio ex nihilo*, in *Primer*, p. 40.

40. Cf. *God the Creator*, p. 77: "That the distinction should be made sharply is the brunt of our argument." Cf. also the short summary of the same idea (contingency has its "ontological ground" in indeterminateness or infinity) in *The Puritan Smile: A Look toward Moral Reflection* (Albany: State University of New York Press, 1987), p. 194f.

41. This is the question, formulated as the problem of *relationality* (cf. *God the Creator*, p. 77: "that would articulate the creator's conditional feature of being creator . . . relational in character"), which attracted our attention already before when we talked about the "point of contact" between the divine and the human, see above, II.3(5)(e).

42. Cf. with regard to this distinction that is also fundamental to phenomenology: H. Deuser, "Die phänomenologischen Grundlagen der Trinität," *MJTH* 6 (1994): 45–67; here, 46.

43. Cf. Westminster Confession (1647), chap. VII, in *Die Bekenntnisschriften der reformierten Kirche*, ed. E. F. K. Müller (1903) (Zurich: Theologische Buchhandlung, 1987), p. 558: "The Distance between God and the Creature is so great, that although reasonable Creatures do owe Obedience unto him as their Creator, yet they could never have any Fruition of him as their Blessedness and Reward, but by some voluntary Condescension on God's Part, which he hath been pleased to express by way of Covenant."

44. Cf. especially *Primer*, chap. 5 (see above, note 12); and his *The Highroad around Modernism* (Albany: State University of New York Press, 1992), p. 194ff.: *Eternity* (see above, note 16), p. 205ff.: *The Truth of Broken Symbols* (Albany: State University of New York Press, 1996), p. 26f.

45. Neville, *Highroad*, p. 195.

46. Neville, *Primer*, p. 52; see above, note 12.

47. This perspective was further developed after *God the Creator* (1968), which indicates a new level of differentiation within the ontological realm of the created, namely the Platonic *Logos*-doctrine, since *Recovery of the Measure* (see above, note 18), chap. 6, esp. pp. 120–28; and *Behind the Masks* (see above, note 8), chap. 1, esp. p. 17ff. However, the foundation remains at the *creatio ex nihilo*, and both acknowledged explicitly in the preface of the *Primer*, p. xii. That means creation theology stands at the beginning, ontologically warranted and sovereign, and covenant theology deals with the following realm of the created. Therefore, nothing has changed with regard to the fundamental questions of the theological interpretation of the cosmological argument.

48. Cf. esp. in *Highroad*, pp. 194–97.

49. Now the ontological function is made available through the fourfold

logos concept (see above, note 47), and followed by the theological unfolding, cf. esp. *Primer*, pp. 56–59; cf. also the short presentation in *Eternity*, p. 205f.

50. Cf. Neville's critical assessment of the individualistic tendencies of this doctrine within the Lutheran tradition, *Primer*, p. 53.

51. In this regard, K. Barth's theology drew the opposite conclusion and placed the covenant idea (without any cosmological or ontological reasoning!) within creation itself; see above, note 11.

52. Cf. *Primer*, chap. 6; *Eternity*, p. 206; *Truth*, p. 79ff.

53. Cf. *God the Creator*, p. 99: "God apart from determinate creation is indeterminate. But the paradox is that to be creator is to be something determinate . . . part of the meaning of being creator is that God must *also* have reality apart from that determinate connection and that this other reality is prior to his reality as creator."

54. Cf. the subtitle of *God the Creator*, and the heading of chap. 4 (94).

55. See note 41.

56. S. Kierkegaard: *The Concept of Anxiety* (1844), chap. I, §5.

57. Cf. H. Deuser, "Grundsätzliches zur Interpretation der Krankheit zum Tode," *Kierkegaard Studies Yearbook*, vol. 1, ed. N. J.Cappelørn and H. Deuser (Berlin/New York, 1996), 117–28.

58. See above, note 25.

59. Cf. *Primer*, 40 (see above, note 14): "In the asymmetry of the act of ontological creation, the source of the act is indeterminate because all determinateness is the result of the act. . . . Insofar as God is conceived, therefore, as abstracted from the trinitarian source-product-act relation, God is utterly indeterminate and unknowable." Cf. the analogous description "of this logical implication" in *The Tao* (see above, note 24), p. 51.

60. Cf. *Primer*, 39: "In the act of divine creation, three elements are necessarily involved: God as source of everything determinate, God as the product or end point of the creative act, and God as the creative activity itself." See also the similar survey in *The Tao*, pp. 54f., 70ff.; also *Highroad*, p. 287n6.

61. *God the Creator*, p. 76: "It does not refer to any fuzziness or chaos in the creator's essential nature." See also p. 101: "Creation of the world from nothing denies that God has an *Urstoff* present in him."

62. See above, note 27.

63. Also in this respect Neville seems to agree with the intention of Dalferth's *theological* critique of Hartshorne and Whitehead, cf. Dalferth, "*Die Theoretische Theologie der Prozeßphilosophie Whiteheads*," and "*The One Who is Worshipped. Erwägungen zu Charles Hartshornes Versuch, Gott zu denken*," in *Gott. Philosophisch-theologische Denkversuche* (see above, note 37), 153–91, 192–12.

64. Cf. Deuser, "Einleitung" (see above, note 4), xxxvii, xl, xliii.

65. Thus it would no longer be a concept of possibility for which would be true (*God the Creator*, p. 100): "Creation cannot be mere actualization of potentialities, for those potentialities would have to stem from something determinate."

66. See above, note 56. Cf. *God the Creator*, p. 115: "Any exercise of creative power that makes something new, or makes something *ex nihilo* (those being the same), is eternal, that is, non-temporal . . . between the moments of

not-being and being, when the creating is going on, there is no time."
  67. See above, IV.2.
  68. See above, note 60. Neville's objection against the immanent Trinity as a "theistic" hypothesis based on Christian Aristotelianism (the unalterability of the first substance) becomes untenable as soon as the Trinity corresponds with a creative *and* metaphysical conception as a whole, symbolizing its structure. Just as demanded by Neville, this case renders God not in terms of an abstract theism "as an individual apart from creation," cf. *Eternity* (see above, note 16), p. 142. It is only in *The Tao*, pp. 73–91, where Neville deals explicitly with the doctrine of Trinity, that the impression is given as if Neville were to correct his reservations against *immanent* Trinity. Here the indeterminateness of the transcendence as such is still maintained (ibid., p. 74), but God is trinitarianly "immanent" *within* his creation (ibid., p. 78). However, this notion of immanence appears to displace the problem, because it merely functions to demonstrate that one cannot conceive of a God as separate from, and "behind," the *economic* trinity: "it must be made clear that the locus of the Trinitarian distinctions is the real and true God" (ibid., p. 78); "God does not have some primordial nature *beyond* the Trinitarian one" (ibid., p. 80). As long as creativity is not understood (as proposed in the following) as creative indeterminateness *within* creation as well as *within* God (and not as a statelike opposite of determinateness), the cut between determinateness, on the side of the created, and indeterminateness, on the side of divine transcendence, is maintained. To put it in the analogy of God's "unspoken" and "spoken Word": Neville cannot count "God's unspoken word" as an analogy for *immanent* Trinity, either, for "the Word unspoken is indeterminate and, consequently, is indistinguishable from any other person in the Godhead" (ibid., p. 81). On the other hand, Neville certainly cannot be blamed for separating the Divine from the world (cf. ibid., p. 82), and for regarding creation as a mere "bridge" between both sides. But the question is how the "connection" between God's transcendence and immanence is to be conceived; and Neville's answer, that there is not only *economic* Trinity (ibid., p. 82), is only directed against the objection that he was to artificially separate God and world. The sentence: "The connection between God and world is internal to God," does not include *immanent* Trinity, strictly speaking; it remains within Neville's conception of the basic ontological distinction of indeterminateness (transcendence) and determinateness (immanence).
  69. Cf. Neville's analogous defense of *harmony* as the most fundamental and qualitative phenomenon as such, see above, II.3(2)(c) and note 28. However, in Neville's ontological or metaphysical scheme (see above, note 18) *harmony* stands for what exists "de facto," and what can be determined through multiple categories, consequently. Unlike the following proposal, Neville himself does not stretch the (Trinitarian) difference between harmony in the (categorically) *original* and the (categorically) *triadic* sense; according to this difference, both *unity* and *harmony* have the double sense of *original* quality and *new* quality, as created by the spirit. Neville's treatment of the doctrine of sin shows that he understands "harmony" primarily in the second sense, i.e., as created by God's "creative power." Cf. *God the Creator*, p. 302. Also with respect to the eternal meaning of human personality, cf. *Eternity*, p. 198: "Persons, like any other determinate thing, are harmonies of essential and conditional features."

PART V

Comparative Issues

CHAPTER 14

On Neville's Understanding of Chinese Philosophy: The Ontology of Wu, the Cosmology of Yi, and the Normalogy of Li

Chung-ying Cheng

Robert Neville's understanding of Chinese philosophy is surprisingly profound and comprehensive. It is not only that he has worked his way diligently into various aspects of Chinese philosophy, but he has also acquired a special feel and insight for Chinese philosophy in his interpretation of the Chinese philosophical concepts and systems. Even in his own philosophical speculation on the most fundamental issues in philosophy, one cannot fail to detect a fine sense of the Dao at work. Is it because being a consummate *Taijiquan* master, his sensibility has penetrated to the very heart of his own being and thinking? Or is it because being an open and creative thinker, his thinking has come to encompass a logic and a dialectic one would naturally find in the creative philosophies of Plato, Whitehead, Laozi, and the *Yijing*? I must say that Neville has both the sensibility and the reflective wisdom to absorb Chinese philosophy and to be absorbed into Chinese philosophy.

It is hence interesting to note that while one could approach Neville from a strictly Western philosophical and theological angle and find him speaking good sense and making good points in the enterprise of reconstructing fundamental Christian theology or Greek value theory, one can equally approach Neville from a strictly Chinese philosophical and perhaps the Daoistic angle and find him also speaking good sense and disclosing a level of understanding that can only be identified in the experience of enlightenment of a great Daoist or a great Chan master.[1] Consequently, I find it possible even to interpret him thoroughly along the lines of Chinese philosophy of the Dao (the way), the *yi* (change), and the *li* (proprieties and rites) just as he is totally at ease in interpreting Chinese philosophy and recovering a hitherto unfathomed depth of meaning from his understanding of God or being, becoming, and justice.

One possible way to understand Neville's view on Chinese philosophy is to understand Neville's efforts in the construction of a system of being, value, theory, and norms. What Neville has in mind is to construct an architectonic philosophy that would comprehend and accommodate everything in the universe and that would also explain the creation and rise of the universe from the very beginning as well as the continuous striving for achieving value and excellence on the part of humans. We may indeed agree that there is a Whiteheadian background in Neville's speaking of quantity, quality, and value in his reconstruction of human thinking,[2] yet one must also point out that there is also a determination to overcome the polarity of the Whiteheadian God in order to guarantee an unbounded and infinite source-fulness (not just the resourcefulness) of creation and creativity. There are, too, no doubt, Neville's efforts to expound and justify the worldliness and humanity of the human person so that the human person will have both the freedom to express itself in culture and the ability to see a plenitude of differences of cultural histories.

Neville is at his best when he aims to preserve genuine creativity on all the four levels of being: the ontological, the cosmological, the sociocultural, and the individual-personal, each with its qualitative features and yet each related to the others based on a dialectic of being (conditions and harmonies of being). As I have suggested, Neville is a disguised master of the *Yijing* ontocosmology with a truly profound vibrating consonance between his own philosophical system, derived largely from Western sources, and the Chinese philosophical wisdom. In fact, one must be amazed at how he could so easily reach a rapport and develop a common measure between Chinese and Western views. To do so Neville has truly mastered the Chinese wisdom of both Daoism and Confucianism at the same time. The creativity of the Dao transcending culture and the creativity of culture immanent in the Dao works in great harmony to exhibit a framework of thinking of multifaceted creativity. Without such philosophical depth and hermeneutical creativity, I do not know how Neville, or for that matter anyone, could reconcile the radical differences between Confucianism on the one hand and traditional Christian theology on the other in relation to essential issues.[3]

Consequently, I must conclude that Neville has been imbued with a

Chinese philosophical spirit in constructing his systematic works equally derived from his spiritual and rational reflections on Chinese philosophy and from the Western sources, the combination and synthesis of which again lead to his insights into both Chinese philosophy and Western traditions. In what follows I shall explore and discuss Neville's contributions to the understanding of Chinese philosophy in three areas that are essential to his system-building, namely, the area of ontological creativity, the area of systematic creativity, and the area of creativity in the cultivation of the human person and human society. I shall elucidate relevant points for the purpose of clarification and elaboration so that one can see how various strains in Chinese philosophy are important for Neville's construction of a comprehensive and fundamental philosophy of reality and value and how they in fact must be important for any construction of a measure of truth in the comparative study of world religions.

ONTOLOGICAL CREATIVITY AND ONTOLOGY OF *WU*

One of Neville's major insights occurs in his revival of the argument for creation *ex nihilo* in the context of Christian theology. In reviving this argument for a necessary understanding of the fundamental creativity of God, he also has introduced new meanings and relevance for any understanding of creation of the world in other great world religions. Neville's reconstruction of the argument *ex nihilo* has the following five highlights:[4]

1. Creation *ex nihilo* is a three-term relation of the created world, the ground, and the act of creation each term of which cannot be separately conceived or known.
2. The created world includes all determinate things, which must be ontologically grounded.
3. The determinateness of a thing is a harmony of essential and conditional properties.
4. Nothingness or emptiness in the creation *ex nihilo* bespeaks the contingency of everything in the world and the world itself.
5. Everything determinate, being a harmony, has a value of a certain kind and a certain degree.

We can see that all these five points are either explicitly verified or implicitly assumed in writings of Daoism and the *Yizhuan* and hence can be said to contribute to a systematic understanding of Chinese philosophy at large. In this regard I see Neville's reconstruction of the theological argument as a reconstruction of a metaphysics of creativity that has an even greater significance for contemporary persons and society in a cross-cultural perspective.

It is a great insight to insist on a fundamental form of creativity in the creation *ex nihilo,* from which other forms of creativity become possible. In general, we understand creativity in terms of creation of something new from something old and preexisting. This is true not only of physical and biological evolution; it is true also of human cultural activities including scientific theorizing, philosophical speculation, and poetic and artistic composition. The new in creativity is based on the old and yet goes beyond the old. When we see life regenerated, we see creativity at work where new form and new structure or hence new function are being developed and yet the old form or structure is preserved to sustain the new.

Human creativity, on the other hand, involves things and actions of the human person. It is an exhibition of an ability to synthesize and to organize a new form, a new structure, and a new function, yet it must be done on the basis of knowledge of the old and understanding of experience. Hence we can see that creativity in general must presuppose something in the past and present in order to present something new. But then we must face the question that if there is nothing to presuppose, could we have creation of something totally new? Furthermore, is there any reason to suppose that we must have something to begin with or rather that we cannot presuppose anything and something has to come into existence by itself? There is no end to the argument for and the argument against a positive or a negative answer to these two questions. For in the nature of logic there is nothing necessary or universal in the following possibilities:

A. Something produces something. (Something dependently comes into being.)

B. Something produces nothing. (Something remains the same.)

C. Nothing produces anything or something. (Something independently comes into being.)

D. Nothing produces nothing. (Nothing comes into being from nothing.)

Without getting into extensive clarification of the meanings of nothing and something in modern logic, all four possibilities could be seen to be separately true as well as jointly true. It is clear that A and C are two basic forms of creativity. But then one may ask whether before something produces something, something has to be something in the first place. Hence the coming into being of something in C must be prior to coming into being from something in A. Hence creation *ex nihilo* is an even more basic form of creativity, which can be titled "ontological creativity." Once we have something in the beginning, one could then argue that all different new things are produced by the something in the beginning. This we can call "cosmological creativity." We can see from this where Neville's insight resides: in a strictly logical sense of presupposition "cosmological creativity" must presuppose "ontological creativity." This is precisely the point made by Laozi in the *Daodejing*: It is the formless and substanceless Dao that gives rise to everything (namely, every form and every substance) in the world. "The Dao gives rise to oneness, oneness gives rise to twoness, and twoness gives rise to threeness. Threeness gives rise to the ten thousand things."[5]

But is the formless and substanceless Dao the nothingness or emptiness (*wu*) in ontological creativity? The answer is positive. As the *Daodejing* puts it: "*Wu* (nonbeing) is to name the beginning of heaven and earth; *yu* (being) is to name the mother of the ten thousand things."[6] But of course such a name is not a constant name and hence the *dao* we speak about is not the constant Dao. What is constant and therefore pervasive is the ground of all activities and all existence and this can be neither named nor spoken of, because in naming and in speaking we will make the Dao a thing or an object. Hence it is not even proper to identify the Dao as the emptiness (*wu*), because in speaking of *wu* we would objectify the *wu* into a thing. Insofar as the Dao gives rise to oneness and so on, it is the primordial source of a limit and a development of a cosmos and a plentitude.

How does the Dao come into being? This question cannot be really answered because it cannot really be asked. If one comes to understand the Dao, the question and the answer will be self-dissolved.[7] Logically we perhaps could say that the Dao is sui generis and self-created. But once there is the Dao, the creativity of the Dao is such that all things will fall in order. Hence we have the Dao as the ontological ground and source of everything. But this is not to say that there is no creativity of things and human persons insofar as they are coming from the Dao. The important insight of the Daoist is that there is creativity of things because there is creativity in things or because there is the Dao in things. The Dao is in things because things are in the Dao. In this sense the Dao cannot be any thing, this thing, that thing, this nothing, that nothing or any nothing, because it is any thing, and at the same time this thing, that thing, this nothing, that nothing. Yet the Dao is not a thing or nothing, but a relation of producing everything from a source, and the creativity of the Dao is a relation involving everything, the source and the creative action. Hence we can also say that the Dao is both absolutely transcendent and absolutely immanent—transcendent beyond everything as the constant ground of activities of things and immanent as the very source of creativity in things.

It is also true that although we can speak of temporal change and transformation of things *in* the Dao, we cannot really speak of the temporal change and transformation *of* the Dao because it is the Dao that creates time and makes the temporal changes possible. In this sense it is constant and hence eternal. But eternity in this sense is not separate from temporality either. They could be seen as two sides of the same thing: as ontological creativity it is atemporal and eternal, and as cosmological creativity it is temporal and changing. This is because the Dao cannot be simply self-produced and then self-destroyed. It has to be constantly self-produced from itself or from nothing (*wu*) so that it can be the constant ground of all creativities of all things, namely, the ground of cosmological creativities. In this sense we come also to another important insight of Daoism, namely, that ontology cannot be ontology alone but must be intrinsically linked to cosmology, and at the same time cosmology cannot be cosmology alone but must be linked to ontology as a consequence of ontological creativity. Hence we need to speak of the creativity of things as cosmo-ontological creativity, and of the creativity of the Dao as ontocosmological creativity as well. In light of this creativity of the Dao we should speak of the ontocosmology and cosmo-ontology of the world.

Although I am not so sure whether Neville will give such a rich meaning of creativity to his argument of creation *ex nihilo*, I feel that what is implicit in the Daoist view of creativity is fully compatible with his intention in bringing out the argument. What remains to be explored is the depth of meaning one may wish to attach to the notion of *nihilo*. Traditional Christian theology gives the appearance of abhorring a vacuum and thinking of *nihilo* as nonproductive or as being a symbol of negativity and darkness. But must we so think? To bring out the argument *ex nihilo* in terms of ontological creativity, cosmological creativity, and eventually in terms of ontocosmological creativity and cosmo-ontological creativity mentioned above will no doubt endow the argument with a much richer meaning, an endowment necessary for a fruitful contemporary understanding of the world and humankind.

As a very important consequence of this understanding, one can see that the source of the creativity is always the ground of any creativity and is not really separate from the creative activity of any determinate thing. The transcendence of the source is made immanent by its continuous creativity, whereas what is immanent in a thing as ground of creativity is actually transcendent as timeless or time-transcending (or "eternal," to use Neville's word) power or source. It is clear that one cannot speak of transcendence without speaking simultaneously of immanence and vice versa. It would be wrong therefore to assume that there is no link between ontological creativity and cosmological creativity of either God or the Dao. Hence the issue raised by Keiji Nishitani, as mentioned by Neville, does not arise.[8]

It is in light of this ontocosmological and cosmo-ontological creativity that we can then explain the creativity of producing something from something or the creativity inherent in the nature of things or the creativity of human mind and human imagination, for it is on all these levels that the original creativity of the Dao is at work. But this is not to say that the creativity of the Dao has determined the way things are. On the contrary, it is precisely the creativity of the Dao that lets things make themselves the way they are, for the Dao itself is undetermined and undeterminable: it is unlimited freedom from which self-discipline and self-limiting are possible. In this sense, things as determinate things, on the one hand, are subject to their formational and transformational conditions (referred to as "essential and conditional features" by Neville); on the other hand, they are free to realize what best possibilities they might have in terms of their creative potentiality and potential creativity. This is also where their value lies: they provide conditions for the realization of cosmological or cosmo-ontological creativity of other things and they can also realize their cosmo-ontological creativity on the basis of their given conditions. It is in this light that Zhuangzi says that things are self-generated, self-created, and self-transformed, because things are in the Dao and the Dao is in things no matter how lowly in value they are.[9]

Neville speaks of the contingency of being of everything. Surely he would include the being of the great ultimate (*taiji*) as the Hebrew God (Yahweh) or the Neo-Confucian supreme principle. I believe that traditional theology would wish to prove the necessary existence of God in a conceivable sense. On the Chinese side, Zhu Xi certainly maintains the principle (*li*) of the great ultimate as a permanent and necessary given. How does the contingency of being as arising from nonbeing square with this aspect of God or the supreme principle? The answer is that the contingency of being is supported by the necessity of emptiness or nonbeing as creative. If being is contingent on nonbeing, and creativity as an aspect of emptiness is a transformation of nonbeing into being, then there is equally a necessity of being similar to the necessity of the nonbeing defined as creativity. That nonbeing can be so conceived is due to the fact that, in the tradition of the *Zhouyi*, the ultimate ground of being cannot but be "ceaselessly creative" (*shengsheng buyi*). This is very clearly expressed in the Xici of the Yizhuan: "To be productive of the productive is called the *yi*; to form forms is called the creative (*qian*); and to present lawfulness of being is called the receptive (*kun*)."[10]

This necessity of ontological creativity in the *yi* is no doubt characteristic of the Confucian metaphysical tradition that is continued in the *Zhong Yong* where the Zhou poetry of "What is mandated from the heaven is ceaselessly active" is quoted and the *Mencius*, which, together, form the foundation of a creative metaphysics of ontocosmology of the "the ultimate of nonbeing (*wuji*) and yet the ultimate of being (*taiji*)" in Zhou Dunyi's *Taiji Tushuo*. But even for the Daoists there is no other way of conceiving the Dao than conceiving it as a necessary or naturally necessary process or framework. Neville is correct to point out that there could be a sense of sequence from *wuji* to the *taiji*.[11] But if this is to be regarded as a statement of the original ontological creativity, as it should, it cannot be a temporal sense of sequence but rather a logical necessity of entailment in light of the defining nature of the *wuji* or the *wu* as the creative.[12]

Neville speaks of the determinateness of a thing as the harmony of its essential and conditional features, an insight making a Confucian point. In fact, he even mentions that Confucianism focuses on the "harmonies among the elements of the primary cosmology, and cites attunement with the ontological creative act as the means to achieve that harmony."[13] But the question is how he understands harmonies as the determinateness of a thing, giving rise to both the being and the value of the thing. He has indicated that conflict and strife are elements of harmony that can work toward either loosening or tightening the pattern. Hence he does not see harmonies as always good. But it appears that these two senses of harmony, the axiological and the ontological, need to be subsumed in a larger theory of harmonization.

Perhaps we can explicitly define harmony as the unity of the polarity of *yin* and *yang* forces or elements in the process of cosmological creation. Any unity of the polarity of *yin* and *yang* is a harmony that carries with it a value; its value is thus its own determinate existence or indeterminate existence in a determinate context. But whether the value of the harmony (or harmony as value) will last or should be broken depends on how a given thing or hence a given harmony may contribute to a larger harmony (both spacewise and timewise) or whether it may hurt or damage a larger harmony such as harmony among harmonies or simply relationships among things. In this way we can see how harmony as ontological creativity and harmony as axiological value could remain the same even though it can acquire two meanings at the same time.

Given ontological creativity, although philosophically we must understand and analyze it in terms of a three-term relation, the inevitable question is how this relation is to be actually conceived or experienced in human history. Is it to be conceived in terms of its source, its act, or its resulting being? Apparently, the Daoist tends to think in terms of the source, namely the Dao as in Laozi, or in terms of its act in nature as in Zhuangzi, whereas the Confucian tends to think of it in terms of its creative being, the great ultimate from which an ontocosmological process will ensue. In the actual historical experience this great ultimate is embodied in the notion of the Lord-on-high (*shangdi*), reflecting the political sovereign on the earth. Later in the beginning of Zhou *Shangdi* becomes the heaven (*tian*), which is less personalized and more comprehensive in scope of influence. Similarly, Judaism also comes to think of ontological creativity in terms of its resulting being-power, which is further identified with the tribal protector God Yahweh for religious reasons.

It is interesting to note that while Judaism has retained the personalistic notion of God and made the hidden ontological creativity more abstract and more transcendent, the Daoist and the Confucian have gradually transformed the full personalistic notion of *Shangdi* into a less personalistic notion of Heaven, and finally has completely depersonalized this notion of Heaven into that of Dao. In this process of depersonalization there is also a process of immanentization that reaches its apex in the notion of the Dao.[14] It is good to see that Neville has distinguished "theological sources" from the "archeology of God" through which one can see how the same or similar notions could come across very different feelings, circumstances, and cultures, depending on the impact of different histories. However, it is through this retrieval of a god (in the sense of the great ultimate) that Neville is able to develop a framework of comparative religion in which he could vividly compare the Western religious tradition with the Chinese metaphysical tradition with regard to their cultural values.[15]

One can easily note that the transcendent personalization of the great ultimate in the Jewish tradition and the immanent depersonalization of the great ultimate in the Chinese tradition are processes which are the reverse of each other. The former leads to a transcendent God whereas the latter leads to an immanent Dao. Are they therefore absolutely incommensurable and completely exclusive of each other? The answer to this question is no. By closely looking into the nature of the transcendent God, as depicted by Karl Barth, we find God as beyond the grasp of human logic. Similarly, by looking into the nature of the immanent Dao, such as in Zhuangzi and Hui Neng, we also find the Dao as beyond the reach of language and logic. Hence, although being the reverse of each other, God and Dao still share something in common and thus could be regarded as extensions of this something in common. What they have in common is the unity of act, source, and result in the original ontological creativity, as suggested by Neville. The difference is a difference of posterior cultures, conventions, and histories, or, as Neville put it, the archeological difference of God and the Dao. The real God is also the real Dao and the real Dao is also the real God.

TRILOGY OF THINKING AND COSMOLOGY OF *YI*

Neville has raised the question as to what the Chinese tradition can contribute to the philosophy of world religions. His answer is that it has brought out a version or versions of ontological creativity "devoid of difficulties of the theism-mysticism split characteristic of the West."[16] In making this answer he has touched on a fundamental feature of Chinese tradition: Chinese tradition is primarily a philosophical tradition, not a religious one. But this is not to say that there are no religions in China in any sense of "religion." The point is that whether Daoistic or Buddhistic, a major Chinese religion developed its theoretical teachings in terms of philosophy, not in terms of theology, as Christianity has done. This may have something to do with the early and continuous effort of the Chinese mind, attuned to an enlightened pragmatism, to naturalize and depersonalize any spirit or god that has no origin in human affairs. Hence philosophy (whether called *weijizhixue*/study of self-realization, *xuanxue*/study of profundities, *daoxue*/study of the way, *lixue*/study of principles, or *xinxue*/study of heart-mind) via the community of scholar-officials plays the same role as theology via a corps of church members.

In this regard one can also see that Chinese philosophy in the above sense also functions religiously, that is, it provides a practical guide to life and presents a goal and a belief system for social practice and self-cultivation, as clearly exemplified in Song and Ming societies and individuals. In this light one can see how the Chinese tradition has presented a straightforward philosophical picture of the ontological and cosmological creativities without being encumbered by a heavy system of religious symbols and institutions.[17] Because of this it is natural to see how ontological and cosmological creativities could be developed more articulately and more clearly in the *Daodejing*, which Neville's understanding suggests. Perhaps, it is not an exaggeration to say that after Neville's efforts the combination of major strains in Chinese philosophy could provide a universal basis for understanding the issue of creation *ex nihilo*, which understanding could serve as a basis for the study of world religions.

We can see that Neville's development of a systematic philosophy of religion is in fact motivated by the need to provide a basis for the study of world religions and their associated theologies or metaphysics. In so doing, he has been influenced by the great Western masters of theology and philosophy (such as Plato, Augustine, Whitehead, and Dewey) as well by the great Chinese masters of Daoism and Neo-Confucianism (such as Laozi and Wang Yang-ming). His effort from the very beginning has been to construct a solid universal foundation of Being and its creativity for the study of human beings and their cultures in their various historical engagements with that foundation. He has taken the challenge to reinterpret traditional arguments, to sort out nuances of meaning, and to explore and creatively propose a profound and comprehensive theory for synthesizing differences and accommodating them with a strong sense of justice in a theoretical framework.

In this light I can see Neville working not as a sectarian theologian, nor a Whiteheadian system builder, but as a truly reflective Neo-Confucian philosopher with a determination to seek the ultimate roots of human thinking that would cover and apply to all the ten thousand things under heaven and thereby inspire a creative life of moral practice at the same time. In this sense we might even say that Neville writes like a Zhu Xi and thinks like a Wang Yang-ming, particularly in light of his central motif, namely to resolve the problem of the one and the many by way of ontological creativity.

One might see that the Neo-Confucian principle "One principle and many manifestations" (*liyi fenshu*) is in fact Neville's hidden guiding light and open challenge at the same time, which provides a key to understanding the development of his systematic views. From the early *God the Creator: On the Transcendence and Presence of God* through his *Creativity and God: A Challenge to Process Theology* to his *Eternity and Time's Flow* one sees his concentration on the problem of the one and the many from the point of view of *one* source. Yet, in *The Cosmology of Freedom, Soldier, Sage, Saint, The Truth of Broken Symbols, The Tao and the Daimon: Segments of a Religious Inquiry,* and *Behind the Masks of God,* one can notice his concentration on the problem of the one and the many from the point of view of the *many* manifestations. The combination of these two points of view is, of course, finally revealed in his recently completed trilogy *Reconstruction of Thinking, Recovery of the Measure,* and *Normative Cultures,* in which one witnesses a systematic progress from a framework of metaphysics of thinking to the founding of a hermeneutical methodology for understanding nature and reality and finally to a theory of theorizing that would lead to a fruitful and harmonizing dialogue over cultural incommensurabilities. In these one also witnesses a Confucian practical reason at work, which makes Neville's philosophy truly ecumenical across time and space.

It is interesting to note that the way Neville developed his philosophy in general and his trilogy in particular can be best interpreted in the

underlying philosophy of the *Yijing*, which is the living source and foun-
tainhead of the development of the Song-Ming Neo-Confucianism. I
shall make five points regarding this interpretation, which is intended to
show that there is a deeper level of meaning in Neville's work, which can
only be caught in this light, and which also demonstrates the significance of his work as a framework of cross-cultural world-thinking for
the twenty-first century.

First, Neville's concern with the argument of creation *ex nihilo* is
implicitly presented in the Duanzhuan of the *Zhouyi* where the Active
Originator (*qianyuan*) is the beginner and creator of the ten thousand
things and rules over heaven. If the *qianyuan* is not the creative act in
the ontological creativity, what could it be? When it is said that all
things are created with its resources, it implies an ontocosmological
beginning of things, as mentioned above. The question has been raised
as to whether the *qianyuan* would form a correlative pair with *kunyuan*
(Conforming Originator) in co-creating the universe and thus lose its
unique originating position. The answer is that the relation between
qian (activity) and *kun* (conformity) needs to be seen with creativity as
a three-term relation, as Neville has argued. *Kun* in fact is primarily
nonactivity or noncreativity from which creativity and action arise, to
which all creations return, and at which all creations would reside.
Hence the sequence from *qian* to *kun* reveals a relation that is implicit
in the ontological creativity of the *qian*. Even in the argument for creation *ex nihilo* we start with creation and then speak of the *nihilo*
because of the nature of the creativity in the initial creation. It is clear
that the first two *guas* of the *Yijing* text have established a paradigm for
all other created *guas* (resulting from combination of *qian* and *kun*) to
emulate thus establishing the ontocosmological nature of the creativity
in a primary cosmology.

Second, we must see the symbolism of *qian* and *kun* as limiting
archetypal symbols abstracted from all creative relationships and thus
applicable to all creative relationships. In this sense we speak of Heaven
and Earth as two concrete exemplifications of the working relationship
of *qian* and *kun* because the former has suggested or disclosed the latter. Perhaps, along the line of a dialectic and semiotic of ontocosmological creativity, we can see *qian* and *kun* as primary symbols that stand
for the relation of ontological creativity and see all other symbols as logically subsequent interpretants of this primary symbolism apart from
being primary symbols for a given reality. The *Yijing* can thus be
regarded as both a methodology of interpretation of nature and an ontocosmology of creativity. What is even more significant is the fact that *yi*
(change and transformation) is best understood as representing both
ontological and cosmological creativity.

Third, the primary cosmology of the *yi* as explained in terms of the great ultimate in the Xici is no doubt a demonstration of the process of cosmological differentiation and ramification with an implicit order derived from the ontological creativity. This *yi*-cosmology no doubt also illustrates how oneness gives rise to many and how many may also relate and return to the oneness in a symbolism far clearer than the abstract notions of Platonic participation or Hegelian objectification. Neville must have had this logic or dialectic of being in mind when he praised the Chinese contribution to his articulation of creation *ex nihilo* in *Behind the Masks of God*.

Fourth, in the Yizhuan one can see a framework of thinking that integrates reality and values in a single ontocosmology of creativity. The very idea of the world as presence of the principle (*li*), which also forms a system in which all things are basically positionable and thus harmonized in the order of complementation and mutual support for furthering creativity is germane to valuational thinking.[18] In a system that caters to an individual's practical action and that regards human action as participatory and as both transcendently and causally effective, all situations are occasions for the valuation of understanding and the evaluation of action. It is not only that reality in a process of change needs be harmonized to avoid conflict and clash, but that even harmonies as a structure and as a relation are subject to change and transformation. Hence the question of how to preserve given harmonies and create harmonies in new situations becomes the challenging concern and burden (called the *yuhuan*) of a creative person. It takes insight and knowledge as well as reflective understanding of the whole in order to reach a good decision and to strive for an end.

In other words, we cannot think of reality without knowing reality in some way, and we can not know reality without valuing reality in some way. Similarly, we cannot value reality without evaluating our relation and action in regard to reality. Hence the cosmology of the *yi* entails or presupposes an axiology of the *yi* that in turn should give rise to a normative understanding of our action with regard to the knowledge and value of *yi*. For valuational and evaluational thinking a correct measure based on one's own life purpose and intention and the whole context of a world philosophy must be entertained and followed.

Fifth, the Yizhuan philosophy of change could also be understood as a "theorizing of theories" as suggested by Neville himself. Neville's concern is to recognize the differences of civilized humanity and different ways or conventions embodying civilized humanity. But to integrate all these differences in an overall theory requires a deep understanding of the roots of the differences in the archeology of religion and the sociology of social practices. To recognize this is to start to think of a comprehensive basis for relating and interrelating and even evaluating these differences. This should lead again to the ontological creativity and ontocosmological creativity in which all levels and dimensions of reality and human activity can be accommodated and positioned. This would be the way of ontocosmological thinking of the *Yijing* as a philosophy of reality and value. To be able to do this would be the basis for finding a practical reason to act in different situations with inherently different demands or norms. This is the wisdom that underlies the basic philosophy of divination for understanding and action in the *Yijing* system of thinking.

For the *Yijing*, to act in a given situation both wisely and in a timely way is to act in view of all the symbolic meanings and implicit values or disvalues of the situation. It requires that a person know the situation not only microscopically but also macroscopically and holistically across all possible situations and to know which goals of life and human responsibilities are allowed or mandated. Hence to act thus is to act creatively in an ontocosmological sense of creativity. I believe that this is the essence of seeking theoretical wisdom across all theories and of seeking hypernorms across all norms in Neville's *Normative Cultures* (1995).

The above serves to show how Neville's philosophical-theological thinking as a whole and his trilogy of thinking, understanding (interpretation), and normative decision in particular could be deepened in meaning in an ontohermeneutical understanding of the philosophy of the *Yijing*. One might also point out that while illuminated by the philosophy of the *Yijing*, the philosophy of the *Yijing* on the other hand might receive illumination from Neville's reflections on those fundamental issues. Specifically, his trilogy reflects a methodology of thinking, interpretation, and decision making that can be said to be essential to the understanding of the *Yijing* in the modern or postmodern light. Together with his fundamental ontology of creativity, Neville can be said to have presented a profound and comprehensive reading of the *Yijing* even though he may not be aware of it. In this light he could also be said to have achieved a "fusion of horizons" across the Western and the Chinese or Eastern philosophical traditions and to have opened new ways toward a global philosophy of humankind in the future.

CONFUCIAN-CHRISTIAN COMPARISONS
AND NORMALOGY OF *LI*

As a philosopher Neville can be best described as a Confucian-Christian or a Christian-Confucian. In terms of theological interests he is no doubt more a Christian than a Confucian and hence a Christian-Confucian. But in terms of philosophical interests he is more a Confucian than a Christian in the traditional sense of the terms and hence a Confucian-Christian. I have noted that Neville has changed his paper on Confucian-Christian incompatibilities into Confucian-Christian comparisons. I see this as a deepening of thinking inclining toward the Confucian ontocosmology as embodied in the Yizhuan of the *Yijing*. But on the other hand, I do not think that he has completely avoided the incompatibilities that exist between Christian theology and the Confucian ontology on a level that still merits our serious consideration.

Of course, Neville's interest is not merely in comparing or eventually integrating the Confucian and Christian philosophical views. He is perhaps eager to establish a universal theory of human thinking and valuation in which all religions and all cultures can be rightfully appreciated and evaluated and, furthermore, in which relevant truths from each tradition can supplement and enrich each other. This is indeed a great task and a great vision, but it is nevertheless not whimsical or impractical insofar as we have no conclusive reason for a postmodern relativism of values, nor do we have a conclusive reason for a Western-oriented modern universalism. To avoid both one needs to open up a deep understanding of world religions and world philosophies and to set one's mind to analyzing issues reflectively and creatively and to formulating frameworks. In this cause Neville argues for the portability of Confucian wisdom into the Western contexts (hence his slogan Boston Confucianism or the Boston School of Confucianism).

I wish to suggest that the portability of Western philosophical thinking apart from Western science has been argued for and in fact implemented since the days of May Fourth 1919 in China. Although there have been many debates on specific issues, the usefulness of introducing Western notions, categories, and methods or methodology cannot be denied in the interests of modernization, rationalization, and revitalization of the native tradition. Similarly, I believe that similar things can be said for the portability of Confucianism or Chinese philosophy to the West, even though the Western tradition is now at its height and the Western culture occupies a dominant position in the world today. Philosophically significant today are questions about how specific points can be made, how specific issues and difficulties of mutual interpretation can be overcome, and how specific issues of incompatibilities can be resolved. It is in this light we can see how Neville has made his contribution toward a Confucian–Christian dialogue.

Neville has located three specific difficult issues regarding the transporting of Confucianism to a modern Western social context: (1) the issue of Confucian filial piety as a holy duty in Christian religion, (2) the issue of Confucian ritual propriety as a moral requirement of Christianity, and (3) the issue of obvious Confucian objections to believing Jesus to be the Son of God in Christianity. How do we understand these issues and how do we resolve them?

Regarding the first issue, filial piety is no doubt rooted in the ancient practice of ancestor worship and must be understood as a reverence toward life and the origin of one's life. It is consistent and necessary that one preserve the respect for one's parents or ancestors so that one can continue the tradition of the past and can look forward to the future as a continuity of the past. Hence for the traditional Chinese family male progeny are considered part of the teaching of filial piety. It is true that in a traditional society in China filial piety as a virtue did contribute to the care for the elderly, but it is certainly not the reason or even the cause for the practice of filial piety. In the *Zhou Rites* (*Rites of Zhou*) and the *Book of Filial Piety* (*Xiaojing*) glorification of the family name and honoring parents with one's official achievements are more the motivating reasons for filial piety than simply nourishing one's parents. Therefore, the issue of filial piety remains even in the present despite the fact that parents normally do not need or wish to have their children's support. Then what is the ultimate value and justification for filial piety as a practice?

The ultimate value and justification for filial piety is derived from the cosmology of the creativity of heaven and earth in which the value of human existence consists. Parents gives rise to the child just as heaven and earth gives rise to humankind. The harmony and unity between heaven and earth and humankind endows and fulfills value in human beings. Similarly, filial piety toward one's parents would actually endow one with value and a sense of rootedness in the world. Hence filial piety is symbolic of the original unity and harmony between heaven, earth, and humankind and should be observed as a supreme norm. It is also true that parents love children without selfishness and to return this love the children should be filially pious, which means care and love of parents without selfishness. In this sense filial piety is seen as an example of reciprocal care and benevolence (*ren*) and together with brotherliness (*di*) forms the root or the base for the practice of *ren*. [19] In this sense filial piety should be regarded as the very core of learning to preserve and extend one's humanity. It is with such understanding that paying respects to one's ancestral spirits and filial piety are linked together and the meaning of doing this is so fundamental that nothing could really compete with it.

On the Christian side, Neville has rightly pointed out that to love God is not to abolish family relations but to transfer love from kinship to community under God. To love God is to love God as the common parent and as the supreme parent under whom all people are related as brothers and sisters. In the *Analects* Confucius has also said that "All men within the four seas are all brothers."[20] This means that all people should love each other because they come from the same roots. But the question is: Which is more fundamental, to love one's parents or to love God? Given the above explanation, I feel that this is a choice of faith, a choice of cosmology, and a choice of ultimate significance or ultimate commitment. It is conceivable that in Jesus' time as in the modern period a Western person from the Christian world would choose love of God over love of one's parents (demonstrated in certain crucial occasions). But this is again a begging of the question.

It ought to be pointed out that it is natural to love one's parents just as it is natural for a parent to love his or her children. To give up this natural feeling for something else requires special consideration and special sacrifice and it cannot be always the case. Hence Jesus' commandment to love God need not be a constant rule by which one would simply abandon one's parents for becoming Christians. Thus I see no conflict between the two requirements, and it would be wrong to assume that there must be a conflict. I have seen many Chinese Christian families in which obligation to parents and obligation to the church are well kept in harmony because each obligation is interpreted as part of the other obligation. Such is the way of harmonization from the Confucian view. It is of course conceivable that one obligation is exclusive of the other from another point of view. But again a metahermeneutical position based on a metaethical attitude is required to make a metadecision of this sort.

There is no denial that the Christian church fosters a community independent of families but which is still a human family from which one could learn love and to which any (believing) individual could join as a member. The advantages of having church-centered communities are many and God-inspired individuals can be great individuals. Perhaps, because of the Christian teaching and Christian community, individuals enjoy more freedom and assume more responsibility, face more challenges and undertake more adventures, all of which have contributed to the promotion and implementation of the values of science, commerce, and democracy in the West. But on the other hand, churches are no substitute for natural families just as communes cannot substitute for natural families. Perhaps they would function best as surrogate families when natural families are broken. This is to assume that the genuine teachings of Jesus prevail. But once the teachings are lost, both communities and individuals are lost. Individuals become rough and tough self-interested and self-serving manipulaters and macho entrepreneurs. Communities become lonely crowds of individuals who do not care for each other and who could become psychologically isolated nomads and disturbed eccentrics. In light of this, it is perhaps not accidental that in present-day America many leaders have campaigned for the promotion of family values. It is also not accidental that philosophers like Neville have also wished to introduce the Confucian proprieties (filial piety and the like) into America.

Neville speaks for the ideal Christian church and the ideal church member who would give love and teach love, with or without families, under any circumstance. Similarly, one could speak of an ideal Confucian family and an ideal Confucian person. It is important to note that the Confucian may extend his love of parents to love of community and then to the love of all people under heaven. Hence for the Confucian, family is the bastion for growing love toward society and even toward all the lives and things under heaven. Thus Mencius speaks of "loving my relatives, caring for people and being friendly to other beings."[21] Wang Yang-ming speaks of "forming one body with heaven, earth and the ten thousand things."[22] In the Datong chapter of the *Liji* (Records of Rites) one also envisions the ideal state of "grand unity" (*datong*) where all less than fortunate people, the handicapped [sic] and orphans, widows and widowers, are to be cared and nourished without fail. These ideal extensions and expansions of love must be seen as rooted in and beginning from the filial piety from a Confucian viewpoint. From this ideal development of love, one can easily see that Confucian philosophy of filial piety could reach the same end as the Christian philosophy of love of God.

Perhaps we could say that the Confucian and the Christian have shared the same ideal goal of love; their differences lie in their conceptions of means and methods for reaching such a common goal of human society, one through a family system and the other through a church system. These differences also are rooted in different conceptions of the ontology and cosmology as already mediated by history and sociology. We have discussed how, in terms of the pure consideration of ontology and cosmology based on creation *ex nihilo*, the West and the East have no disagreement, and Chinese ontology and ontocosmology have specifically and thoroughly supported this thesis of ontological creativity. But then, history and culture have given different forms to this ontological creativity and have caused the great divide between them—the theology of God and the cosmology of the Dao.

Our discussion of filial piety as holy duty has led us to a recognition of the holistic character of the underlying philosophies of filial piety and holy duty. They are compatible insofar as their ultimate social goals and understanding of creativity are concerned. Nevertheless, they are incompatible with regard to means and methods and to historical symbolism and belief systems requiring different practices and institutions. However, we must also note that in regard to means and methods we could still find some similarities, for example, between the self-cultivation theory of Confucianism, and the self-sanctification theory of Christianity.[23]

The question can arise as to whether these two apparent differences make any real difference. The answer is both yes and no. It is no if the two communities or traditions do not meet, or when they do, they respect each other and make no attempt to impose one's system on the other. On the other hand, the answer is yes, if one community or one belief system tries to impose itself on the other, or if one believes itself to be the ultimate truth and thus ignores or devalues the other. It is perhaps because of the nature of this question and answer that Neville shows a great interest in promoting the Confucian culture of ritual propriety (*li*) as a way of realizing concrete universalism.

As the *Analects* has it, the most precious function of *li* is its harmonizing function.[24] But Yuzi also says that "Knowing harmony and harmonize without modulating it with the *li*, it is also not the right thing to do."[25] So here *li* at least has two important functions for relating people: to harmonize and to modulate, both achievable at the same time. This is because to *li* belongs the rules, institutions, and forms of behavior or relationships that embody respect for other persons, groups of persons, or even systems, customs, or practices that have been respected by people.[26] To have respect is to recognize the others' position, role, and what they stand for. It is to do the right thing according to the rules for special behavior. Hence *li* involves a dimension of assumed understanding and trust in others. Finally, the question of how to show respect for others also depends on the concrete situation in which *li* is performed. One must take into consideration the relevant factors of time and locale in order to properly articulate one's *li*. Hence to keep a promise and to keep it in a proper or fitting way is a matter of acting according to *li*.[27]

With this understanding of the *li* based on the Four Books and the *Liji*, I see Neville's reliance on Xunzi's explanation of *li* as basically correct and needed. For it is Xunzi who came to synthesize all the many factors into a coherent theory of the *li* in his essays "Lilun," "Zhenglun," "Wangzi," and other related essays. Espousing a rationalist philosophy, Xunzi observes that human persons have rational minds to recognize, organize, and plan human ends and capabilities in connection with the given resources from nature. The system of *li* is precisely a result of rational organization and planning that would serve the advancement of human ends and development of human persons for both their individual and social needs. This rational and social utilitarian justification of *li* will also give it the proper authority and sanction for implementation and observance. *Li* is indeed what Neville calls "humanity-defining conventionality" for it is by *li* that a human person becomes functional in a human context and learns how to express herself or himself as a human person. Hence *li* can be seen as a catalyst for the humanization of the person and the society. But the question is whether we can understand the breach of order or the promise to God in the Bible as a matter of failing to observe *li*. In one sense it is, but in another sense it is not. Adam could ask God before acting on his own. Besides, he knows that God forbids him to eat the apple. It is a failure to observe an implicit *li*. But on the other hand, as a system of rules of behavior that has not been fully established and explained by God, Adam and Eve have no particular explicit rule to obey. To me their sinfulness lies in their violation of a specific order from God.

Neville has followed Xunzi closely to give a significant construction of the continuum of ritual conventionality. For Xunzi as for Neville, *li* acquires a transforming power of cultivation and reformation; it is not simply a matter of harmonizing and modulating. It is also a matter of legislation and establishing norms and laws.[28] For Xunzi the setup of *li* in this sense is needed because he regarded human nature as basically selfish and greedy. But for Mencius human nature, with the mandate of heaven immanently endowed, is not to be controlled in this fashion; *li* has to be understood as expression of the *yi* (rightness) from within the heart of humankind. For Mencius *li* becomes more a matter of harmonizing social orders and realizing and maintaining the goodness of the human person. Perhaps, it is in Xunzi's strong sense of *li* that Neville can speak of "repairing the covenant" with God, but certainly not in Mencius' sense of *li* as expression of the *yi*. For in light of Xunzi's theory, humankind has to learn to obey institutions and orders from the sage-king in order to eliminate selfishness in its humanity and to avoid falling into chaos. I see how Neville may be attracted to Xunxi in light of Xunzi's theory of human nature. But one need not forget that before the Fall, humankind was supposed to have been given a good nature by God and hence need not have the system of *li* in Xunzi's sense. Xunzi's *li* is needed for reform only when man has become bad in nature or, for Christianity, only after he has fallen from Eden. Despite Neville's good intentions, unfortunately, there is an inconsistency in Neville's argument for compatibility or agreement between the Confucians and Christians by capitalizing on Xunzi.

At this crucial point we could come to see a more fundamental cleavage between the Confucian and the Christian in their understanding of ritual behavior as a system of observing *li*. Strictly speaking, for the Confucians in a classical sense the ultimate *li* consists in serving parents for filial piety, in serving ancestral spirits by paying respects at the family altars, and in serving heaven by worshiping heaven at the tem-ples.[29] All these are consistent with the doctrine of trinity of heaven, earth, and the human in a philosophy of onto-cosmological creativity. But all these may actually run counter to the liturgy and ritual developed by Christians. Not only does the historically rich and culturally loaded symbolism of the Christian system run counter to the Confucian system, but also at the primary symbolic level, the respect for heaven and earth and the love of God are often intentionally interpreted to show difference rather than similarity. Hence we can see how the great Rites Dispute in the seventeenth century led the Roman Catholic pope to forbid Chinese Christians to worship ancestors and how as a reprisal Emperors Yongzheng and Qianlong ordered all missionaries to be expelled from China in 1723 and 1747, respectively.

I have attempted to stress how things really stand, burdened as they are by history, archeology, and the various systems of social and religious symbolism and practice. Philosophically, we could still speak of an ideal system of *li* to which both Confucians and Christians could agree. We could further require or hope that both Confucian and Christian would reform their traditions and confront the need for communication, equal learning, and mutual enrichment toward reconciliation and integration. Perhaps, this is the goal of Neville's trilogy, particularly as seen in the last book in the trilogy. We could establish common norms or norms of norms among different or even clashing normative cultures. We can do this because we share a foundation deep enough to go beyond our primary symbolism and historical differentiation. We share also a creative reason that would enable us to see and transcend our biases and to show respect for and trust each other. It is perhaps in this that we find the deepest meaning of *li*, *li* as a way of realizing *ren* (unselfish love) and relating and reconciling even radically different and incommensurable traditions or communities in the interest of common visions and in view of common roots. This may take a long time to implement, but if philosophers do not begin to think, to persuade, and to articulate, who will?

In the interests of fulfilling *ren* and seeking development of the human potential, models are necessary. Neville is right in arguing for Jesus as a model of perfection of humanity. Similarly, we can say the same for Confucius as a model of perfection of humanity. I do not see any real objections to this comparison for either classical Confucians or modern Christians. This is because a model of perfection has to be understood in terms of actual exemplary behaviors. But when we come to theological and religious issues that bear on matters of faith and belief, we should not expect accord, which, perhaps, is what cultural and religious pluralism means. Neville has wisely appealed to a pragmatism of practical significance to resolve or cast aside the differences between the transcendent Christian models and the immanent Confucian models of perfection. We need to be aware, however, that historical, cultural, and even ontological differences do often make a real difference. The issue therefore remains unresolved.

NOTES

1. I know that Neville sees himself as a scholar-official in the best tradition of Confucianism as indicated in his explanation of the workings of the Boston Confucianism.

2. See the first book of his trilogy, *Reconstruction of Thinking* (Albany: State University of New York Press, 1981).

3. One sees the changing of the title of his recent paper on Confucianism and Christianity from "Confucian-Christian Incompatibilities" to "Confucian-Christian Comparisons" in about a year, 1994–95.

4. Neville has formulated the logic of creation *ex nihilo* in his various writings, but the most pronounced statement of it is given in his 1991 book *Behind the Masks of God* (Albany: State University of New York Press, 1991).

5. See the *Daodejing*, section 42.

6. Ibid., section 1.

7. *Daodejing* says that "The Dao follows the nature (*ziran*)" which in a sense means simply that the Dao exists and functions of its own accord, without any external or internal restriction or limit.

8. See Neville, *Behind the Masks of God*, pp. 94–95.

9. Although Neville has referred to Zhuangzi a couple of times in his book *Behind the Masks of God*, the importance of pervasive presence of the self-creativity of the Dao in the sense of ontocosmological/cosmo-ontological creativity has not be recognized by him for explaining the sense of creativity in Neville. See Chuangzi's essay "Qiwu Lun" (On equalizing things).

10. See *Yijing*, Yizhuan, Xici, section 5.

11. See his recent paper "The Dialect of Being in Cross-Cultural Perspective," a typescript.

12. I think that when one recognizes creativity as defining nature of the *wu*, *wu* would become the ultimate of the *wu* and hence the *wuji*. But this is not to say that *wu* must be so conceived, yet as an ontological intuition it has been so conceived from the earliest founder of Neo-Confucianism to the founding father of the contemporary Neo-Confucianist Xiong Shili. Another point is: Why cannot the ontological creativity be both contingent and necessary just as it is both transcendent and immanent?

13. See Neville, *Behind the Masks of God*, p. 83.

14. For the process of transformation of depersonization from *shangdi* to *tian* and then to Dao, see my article "Dialectic of Confucian Morality and Metaphysics of Man," in *Philosophy East and West* 21.2 (1971): 111–23.

15. Neville has recognized the abstract nature of the ontological creativity in the argument of creation *ex nihilo* and considered religious symbols and significations far more interesting than an abstract theory of God as ontological act

or source and outcome. But I disagree with this evaluation: the abstract analysis of the divine creativity sheds light on the hidden nature of any major religion and reveals common ground or differences among all major religions. Furthermore, the three-term of the creativity as a relation illustrates the hidden relationship of the terms of the trinity of God the Father, God the Son, and God the Holy Spirit, which can be reinterpreted as the creative act, the created result, and the implicit ontological ground or source. Similarly, the trinity of heaven, earth, and the human can be also identified as that of the ontological creative act, the ontological creative ground or source, and the created result, which is endowed with the ability and the nature to act creatively in the environment of heaven and earth.

16. See Neville, *Behind the Masks of God*, p. 83.

17. Despite fancy names being given to directions and states of reality, it remains basically a matter of philosophical understanding. However, this is not to say that the lack of an organized transcendent religion with its theology in traditional China must be an absolute blessing. On the contrary, one might argue that this lack deprives traditional China of a balancing power against the despotism of emperors and prevents forces in favor of the development of science and democracy.

18. See my article "Philosophy of Position (*Wei*) in Zhouyi," forthcoming *Orient extreme, Occident extreme*, 18, 1996, Paris, 149–76.

19. See the *Analects*, 1.

20. See the *Analects*, 12.9.

21. See the *Mencius*, 7A.45. Zhang Zai also speaks of "treating people as my brothers and things as my companions" in his well-known essay "Ximing" (Western Inscription).

22. See his essay "Taxuewen" (On the Great Learning).

23. See discussion on this subject in Neville's *Behind the Masks of God*, pp. 116–25.

24. See the *Analects*, 1.12.

25. Ibid.

26. Mencius simply puts it: "The heart/mind of respectfulness is *li*." See the *Mencius*, 6A.6.

27. I have enumerated eight senses of *li* in my earlier comments on Neville's book *Normative Cultures* (Albany: State University of New York Press, 1995).

28. See Xunzi's essay "Wangzhi" (Institutions for a Kingdom), which certainly goes beyond what Confucius and Mencius explicitly would articulate.

29. In traditional China it is only the rulers who are to perform the *li* of worshipping heaven or *jitian*.

CHAPTER 15

The Culture of Metaphysics: On Saving Neville's Project (from Neville)

David L. Hall

The strange family resemblance of all Indian, Greek, and German philosophizing is explained easily enough. Where there is an affinity of languages, it cannot fail, owing to the unconscious domination and guidance by similar grammatical functions, that everything is prepared at the outset for a similar development and sequence of philosophical systems.
—Friedrich Nietzsche, *Beyond Good and Evil*

In the remarks that follow I want to juxtapose certain elements of Robert Neville's philosophical project with notions contributing to the thematics of the Chinese philosophic sensibility. My purpose is, first, to suggest that the mere existence of the Chinese sensibility relativizes and encapsulates the speculative tradition of Western thought. That is to say, the Chinese inventory of issues, problems, and ideas is so uncongenial to Western understandings as to suggest real incommensurability. The effort among speculative philosophers in the West to successfully construct general interpretations of the world as we experience it is presently stymied by the exotic nature of the Chinese sensibility. Second, I wish to recognize the fact that Neville is among the few speculative thinkers in the West who have begun to accept the challenge represented by the esoteric character of Chinese intellectual culture, and to take seriously many of the themes comprising the Chinese sensibility. Third, while acceding to the brilliance and cogency of Neville's comparative efforts, I wish to challenge the adequacy of his understanding of Chinese thought. My questions will concern the relevance of two notions central to the Western speculative tradition, and to Neville's thought as well, to the understanding of Chinese intellectual culture. These notions are "Being" and "Truth."

I want to suggest that Neville's inadequate treatment of the Chinese tradition is a consequence of his "metaphysical faith," which leads him to assume that the speculative vocabularies of the West bespeak a universal tendency in human beings. This belief precludes Neville from entertaining the idea that cosmology and metaphysics are contingent, local, historically determined phenomena that, however well they might have served us for the past two and one-half millennia, may have influenced the Chinese very little, if at all.

I need to defend the nature of my method on at least two grounds. First, the suggestion that there is *a* Chinese way of thinking about "Being" and "Truth" will not, I believe, seem so absurd since I shall be dealing with a "family" of perspectives that, however distinctive among themselves, share a common contrast with the analogous family of Western significances. Second, I will be highlighting certain general assumptions of the speculative tradition regarding the topics under discussion, with only a brief rehearsal of Neville's particular interpretation of these notions. I have not done a detailed exegesis of the particular character of Neville's philosophy for the following reasons: Based upon my understanding of his thinking, I believe that his particular characterizations of "Being" and "Truth," though slightly less pernicious from the Chinese perspective than those of the Western mainstream, are themselves finally trapped inside the Western problematic and must be found wanting by the Chinese. Since, however, I wish to keep an open mind, I have chosen to minimize recourse to my own interpretations and to assume that Neville knows at least as well as I do what he thinks, and to ask him to respond at length to certain issues to be found in Chinese thought that are interestingly allied to those he has presented in his work. This method has the advantage of allowing us to reduce the amount of time spent on the "that's really *not* what I meant" phase of the discussion.

While I have tried to avoid romanticizing the "otherness" of Chinese thought, I do admit that I have been more concerned to guard against any sort of easygoing assumption that the Chinese think pretty much as we do, only are not yet so sophisticated in their theoretical constructions. I am even more concerned to struggle against any sort of metaphysical colonization of China, which is no less suspect than are the commercial, political, or technological incursions that are its concrete correlates. In the following two sections I will be urging Neville away from what I take to be his tendency to sympathize with that metaphysical takeover.

A QUESTION THE CHINESE NEVER ASKED

Parmenides conflated existential and predicative senses of "be," and Lo! Metaphysics was born. Whether this conflation was the consequence of profound insight, or simply of the sort of muddle-headed thinking that some metaphysicians have since made famous remains a matter of dispute. Whatever the truth of the matter, the "Question of Being," in one form or another, has haunted the Western speculative tradition well-nigh from its beginnings.

Neville has added his own peculiar twist to this question by making the notion of creative activity prior to either "Being" or "Nonbeing." The primordial relationship, then, is not between Being and Nonbeing but between God as indeterminate creative ground and the determinate things so grounded. There is a three-termed relationship between "ground," "act," and "determinate things." Any determinate thing is a harmony of essential and conditional features. The togetherness of things characterized in terms of their essential features is "ontological togetherness." Cosmological togetherness is relative to the conditional features of things. "The question of Being can be raised . . . by referring to the togetherness of different things each with its essential features. . . . Ontological togetherness is the ground of the possibility of the very being of things that are different and yet cosmologically related."[1]

For Neville, Being is not primarily a common property of things; and it definitely is not a container that relates things by placing them within its own structure. Instead, "Being is a single creative act the end products of which are the various determinate beings with their cosmological connections ontologically together in the act itself."[2] This view nicely sublates the differences of the "common property" and "container" views, thus clarifying the intuitions contained in both and saving what one must take to be the essential intention of each.

Neville has gone to some lengths to demonstrate the efficacy of this formulation of ontological grounding to alternative religious and philosophic sensibilities in Eastern cultures. With respect to the Confucians and Daoists of China, I believe that he has not made his case. The problem is that the workable senses of Being in the Chinese traditions—Confucian, Daoist, that of the Mohist logicians, the Neo-Confucians, and even the Chinese Marxists—do not well resonate with either traditional Western understandings of Being or Neville's particular specification of that tradition. The key feature of Neville's formulation as it applies to the Chinese sensibility is that of the asymmetry of *ground* and *determinate things*. The disposition of the Chinese from the beginning to the present is highly inhospitable to asymmetrical relations of any kind. It is true that every relation is hierarchical, but the terms of the hierarchy are always in transition.

To see the difficulty of relating Neville's discussions of asymmetry of ground and determinate things to the Chinese sensibility one must begin with the meaning of Being in the Chinese tradition. The sinologist Angus Graham has pointed out that the Chinese existential verb, *you*, "being," overlaps with the sense of "having" rather than the copula, and that, therefore, *you*, "to be" means "to be present," "to be around," while *wu*, "not to be," means "not to be present," "not to be around." The Chinese language is an aesthetic, correlative language to the extent that it privileges the classical meanings of *you* and *wu*. This means that *wu* does not indicate strict opposition or contradiction, but absence. In classical Chinese philosophical discourse, the distinction between "not-p" and "non-p" is understandably elided. Thus, the *you/wu* distinction suggests mere contrast in the sense of either the presence or absence of *x*, rather than an assertion of the existence or nonexistence of *x*.

An important implication of this exotic sense of the *you/wu* relation has been noted by Graham: "In the absence of an affirmative copulative verb, there is no being an ox, any more than there is being white, and so no essence intervening between name and object; the term closest to Aristotelian essence, *ch'ing [qing]*, covers everything in the ox without which the name 'ox' would not fit it, not everything without which it would not be an ox."[3]

Another interesting illustration of this point is easily provided by recalling the Daoist sentiment, often rendered in English as "Not-being is superior to Being." A better translation is "Nothing is superior to something." But even this might suggest presence and absence in some absolute sense. For the Being-intoxicated Western thinker, an even better translation would be "Not-having is superior to having"—or as a contemporary Chinese Marxist translation reads: "Not-owning is superior to owning."

The *you/wu* problematic yields a vague supplement not only to modern Western notions of reason but to the late modern critiques of reason as well. For there is no need to overcome the "logocentrism" of a "language of presence" grounded in "ontological difference" if no distinction between Being and beings, or beings and their ground, is urged by the classical Chinese language and its philosophical employment. A Chinese "language of presence" is a language of making present the item itself, not its essence.

Language that does not lead one to posit ontological difference between Being and beings, but only a difference between one being and another, suggests a decentered world whose centers and circumferences are always defined in an ad hoc manner. The mass of classical Chinese philosophical discourse, then, is already deconstructed. Or better said:

the *you/wu* problematic does not urge the creation of texts that can be victimized by the deconstructor. According to Angus Graham, "the reversals in Lao-tzu have a modern parallel in Derrida's project of deconstructing the chains of oppositions underlying the logocentric tradition of the West." But there are clear differences as Graham suggests. Whereas the West tends to see a contrast of *A* and *B* as conflictual, China interprets the contrasts, as in yin/yang terminology, as complementary. For example, Graham emphasizes that Laozi wouldn't share Derrida's conclusion that Western philosophy, having failed to discern "the full presence of *A* has to be satisfied with the trace of it, which on inspection turns out to be only the trace of a trace of *A*. . . . Perhaps Lao-tzu's Way is how the Trace will look to us when we are no longer haunted by the ghost of that transcendent Reality the death of which Derrida proclaims."[4]

In the light of this analysis it is difficult to make sense of Neville's claim that "the *dao* that cannot be named underlying the *dao* that can be named" (*NC* 89) is an affirmation of the inexpressible unity of all things and their infinite ontological value. Nameless Dao is not an ontological ground; it is merely the noncoherent sum of all possible orders. The natural cosmology of classical China does not entail a single-ordered cosmos, but invokes an understanding of a "world" or Dao constituted by a myriad of unique particulars—"the ten thousand things." Dao is, thus, the process of the world itself.

In Daoism, the relevant contrast is not between the cosmological whatness of things and the ontological thatness of things, but rather it is a contrast between the cosmos as chaos—the sum of all orders, Dao—and the world as construed from some particular perspective—that is, any particular one of the orders.

Dao is not organic in the sense that a single pattern or telos could be said to characterize its processes. It is not a whole, but many such wholes. It is not the superordinate One to which the Many reduce. Its order is not rational or logical, but aesthetic—that is, there is no transcending pattern determining the existence or efficacy of the order. The order is a consequence of the particulars comprising the totality of existing things.

This interpretation of Dao makes of it a totality not in the sense of a single-ordered cosmos, but rather in the sense of the sum of all cosmological orders. Any given order is an existing world that is construed from the perspective of a particular element within the totality. But, as a single world, it is a selective abstraction from the totality of possible orders. The being of this order is not ontological in a foundational sense, but *(acosmotically)* cosmological. Such an abstracted, selected order cannot serve as fundament or ground. In the Daoist sensibility, all differences are cosmological differences.

I would contend that one does not have to think of Dao as ground of the determinate things in order to experience the kind of *tremendum* associated with religious or mystical experience. *Dao* as the sum of all orders, as the complex set of ways things are, is pretty mysterious, and not a little fascinating, in itself. Thus the "mystical" character of certain aspects of Daoist thought is perfectly understandable.

If Dao lacks ontological significance, then the act of understanding and articulating the Dao of things—*daoli* [the grasp of the patternings (*li*) of Dao (the ways of things)]—cannot have ontological reference either. The closest to our typical understanding of "reason," or "reasoning" is to be found in "seeking the *li.*" *Wuli xue* in modern Chinese is "the investigation of the patterns of things and events"—what we term "physics." "Psychology" is *xinli xue*—"the investigation of the patterns of the heart-mind." In general, to be *he li,* to be "in accord with *li,*" is to be reasonable or rational.

Li was translated "principle" by Wing-tsit Chan, one of the pioneer interpreters of Chinese culture to the West. This translation has created vast confusion on the part of a generation of Western interpreters of Chinese, many of whom just assume that *li* must, at some level, be transcendent. But *li,* as a "making sense of things," cannot be understood as a process of seeking principles as determining sources of order, or of discovering essential categories inclusive of particular things. It is, rather, an activity that constructs categories (*lei*) analogically, then traces, again by analogical means, correlated details that manifest patterns of relationships immanent within things and events. This sort of reasoning depends upon noninferential access to enlarged and deepened patternings. Inclusion or exclusion of items within a "category" are never associated with notions of logical "type" or "class." The sortings are "analogical," not "logical."[5] This understanding of "reason" and "reasoning" is one more implication of the fact that the Chinese never asked "The Question of Being."

The Chinese understanding of the *you/wu* relationship has profound implications for the manner in which philosophic discourse is shaped throughout the Chinese tradition. In the absence of the senses of "Being" associated with Western speculative philosophies, assumptions we take for granted as conditions for philosophizing are simply not present. Though some explanation of these claims would need to be made in order to render them finally plausible to Western philosophers, it may be said that the proper understanding of "being" in the Chinese tradition helps us to account for the fact that there is no real "metaphysical" tradition in China if we mean by metaphysics anything like *scientia universalis* or *ontologia generalis*. In addition, there is no ontological tradition that deals with the question of why these real things exist at all.

And when we arrive at cosmological questions, such as "What kinds of things are there?" or "What are the basic categories that make up the world as we know it?" the situation is the same. While it is true that Chinese thinkers, particularly the Daoists, ask about things, they do not ask about "categories" or "kinds" in any manner that would suggest that things have "logical essences" or constitute "natural kinds." Since there is nothing like "Being" that shines through the "beings" of the world, but only the beings of the world, there is no effective impulse to handle cosmological issues as we do—namely, by asking after the *logos* of the *cosmos*.

The principal reason Chinese thinkers are not apt to ask after the *logos* of the *cosmos* is that they lack an operative sense of cosmos. And their sense of *logos* (*li*, "pattern") is a *radically situated* notion. The Chinese understanding of "cosmos" as the "ten thousand things" means that, in effect, they have no concept of cosmos at all, insofar as that notion entails either a coherent, single-ordered world that is in any sense enclosed or defined, or a congeries of entities with essential features or essential modes of connectedness. The Chinese are, therefore, primarily, "acosmotic" thinkers.

I have tried to demonstrate the questionable relevance of Western ontological speculations, including those of Neville, to the Chinese sensibility. Being unable to rehearse the entire sweep of the Chinese tradition, I have had to rely upon the a fortiori mode of argumentation. For instance, if Dao and *li* cannot be interpreted along ontological lines, there is little chance that anything else in the Chinese tradition can.

THE WAY AND THE TRUTH

The second subject that challenges the universality or philosophical adequacy of Neville's enterprise involves the question of truth. It is rather obvious that Neville's handling of the question of "Being" will determine in large measure the manner in which he approaches the subject of truth.

One of the fundamental historical loci of the distinction between Appearance and Reality is to be found in Parmenides' efforts to reconcile the claim "Only Being is," with the deliverances of sense perception. Oddly, it is the question of the presence or absence of formal concepts or theories of truth that looms largest in this discussion. For merely suggesting, along with Aristotle, that to speak truly is "to say of what is that it is and what is not that it is not" merely states what is for (nearly) all of us quite obvious. The interesting and important issues generated by the search for truth are consequences of the strong motivation of Western thinkers to move beyond the obvious. Likewise, with the seemingly innocent notion of "concepts." In a formal sense, a concept expresses the sense of a "term." A term is a word with a stipulated meaning. The contexts of stipulation are, ultimately, theories. Thus a concept of truth has its locus within a particular theory.

There is really no useful sense in which we could refer to the statement of Aristotle just cited, taken simply by itself, as stating a "concept" or a "theory" of truth. This is the case even though the sentence is often taken as a succinct statement of the correspondence theory. It is only after placing this claim within the context of Aristotle's metaphysical and epistemological assertions that we may say such a thing.

In accordance with his view that truth involves the "carryover of value," Neville glosses Aristotle's notion of truth in the following manner: To say of what is that it is implies a notion of "isness," which Neville elaborates in terms of the notion of the achievement of value. Thus an entity is the values it achieves. And in the course of the "saying" that characterizes a thing truly, a number of perspectives are involved—namely, the biological, cultural, semiotic, and purposive. "Truth, then, according to the traditional formula, is translating the nature of reality [as an array of achieved values] into the biological, cultural, semiotic, and purposive terms of interpretation."[6] That is to say, "truth is a relation between the objectification as an intentional object and that to which the intentional object 'corresponds,' the thing with its achieved value."[7]

Neville's is a truly punched-up correspondence theory. He substitutes "value" for "form" as the standard of "reality," and introduces "translation" and "causation" in the place of mere "representation." This causal, pragmatic theory of truth would have strong affinities with certain Chinese understandings, particularly the Daoists, were it to eschew resort to essential features in defining the character of real things. But Neville's concern with ontological ground and cosmological reality as standards in accordance with which truth-relations are to be assessed would disqualify his theory in the view of the Chinese.

Theories defining truth in terms of a conformation of appearance and reality, or "language" and "world," or "propositions" and "facts" ("states of affairs") or, as in Neville's case, between intentional object and "real" object as something with achieved value, all presuppose a distinction between things as they "are" and as they "appear," or are asserted, or interpreted, to be. In Western philosophy this distinction has been implicit from its beginnings in classical Greece. When Thales claimed, "Everything is water," a natural response on the part of his communicants would have been, "Well, not everything appears to be water. What about mountains and olive trees?"

With Parmenides, this distinction is most explicit. "Only Being is; Not-Being is not." The first half of this proposition conflicts wildly with the way things appear to be for most individuals. Parmenides had to write a sequel to his "The Way of Truth" entitled "The Way of Opinion" in order to provide some characterization of the familiar world of "appearance." Being able to connect the way things are or must be, with the way they appear, is a function of our ability to think and speak rationally—that is, to draw out the consistent and formal (logical) implications of the proposition that states the being of Being and the not-being of Not-Being.

As Roger Ames and I have discussed at some length in our *Anticipating China*,[8] Zeno's challenge to the rational understanding of motion and change, expressed in the form of a set of logical paradoxes, had incaluable influence on subsequent cosmological speculations. The disjunction between our experience of the world and our rational understanding of it, the disjunction that those inclined toward the rational understanding of things soon saw as the separation of "Appearance" and "Reality," became a fundamental characteristic of our cultural self-understanding.

Correspondence theories of truth require that a proposition must have some independence from the state of affairs it characterizes. On the one hand, this argues for the transcendence of principles and, on the other hand, for the dualistic relations of propositions and states of affairs. Without such independence, both in the sense of dualism and transcendence, nothing like strictly logical truth may be formulated.

For the last several years a debate has taken place between sinologists and comparative philosophers over the claim that the Chinese do not have a concept or theory of "truth." Scholars from China, America, and Europe are to be found on both sides of this debate. While on the surface the claim may appear rather outrageous (surely Chinese tell the truth as often as we, and lie as often), the issue turns out not to be as easily settled as one might think.

In his introduction to *Disputers of the Tao*, Angus Graham distinguishes the central philosophical concern of the emergent literati class in classical China from that of the traditional Western philosopher by saying that their question was not that of the Western philosopher—namely, "What is the Truth?" but "Where is the Way?" This statement very succinctly contrasts the problematics of Western and Chinese cultures with respect to the issue of how one might orient oneself within the natural and social worlds.

Some comparativists have claimed that the Chinese concern for the Way was a consequence of the breakdown of moral and political order at the very period in which reflective thinking began in China. The argument is that the Chinese, in contrast to the more speculative Greeks, were forced to concern themselves with social order and harmony rather than with a dispassionate search for Truth. But, as Roger Ames and I have argued in our *Anticipating China*, there is every reason to believe that the search for Truth—for a reality beyond appearance, for some standard in accordance with which a plurality of distinctive beings might be measured—was itself a response to the problem of creating or discovering a social and natural order within which individuals might find a secure and harmonious existence.

The suggestion that the Chinese sought the Way because of their more practical and urgent political and social concerns, while in the West we went adventuring after Truth because we somehow had the luxury to be speculative, is on reflection, highly questionable. A more pragmatic interpretation seems equally plausible. The philosophical discourse shaped in large measure by the search for Truth itself had an ethical and political cast from the beginning.

In pluralistic, ethnically diverse societies, it is not so easy to chart a concrete and specific Way among the many ways suggested by diverse languages, myths, customs, and rituals. Harmony must be sought through assent to abstract, and ultimately universalizable, principles and standards. The quest for capital "T" Truth serves the aims of social and political stability in both positive and negative manners. Positively, it promises, down the road, a standard of common assent that can ground values and practices. Negatively, it suggests the necessity of a certain tolerant circumspection in the treatment of those who do not share our present truths.

By contrasting the Way and the Truth as goals of philosophical reflection, I do not wish to perpetuate the clichéd interpretation of the West as theoretical and dispassionately reflective, and Chinese thinking as vested in the need for social harmony. In my view, the two cultures shared the only sensible goal for social human beings—the attainment of social stability and, possibly, of harmony.

The series of events that has made the question "What is Truth?" one of the defining concerns of the Western tradition constitutes a fascinating narrative, not the least because it could all have been different. The complex senses of truth encountered in the *Oxford English Dictionary* divide rather naturally into two categories: There is one class of meanings associated with notions of rectitude, integrity, wholeness, lack of distortion, and so on, and a second class associated with the comparison of what appears to be the case and the reality itself: "conformity with fact," "real contrasted with imitation." It is the first class that resonates with the "Way" metaphors we associate with the Chinese sensibility—the true course of an arrow, following the true path, having a true heart, and so on.

If we look to the Hebraic tradition at the time of the major prophets (eighth–sixth centuries B.C.E.), the senses of truth are related to wholeness, integrity, the ability to maintain oneself as healthy and whole in all circumstances. "Truth is that which can be maintained by the soul, that which has the strength to exist and act in the entirety of the soul."⁹ The prophet is one whose words, being true, have efficacy. "A prophet must be true in order to be a prophet, to have the necessary strength of soul, that his words shall not fail to take effect."¹⁰

The sense of truth as "the strength to maintain oneself" contrasts readily with the notion of truth as signaling a correspondence between appearance and reality. Indeed, in the Western tradition, that sense was a gift of the post-Homeric Greeks. Philosophically, it is the Greek *aletheia* and the Latin *veritas*, as influenced by the Greek thinkers, which have come to determine the dominant uses of the terms in philosophical discourse. At the beginning of our *Anticipating China*, Roger Ames and I tell the story of the manner in which the presumption of the construal of a single-ordered cosmos from out of chaos provided the grounds for the assumptions of an ordering agency, the belief in an appearance/reality contrast, the preference for being and permanence over becoming and process, and the presumed disjunction between the claims of reason and those of sense experience. It is this complex of beliefs that motivated the development of the distinctive senses of truth in the Western tradition.

By claiming that Chinese philosophers concern themselves with the Way rather than the Truth, I certainly do not wish to deny that the Chinese are concerned with questions of fact. Whether or not the check is in the mail is a significant question in both Chinese and Western cultures. But this in itself does not touch the issue of whether a concept of truth is present. Indeed, Graham holds it to be obvious that the Chinese have no concept of truth. His argument is this: In the West we have developed a concept of truth by extending the meanings of "fact" from questions such as "whether the money, as you told me, is already in the bank"¹¹ to such nonfactual issues as the truth of tautologies, the truth of narratives, and so on.

Thus the semantical range of "true" and "truth" comes to extend far beyond first-order questions of a factual nature to logical, historical, and literary issues that are expressed in propositional form. What this means is that truth comes to be a second-order concern involving the comparison of propositions with states of affairs—or "facts." As for the Chinese, Graham notes that:

> such words as *jan* [*ran*], *yu* [*you*], and *hsin* [*xin*] would not be expected to, and do not, have the same metaphorical spread as "true." . . . To

say that Chinese philosophers display a "lack of interest in questions of truth and falsity" amounts then to saying that like Westerners they are not primarily concerned with the factual, but unlike Westerners they do not use a word that assimilates other questions to the factual. That they would have no concept of Truth would be taken for granted, but is trivial.[12]

The reason this conclusion—though trivial for the grammarian concerned primarily with the nature of *langue*, could not be so for the comparative philosopher more interested in the nature of the Chinese *parole*—lies in the fact that the latter is concerned with the broadest of cultural evidences that shape the construction and expression of values and visions. Thus, the distinctive treatment of "facticity" in the Western and Chinese traditions noted by Graham is of greater interest to the philosopher of culture than it would be to the grammarian.

If we look at our question from the perspective of translatability, two problems emerge: The first is the obvious one of whether we can find a word or words that we are justified in translating as "truth." The second is this: If we do translate some Chinese locution as "truth," do the Chinese conceptualize or make up theories explaining this term and account for the phenomena it represents or to which it alludes?

When we look at the Chinese culture, therefore, we do so armed with the assumptions highlighted by the importance Western philosophers have given, both tacitly and explicitly, to the notion of "truth." We presume the Chinese must have a concept or theory of truth because we, quite rightly, assume that the Chinese are as concerned as we are as to whether or not the check is in the mail. We further believe (with far less justification) that in the background of this concern is a worry about saying of something that is, that it is. And we then take for granted (this time with no justification at all) that such a worry requires, yet farther in the background, some theory of truth.

The presence of transcendent beings and principles in the formation of Western culture is uncontroversial. The dualism entailed by this transcendence, though discomforting to the theologically doctrinaire, is also a widely accepted characteristic of the rational interests of Anglo-European societies. The polar, interdependent, *yin/yang* relations of terms and concepts within the Chinese tradition is unquestioned. These correlative terms—Heaven and humanity (*tian/ren*), knowing and doing (*zhi/xing*), change and continuity (*bian/tong*), speaking and doing (*yan/xing*), fullness and emptiness (*shi/xu*), name and performance (*ming/xing*), stuff and function (*ti/yong*), body and heart-mind (*shen/xin*), and so on, constitute a vocabulary that in one form or another, pervades the classical Chinese corpus, insuring a correlation between these complementary terms and a vision of things.

For a proposition to have a univocal sense, terms must be strictly delimitable. This is a familiar condition of an asymmetrical worldview. The Chinese polar sensibility on the other hand, renders the defining vocabulary porous and interdependent, precluding such delimitation in any but the grossest terms. "As different as night and day" in this world becomes "as different as night-becoming-day from day-becoming-night." Precisely where does the difference lie? In a polar sensibility terms are clustered in such a way as to be essentially incomplete unless paired with opposing or complementary "alter-terms." Classical Chinese may be uncongenial to the development of univocal propositions for this reason. And without such propositions, theories of truth that presume, however tacitly, a distinction between "propositions" and "states of affairs" are ultimately untenable.

There are, in fact, some Chinese sources that would seem to serve as the basis for discussions of theories of truth in the most formal of senses. But to find significant discussions of the notion of truth in a form we would recognize, we would have to find at least the beginnings of truth-functional logic. Some scholars seem to believe that there are promising resources among Chinese thinkers associated with the so-called Mohists, Legalists, and the School of Names. Those scholars disposed to argue for truth theory in China do in fact employ these sources. The problem, of course, is that these resources come from thinkers and schools whose ideas were effectively abandoned by the second century B.C.E. Appeal to such sources is analogous to our appealing to the insights of Heraclitus or Empedocles, equally neglected thinkers, to say something about the general character of our culture.

The conclusion is that it might well be possible to discover structural similarities between Western and Chinese languages such that a theory of truth could be claimed possible for the Chinese. I would further stipulate that some thinkers might be found who have at least adumbrated such a theory. Clearly, after the incursions of Buddhism into China and after the development of the great Neo-Confucian syntheses of Zhuxi and Wang Yang-ming, the grounds for theories may be thought to be even more prominent in philosophical and literary texts.

Having said this, however, the broadest evidences favor the conclusion that interest in truth in the traditional Western senses of that term was notably absent among Chinese thinkers. Those traditional senses, of course, are expressed in terms of the notion of truth grounded in either a correspondence or a coherence theory. Even the counter-examples to this claim are of limited value. Mozi himself subordinated logical and rational argumentation to what we would term ethical considerations. He sought principles of ethical utility in a manner that would align him with certain rather broadly conceived forms of pragmatism. There is little by way of dispassionate rationalism to be found even in the early Mohist doctrines.

Many of the discussions found in later Mohist thought, expressed in the work *Names and Objects* recovered in the sixteenth century, come closer to what we in the West would recognize as rationalism. But, even here, there is a crucial difference. The paradigm of Western rationality is the employment of a logic of definitions in the search for necessary truths. Plato's development of a theory of definitions in the *Theatetus, Sophist,* and *Statesman* originated the account of knowledge as "justified true belief." Aristotle's development of categorial definitions and the logic of the syllogism further formalized the interest in truth. Leibniz began his philosophical reflections from the logical form we call the "principle of identity" (A = A). Hegel may be said to begin his dialectical arguments from an interpretation of the "principle of noncontradiction" ["not (p and not-p)"]. Updated forms of Anselm's ontological argument for the existence of God employ modal logic to demonstrate that "perfection (God) exists." The point here is that Western modes of rationality have closely tied rational and logical discourse.

Even in later Mohist philosophy, which is the closest thing to representing something like what we call rational thinking, discourse and logical argumentation remained distinct. Neither in the part of *Names and Objects* dedicated to discourse nor in that concerned with argumentation, is the Mohist interested in establishing logical forms. Chinese reflections and conversations were conducted without the benefit of those sorts of distinctions that identify logical or grammatical relations. The principal aim was to produce a discourse shaped in such a manner as to guard against the expression of incoherent or unproductive analogies. Though the Mohists were able to develop procedures for testing the viability of descriptive expressions, they did not see the relations of such discourse shaped by the criteria of logical necessity. As a consequence, whatever development of logical forms took place, these forms did not contribute to the construction of more rigorous modes of discourse.

Questions of truth and falsity in the strict sense depend upon notions of the necessity of the conclusions of argument-forms, such as the syllogism, by which this necessity may be expressed. Without an attempt to render explicit the logical forms of argumentation, discourse establishing the truth of this or that would not be possible. To the extent that there is a split between discourse and argumentation, as in later Mohism, there can be no efficacious concern with strictly necessary truth as formal coherence or correspondence.

The failure of the Chinese to develop modes of logical analysis directly related to discursive argument is strong evidence that attempts to interpret Buddhist-influenced doctrines of the Neo-Confucians along metaphysical lines are likely wrong-headed. And the slightest examination of Maoist versions of Marxist and Hegelian dialectics demonstrates the fact that the traditional separation of logic and discourse has dominated China from its beginnings.

By the time of the Later Han dynasty, classical Chinese culture contained an inventory of ideas from which concepts of propositional truth might have been derived. It does seem, however, that the import of classical Chinese thought lay on the side of alternative notions that, from the perspective of the Western truth-theorist, must seem most exotic.

It is plausible to suggest that we ought to translate a Chinese term "truth" only if the Chinese have essentially the same beliefs about, and with respect to, that term. This is to say, we might expect the Chinese to assert essentially the same things as do we when we address the term "truth." If the Chinese do not treat the locution(s) in their language that are translated by the term "truth" in the same manner, we are thereby urged to believe that we are dealing with different things.

Of course, the same is true intraculturally: There are sufficient differences between the attitudes toward, and characterizations and uses of, the term "truth" among Anglo-European philosophers, as to signal that different terms ought to be used. Part of the animus between the realist and pragmatist understandings of truth is due to the fact that they are really talking about altogether different things.

I should recall the observation made earlier with respect to Neville's concept of truth as "the carryover of value." There is certainly a sense, as I have said, in which the pragmatic aspects of Neville's translational or causal theory of truth resonate with Chinese understandings. But, to the extent that "Way" metaphors dominate the Chinese sensibility, carryover of value must be seen strictly in terms of practical consequences having to do primarily with moral self-development and the realization of social harmony. A concern for propositional truth is hardly a dominant feature of the Chinese tradition.

Why would it matter that the Chinese have no articulated understanding of propositional truth if, as is certainly the case, there is a serviceable recognition of the facticity of matters of practical import? That is to say, since the Chinese can certainly recognize whether or not the check is in the mail, or the money is in the bank, and are likely to be aware of the precise date of Chairman Mao's death, why do they require a self-conscious articulation of propositional truth?

The lack of interest in propositional truth is no more a sign of cultural defect than is the Western stress on the notion of truth as correspondence or coherence at the expense of a concern for the understanding of truth as the way of things. The issue, rather, involves the question of how mutual understandings between these traditions may fare in the absence of self-consciousness about the differences in cultural invento-ries. It is, after all, clear that Western intellectuals hold a rather quali-fied respect for Chinese scientific and historiographical methods rooted in traditional values rather than objective standards of evidence. Indeed, the speculation concerning reasons for the retardation of scientific devel-opment in China are most often addressed in terms of the relative unconcern of the Chinese for objective assessment of the natural world. For their part, the Chinese question the moral sensibilities of Western societies who are seemingly unconcerned with the more human tasks of realizing a harmonious way of living.

A MODEST PROPOSAL

I have argued that the Western metaphysical tradition, including Neville's particular stipulation of it, is broadly irrelevant to Chinese philosophical concerns. Now, I wish to qualify that claim in the follow-ing manner: It is certainly possible for the Chinese concerns to shift, par-ticularly since it appears that China is presently being forced to confront the Western world in its political, economic, and technological guises. If the Chinese, contrary to their history and tradition, wish to begin the task of global thinking, it may be that they will warm more readily to issues of generality, universality, theoretical adequacy, and so on.

But my personal view is that the next century (at least) belongs to China and that the burden of understanding, and of intellectual and practical adjustment and compromise, will be placed upon us Western-ers. As the "people of the Center," the Chinese are ill-disposed, and even more ill-equipped, to join the "Community of Nations." Our ability to accommodate the Chinese insistence upon its own centeredness depends upon our willingness to understand the Chinese sensibility from within. Such willingness can only be underwritten by the kind of modesty that has always spelled disaster for the speculative philosopher.

If we are to survive the coming century, we are called upon to have a grasp of the distinctive intellectual and spiritual resources that have sustained the Chinese community from its beginnings. This is the pri-mary reason I am doubtful that the apologetic and constructive tasks of Robert Neville as a comparative philosopher will be helpful in shaping the pattern of future engagement among Chinese and Western intellec-tuals.

I believe that the claim of the Western theorist to universality, or adequacy, must finally be found false in the face of the very real outsid-edness of the Chinese tradition. In my view, the only way Neville can save his philosophy from encapsulation and relativization by the all-too-exotic Chinese tradition is by giving up any hint of the "transcendental pretense,"[13] thereby moving his project a great deal closer to something like that of the historicist forms of American pragmatism and closer, as well, to the Chinese modes of thought. In doing this, of course, he will move beyond the pale of the Western metaphysical tradition. The good news is that he will still be able to hang out with nominalist-pragmatists-historicists such as myself. Thus, I may rightfully be expected to have a selfish motivation in this paper, for were Neville to accept my proposal, we could then be, in addition to good friends of long-standing, fellow-travelers, as well.

The massive excellence of Neville's philosophy makes praising him appear an exercise in the obvious. This much needs to be said, however: If Whitehead was correct in claiming that it is more important that a proposition be interesting than that it be true, then Neville's philosophic reflections, entertained as a complex proposition, have achieved a level of importance that renders questions concerning the truth of this or that aspect of his thought as close to irrelevant as such questions ever become. In particular, the value of Neville's speculations for my own thinking has been unexcelled throughout my entire professional life. So valuable, in fact, has been his persistent illumination of the path I didn't take, it is certainly the case that, had he not existed, I would have been required to invent him!

I end, therefore, with this modest hope: If Neville remains stubborn and unyielding and proceeds along the path he has so long traveled, I can only wish that his thinking comes to serve his Chinese interlocutors in the same manner as it has served me over these many years.

NOTES

1. *Normative Cultures* (Albany: State University of New York Press, 1995), pp. 88–89. Hereafter, *NC*.

2. Ibid., p. 89.

3. *Disputers of the Tao* (LaSalle, Ill.: Open Court, 1989) p. 410.

4. Ibid., p. 228.

5. Tony Cua's work *Ethical Argumentation—A Study in Hsun Tzu's Moral Epistemology* (Honolulu: The University of Hawai'i Press, 1985), is an excellent examination of the dominant Chinese understanding of "type" and "category."

6. *Recovery of the Measure* (Albany: State University of New York Press, 1989), p. 69.

7. Ibid.

8. Albany: State University of New York Press, 1996.

9. Johannes Pedersen, *Israel: Its Life and Culture* (London: Oxford University Press, 1959), p. 339.

10. Ibid.

11. Angus Graham, *Disputers of the Tao* (LaSalle, Ill.: Open Court, 1989), p. 396.

12. Ibid.

13. See Robert Solomon, *The Bully Culture: Enlightenment, Romanticism, and the Transcendental Pretense, 1750–1850* (Lanham, Md., Rowman and Littlefield, 1993).

PART VI

Robert Neville Replies

CHAPTER 16

Responding to My Critics

Robert Cummings Neville

The first "reply" to this collection of essays is an expression of my gratitude. So many things deserve thanks, four of which I shall mention at the beginning. First, is the honor of it and for this I am deeply grateful to the editors, Nancy Frankenberry and J. Harley Chapman. Second, is their sagacity in picking the range of authors who approach my work from so many angles. Third, is the extraordinarily high quality of the essays themselves, reflecting the fact that the authors are all serious thinkers with agendas of their own: this collection is a dialogue among positions, not merely an expository and critical examination of one, though the exposition and criticism in all the essays is acute and responsible. Fourth and perhaps most important is the fact that this book exhibits a generation of thinkers who can handle the great issues of philosophy and philosophical theology, East and West, as well as any generation ever. Neither Zhuxi's group in the twelfth century nor Thomas Aquinas' at the University of Paris in the late thirteenth has an edge over the circle represented here for disciplined original thinking about the deepest and most perplexing questions in human intellectual culture. I am grateful for all these things and many more that will be highlighted in the discussion below.

My plan for this Response is to discuss each of the papers briefly, but as I go along to develop more extended discussions on thematic lines that bring the essays together. Four of these essays, those by Robert S. Corrington, Delwin Brown, Hermann Deuser, and David Hall, have been published with a reply in *American Journal of Theology and Philosophy*; my responses there focused on methodological issues and here those essays will be discussed more in terms of their dialectical relation to my thinking.

GEORGE ALLAN

George Allan's paper is a *tour de force* of creative analysis of the most difficult writing I have done, the *Axiology of Thinking* trilogy. I wish I could write with his clarity and wit, especially because, to my mind, the *Axiology* is the center of my system. If we cannot find an axiological alternative to the fact-value split that was assumed along with the invention of early modern science, then there is no way to surmount Kant's foundationalist reductionism so as to make speculative philosophy plausible. And if speculative philosophy is not plausible, the problematic of God and creation I have pursued is not plausible, the realism of moral, political, aesthetic, and religious experience I have defended is not plausible, and the comparative interest that brings Western culture and values—not just science and technology—into relation with other cultures is not plausible.

The hallmark of my own axiology, which Allan teases out with such cunning, is the claim that valuative thinking, in the forms of imagination, interpretation, theorizing, and the pursuit of responsibility, is always a function of human life as part of nature. Thus my axiology needs to develop at length and integrate

1. a theory of value that can be found in nature and carried over into imagination, interpretation, theorizing, and responsibility;
2. a philosophy of nature dealing with basic topics such as space, time, and movement that can exhibit human personal and social realities as complex natural things; and
3. a theory of *intentionality* that can illumine imagination with the depths the Romantics found in it, of *interpretation* with the subtleties that the pragmatists and hermeneuts develop, of *theorizing* that includes science on the one hand and philosophy of culture on the other, and of *practical reasoning* that integrates personal and social dimensions while dealing with the large questions as well as the immediately practical.

Allan's essay lays all this out with genius, for which I thank him with much envy. I shall respond to some of his specific points in treating certain themes below.

EDITH WYCHOGROD

Edith Wyschogrod's essay is a brilliant irenic counterpoise to my polemics against modernism and postmodernism in *The Highroad around Modernism.* She herself is one of our most distinguished postmodern thinkers who has made important contributions to philosophy and religious studies, and her own work embodies the irenic spirit she would have me develop. Whereas most of her postmodernist colleagues say "you can't do this anymore" and "it was never legitimate to do that," and therefore never get inside the proscribed intellectual projects such as speculative pragmatism or process philosophy, she is at home in all the currents of contemporary thought and interprets them with insight and passion.

She is right, of course, that my rejection of postmodernism is hasty and polemical; several other authors here note that I once called my own project "postmodern." Heidegger was an important influence on my thinking in college and graduate school.[1] His "ontological difference" was the initiating problematic for my concern with being-itself and the problem of the one and the many, although I moved away from his specific distinctions fairly early to a theory of creation *ex nihilo*.[2] Heidegger was also a major influence on Paul Tillich, whose ideas about symbolizing the Other are the germ for my *The Truth of Broken Symbols*. I am grateful also for the parallels Wyschogrod finds between my work and that of Derrida and Deleuze, parallels made possible in part by her extraordinary genius at finding deep metaphysics in authors who would be surprised to know that is what they are doing.

So I accept Wyschogrod's corrections with apologies so long as I am allowed one last polemical fling. Why is it that so many postmodern authors, including Heidegger, fail to engage intellectual projects other than their own with respectful detailed criticisms (of the sort found so often in the present volume)? Why do they assume that every other project must be a repetition of the particular past that they already have decisively debunked? Neither process nor pragmatic metaphysics is like the Wolfian scholasticism Kant attacked, and they are not subject to the antifoundationalist arguments of postmoderns. Yet they are dismissed as illegitimate without a hearing, read right out of the conversation, except by rare postmoderns like Edith Wyschogrod (and I cannot think of another example; Derrida read Peirce on semiotics but missed the metaphysical part). So my pique is the personal one of being dismissed and therefore delegitimated as a thinker by those with whom I would like to be in conversation and who control much of the means of communication (analytic philosophers control most of the rest); it's a righteous pique felt by nearly every philosopher and theologian who is not part of the postmodern or analytic programs. Intellectual concern for the Other, so important to many postmoderns, ought not delegitimate one's intellectual others but bring them into a community of inquiry.

PATRICIA COOK

Patricia Cook's essay is the first of several that attempt to locate my pedigree. Her question is whether I am as much a Platonist as I think, or rather am an Aristotelian because I am a systematic thinker. Now, to be compared positively with Aristotle is not a bad thing, even for a Platonist, and I thank her for that. But there are three points in which I want to defend the importance of my Platonism over against what Aristotle would like.[3]

First, she and I disagree about Plato's conception of the role of philosophy in public life. I am not persuaded by her claim that Plato believed that philosophy's "relentless questioning" is ultimately subversive to public life and the political process; perhaps she has more affinity with Straussians than I, or gives more credence to the authenticity of the *Seventh Letter* as Plato's last word. At any rate, with Whitehead I take Plato to regard the function of reason to be the wise guidance of life, social as well as personal; this was the point of the return of the enlightened philosopher to the cave in the *Republic*, as well as of the need of the philosopher-statesman for "normative measure" in mixing incommensurables in the *Statesman*.[4] Plato's own attempts at politics were disasters, but that might simply have been a function of the problems of his time relative to his practical talents; he did invent the university, a considerable contribution to public life. The most important contrast between Plato and Aristotle in this regard was that the former believed reason to be part of a larger harmony of human life, its servant and guide, whereas the latter had a hierarchical view of the self in which theoretical reason is higher than practical reason whose purpose is to make life safe for contemplation (*Nichomachaean Ethics*, book 10). Plato, perhaps in distinction from the real Socrates, did not believe that "relentless questioning" is the ideal of reason, but only a part of it and sometimes a merely playful part. Reason for Plato rather has to do with discerning appropriate forms for life and harmonizing them with ongoing political and other processes with good timing. Remember that the philosopher-king aspirants in the *Republic* need to supplement their mathematical and dialectical training with fifteen years in the provinces as petty bureaucrats. Plato surely saw the usefulness and fun of pursuing ideas critically for its own sake; but when philosophy is engaged in public life, he would have approved Peirce's dictum that doubt needs to arise from a reason, not be doubt "in principle," because the function of philosophic reason is to harmonize ongoing processes according to the best discernible ideals, not to establish indubitable truths.

Second, Cook is right that I am Platonic in developing a theory of value based on notions of aesthetic intensity. She is also right that my specific way of doing that, with a theory of harmonies as having essential and conditional features mixed according to simplicity and complexity, is not to be found as such in Plato. It derives from Leibniz, Whitehead, and Weiss, but is put together in ways unique to my own argument. Leibniz contributed the notion that goodness is intensity of being insofar as it has simplicity and complexity, Whitehead the rudiments of a theory of harmony, and Weiss the distinction between essential and conditional features. The audacity to give *harmony* such a central metaphysical place comes from Confucian and Daoist philosophy in which it would be audacious not to give harmony such a place.

The contrast with Aristotle is just here: instead of using the idea of harmony he characterizes value in terms of completeness, perfection, and structural fulfillment: the greatest value is not having to move or fulfill more potential, like God as Thought Thinking Itself, imitated best by the rotation of the stars that move in no other way, and by the human contemplator whose material potentials are stabilized to allow for thinking thoughts that are fully fulfilled in being thought. I surely side with Plato on this point and, as Allan pointed out, that form of axiology is central to my work. If I were an Aristotelian, I would have to define truth as the carryover of form, not value, because for Aristotle value is the actualization of form.

Third is the matter of the nature of systematic philosophy. Perhaps because of his emphasis on structure rather than harmony, Aristotle developed his philosophic theories as structured systems of categories, as Cook so neatly describes and attributes to me. I admit that my one essay, "A Sketch of a System," in *New Essays in Metaphysics* does present my system in the rhetorical form of a structural laying out of categories; that was because Paul Weiss, an Aristotelian in that sense, asked me to express my thought that way. But precisely because I think "systematic philosophy is the critical attempt to comprehend everything in one discursive view," no system of categories alone can constitute a philosophic system. Categories leave out what is categorized and by themselves do not indicate their own relativity to context and purpose. For that reason my own "system" is a vastly complicated dialectical relating of categories to experience in many different fields, including religion, education, ethics, and many other approaches to interpretive life. Even such basic categories as harmony and essential and conditional features take their meaning from their cumulative definition in many different contexts. The system includes careful interpretation of experience and other theories, the imaginative elaboration of ways of saying positive things that do not commit you to unwanted positions, and comparative study of alternative cultural systems with their philosophies. Because systematic philosophy requires coming at reality from all the angles you can find, there can be no one statement of the system. Isn't this just what Plato meant by dialectic? "One discursive reflective view" means the singular cumulative process of coming at things from as many angles as you can manage, giving meaning to central categories and strategies through the process, not through Socratic definitions.

Of course I have learned from many besides Plato and never would think a philosopher would want to repeat Plato rather than develop a view appropriate for the enlightenment and guidance of the philosopher's own time. We are all global philosophers in ways Plato did not imagine. But I am a Platonist beyond what Cook stresses, I think, with regard to three of his "doctrines": the function of reason as the guide to harmonizing life so as to realize the best, the aesthetic approach to value as harmony, and the systematic character of philosophy as the vigorous probing of reality from as many angles as possible.

SANDRA ROSENTHAL

Sandra Rosenthal comes at my pedigree from a contemporary perspective, asking whether I am more a pragmatist or a process philosopher. Of course I have learned from both movements. Because of the centrality of Peirce's philosophy for my theory of signs (say in *Recovery of the Measure* and *The Truth of Broken Symbols*), I consider myself a pragmatist, the orientation of my major teacher, John E. Smith. But George Lucas, Lewis Ford, and Delwin Brown here, centrally committed process philosophers, as well as Rosenthal, a pragmatist, put me in the process camp.

Rosenthal analyzes my pragmatic commitments with great discernment, sharing as we do a penchant for "speculative pragmatism."[5] I take issue with only one point of her interpretation, namely, her claim that I believe "that the question of truth is not relevant to philosophic systems," which instead are supposed to enlarge and interpret experience. I do follow Peirce in holding to a correspondence theory of truth, though the criteria for truth are pragmatic.[6] Philosophic systems are large-scale representations developed over time with which to engage reality, and they should get reality right in the respects in which they interpret it. This is consistent with pragmatism.

The genius of Rosenthal's paper is its critical analysis of time as construed by pragmatism and process philosophy. She acutely describes my rejection of the pragmatic theory of continuity in favor of the process theory of atomic moments of present concrescence. She also accurately and with extraordinary sensitivity to detail traces my rejection of the process theory that atomic moments are the *res verae* in favor of a theory of time in which past, present, and future need to be together (eternally, not temporally) in order for time to flow, thus coming back to continuity from another direction.

Rosenthal's most important contribution is the identification of a major contrast between process philosophy and pragmatism at the level of root metaphors, if you will. For process philosophy, and me, temporal creativity, indeed the very meaning of temporal existence, is based on the model of "coming-together-of." This is exactly right, a function of the Platonic theme of harmony and a point traced in other matters by George Allan. To this Rosenthal contrasts pragmatism's model of "emerging elements within," a theme Peirce elaborated in his theory of infinitesimals and that is common to Dewey, Mead, and James. I had not thought of the contrast between process philosophy and pragmatism on this basic a level before, and am grateful to Rosenthal for spelling it out with such precision.

Though Rosenthal does not attempt to adjudicate the dispute between pragmatism and process philosophy here, she is famous for her defense of pragmatism and I accept her characterization of me as a process philosopher on the point here of harmonization rather than emergence. The fulcrum of the disagreement is whether the past has to be fully determinate in order for the present to make an advance upon it. Her pragmatism says that a concrete moment of processive emergent change does not need to have the past be fully determinate, whereas my process theory does, treating past and present (and future) as distinct modes of temporal reality that therefore have to be harmonized for flow to take place. My negative defense is to say that, if a stretch of time contains indeterminacy when past, then in precisely those indeterminate respects it is impossible to say which parts of the process are earlier or later, and thus time's flow is lost, or at least confused. My positive defense is to argue that temporal passage is causal, with the antecedents functioning as determining conditions for the consequents, which requires their being determinate in the causal respects. But I am not sure we have gotten to common ground to settle the dispute. Rosenthal would argue that the process of emergence is what creates separations so that we get temporal extensionality; I say that we have to have the separations brought into harmonious connection in order to get extensional continuity. I say that her emergence is temporally unextended, with no discrimination of earlier and later, in the respects in which it is indeterminate; she would say that my account cannot be phenomenologically accurate with respect to the feeling of emergence. This issue deserves much more thought, and I thank her for framing it.

GEORGE R. LUCAS JR.

I owe special thanks to George Lucas for focusing attention on my moral and political thinking, which I take to be integral parts of my system. Indeed, to return to the discussion of Cook's points about public life and Platonic dialectic, I would consider the more speculative parts of the system to be defective if they could not be in a critical connection with social philosophy. Lucas is exactly right in seeing the connection between speculative thought and the practical, and I appreciate his recognition of my early defense of what would later be called "communitarianism." He is accurate in characterizing the use to which I have put the notion of "discursive individuals" over the years and he gives a fine account of my reversal of the liberal accounts of freedom and responsibility, or privacy and publicness, or individualistic and communal definitions of obligation.

Lucas raises Cook's important questions of the role of philosophy in public life from a different angle from her Platonic perspective. He rightly notes that much of my sense of philosophy's public role is fueled by Dewey's philosophy, which he then characterizes as "modernist social engineering." The modernist accusation is not quite right, I think, because in books such as *Liberalism Old and New* Dewey criticized modernist individualism in much the same way that Lucas lauds in my work and the communitarians'. That Dewey believed in social engineering is quite true, and we would consider many of his projects now as naïve, as innocent of traditional values that would be lost through engineered change, and as somewhat foolish with regard to whether we can understand enough about what is going on to predict the value of the consequences of change. My appeal to Puritans and Confucians is a traditionalist counterweight to that kind of social engineering, and so is the traditionalism of communitarians such as Alasdair MacIntyre and Charles Taylor. But Dewey rightly saw that there are conditions that ought to be changed, often conditions of poverty and inequality of opportunity; he also held that it is the function of government as the representative of the public to use public resources to redress injustices and positively to enhance stability and social value. Dewey died before the concerns for the environment became so pressing, but he would not have feared to use the government to enforce modesty on human impulses to control and consume. The heart of Dewey's argument for philosophy was that by providing a bigger picture in which people could see and imagine concretely what the consequences of this or that process would be, the public order could be brought to more consensual responsibility. I do not share his confidence that vision will overcome selfishness. But I do believe that public *leaders* need philosophy for the changes they should engineer.

Lucas raises a crucial question about the use of comparative philosophy, and suggests that the moral and political contributions of my philosophy could have been developed out of reflection on the West alone.
He makes the additional important points that, because of modernity's
future-orientation it is easy for our culture to develop amnesia about its
own past, and that the effort to recover that past might be more important than the effort to engage the Chinese or Indian. In respect of the
first point, I agree that my political thought has a solid grounding in
Western thought and could be given expression without appeal to the
Chinese. The advantage of the Chinese perspective here is only to make
modern individualism nonobvious. In respect to the second point a more
serious issue is at stake: Who are *we* and what is *our* culture? I think the
time for us to consider ourselves Westerners as opposed to the other cultures of the world is coming to an end. The argument is this. Individuals are defined not only or mainly by their individual histories and ambi-
tions but also and more importantly by their communal responsibilities
and interactions. Because of the global economy, global political and
military situation, global scientific and technological community, global
means of communication, and global educational enterprises, our communal responsibilities and interactions are global, not just Western.
Therefore *we* are the people of the world, not just the West, and *our* culture is the human tradition, however fragmented. Never is there an
excuse for not knowing something, to be sure, and we should know
Plato and Aristotle. So should everyone, just as we should also know
Confucius and the *Bhagavad Gita*. Every past needs to be recovered, and
it is as hard to teach Plato and Aristotle to students in Boston as it is to
teach Confucius and Xunzi. Because of the global character of our
world, and hence our communally defined obligations and responsibilities, we need to make our own a past appropriate to our global identity
as living in the human condition. Perhaps this claim is premature,
because we have a lot of nonglobal defining conditions; but I am convinced that the claim will become true very soon. Therefore, the importance of weaving the study of Confucianism and other cultural traditions
into our own philosophic reflection is that it is required for the living
discourse of a community that includes all cultures.

NANCY FRANKENBERRY

Nancy Frankenberry has contributed the most exciting thoroughgoing
challenge to my thought in this volume, a truly brilliant representation
of what my theory of symbols looks like when read through the assumptions of the semiotic discussions deriving from Saussure and from ana-

lytic philosophy, with trenchant criticisms of some of my main positions that are entirely valid assuming those assumptions. In my response I shall take the opportunity to show how far I reject those assumptions and will suggest, albeit briefly and cryptically, that with my far better assumptions her criticisms do not hold.

Frankenberry interprets me as holding that meaning is reference, whereas she holds that meaning does not involve reference for the reasons given in the postmodern discussion that she neatly lays out (*pace* Wyschogrod). But to the contrary I follow Peirce in sharply distinguishing the problematics of meaning, reference, and interpretation. Perhaps the fact that I put the discussion of reference before that of meaning in *The Truth of Broken Symbols* has been misleading in this regard, although I suspect the real problem is that the postmodern assumptions about meaning preclude its relation to reference.

In fact, I advocate an entirely different model from hers for understanding interpretive experience. Isn't it the case (I suggest in advocating my assumptions) that human beings are intelligent animals who engage their environment aided not only by the discernments made possible by their senses and the organs of touch and motion that let them explore things but also by the semiotic systems that focus attention, that allow certain things to register while not picking up on others, and that embody many levels of judgment about what is important? Human beings engage their environment with their semiotic systems in developing and living out their purposes, from following the instincts for bare survival to enjoying the arts of high civilization. The semiotic systems in one sense are in the minds and habits of individuals, and in other appropriate senses are developed and resident in the cultures of communities. The semiotic systems are relative to the environment of specific cultures. My own semiotic system is not very good at all for picking up on what is important in a jungle, where a native of the jungle sees and appreciates far more than I; on the other hand my semiotic system makes me a skilled driver in Boston, where a person from a jungle culture, or Des Moines, visiting Boston for the first time would be baffled about what is important to notice.

A semiotic system needs to be understood in two complementary ways, the language of which might be confusing. What I call the *intentional* understanding has to do with how the semiotic system is an instrument in the natural process of human engagement of reality. As an instrument it supplies the signs or symbols used in the engagement, for instance for distinguishing a snake from a vine, or discerning from its lean whether an oncoming car is braking or accelerating. Those signs or symbols have their meaning only as that is defined or coded within the semiotic system, however, and therefore the whole system is taken to be in play when specific interpretive engagements are made. Thus, human beings suppose that their semiotic systems as a whole give access to or are iconic of reality; where engagements themselves are problematic, human beings know that their semiotic systems might be at fault. Systems continually are modified by the feedback involved in engagement. Intentional interpretation is actually engaging something, interpreting it to be as the semiotic system's signs say in the respect in which those signs interpret the reality. We are limited to interpretively engaging reality only in those respects in which our signs allow us to interpret it; when reality has important respects that our signs miss, we get bumped.

Semiotic systems also are to be understood in terms of their internal extensional structures as meaning systems. The basic pragmatic structure of a meaning system is that within it certain signs can be taken by other (propositional) signs to represent yet other (objects) signs in certain respects. This is an analogue of the intentional structure of interpretation, but only an analogue. Intentionality is real interpretive engagement; extensionality, in my usage, is the structure of the semiotic code. The semantics and syntactics of signs articulate just what other signs can be related as objects of the signs when interpreted by what other signs. Semantic meaning systems are the kinds of things a scholar can study by looking at the meanings alone, without seeing how they are used or function in intentional interpretive engagement. "Use" is a fairly thin concept to designate the intentionality of engagement, in contrast to extensional "mention," but it does note the distinction.

The "holism" for which Frankenberry calls fits entirely within the extensional analysis of semiotic systems as I understand that. So, for instance, she is right to begin by pointing out that symbols are broken off from other symbols that postmoderns like to track down through traces, an extensional concern, whereas I use the phrase "broken symbols" to refer to their intentional use. Her general call for the exploration of symbols and systems of symbols through the explication of their meanings is a crucial task. Moreover, she is right in citing Sperber about the limitations of decoding as an adequate means for analysis of symbols. Semiotic systems are not consistent totalities but collages of overlapping, partly congruent, sometimes contradictory and sometimes incommensurable symbol systems, and they usually are changing as people engage life differently. Some of our symbol systems, such as those that make up philosophic or sophisticated theological language, are highly self-referential in the sense that the main symbols have many other symbols within the system that interpret them; philosophers more than most can say what they mean in other words. Other symbol systems, including many deeply important in religion, are very powerful in people's religious engagement but are not elaborated in other explanatory symbols; hence Sperber's point that many deeply religious people cannot explain their symbols but just live religiously with them. In religions with long interpretive traditions, most symbol systems are in between in matters of explanatory interdefinition. Encountering people with very different religious symbol systems, and coming to suspect that one's system might be sorely lacking, are powerful motives for expanding a religious symbol system to become more interpretively self-conscious; Christian encounters with Hindu avatar theory and Jewish responses to the Holocaust are recent examples of pressures to change or augment inherited symbol systems.

Extensional analysis of semiotic systems, especially their religious symbol systems, in principle if not in practice, can be an "objective" study, noting how the symbols do and do not connect. But no amount of extensional analysis will deal with the questions of how the symbols refer in actual interpretation, whether they have real referents, or whether they represent their referents rightly in the respect in which they interpret the referents. Those are all questions of truth, of whether the interpretations in the engagement pick up on what is important in reality so that this is registered appropriately in the interpreters. These are "pragmatic" considerations of truth of the sort I treated at length in *Recovery of the Measure* and *The Truth of Broken Symbols,* treatments Frankenberry cites but does not analyze.

I think the underlying reason why many people believe that religious symbols do not have real referents, whereas almost nobody doubts that the symbols involved in distinguishing snakes from vines or driving a car do, is that religious symbols refer to such funny referents, not substances or measurable things but boundary matters. Frankenberry is mistaken in attributing to me the view that all religions (or any for that matter) attempt to refer to the infinite flat out. Rather, I say they refer always to finite-infinite contrasts: you never get the infinite without the finite, which is why I agree with her that any apophatic claim must be based on something kataphatic. Moreover, it is important to distinguish the generality of my claim about finite-infinite contrasts from the specific one I have analyzed so often, that of divine creation of the world. Let me explain.

A finite-infinite contrast involves a finite something that a culture (or person) takes to be defining or foundational for the culture's sense of the world. The "infinite" is what would be the case if that finite something were not real or were not foundational. Obviously, the very physical existence of the world is important in this sense, and most religions have symbols referring to it. I have argued for a particular version of creation *ex nihilo*, examined by several papers here, as the best theory of the foundational nature of cosmic existence; in that theory I claim that the creator would be wholly indeterminate (infinite) if there were no creation: but because there is the creation of the world, God the creator is what makes that difference—a finite-infinite contrast—and is determinate as the creator of this world. But there are many other finite-infinite contrasts among religious symbols, those having to do with whether life has meaning, whether the world has value, whether we have company in the universe. The finite side of a finite-infinite contrast is always a function of a culture's semiotic system. If the Shinto world has sacred points of punctuation it is because of the cultural construals of the kami stones, which thus are finite-infinite contrasts for defining a sacred space.

It is very important to consider the philosophical theory of finite-infinite contrasts as the referents of religious symbols separately from the very different questions of whether my theory of creation *ex nihilo* articulates a candidate finite-infinite contrast and whether that theory might also be true. That a culture's religious symbols refer to a culturally defined finite-infinite contrast by no means entails that an actual such referent exists. My philosophic theory of symbols is intended to explain interpretive reference, not to defend a theory of a particular referent. Frankenberry's criticisms of my theory of reference separate the infinite from the finite, and hence give rise to her concerns with unsayable meanings; they also confuse the philosophic theory of finite-infinite contrasts with my ontology of creation *ex nihilo*.

This brings me to a final issue to discuss here, though her rich paper calls for a page-by-page response. Frankenberry makes much of the distinction between the symbolic and the literal. Although there is some distinction to be made here, I should say that I use the word "symbol" to mean any kind of sign, particularly religious signs. Some symbols can be interpreted quite literally, which is to say, the intentional use of the symbol to engage reality can use without alteration a propositional or other extensional form from the semiotic system. Religious symbols with a heavy dose of apophasis built in, such as Plotinus' theory of the One, Aquinas' analogical pure Act of Esse, Tillich's Ground of Being, and my creation *ex nihilo*, can all be used to engage reality literally once one has grasped the extensional definitions that state what is kataphatic and what is apophatic. What is the point of careful metaphysics, lining up what the meanings of terms are and are not, if the terms are not to be used experientially with those qualifications? Other symbols indeed are used metaphorically, where the extensional form is used intentionally to refer to and interpret a referent different from what is extensionally allowed. If my extensional system says God creates the conditions for goodness, then it can be only metaphorical to say that God is good. Often metaphors then become familiar parts of the extensional system, so that people forget, for instance, that the stem of a goblet is a metaphor deriving from flower stems. Most living religious symbols are of this extensionally reinscribed sort, recording in the inheritable symbol system a metaphoric leap that once creatively effected a new engagement, like conceiving nirvana as the extinction of a flame.

Though symbols can be used literally, there are two important senses in religion (and other domains) in which symbols can involve an unsaid reservoir of meaning. One is where (1) a symbol is used metaphorically to facilitate a new or improved engagement that articulates reality in some newly framed respect and (2) the metaphor has not yet been made part of the extensional system with careful qualifications and paraphrases; the limitations of calling Yahweh a warrior or father are fairly well understood in contemporary inherited Christian symbol systems, whereas the implications of saying God has a preferential option for the poor or is incarnate in our ecological environment are still somewhat mysterious. Maybe theologians will eliminate these mysteries. The second sense of unsaid mystery comes from the fact that symbols interpret their referents only in the respects involved in the interpretation, and the referents can also be interpreted in other respects; many religious symbols, precisely because of the subjunctive finite-infinite quality of their referents, include within their meaning the suggestion that there are other respects in which the referents might be interpreted. The apophatic element in religious symbols, to which I shall return in the discussion of Delwin Brown's paper, recognizes that the positive element in asserting the importance of the finite side is contingent on the infinite side being merely subjunctive—what the case would be without the finite world-making element.

I am grateful to Frankenberry for the occasion to draw out some of the differences of my view from the more common one regarding religious symbols.

J. HARLEY CHAPMAN

I thank Harley Chapman for his wonderful "teasing" essay. He has done me a good service in pulling together thoughts from many places to construct a theory of the self for me. He is surely right in his interpretation of my relation to Whitehead and Weiss on this point, and I appreciate how he has not gotten flummoxed by my claim that selves are eternal as well as temporal, not one without the other.

Why have I not written more directly and systematically on the self? That was the main topic of my undergraduate studies where the question was framed in the language of German, British, and American idealism, especially Royce, and in the work of Kierkegaard to whom I was much devoted. My explicit attempts to distance myself from idealism and the individualism of existentialism probably account for my failure to thematize the self.

But to follow Chapman's psychoanalytic lead, there was probably a deeper reason. The very early dialogue that he analyzes at the beginning of his essay of course expresses my deep motives in both of its characters, not just Dr. Thomas. I surely am the young existentialist as much as the spiritualizing naturalist. Considered as a remake of the *Kathopanisad*, it is interesting that the boy Naciketas becomes a young woman in my dialogue, an affirmation of feminine identification; but of the two characters, it is the woman, Nonscivi, who represents the spirited, agential side of the self while Dr. Thomas (Yama, god of death) represents more of the soul that rests on its inner processes (Marjorie Suchocki would say that both Chapman and I need to talk to her about feminine and masculine stereotyping). I conclude from this, upon present reflection, that soul and spirit, in Chapman's language, are tightly interwoven, reflect in each other, and perhaps substitute for one another in various contexts. All of this means that I should have sorted it out better, as Chapman urges.

I fully accept his suggestion that what he calls "soul" is important and is not adequately dealt with under the rubric of spirit. As he indicates, my own greatest use of "soul" language comes in discussions of inner transformations, such as the treatment of realizing our eternal identity in *Eternity and Time's Flow* and in the treatment of spiritual formation (should be "soul formation") in *The Truth of Broken Symbols*, chapter 5. Without having in mind his technical distinction between soul and spirit, I had some feel for its force.

Chapman's distinction between spirit and soul is a bit like the distinction I draw concerning the logos (say, in *A Theology Primer*) between order that needs to be worked into or imposed upon less ordered elements and the components of things that need to be harmonized with order but that themselves have their own order and direction, perhaps not in full congruence with the harmony of the whole. With respect to the self, what I call piety is the cultivation of soul. But these categories are not sufficient to recognize the soul in Chapman's full sense because that would require imaginative representations of the whole of the self from the standpoint of the soul representations of Hillman's sort. It is a failure of my thought so far that I have not developed sufficiently elaborate models or images of soul like those for more "spirited" parts of the self. I am grateful to Chapman for pushing in this direction, and look forward to more of his own work on this topic.

ROBERT S. CORRINGTON

With Robert Corrington's essay this collection turns to matters of philosophical theology, and what an introduction that essay makes! Never have I encountered as penetrating an analysis of my complex and cumbersome theory, dealing with both the categoreal and experiential elements; Corrington's power probably comes from the fact he has wrestled with the same issues and has developed his own theory, as complex if not as cumbersome as mine. He says that he "devoted a great deal of energy to the task of exposition because of the painfully reiterated experience that philosophers rarely take the time and care to *truly* understand each other," and I am very thankful, awed in fact, for his courtesy. I shall discuss here the three issues he raises at the end of his essay.

The first is whether my quasi-process naturalism escapes the mentalism and idealism he associates, rightly, with more orthodox versions of process philosophy than mine. He argues that the notions of harmony and value I employ are a Trojan horse that sneaks mentalism into the naturalist settlement. To this I reply several things. One, the question of what nature is should not be settled before it is settled, and the issue here is whether value is in things naturally. Corrington supposes that a true naturalism will take things to be "opaque or semiotically dense" and that value is a function of human experience guided by human feelings and aspirations. He says that nature, for a true naturalism, should be *described*, whereas idealism fudges by describing with honorifics. But what if nature is made of things that really are achievements of value and our experience gets that value with the same accuracy or misinterpretation that it gets the semiotic forms of things? I believe my theory of value has shown how it is *possible* that nature is value-bearing and that with this theory as a sign we can engage nature or reality doing prima facie justice to our experiencing of the world as valuable (or dis-valuable where sadness is a realistic response, as Corrington would say). My overall argument takes the form of "saving the appearances."

For another reply, some dialectical considerations help. Corrington and I agree on the importance of Spinoza's distinction between *natura naturata* and *natura naturans*. He, but not I, accepts Spinoza's account of *natura naturata* as a value-free process of determinations. This is reinforced in his thought by Justus Buchler's theory of things as "natural complexes" that are analyzed in terms of *positions* in *orders* that are subject to judgmental *discrimination*. For neither Spinoza nor Buchler is value something conceived to be an intrinsic property of existence. They both aim philosophy to be in accord with modern science and accept the fact-value distinction associated with that; the result is scientism. My axiology, as Allan argued, is a counterposition that attempts to show that the fact-value distinction is a scientistic abstraction that can be accepted only in very limited scientific usages. Corrington and I agree that Spinoza is wrong about the deterministic character of natural process and instead read that process in semiotic terms. But Corrington's semiotic theory is value-free, as was Peirce's, whereas I have argued in the *Axiology of Thinking* that semiosis is valuing the values of things. My point is that form is a function of the achievement of value in a medium, rather than value being a function of the (Aristotelian) completion of form. So my response to Corrington's first point is that the "true naturalism" is the one that gets nature right, and because natural things are achievements of value, it should be an axiological naturalism. For all its appeal to psychoanalytic motifs (mentalism?), and contrary to his own intention, Corrington's is a quasi-scientistic naturalism.

The second issue is "the nature of the indifferent ground [of the natural world] and its relation, or lack thereof, to unity." I shall discuss unity in connection with the third issue and here want to concentrate on the *indifference* of the ground. Corrington and I agree in rejecting anthropocentric philosophies of nature and anthropomorphic theologies. There is no realistic way of saying that God is a being apart from the world who has purposes for it and us. There might indeed be occasions where personalistic religious symbols have a place, but they need to be "broken symbols," which I discuss in connection with Frankenberry's essay.

To use the language of *indifference*, however, is to suggest that the matter should be otherwise, namely, intentional. In our time we need to look at the scale of the cosmos to derive our "images" of God, a cosmos begun in a big bang, consisting of expanding gases, and headed toward infinite entropy and heat death (according to the recent theory). In some middle state of expanding gases they clump briefly, cosmically speaking, to form the garden-world within which life, including human life, arises. One of the characteristics of human life is that it sometimes can discern the difference between better and worse courses of action, and therefore lies under obligation to be better by doing better. In this context, the ground of all does indeed give us purposes and it can be schematized in the imagination as a judge of our merits. Religions have focused more on the domestic economy of the obligatory scale of human life than the vaster scale of cosmic forces that are indifferent to the human economy. With Corrington I believe we need to focus now on the latter, the wild God, in order to do justice to our scientific sense of the cosmos.

But because even distant gases have value, and the values in our neighborhood are differential for our purposes and obligations, we need also to think about the creator as ground of the human economy, not intentionally so but ground nevertheless. Because the values relevant to our possible actions are indeed differential, we are not merely ejected clumps of expanding gases but such clumps as are moral agents. In face of this, it is a bit too anthropomorphic to object that the creative ground is "indifferent." It's the cosmic processes—the plate tectonics, the ecology of germs, the inertial trajectories of colliding automobiles—that are indifferent. The creator is just creator.

The third issue is the relation between God and the world and Corrington's claim here is that I privilege thirdness among Peirce's categories, providing too much mediating intelligibility and purpose to human life. I have not much developed my own theory in terms of Peirce's categories, but if I were to do so I would have to deny any privileging of any category. All categories together are products of creation, I would say. Our dispute centers on firstness, about which he says that it "is that 'within' each thing that pulls it back to the origin that has no semiotic density, nor any possible relation to Logos or thirdness, however defined." This is a bit of an exaggeration. Peirce does give firstness something of this role in his evolutionary theory because firstness needs less explanation than secondness or thirdness. But the general meaning of firstness is "that which is what it is without reference to anything else," and this is immediacy. There is a firstness to thirdness and to secondness, their immediate characters. But there is no firstness to nothingness, the ground from which all categoreal distinctions arise (for both Corrington and me). Corrington brilliantly sees that there is an "ontologically unique space of betweenness" in which things, including the Peircean categories, are together; this is what I call the "ontological ground for mutual relevance." I have argued that this ontological ground can be nothing other than the divine creative act that makes genuinely "other" things exist together, a "unique *space*," an *eternal* ground for *temporal* flow, and so forth. Corrington rightly recognizes a fundamental human hunger to "return to the . . . ground." But he describes the act of creation as "ejective" and "nonnurturing." These are potent dis-honorifics. Only if we had wanted to be kept as fetuses within Mother-God would we be disappointed at our creation.

Ejection is a peculiarly bad description of creation or grounding because it supposes that we and the rest of nature can be disengaged from the creative act. But there is no medium for disengagement. Nature is the terminus or actualization of the singular and eternal creating act (as Spinoza knew). Therefore we bear not only traces of our creative ground but the actual creator as functioning within our limits. The unity of creatures and creator is different from the kind of unity that consists in cosmological harmonization (see Vaught's and Ford's essays on ontology versus cosmology, and Rosenthal's on harmonization). It is rather the unity of an act which creates determinate reality in no medium save the act itself. In this sense Spinoza was right about there being only one substance, God-with-the-world. For all the cosmological suffering we endure, the hunger for return to the ground is a doubled joy: an ecstacy in our own existing and a bliss evoked by the loveliness of the creator. It is an eros, as Corrington says, but not necessary melancholy as if affected by loss.

CARL G. VAUGHT

Carl Vaught pushes my philosophical theology from the opposite side of Corrington's thrust. As he says, our debates are very old and in fact I developed the early versions of my theory of creation *ex nihilo* in response to his arguments in graduate school. Whereas Corrington comes at my thought from the side of a theory that is a more radical departure from traditional religion than mine, Vaught brings the resources of the Christian tradition itself to criticize and present a viable alternative. His exposition of my view is exactly on the mark, like Corrington's, and it is interesting to contrast his with Corrington's to see the differences wrought by their interpretive perspectives. Vaught, for instance, is not at all afraid of personal rhetoric for God even though he, as much as Corrington and I, rejects anthropomorphizing personalism; in my discussion here I will adopt Vaught's expressions. I especially appreciate his careful delineation of the connections between theology and philosophy, a topic that Hermann Deuser also treats. My responses here shall be to his specific difficulties with my theory and to his own alternative, which revives the *analogia entis* to interpret creation *ex nihilo* and give us more positive knowledge of God than my heavily apophatic theory allows (see Delwin Brown's paper).

Vaught's first objection is that "being and absolute nonbeing collapse into one another, where God as he is in himself is indistinguishable from nothing at all." I admit the accusation but no longer believe it to be an objection. When I wrote *God the creator* I was affected by two relevant interests. One was to pursue the question of Being in the context of the problem of the one and the many, and in this context was anxious to keep the priority of Being over nothingness. The other was to connect with the language of the Christian tradition associating God with Being and, following Tillich, to understand nothingness as something Being overcomes. Over the years I have come to accept the force of Vaught's dialectical point about the identity of Being and nothingness, and also to realize that the mystical traditions of Christianity as well as of others of the world's religions give experiential support to that identification. But more important, I have realized that, given the creation, God or Being or Absolute Nothingness is not by itself. Therefore there is no absolute nothingness but the singular creator of the determinations of being; without the creation, of course, there *would be* nothing. Being is not indeterminate but the actual creator of this world, though it *would be* indeterminate if there were no creation. To speak of God in himself is always to speak subjunctively, counterfactually to the creation. So in one sense I am willing to abandon the exclusive "Being" language of the Christian tradition, and in another sense I am more able than I was in *God the Creator* to use the theistic language of singularity for the creative act and its asymmetrical structure so ably described by Vaught.

His second difficulty is that on my theory God collapses into the act of creation itself, another point I admit without believing it to be a difficulty; in fact it follows from the first point. There is no intelligibility to God apart from creation (as Vaught wants to hold) but only to God the creator. Vaught is right that source, product, and act are abstractable aspects of God, but no less real for all that. From a religious standpoint, I want to point out that God apart from creation is not interesting or ever even mentioned in such writings as the Bible; God is interesting precisely as creator and as functioning more specially within that role.

Vaught's third difficulty is that my theory collapses the immanent Trinity into the economic one. Again, this is what religion is interested in—God's relation to the world. My only qualification of his expression of this point is that the phrase "economic Trinity" might suggest that it makes sense to say that God is something immanently; but God is nothing immanently, apart from creation. These first three "difficulties" are difficulties for Vaught but "advantages" for me.

Vaught's fourth difficulty is that my theory of dialectic collapses into *analogia entis*. This is a serious claim, for my argument depends on the principle of the univocity of being. Vaught holds that the sense of causation involved in the cosmological processes of the world is analogically related to the sense of causation involved in the cosmogonic divine creation of the world. To this I reply the following. First, Thomas Aquinas hoped analogy would work to connect God in himself to the world understood on its own terms. But I say nothing about God in himself, which, as Vaught himself says, is equivalent to absolute nothingness on my view; my sole concern is with God as creator, there being nothing else to divinity. Second, the connection between God and the world is through creation, which I claim is a univocal sense of causation that is pure in God's case and subject to limitations in the instances of causation within cosmological processes. (I said this in *God the Creator* but perhaps was not clear about applying the univocity argument to causation.) So, divine cosmogonic creation is the bringing into being of all finite determinations, including the extensive temporality and spatiality of the world; each creature is a harmony of essential and conditional features, and through the latter is connected with other creatures; most creatures change through time and I attempted to account for this and their relation to the singular eternal act of creation in *Eternity and Time's Flow*. A cosmological causal act within the world is a part of the divine creative act with these limitations: its *ex nihilo* spontaneous creation of a new determination picks up past or environing determinations as components to be harmonized, though the harmony of them is new; God, by contrast, picks up no previously made components but creates all at once. For a finite causal act, the past components once had their own spontaneous present in which they were parts of the singular divine act, and their own previously determined components in turn once had their own present, *ad infinitum*. Nothing functions as a causal antecedent for a present spontaneous act that did not have its own parcel of spontaneous harmonization of more remote antecedents that in turn had their part of the divine act, so that God is the source of all. The limitations of finite causation are given by the conditions of temporality expressed in conditional features. (This account is a simplification of a fuller account of temporality that would deal with the future as well, as in *Recovery of the Measure* and *Eternity and Time's Flow*.) So not only is there univocity in the sense of causation connecting divine and finite causation, there is singularity to the one temporally manifold act. To put it another way, repeating Spinoza's theme, only God is and we live within that.

This brings the discussion to Vaught's own analogical theory in which he denies that last point by saying creation *ex nihilo* "means that God creates everything other than himself out of absolute nonbeing, where the creator and the product are not only different in 'kind,' but also different in the senses in which they are what they are." (For me, there is nothing really "other" than God.) There is too little space here for an adequate interpretation and consideration of his brilliant theory that allows him to reconstruct much of the Christian tradition's language about God as a Being to whom we are related. He does not hold to a strong Thomistic sense of analogy in which the character of the divine is inferred from the character of the world; he rather makes the incisive claim that a three-figured analogy of structure, power, and mystery needs to hold between God, the world, and the act of creation, in order for any transition to be viable from estrangement to fulfillment. His fundamental motive thus is soteriological.

God, world, and act of creation are the subjects of ontology, cosmology, and cosmogony respectively in Vaught's view, and each exhibits structure, power, and mystery. He claims that structure, power, and mystery "are analogical terms because they mean different but related things at all three levels." They must be understood together before they can be separated for the respective levels, and yet this does not reduce to univocity. His crucial thesis is "that mystery, power, and logos are analogical concepts from the outset; . . . they apply to three regions that are first understood together and only later understood apart from one another; and . . . both univocity and equivocity are abstract degenerations of analogy rather than the ontological and semantical superstructure upon which the analogy of being depends." I hope that in subsequent work he develops and defends this at length as true analogy, because it seems to me like a plain univocal distinction of different senses of structure, power, and mystery based on the distinctions between God, world, and act of creation.

There are many advantages to Vaught's view that he details, especially with regard to the problem of the one and the many, which he regards as at least three problems, one for each level and analogically related; is an analogical connection among them a sufficient unity for *that* many? Perhaps the most brilliant part of his theory is the richness he can give to the question why there is something rather than nothing. He can give an answer, which I cannot, to the effect that God's immanent life provides intelligible reason for why there is a world, which he interprets as an unending spiraling of being; I hope Vaught develops this at length to show how this is not a version of the Neoplatonic overflow of the plenitude of Being. Vaught's theory allows for us to consider God, the world, and the act of creation in relation but not reduced to one another; I would ask how he would find confirming evidence for the importance of structure, power, and mystery in the world (or the others) without begging the question, a crucial issue when it comes to relate the theological account of the world to science. A similar question should be asked of the application of his analogies to comparative theology: Do structure, power, and mystery play important roles in other religions' theologies, or do we illegitimately find traces of them in other religions and just say that those categories with analogical structure are the important ones? The relation between theoretical constructs and empirical description, both of which are required for comparison, is delicate.[7]

Vaught's most important contribution here, I think, is the defense of a conception of God that provides conditions for the intelligibility of God apart from the world while holding to a very transcendent view of God as creator. My counterposition is that his distinction of God (immanently considered), world, and act of creation collapses into my theory of the singularity of God the creator as source, world, and act because the analogy of being he employs is not sufficient to separate them. They fold in on one another in analogical connection, which reduces, I think, to merely univocal distinctions of elements in the singularity. His distinction, for instance, of structure, power, and mystery in God from those categories in the world is rather like my distinction of God's total act of creation from the finite parts of that act that constitute causal acts within the world. I await his counterarguments with delight!

LEWIS S. FORD

Lewis Ford is the most creative process theologian of our time, developing Whitehead's initial insights in directions far more radical than Hartshorne and his students. It is a great honor to have him think so carefully about my own philosophical theology so as to interpret it from a Whiteheadian perspective. His exposition and interpretation is as penetrating and incisive as Corrington's from his perspective and Vaught's from his, and it has been an extraordinary education for me to see my theories reflected in those three very different angles of vision. I am very pleased by the extent of agreement I have with each of those positions—the naturalist, the Thomist, and the Whiteheadian—on matters where they do not agree with one another.

In this response I will focus on his main issue: "Does God create the spontaneous features of each occasion, or does the occasion create itself by actualizing the creativity it receives from God?" The former is my view, expressed in different language above in the discussion of causation in Vaught's paper, and the latter is Ford's own, based on his original theory of God as the future providing possibilities ready for finite occasions' actualization.[8]

I am particularly pleased that Ford is happy with the language of creation and that he agrees that God's nature comes from God's act of self-creation. His root argument is that self-creation creates *like*; if there is something *different*, it must be by other-creation. God is nontemporal and thus creates only the nontemporal metaphysical principles or conditions; temporal things, being other than nontemporal, cannot be created by God's self-creation but must create themselves in their own temporal acts of self-creation. Ford has a brilliant theory of how God's self-determination as nontemporal form constitutes the future that can be actualized in finite things' own acts of temporal self-creation. The dilemma he poses for me is to defend a view of other-creation in which a nontemporal or eternal God can create temporal things. Let me treat his argument in several steps.

First, there is the issue of what Ford calls independence and interdependence. Whereas I have argued that connected or interdependent things need an ontological context of mutual relevance, he argues that things that are mutually dependent on one another form a metaphysical stability that is a tight unity. But their unity does not account for their determinateness, he admits, and this needs determining by ontological creation in some sense. He is happy with nontemporal determination by God of nontemporal things such as metaphysical categories, but wants to say that these (God, nontemporal creation, and nontemporal things) are interdependent with temporal things and their causal occasions. I would say that because the nontemporal and temporal are determinate with respect to one another (interdependent) they must be created by a larger act with both nontemporal and temporal products. He objects that my conception of God makes God "not dependent on the world in any way" and that the world has solely one-way dependence, which he takes to be arbitrary and irrational. But I say that God's *nature* as creator is interdependently defined with reference to the world (and act of creation) and that all arise with the creative act. Therefore God as God is interdependently defined and thus rationally intelligible. The sole one-way dependence is the ontological existence of all intelligible or determinate reality whatsoever dependent on the primal creative act. Thus the symmetrical interdependent product of world and divine nature, rationally intelligible, expresses the asymmetrical ontological act of existence. The process claim that God's abstract necessity is dependent on the world for concrete actuality, and vice versa, is a variant on the interdependence I affirm in the ontological product, once the existential act is acknowledged.

Second is the issue of necessity and contingency. Ford defines the necessary as "that which is common to all things without exception" and whose alternative cannot be conceived. This is fine, but I would call this logical or determinate necessity. That there is a world with logical necessity and the intelligibles is itself contingent. So it is necessary in an ontological sense for that world to be existentially determined. I would be careful not to say that the ontological contingency of the world depends on some other thing that in itself is necessary; if it did, that would be mere interdependence in Ford's terms and would require an even larger ontological context of mutual relevance to connect them. On the contrary, the reality of the world is contingent upon an ontological act that creates it, and in so doing gives the act the character of God creating *ex nihilo*.

Third, on the issue of self-creation I stand rather far from all process theology, and on two levels. My position on the ontological level should be clear from what has been said so far, namely, that the relation between God and the world or finite creatures is not that between two selves or substances but that between the ontological creative act and its product, which includes selves in the cosmological sense. Thus our particular finite selves have their own responsibility that at the same time participates in the divine creative act. God is not a big self relative to us little ones, on my view, but the ground of our being; we should be careful not to attribute knowledge or consciousness or intention to God except in very particular contexts where those symbols have controlled metaphoric meaning. God is not a self whose actions produce the world: God is the creator of a world with selves in it.

My position on the cosmological level was spelled out in *Recovery of the Measure*, in which I argued that temporally thick processes have many different kinds of unity through time, from the looseness of a landslide to the complexity of an evolving political crisis to a personal self with moral identity and responsibility forged through a lifetime. Because all things on my view are harmonies of conditional as well as essential features, their harmonic unity is highly variable with regard to various environing conditions. Process philosophy believes that actual occasions are the true units of reality, the *res verae*. It often makes the assumption that different actual occasions are each selves. The process argument for protecting individual freedom by sequestering the subjectivity of concrescence within an individual occasion depends on this assumption. But selves in the personal sense are societies, in Whitehead's sense, and societies can interweave, which allows for accounts of intersubjective and conjoint responsibility. I supplement Whitehead's account of personally ordered societies with my notion of discursive harmonies in order to get greater tightness of moral identity over time than his account allows. I take actual occasions to be abstractions from a temporally thick process. But still I would agree that selves in the personal sense have no strict ontological borders, being harmonies of components rather than singular acts.

Ford thinks that the integrity of finite selves over against God derives from the independence of their decision-making acts which, on his own theory, take up the possibilities God forms for them with some indetermination. But no human self is such a singular act, or even a bunch of those acts with inherited common character. A human self is a harmony worked out in connection with other selves, social roles, environmental conditions, moral obligations stemming from past actions, and responsibilities for the future stemming from the value of what might be influenced by action, mostly conjoint action with others (see Chapman's paper). Thus one's orientation to God, though it might have many starting points, needs to see God as the creator of the whole world in terms of which one's identity is interdependently defined, including the divine nature.

Ford has many other important things to say in his ongoing debate with me, but for sake of space I shall postpone their discussion to comments on the papers of others, especially Delwin Brown.

DELWIN BROWN

Delwin Brown is both an academic and a church theologian, like me, and thus picks up on a dimension of my philosophical theology passed over by Corrington, Vaught, and Ford, namely its impact on religious practice, especially organized practice. Moreover, he homes in exactly on the tenderest spot: my theology is strongly apophatic, a trait deeply distrusted by organized religion, which wants much more positive or kataphatic knowledge. The mystical traditions with which I identify have never found a comfortable home in organized religion and yet here I am, a seminary dean.

Brown is exactly right about the apophatic force of my claim that God apart from creation is indeterminate, indistinguishable from nothing, and that even the divine nature is part of what is created; anything we know about the created determinate world is known fallibly. I thank him for stressing this point and have said enough above to indicate my agreement with his account.

Brown himself, contrary to most seminary professors, wants to protect the apophatic element and forestall any kataphatic theological claims except of the most provisional fallible sort. His motive is an historical observation about the evils of dogmatic belief, especially in religion, a motive shared with Hall. This thus sets him at odds with Vaught and Ford, who believe I am soft on the rational intelligibility of God, and puts him in league with Corrington, who believes I have smuggled in too much idealistic comfort and intelligibility. Let me argue that I have it just right, with the general qualification that all knowledge is fallible and that I am presenting my views as hypotheses for consideration, vulnerable to correction.

Brown has caught a serious mistake in the presentation of my view when I claimed that the theory of God as creator *ex nihilo* has little religious import. His essay is entirely persuasive to me now that the ontological question is a compelling one in many cultures and that the transcendence required to address it theoretically has existential importance, both negative in warding off dogmatism and positive in funding mystical experience. What I had meant in that unguarded claim is that the theory of creation *ex nihilo* allows for the created world to be anything that science or religion (or any other inquiry) finds it to be, and that most religious interests have to do with the character of the world created and what that says about their creator. Ford and others have picked up on that point, which surely ought to be corrected and supplemented by Brown's.

Nevertheless, I want to argue that a certain positive, albeit hypothetical and fallible, knowledge of God is to be found in between the apophatic transcendence of God as source and the empirical contingency of the world's details as expressive of the creative act. This is to be found in the eternal character of God as creator of the temporal world. Corrington had this point right, and Ford too noticed it and objected to its intelligibility on the grounds God cannot create self and other at once. My claim is that there is a complex transcendental logos, to use Vaught's term, with two levels. One is the transcendental conditions of harmony involving form, components, mixture, and value; this is the basis of my theory of covenant that Marjorie Suchocki analyzes and that I shall discuss in that connection. The other is God's singular creation of temporally changing things that I will reaffirm here.

Contra Ford, the vague point that the singular act of creation gives rise to all things in whatever kinds of togetherness they might have can be given concrete specificity with a more detailed account of time and temporal things. Rosenthal, Chapman, and Corrington have traced my theory in detail and I do not need to repeat their exposition. Let me draw out but one implication. The temporal theory says each date of things has three modes: as dated past things are fixed and actual, as dated present they are in process of determining indeterminate possibilities into actual singulars, and as dated future they are myriad shapes of possibility varying with every present decision that conditions them. Within time the various dates of a thing are ordered temporally, with the earlier ones actualized before the later ones. But because the modes of temporality have integrity over against each other, that is, they have separate essential features, they are together within the singular divine creative act in nontemporal or eternal ways. There is no point within that eternal creative act where they are together *at once*, as if the future were fixed in the divine mind's eye before it is actually fixed within time. Rather the various dates of a thing, including highly unstructured processes, are simply eternally together within the singular divine act; otherwise, they could not be conditionally related to one another as required by the process of things in time's flow. Therefore, the internal composition of the eternal divine act has an extraordinary dynamism that fully justifies calling it a "divine life": past-dated things are eternally accruing new meaning with the accretions of actuality, present-dated things are eternally making creative decisions, and future-dated things are eternally shifting in a kaleidoscope of forms relative to different presents. To hold in mind this theory of temporality-in-eternity as a complex symbol for engaging God is extremely difficult. But it is the most powerful mystical symbol I have encountered and combines the apophatic and kataphatic dimensions of knowledge of the divine. God can be encountered as the singularity within which we live and move and have our being, and in this encounter we discover our own identity to be more than the temporal identity of the present date but rather an eternal identity in which we live *coram dei*.

To symbolize this as fulfillment at the end of time is a thin metaphor biased by thinking that past-dated temporality includes the rest. To symbolize it as living in the *totum simul* of divine consciousness is biased by present-date temporality. To symbolize it as living in eschatological hope is biased by future-dated temporality. Eternity requires breaking those symbols and investing those proper to the singularity of the eternal creation of temporal creatures. The difficulty of holding this middle position between wholly transcendent apophaticism and arbitrary empirical created detail is that we have so few good symbols of eternity. This point about eternity, the divine life, and the eternal identity of our temporal lives, is my alternative to Vaught's analogy of structure, power, and mystery.

Brown, like Corrington and Suchocki, raises the question whether my view sufficiently acknowledges tragedy, and Suchocki answers Yes and wants it applied to eschatology. After the discussion of eternity, it is clear now that in one sense I do not give ultimacy to tragedy. We all have our identities in God, and in this light participate in the divine creative glory such that our own specific characteristics are trivial by comparison. On the other hand, in eternity we eternally are who we are, short-lived, full of pain, frustrated in our projects, and often not adding up to much that a biographer would call an integrated life with a story. It's not that in eternity we live longer, that dead infants get a full lifespan through which to grow, or that those who suffered in temporal life will enjoy good food, polymorphous sex, and Jacuzzis. The only "advantage" to eternity is the fullness of God in whom we live insofar as we live temporally at all.

Religions sometimes tempt us to bliss out on eternity to the neglect or denial of the specificity of our temporal lives. This temptation should be blunted by my view that the times of our lives are the only reality we have, however contextualized in the divine creative act and connected through conditional features with other things. We are indeed temporal creatures. And because of this, much of life is tragic and that cannot be gainsaid. Corrington says this should require our theology to express ultimate sadness, whereas I say our theology should recognize this but focus ultimately on God, whose singular creative act creating the world *ex nihilo* is glorious, not sad. Brown says all this is to say too much, but I say that saying this much does not compromise the apophatic transcendence upon which he rightly insists.

MARJORIE HEWITT SUCHOCKI

Marjorie Suchocki is also a church theologian as well as an academic one and writes here from an explicitly feminist perspective. I apologize for making her angry with my claim to have built more of an explicitly feminist symbology into my philosophical and theological ontology than other feminist theologians. But she is a little hard on me at that point. I only said that I explicitly developed structural components of my theory of the logos that register the Earth Mother in parallel with components that register the Sky God, not that I am a better feminist than women feminists. I admitted that not all feminists like the symbolism of the Earth Mother or feminine names for God. And I surely recognize the important work of Mary Daly, Sallie McFague, Rosemary Ruether, and Suchocki herself. My *Primer* gives chapter assignments in Ruether and I have regularly taught Suchocki's work in the classes where I use the *Primer*. As to the structural point, Daly, McFague, and Ruether are Tillichians in their philosophical theology and ontology, and the last two do not explicitly go beyond him to develop a structure that recognizes both feminine and masculine symbolic categories or metaphors; Daly comes closest to my approach by developing elaborate feminine interpretive categories in direct opposition to masculine ones, though she does not elaborate this metaphysically. Suchocki herself is a process theologian who stays with Whitehead's view of God as the eliciter of order, usually interpreted as a masculine function, the yang work of Heaven in Chinese cosmology rather than yin Earth. In making these points I surely do not mean to confirm her view that "Neville overlooks—and thus disqualifies—theologies written by women as properly meeting the criterion of incorporating major feminist concerns." I just wish she had noted that *A Theology Primer* contains an entire separate bibliography of feminist writings in theology and religions.

Suchocki's anger comes from a more profound motive also, however, because she rejects any symbolic use of feminine and masculine traits. She thinks they should be applied plainly and exclusively to women and men respectively because of the history of oppression of women that has been rationalized by a demeaning depiction of feminine symbolism. I appreciate her historical point, and her strategy is one way to go. Its cost is the abandonment of deep and rich treasures of the imagination regarding sex and gender in every culture I know about, a treasure to which Chapman appeals. Another way to go is to criticize and correct the symbolism so that it is not demeaning to women. The same thing should be done for symbols applied to gay and lesbian people. Part of the correction of such symbolism would be to give philosophical reconstructions of the symbols with parallel dignity, such as the complementarity of yin and yang in Chinese thought. I agree with Ruether's strategy Suchocki cites in *Gaia and God*. That was like the strategy of my treatment of the symbols of the Sky God and Earth Mother in the logos.

Suchocki's interpretation of my position focuses on the logos insofar as that underlies my development of the biblical symbol of the
covenant as a Christian way to understand the relation of people to God
and to the rest of creation, especially nature, other people, and institutions. She rightly sees this as an alternative to the individualism of much
Christian theology. I do not believe, as she suggests, that "each creature
is ex nihilo," but rather that the entire world is created in mutual relations of parts, via conditional features, a point I learned well from process philosophy.

Suchocki very nicely exposits my view of the covenant and its connection with the logos of the transcendentals form, components, mixture, and value. The covenantal character of human life is that we live
under obligations to have the right form, proper deference to the component processes of nature and society, proper engagement of our existential situation, and proper intention to achieve the best values for our
situation, giving rise to righteousness, piety, faith, and hope respectively,
integrated by love. This is just a scheme for exploring the normative
dimensions of these virtues and the consequences of sin when they are
mishandled. My claim is that every thing, including every person, has all
four traits of the logos and hence all four forms of obligation plus the
need to integrate them. Suchocki, however, reads back the restriction of
feminine traits to women alone and masculine traits to men alone, and
thus associates women with piety and men with righteousness, the very
opposite of my argument. Moreover, she reads a stereotypical model of
the greater value of righteousness over piety into my position, which
was the very point I have tried to fight in putting form, components,
existential mixture, and value on a par; I have treated these four as interdependent in precisely Ford's sense. She adds to the stereotype by saying that men are supposed to be active, and hence righteousness and
unrighteousness are active, whereas women are supposed to be passive
(she knows my wife—how can she say that?!), and hence piety and impiety are passive. But unrighteousness comes from failures to act as often
as not, and impiety often comes from brutalizing the environment or
social institutions in the name of supposedly higher righteousness.

I do not know how to adjudicate our dispute here. She insists that
the gendered symbols necessarily have the connotations I work so hard
to correct. But symbols of race have changed radically in our generation,
and it seems to me that gendered symbols have also changed much;
should we not keep trying so as to be both just and appreciative of the
imaginative depth of the symbols? Doubtless neither Suchocki or I will
live long enough to know who is right.

Suchocki also raises an important question, this time from her own
process theology perspective—Brown notes her uniqueness among pro-

cess theologians—about eschatology as a theological problem. She is right that this is not a major theme in *A Theology Primer*. But it is the exclusive religious focus of *Eternity and Time's Flow*, and I summarized its eschatological position in the discussion of Brown above. Suchocki's own view emphasizes the continuation of history beyond ordinary time within God, whereas I say that history is only within time and that time itself is within God; she has a strong doctrine of immortality whereas mine is of eternal life. Her theory is an interesting contrast to Brown's insistence on apophatic mystery, especially interesting because both are developments of process theology.

HERMANN DEUSER

Hermann Deuser's paper brings the European perspective to my peculiar systematic theology and I am very pleased indeed that he finds it to be a substantial dialogue partner with the current developments in the German theological scene. For American theologians of my generation, so fearful of being thought lightweight by the heavyweight Germans idolized by our teachers, Deuser's careful and erudite response is gratifying indeed. His detailed analysis of my careful argument in *God the Creator* for considering things to be harmonies of essential and conditional features, and the reality of God this entails, is one of the best I have seen. His analysis reinforces Brown's with respect to the importance of the indeterminate transcendence of God. I am particularly delighted with how he traces my way around Kant. So often commentators (though rarely in this volume) outline my conclusions and contrast that with what they otherwise believe to be the truth. That takes the fun out of careful argument!

In this response I want to focus on his extremely subtle argument contrasting his Kierkegaardian-Lutheran with my Reformed Christian sensibilities (understand that I am really a Methodist, that is, *Arminian* reformed, with ties to Roman Catholic spirituality and Eastern Orthodox theology à la Wesley!). The critical point Deuser makes is brilliant. How do we articulate the religiously important relation between God and human beings? He is right that in the *Primer* I present the covenant idea as a kind of metaphor for understanding the human role in that relation. He is also right that there I reject or subordinate the idea (metaphor) of the *imago dei* in human beings because it seems to me to recommend too strongly an individualistic relation of each person to God without the others; the covenant idea requires a social as well as individual conception, the point made so well by Lucas.

But a mere metaphor is insufficient to articulate a serious religious relation between God and people, Deuser argues, and he is right about the covenant metaphor as so developed (other metaphors are not so mere). He recommends instead the powerful Kierkegaardian development of the personal and religious significance of freedom as the human image of divine creation, with all the anxiety of indeterminateness and force of self-determination this entails. I accept this recommendation with qualifications, and confess that my own original thinking about individuality came out of Kierkegaard. Part of my affection for process philosophy is that its conception of concrescence gives a metaphysical account of existential freedom; my discussion of divine and finite causation in connection with Vaught's paper can be taken as a defense of freedom as *imago dei*. Moreover, Kierkegaard is the *only* modern thinker I have encountered for whom the symbols of eternity are central and not strained.

My qualifications of this *imago dei* doctrine stem from my claim that even our ownmost subjective identity is a matter of essential and conditional features connecting us with others. So, we do not act in freedom alone, but conjointly; Kierkegaard ought to have married Regina! The very terms of freedom should be defined covenantally, drawing out the insistence that the norms of righteousness, piety, faith, and hope apply to us in our social interconnections. From now on I will affirm an *imago dei* doctrine, claim that my metaphysics has supposed it all along, and qualify it with the covenantal setting!

Deuser agrees with Vaught in hoping to sustain a doctrine of the immanent Trinity. But he does not take Vaught's line of distinguishing God from the world and drawing out analogies to make God intrinsically intelligible. Rather, he appeals to the distinction between the two kinds of relation I attempt to articulate, the symmetrical relation between source, world, and act produced in the creative act (an economic Trinity) and the asymmetrical relation that symmetrical relation asserts, namely that God is the self-constituting of God as economic Trinity. The latter, God's creating so that God is source, world, and act, is God's immanent trinitarian nature expressive of the freedom of creation *ex nihilo*. The brilliance of Deuser's paper is that his discussion of the Trinity is the obverse of his discussion of *imago dei*: his immanent trinity is the freedom of which the human vestige is an image. And I accept the point here too. I should not say that God is not immanently a Trinity, especially if I say that in the ontological respect there is only one thing: God creating and self-determining as source, world, and act. I'm not sure that those with Vaught who believe the immanent Trinity is supposed to articulate God's independence of the world will accept this. But Deuser has supplied many reasons why they should, including the requirement that they abandon the idea of God as a separate being.

As a German theologian, Deuser has shown me to be closer to the customary reading of Christian tradition's center than I had dared to hope, and for that I am grateful.

CHUNG-YING CHENG

What a treat, then, to discover from Chung-ying Cheng that my work also successfully engages some of the spirit and themes of Chinese philosophy that seem so enlightening to me! (Particularly in light of David Hall's paper that I shall discuss shortly.) Without turning me into a Chinese philosopher, and fully appreciating the Western sources for my major intellectual impulses, Cheng is able to translate my discussion of creativity, even creation *ex nihilo*, into a multileveled ontological picture that takes the most ancient classic, the *Yijing*, as a core text for contemporary philosophical and religious development. I deeply appreciate this reading of my work, and especially his application of it to my own reading of *li* as ritual propriety in contemporary society.

The original work in this regard is Cheng's, for I have always regarded the *Yijing* to be so shaped by metaphors and sensibilities alien to my own that I have avoided serious interpretation of it. The *Yijing* has its roots in pre–Axial Age thinking, and I have no handle on that in China or elsewhere. The classic texts of ancient Daoism and Confucianism, however, are basic Axial Age creations, building on the *Yijing* as their core text and becoming core texts themselves for subsequent Axial Age traditions. I have learned much from the study of those Daoist and Confucian texts and have treated them as very relevant resources for contemporary philosophical and theological thinking. It is through those treatments that Cheng sees my affinity with the *Yijing*.

From his perspective, Cheng provides yet one more take on my differences with process theology, namely, that they seek to overcome the polarity in the process God with a different model for relating infinite and unbounded creativity to finite created things. That he sees the same logic working in my treatment of culture and personal-individual life as well as ontology and cosmology is helpful for me to understand. Because he accepts my suggestion that creation *ex nihilo* conceives the same ontological reality as Laozi's point about the fecundity of the unnamed Dao, Cheng is able to avoid the common reaction of most Chinese scholars who object that "causation" metaphors are used differently in China and the West. The metaphors are different, true, but the same point about creativity is made in both cultures, I agree. I especially appreciate Cheng's discussion of the *nihilo* in terms of Chinese *wuji*, and his appreciation of the Confucian orientation of my insistence that determinateness requires both essential and conditional features, *zhongyong*. Cheng has an extraordinarily musical mind for hearing common resonances and counterpoint, as illustrated in these points and also in his unusual but very enlightening treatment of Yahweh.

Cheng rightly notes that I might have exaggerated the differences between the family orientation of Confucianism and the organization of Christianity as a church community. I agree that ideal natural families have no substitute, and that though a church community might be the best alternative for widows and orphans it still is not a real ideal family. The Christian conception of the church, however, has another dimension he does not discuss, namely, that it is an organization with a mission or ministry. The family does not have an historical mission. If Christianity were ever fully and forever successful in its mission, the church would deconstruct itself (there is no temple in the New Jerusalem). The Christian universalizing of family relations, according to which God is parent of us all, does not have to wash out the intensity that Confucians have found in filial piety, nor the role of filial piety in personal individuation; Cheng is right about this.

I am grateful to Cheng for stressing the importance of ritual or propriety in my thought, especially in late writings where I attempt to give a positive alternative to the individualism of existentialists and idealists. Ritual propriety, I argue in *Normative Cultures*, is crucial for practical reason. If I do take a few steps in the direction of Cheng's claim that I successfully combine Western and Chinese modes of thought, it is in seeing all the forms of thinking as serving practical reason, thus embracing the Western speculative tradition within a contemporary Confucian project.

DAVID HALL

For at least twenty-five years David Hall and I have argued over whether we are in fundamental agreement or disagreement; we have each held both sides of the issue at various times, and have never come to consensus. We have tried indirect as well as direct devices to clarify the issue, as when I footnoted him in *Behind the Masks of God* by the name of a quasi-autobiographical character, Michael Evers, in one of his novels. In this paper he has a wonderful new strategy, namely, the claim that I cannot possibly mean what I say in developing a philosophy drawing on an integration of Western and Chinese philosophy because those traditions are virtually incommensurable. This is stronger than saying simply that I misunderstand Chinese philosophy. Not to let our argument die, I shall turn the tables and argue that *he* misunderstands Chinese philosophy because he reads it too crudely with too many overgeneralizations from a limited Western perspective. Moreover, his limited Western reading of Chinese philosophy is unnatural to his own philosophic instincts and talents: he has been seduced! His seduction has been to go down for Analytic Philosophy in China.

Analytic Philosophy in China is an unlikely cultural phenomenon, let alone a seductive one. Only the great genius of A. C. Graham, a truly distinguished philologist who brought Mohist and other non-Confucian-or-Daoist texts to philosophical attention, could bring it about and make it seductive. As an analytic philosopher he was antimetaphysical, and hence worked overtime to overthrow the metaphysical Neo-Confucian interpretation of the Chinese tradition represented by Wing-tsit Chan, for instance. Like most analytic philosophers he assumed that nominalism is true. And it was as an analytic philosopher, not just a philologist, that he thought arguments about words determine conclusions about ideas. David Hall, after an unfortunate encounter with Chicago Aristotelianism at the University of Chicago, became a Yale Platonic Whiteheadian under the influence of William Christian and Robert S. Brumbaugh.[9] So it is hard to see how he was seduced by Graham's style of argument. But he was, and I want to comment on the issue of words and ideas here.

Hall is right that the concern for Being is a motif of some Western philosophy (though not analytic philosophy) and that China does not have that motif. Western philosophy also has a motif concerning the one and the many on which certain streams of philosophers have commented, which does not have a parallel in China. My own dialectical treatment of Being-itself and the one and the many in *God the Creator* was presented strictly in terms of a dialogue with Western thinkers. But my theory for *solving* "the problem of being" and "the problem of the one and the many" is that of creation *ex nihilo* according to which the act creating the many determinate things of the world proceeds from an indeterminate starting point, the asymmetry of creation and dependence that Hall notes. For this theory, there are a great many parallels in Chinese philosophy. Hall himself cites my citation of the beginning of the *Daodejing*, which says that the Dao that can be named is not the true Dao and that the true Dao underlies and is the "mother" of that Dao of process. There are also many discussions of nonbeing (*wuji*) and the Great Ultimate or Being (*taiji*) in Zhuangzi, Wangbi, and the Neo-Confucians, as well as in Chinese Buddhism (which after all dominated Chinese thinking for 800 years!). My ontological conversation with Chinese thought has been at this level, not at the level of asserting that the Chinese have a theory of Being or a Plotinian dialectic of the One and the Many. I think Chung-ying Cheng has correctly moved from my explicit Western discussions of Being and creation to the Chinese problematic of creativity on ontological, cosmological, social, and personal levels.

Hall argues that these Chinese conceptions of Dao, *wuji*, and the like, ought not be taken as they usually have been, but instead have wholly non-ontological meanings. Following Graham, he points out that the Chinese word for being, *you*, also has the connotation of having, and that is right. But then he concludes "that, therefore, *you*, 'to be' means 'to be present,' 'to be around,' while *wu* [the negation], 'not to be,' means 'not to be present,' 'not to be around'." What does "having" have to do with "being present"? Nothing. Many Chinese texts have a very complicated supposition about time, combining flow and extension within a moment as part of a process with a sense of spontaneous arising; for the *Yijing*, existential units are changes, passing through time, not substances or objects that can be simply present or absent. It is very difficult indeed to get a Western-style "metaphysics of presence" out of Chinese texts. I believe that a far better Western construction for *you* as both *being* and *having* is my theory that to be is to be a harmony of essential and conditional features, with the relational qualities of conditional features pointing to the "having" of things in context. Hall's anti-ontological construction of *you* is unpersuasive in the face of the several long traditions in China of giving it an ontological construction.

He also defends his anti-ontologism by construing the Dao as "merely the noncoherent sum of all possible orders." That might be an imaginative interpretation if we knew in advance that the Dao could not possibly mean an underlying or intrinsically harmonizing principle; on his side is the story of Hundun, the chaotic glob who was killed when his friends drilled him eyes, ears, nose, and mouth. But we do not know the truth of that anti-ontological claim in advance—indeed, that is what the debate is about—and have to do justice to the texts. How could the Dao be the noncoherent sum of all orders if it is the way to cultivate the nature given humans by Heaven (*Doctrine of the Mean*)? How could it mean that if it is the source of nameable orders (*Daodejing*)? The Chinese from earliest times have believed that the cosmos is one and articulated by countless interrelated processes; sometimes the processes can get out of harmony in the sense that legitimate concern for providing for the future can turn to greed and hoarding, or eating too much of one kind of food can throw off one's digestive harmony. But where in Chinese thought can you find diverse orders *chaotically* related? There are many expressions of the theme that determinate orders arise out of less determinate ones, as in the supposition that things are made up of the five elements, which in turn come from yin and yang, which arise from the *taiji*.[10] But there are no unrelated or noncoherent orders awaiting supervening order. I myself have argued that the idea of totality is a bad one, for the West as well as for the East.[11] Hall is right to claim that a single-ordered cosmos is not a good conception for the Chinese or for the West. But this does not mean that the cosmos is not conceived by the Chinese as always having some kind of pervasive though complex harmony.

Hall also has an argument against my concern for truth, claiming that the Chinese do not have such a thing in a sense I am supposed to insist upon, namely, that there is always a reality beyond the appearances. But I don't insist upon that, and Hall nicely describes my view that truth instead is the carryover of value. If he had put that more in the context of interpretation in which I always treat it, the resonance of truthful living—as living in appropriate accord with the values of things—with Chinese conceptions of the way should be obvious. I am in thorough agreement with the view that the pursuit of truth is like learning to dance better with the cosmos, noting that dancing is shaped by rituals of conventional semiotic systems; this is a Platonic point, as I argued in connection with Cook above, as well as a Confucian one. Here is a case in Hall's argument in which he says I cannot mean what I say because Westerners have to mean something else by truth.

One of the ways by which Hall has characterized the difference between Western and Chinese cultures over the years is to say that Westerners like to impose principles of order on things, whereas the Chinese like to move by adjusting balances, what he calls, after Graham, "correlative thinking." OK. Suppose that is true. Then treating Western and Chinese cultures as having sharply different traits, so sharp as to apply with great generality, is a Western move. Philosophy of culture of the sort Hall employs is a Western, objectifying, distancing, and ultimately violent manipulation of traditions to fit one's categories. This is why I say he is a Western reductionist. My own practice is to work within the environment funded by all the cultural resources to which I can find access, balancing different metaphoric systems and attempting to weave a garment fit for our time; for me, philosophy of culture is internal to a much larger philosophic enterprise with many checks on consistency and faithfulness before getting to cultural generalizations. In this approach to systematic philosophy, I feel more akin to the sensibility he attributes to China than to the categorization problematic he attributes to the West.

The metaphor of a dance fits my response to these essays. I have had the pleasure of many dancing partners here, each with her or his own steps and style, but coordinated by their perspectives on my texts. I look upon my own work now as a dance; it has no one pattern as an Aristotelian or Hegelian system might, but many patterns depending on where in the dance they come and on who it is with whom I am dancing. Thank you for the dance. As I come to the end, conscious of the great length of this response, I am also conscious of many other things I ought to have said, points that should be more developed, arguments answered more thoroughly. Perhaps there will be other dances.

NOTES

1. My conception of creation *ex nihilo* was developed through many conversations with Steve Erickson and Carl Vaught, the former being then a committed Heideggerian and the latter a recovering analytic philosopher.

2. See, for instance, my "Wang Yang-ming and John Dewey on the Ontological Question," chapter 9 of *Behind the Masks of God* or (in a slightly different form) in *The Journal of Chinese Philosophy* 12 (1985): 283–95, for the continuing positive influence of Heidegger.

3. I admit to being no Plato scholar, as Cook is. My interpretation was influenced very strongly by Robert S. Brumbaugh, who was one of those to whom I dedicated *Normative Cultures*, which expresses my pro-Platonic contra-Aristotelian theory of practical reason.

4. I argued this in some detail in *Reconstruction of Thinking*, chapter 2.

5. See her *Speculative Pragmatism* (LaSalle, Ill.: Open Court, 1986).

6. See, for instance, *Recovery of the Measure*, chapters 3–4, or *The Truth of Broken Symbols*.

7. This is the point of my discussion of theory in *Normative Cultures*.

8. See his own footnotes.

9. See my reply to his paper in *American Journal of Philosophy and Religion* 18/3 (September 1997): 281–94.

10. I discuss several in *Behind the Masks of God*, chapter 3.

11. *The Highroad around Modernism*, chapter 5.

PUBLICATIONS
OF
ROBERT
CUMMINGS
NEVILLE

I. BOOKS

God the Creator: On the Transcendence and Presence of God. Chicago: University of Chicago Press, 1968. Reprinted with corrections and a new preface, Albany: State University of New York Press, 1992.

The Cosmology of Freedom. New Haven: Yale University Press, 1974. New edition, Albany: State University of New York Press, 1995.

Soldier, Sage, Saint. New York: Fordham University Press, 1978.

Creativity and God: A Challenge to Process Theology. New York: Seabury Press, 1980. New edition, Albany: State University of New York Press, 1995.

Reconstruction of Thinking. Albany: State University of New York Press, 1981.

The Tao and the Daimon: Segments of a Religious Inquiry. Albany: State University of New York Press, 1982.

The Puritan Smile. Albany: State University of New York Press, 1987.

Recovery of the Measure. Albany: State University of New York Press. 1989.

Behind the Masks of God. Albany: State University of New York Press, 1991.

A Theology Primer. Albany: State University of New York Press, 1991.

The Highroad around Modernism. Albany: State University of New York Press, 1992.

Eternity and Time's Flow. Albany: State University of New York Press, 1993.

Normative Cultures. Albany: State University of New York Press, 1995.

The Truth of Broken Symbols. Albany: State University of New York Press, 1996.

The God Who Beckons: Theology in the Form of Sermons. Nashville, Abingdon, 1999.

II. BOOKS EDITED

Operating on the Mind: The Psychosurgery Conflict, edited, with Willard Gaylin and Joel Meister. New York: Basic Books, 1975.

Encyclopedia of Bioethics, Associate Editor, for the Behavioral and Neurological Sciences. Warren Reich, Editor-in-Chief. New York: Macmillan–Free Press, 1978.

Tiai-Chi Chíuan: Body and Mind in Harmony. The Integration of Meaning and Method. By Sophia Delza. Revised edition, edited with a foreword by Robert Cummings Neville. Albany: State University of New York Press, 1985.

New Essays in Metaphysics. Albany: State University of New York Press, 1987.

The Tíai-Chi Chíuan Experience: Reflections and Perceptions on Body-Mind harmony. By Sophia Delza, edited with a foreword by Robert Cummings Neville. Albany: State University of New York Press, 1996.

Evangelism: Crossing Boundaries, an issue of the *Circuit Rider,* February 1997, edited by Robert Cummings Neville.

The Recovery of Philosophy in America: Essays in Honor of John Edwin Smith. Edited with Thomas P. Kasulis. Albany: State University of New York Press, 1997.

III. ARTICLES AND CRITICAL STUDIES

"Man's Ends." *Review of Metaphysics* 16.1 (September 1962): 26–44.

"Ehman's Idealism." *Review of Metaphysics* 17.4 (June 1964): 617–22.

"Some Historical Problems about the Transcendence of God." *Journal of Religion* 47 (January 1967): 1–9.

"A Critical Study of Edward G. Ballard's Socratic Ignorance: An Essay on Platonic Self-Knowledge." *International Philosophical Quarterly* 7 (June 1967): 340–56.

"Reply." *The Christian Scholar* 50.3 (Fall 1967): 324–25.

"Intuition." *International Philosophical Quarterly* 7 (December 1967): 556–90.

"Improving What We Are." *Fordham Magazine* 2 (March 1968): 18–23.

"Can God Create Men and Address Them Too?" *Harvard Theological Review* 61 (1968): 603–23.

"Current Issues in Christian Ecumenism." *World Order,* Winter 1968–69.

"Creation and the Trinity." *Theological Studies* 30 (March 1969): 3–26.

"Nine Books by and about Teilhard." *Journal of the American Academy of Religion* (1969): 71–82.

"Father Gibson's Pop Culture." *Commonweal,* October 31, 1969.

"Neoclassical Metaphysics and Christianity: A Critical Study of Ogden's Reality of God." *International Philosophical Quarterly* 9 (December 1969): 605–24.

"Whitehead on the One and the Many." *Southern Journal of Philosophy* 7 (Winter 1969–70): 387–93.

"The Impossibility of Whitehead's God for Theology." *Proceedings of the American Catholic Philosophical Association,* 1970, 130–40.

"The Faith of Easter." *The Lamp* 58 (March 1970).

"The Social Importance of Philosophy." *Abraxas* 1.1 (Fall 1970): 31–45.

"Paul Weiss's Philosophy in Process." *Review of Metaphysics* 24 (December 1970): 276–301.

"Genetic Succession, Time, and Becoming." *Process Studies* 1.3 (Fall 1971): 194–98.

"The Cumulative Impact of Behavior Control." *Hastings Center Report* 2 (September 1971): 12–13.

"Where Do the Poets Fit In? A Study of B. F. Skinner's *Beyond Freedom and Dignity.*" *Hastings Center Report* 3 (December 1971): 6–8.

"Experience and Philosophy: A Review of Hartshorne's Creative Synthesis and Philosophic Method." *Process Studies* 2 (Fall 1972): 49–67.

"Response to Ford's 'Neville on the One and the Many'." *Southern Journal of Philosophy* 10.1 (Spring 1972): 85–86.

"Contemporary Schools of Metascience by Gerard Radnitzky: A Critical Review." *International Philosophical Quarterly* 12.1 (March 1972): 131–36.

"Knowledge and Being: Comments on Griesbach and Reck." *The Review of Metaphysics* 25 (June 1972): 40–46.

"The Limits of Freedom and the Technologies of Behavior Control." *Human Context* (Winter 1972): 433–46.

"Creativity and Fatigue in Public Life." In *Toothing-Stones: Rethinking the Political,* edited by Robert E. Meagher. Chicago: Swallow Press, 1972.

"A Metaphysical Argument for a Wholly Empirical Theology." In *God: Knowable and Unknowable,* edited by Robert J. Roth, S. J. New York: Fordham University Press, 1972.

"Statutory Law and the Future of Justice." *The American Journal of Jurisprudence,* 1972, 92–110.

"The Contours of Responsibility: A New Model," with Harold F. Moore and William Sullivan. *Man and World* 5.4 (November 1972): 392–421.

"Blood Money: Should a Rich Nation Buy Plasma from the Poor," with Peter Steinfels. *Hastings Center Report* 2.6 (December 1972): 8–10.

"The Physical Manipulation of the Brain: A Conference Report," edited. *A Hastings Center Report,* 1973. Republished in *Dissent,* Summer, 1973.

"Brain Surgery in Aggressive Epileptics: Social and Ethical Implication," with Vernon H. Mark. *Journal of the American Medical Association* 225 (11/12/73): 765–72. Reprinted in *Physiology of Aggression and Implications for Control: An Anthology of Readings,* edited by Kenneth Evan Moyer. New York: Raven Press, 1976, pp. 307–20. Reprinted in *Ethical Issues in Modern Medicine,* edited by R. Hunt and J. Arras. Palo Alto, Calif.: Mayfield, 1977, pp. 383–402.

"Behavior Control: Need for New Myths." *Engage/Social Action* 1.10 (October 1973).

"Specialties and Worlds." *Hastings Center Studies* 2.1 (January 1974).

"Pots and Black Kettles: A Philosopher's Perspective on Psychosurgery." *Boston University Law Review* 54 (April 1974).

"Controlling Behavior through Drugs," edited with an introduction. *Hastings Center Studies* 2.1 (January 1974): 65–112.

"Vanity and Time." *The Cord,* April 1974.

"A Study of Charles E. Winquist's *The Transcendental Imagination.*" *Process Studies* 5.1 (Spring 1975): 49–60.

"Teaching the Meno and the Reformation of Character." *Teaching Philosophy* 1.2 (Fall 1975): 119–21.

"Gene Therapy and the Ethics of Genetic Therapeatics." *Proceedings of the New York Academy of Science,* 1975.

"Freedom's Bondage." *Proceedings of the American Catholic Philosophical Association,* 1976, 1–13.

"In Defense of Process." In *First Considerations*, edited by Paul Weiss. Carbondale, Ill.: Southern Illinois University Press, 1977, 208–22.

"Pluralism and Finality in Structures of Existence." In *John Cobb's Theology in Process*, edited by David Ray Griffin and Thomas J. J. Altizer. Philadelphia: The Westminster Press, 1977, 67–83.

"Defining Death." In *Human Life: Problems of Birth, of Living, and of Dying*, edited by William Bier, S. J. New York: Fordham University Press, 1977, 181–91.

"Environments of the Mind." In *Mental Health: Philosophical Perspectives*, edited by H. T. Engelhardt Jr., and S. F. Spicker. Dordrecht, Holland: D. Reidel, 1977, 169–76.

"Suffering, Guilt, and Responsibility." *Journal of Dharma* 2.3 (July 1977): 248–59. Reprinted as "Suffering and Evil," by Stauros International, 1981.

"Wang Yang-Ming's Inquiry on the Great Learning." *Process Studies* 7.4 (Winter 1977): 217–37.

"Behavior Control." In *Encyclopedia of Bioethics*. New York: Macmillan–Free Press, 1978, 85–93.

"Drug Use, Abuse, and Dependence." In *Encyclopedia of Bioethics*. New York: Macmillan–Free Press, 1978, 326–33.

"Psychosurgery." *Encyclopedia of Bioethics*. New York: Macmillan–Free Press, 1978, 1387–91.

"The Taste of Death." In *Philosophical Aspects of Thanatology*, edited by Florence M. Hetzler and Austin H. Kutscher. New York: Arno Press, 1978. Vol. 1, 177–89.

"Sterilization of the Retarded: In Whose Interest? The Philosophical Arguments." *Hastings Center Report* 8.3 (June 1978): 33–37.

"Critical Study of *Psychosurgery and the Medical Control of Violence: Autonomy and Deviance*," by Samuel I. Shuman. *American Journal of Orthopsychiatry* 48.4 (October 1978): 732–36.

"Philosophic Perspectives on Freedom of Inquiry." *University of Southern California Law Review* 51.5 (July 1978): 1115–29.

"On the National Commission: A Puritan Critique of Consensus Ethics." *Hastings Center Report* 9.2 (April 1979): 22–27.

"Reply to Philip H. Rhinelander's 'Critique of the Puritan Ethic'." *Hastings Center Report* 9.6 (December 1979): 49–50.

"Authority and Experience in Religious Ethics." *Logos* 1.1 (1980): 79–92.

"Metaphysics." *Social Research* 47.4 (Winter 1980): 686–703.

"From Nothing to Being: The Notion of Creation in Chinese and Western Thought." *Philosophy East and West* 30.1 (January 1980): 21–34.

"Various Meanings of Privacy: A Philosophical Analysis." In *Privacy: A Vanishing Value*, edited by William Bier, S. J. New York: Fordham University Press, 1980, 22–33.

"The Space of Freedom." *Notebook*, Fall 1980, 17–21.

"The Art of Beth Neville." In an Exhibition Catalogue, April 1980.

"The Sun and the City." In an Exhibition Catalogue, April 1980.

"Sterilization of the Mildly Mentally Retarded without Their Consent: The

Philosophical Arguments." In *Mental Retardation and Sterilization: A Problem of Competency and Paternalism*, edited by Ruth Macklin and Willard Gaylin. New York: Plenum Press, 181–93.

"The Buddha's Birthday." *The Joong-Ang Daily News*, Thursday, May 7, 1981, p. 15. Translated into Korean by Sung-bae Park.

"The Holy Spirit as God." In *Is God God?* edited by Axel D. Steuer and James Wm. McClendon Jr. Nashville, Tenn.: Abingdon Press.

"Concerning Creativity and God: A Response." In *Process Studies* 11.1 (Spring 1981): 1–10. In reference to "Three Responses to Neville's Creativity and God," by Charles Hartshorne, John B. Cobb Jr., and Lewis S. Ford, in *Process Studies* 10.3–4 (Fall–Winter 1980): 73–88.

"Missions on an Ecumenical Globe." *Jeevadhara* 13.77 (September 1983): 335–42.

"Responsibility, Rehabilitation, and Drugs: Health Care Dilemmas," with Jay Schulkin. In *Ethical Problems of the Nurse-Patient Relationship*, edited by Catherine P. Murphy and Howard Hunter. Boston: Allyn and Bacon, 1983, 166–82.

"Whitehead on the One and the Many." Reprinted with extensive alterations in *Explorations in Whitehead's Philosophy*, edited by Lewis S. Ford and George L. Kline. New York: Fordham University Press, 1983, 257–71.

"Ethics in Medical Donations." Abstracted in *American Paralysis Association/Research in Progress* 6 (September 1983): 3ff.

"The State's Intervention in Individuals' Drug Use: A Normative Account." In *Feeling Good and Doing Better*, edited by Thomas H. Murray, Willard Gaylin, and Ruth Macklin. Clifton, N.J.: Humana Press, 1984, pp. 65–80.

"Buddhism and Process Philosophy." In *Buddhism and American Thinkers*, edited by Kenneth K. Inada and Nolan P. Jacobson. Albany: State University of New York Press, 1984, 121–42.

"New Metaphysics for Eternal Experience: A Critical Review of Steve Odin's Process Metaphysics and Hua-Yen Buddhism." *Journal of Chinese Philosophy* 11.2 (June 1984): 185–97.

"The Valuable and the Meaningful: A Critical Study of Robert Nozick's *Philosophical Explanations*." *Modern Age* 27.3–4 (Summer–Fall 1983): 322–25.

"Body, Mind, and Health in Salvation." *Listening* 19.2 (Spring 1984): 91–102.

"Uncertain Irony." *Process Studies* 14.1 (Spring 1984): 49–58.

"Philosophy and the Question of God." *International Philosophical Quarterly* 25.1 (March 1985): 51–62.

"Wang Yang-ming and John Dewey on the Ontological Question." *Journal of Chinese Philosophy* 12 (1985): 283–95.

"From Légumes à la Grecque to Bouillabaisse in Early Taoism." *Philosophy East and West* 35.4 (October 1985): 431–43.

"Hegel and Whitehead on Totality: The Failure of a Conception of System." In *Hegel and Whitehead: Contemporary Perspectives on Systematic Philosophy*, edited by George R. Lucas Jr. Albany: State University of New York Press, 1986, 86–108.

"The Scholar-Official As a Model for Ethics." *Journal of Chinese Philosophy* 13.2 (June 1986): 185–201.

"John E. Smith as Jeremiah." *Transactions of the Charles S. Peirce Society* 22.3 (Summer 1986): 258–71.

"Comments on Girardot's 'Response'." *Philosophy East and West* 36 (July 1986): 271–73.

"A Thesis Concerning Truth." *Process Studies* 5.2 (Summer 1986): 127–36.

"On the Relation of Christian to Other Philosophies." In *Being and Truth: Essays in Honour of John Macquarrie*, edited by Alistair Kee and Eugene T. Long. London: SCM Press, 1986, 276–92.

"Behavior Control." Reprinted in an edited version from *The Encyclopedia of Bioethics* in *The Westminster Dictionary of Christian Ethics*, edited by James F. Childress and John MacQuarrie. Philadelphia: The Westminster Press, 1986, 55–57.

"Achievement, Value, and Structure." In *Creativity and Common Sense: Essays in Honor of Paul Weiss*, edited by Thomas Krettek. Albany: State University of New York Press, 1987, 124–44.

"Contributions and Limitations of Process Philosophy." *Process Studies* 16.4 (Winter 1987): 283–98.

"Sketch of a System." In *New Essays in Metaphysics*, edited by Robert Cummings Neville. Albany: State University of New York Press, 1987.

"Units of Change—Units of Value." *Philosophy East and West* 37.2 (April 1987): 131–34. Reprinted in *Nature in Asian Traditions of Thought: Essays in Environmental Philosophy*, edited by J. Baird Callicott and Roger T. Ames. Albany: State University of New York Press, 1989.

"The Depths of God." *Journal of the American Academy of Religion* 66.1 (Spring 1988): 1–24.

"Motion in Causal Agency." *The Journal of Speculative Philosophy* 2.3 (new series, 1988): 175–91.

"Beyond Production and Class: A Process Project in Economic Theory." In *Economic Life*, edited by W. Widick Schroeder and Franklin I. Gamwell. Chicago: Center for the Scientific Study of Religion, 1988, 141–63.

"Between Chaos and Totalization." In *Harmony and Strife*, edited by Robert Allinson and Liu Shu-hsien. Hong Kong: Chinese University of Hong Kong Press, 1988, 49–58.

"A Christian Response to Shu-hsien Liu and Pei-jung Fu." In *Religious Issues and Interreligious Dialogues: An Analysis and Sourcebook of Developments since 1945*, edited by Charles Wei-hsun Fu and Gerhard E. Spiegler. Westport, Conn.: Greenwood Press, 1989, 555–70.

"The Chinese Case in a Philosophy of World Religions." In *Understanding the Chinese Mind: The Philosophical Roots*, edited by Robert E. Allinson. Hong Kong: Oxford University Press, 1989, 48–74.

"Confucian-Christian Dialogue." *China Notes* 27.2 (Spring 1989): 524–28.

"Freedom, Tolerance, and Puritan Commitment." In *On Freedom*, edited by Leroy S. Rouner. Notre Dame, Ind. University of Notre Dame Press, 59–76.

"Neville's Review of The Boston Personalist Tradition," with Rufus Burrow Jr., *The Personalist Forum* 5.2 (Fall 1989): 145–47.

"Individuation in Christianity and Confucianism." *Ching Feng* 32.1 (March 1989): 3–23. Reprinted in *Confucian-Christian Encounters in Historical and*

Contemporary Perspective, edited by Peter K. H. Lee. Lewiston, N.Y.: Edwin Mellon Press, 1991, 274–94.

"The Call to and Practice of Ordained Ministry." *Tower Notes* 1 (Spring 1990). Republished as "The Apostolic Character of Ordained Ministry," in *Quarterly Review*, Winter 1990, 1–18.

"Technology and the Richness of the World." In *Technology and Religion*, edited by Frederick Ferre. Vol. 10 of *Research in Philosophy and Technology*. Greenwich, Conn.: JAI Press, 1990, 185–204.

"World Community and Religion." In *Ilyu munmyong gwa Won Bulgyo sasang* [Civilization of Mankind and the Thought of Won Buddhism]. Korea: Won'gwangch'ulp'ansa [Won'gwang Publishing Co.], 1990, 1565–92.

"Time, Temporality, and Ontology." In *The Philosophy of Charles Hartshorne*, edited by Lewis Edwin Hahn. The Library of Living Philosophers, vol. 20. Lasalle, Ill.: Open Court, 1990, 377–95.

"On the Architecture of No-Man's Land: A Response to Hartt and Gustafson." *Soundings* 73.4 (Winter 1990): 701–18.

"On Buddha's Answer to the Silence of God." *Philosophy East and West* 41.4 (October 1991): 557–70.

"The End of Philosophy in the West." *Sino-American Relations* 18.3 (Autumn 1992): 62–80.

"Body-Thinking in Chinese Philosophy." *Journal of National Chung Cheng University* 3.1 (October 1992): 149–70.

"Body-Thinking in Western Philosophy." *Journal of National Chung Cheng University* 3.1 (October 1992): 171–91.

"The Puritan Ethic in Confucianism and Christianity." *Pacific Theological Review* 25–26 (1992–93): 30–32.

"The Role of Religious Studies in Theological Education." School of Theology at Claremont Occasional Paper No. 8, 2.4 (December 1992): 1–8.

"The Symbiotic Relation of Philosophy and Theology." In *Philosophical Imagination and Cultural Memory: Appropriating Historical Traditions*, edited by Patricia Cook. Durham, N.C.: Duke University Press, 1993, 149–64. Portions published also in *The Highroad around Modernism*, chapter 8.

"Chung-kuo che-hsueh te shen-t'i ssu-wei." Translation by Yang Ru-pin of "Body-Thinking in Chinese Philosophy." In *Chung-kuo ku-tai ssu-hsiang chung te ch'i lun nai shen-t'i kuan* [Ancient Chinese Interpretations of Matter-Energy and the Body], edited by Yang Ru-pin. Taipei: Chu-liu Publishing Company, 1993, 193–212.

"World Community and Religion." A shortened version in English of the article above with the same title, in *The Journal of Ecumenical Studies* 29.3–4 (Summer–Fall 1992): 368–82.

"The Puritan Ethic in Confucianism and Christianity." *Pacific Theological Review* 25 (1992)/26 (1993): 30–32.

"Religious Studies and Theological Studies: The 1992 Presidential Address to the American Academy of Religion." *Journal of the American Academy of Religion* 61.2 (Summer 1993): 185–200.

"Religious Learning beyond Secularism." In *Can Virtue Be Taught?* edited by Barbara Darling-Smith. Notre Dame, Ind.: University of Notre Dame Press, 1993.

"God the Witness." Sermon on Micah 1:2; 2:1–10; Luke 17:11–19; 2 Timothy 2:8–15, excerpted and commented on in Donald K. McKim, *The Bible in Theology and Preaching: How Preachers Use Scripture*. Nashville, Tenn. Abingdon Press, 1994, 112–14.

"Confucianism as a World Philosophy." Presidential address for the 8th International Conference on Chinese Philosophy, Beijing, 1993. *Journal of Chinese Philosophy* 21 (1994): 5–25.

"Report on the Roundtable 'Chinese Philosophy at the Turn of the Century'," at the Nineteenth World Congress of Philosophy, Moscow, Russia, August 23, 1993. *Journal of Chinese Philosophy* 21 (1994): 67–69.

Review of "The Human Predicament: Its Changing Image: A Study in Comparative Religion and History," by Jaroslav Krejci, assisted by Anna Krejcova. *Philosophy East & West* 44.4 (October 1994): 741–43.

"Confucian-Christian Incompatibilities." *Ching Feng* 37.4 (November 1994): 195–216.

Feature Review: "Discourse and Practice," edited by Frank Reynolds and David Tracy. *Philosophy East & West* 45.1 (January 1995): 115–19.

"The Classical Challenge." In *Christianity and Civil Society: Theological Education for Public Life*, edited by Rodney L. Petersen. Maryknoll, N.Y.: Orbis Books, 1995, 150–60.

"Truth and Tradition." In *Truth and Tradition: A Conversation about the Future of United Methodist Theological Education*, edited by Neal F. Fisher. Nashville, Tenn.: Abingdon, 1995, 37–58.

"Truth's Debt to Value," by David Weissman, a Review in *American Catholic Philosophical Quarterly* 69.1 (Winter 1995): 116–19.

"Bostonskoye konfutsianstvoï—korni vostochnoi kulturyi no zapadnoi pochve" [Boston Confucianism—The Roots of Eastern Culture on the Western Soil]. In *Problemyi Dalnego Vostoke* [Far Eastern Affairs], translated with a commentary by A. Lomanov 1 (1995): 138–49.

"Religions, Philosophies, and Philosophy of Religion." *International Journal for Philosophy of Religion* 38 (1995), special volume "God, Reason, and Religions on the occasion of the 25th anniversary of this Journal," edited by Eugene Long, 165–81.

"The Last Words of Sisera: A Libretto." *Soundings: An Interdisciplinary Journal* 78.3–4 (Fall/Winter 1995): 439–62.

"Paul Weiss's Theology." In *The Philosophy of Paul Weiss*, edited by Lewis Edwin Hahn. The Library of Living Philosophers, vol. 23. LaSalle, Ill.: Open Court, 1995, 389–414.

"Some Confucian-Christian Comparisons." *Journal of Chinese Philosophy* 22 (1995): 379–400. An academic revision and expansion of "Confucian-Christian Incompatibilities," above.

"The Temporal Illusion of Eternity: A Pragmatic Theory of Spiritual Insight." In *Weisheit und Wissenschaft*, edited by Tilman Borsche and Johann Kreuzer. Munich: Wilhelm Fink Verlag, 1995.

"A Confucian Construction of a Self-Deceivable Self." In *Self and Deception: A Cross-Cultural Philosophical Enquiry*, edited by Roger T. Ames and Wimal Dissanayake. Albany: State University of New York Press, 1996, 201–17.

"How Far We Are from a Confession: Tasks for Theological Education in Church and Society." *Quarterly Review* 16.2 (Summer 1996): 117–25.

"The Emergence of Historical Consciousness." In *Spirituality and the Secular Quest*, edited by Peter H. Van Ness. Volume 22 of *World Spirituality: An Encyclopedic History of the Religious Quest*. New York: Crossroad, 1996, 129–56.

"Kitaiskaya Filosophiya v sovremennom mire [Chinese Philosophy in the Contemporary World]." *Problemyi Dalnego Vostoka* 96.4 (Fall 1996): 49–55.

"Puritanskya Eteka c Konfusianstvo a Christianstvo." Translation by Alexander Lomanov of "The Puritan Ethic in Confucianism and Christianity." In *Chinese Philosophy and Chinese Civilization*, The Second All-Russian Academic Conference, Moscow, Institute of Far Eastern Studies, Russian Academy of Sciences, May 22–24, 1996.

"Uniting Two Images" and "Evangelism Across Boundaries." *Circuit Rider*, February 1997.

"Commentary on the AAS Panel: Shun, Bloom, Cheng, and Birdwhistell." *Philosophy East & West* 47.1 (January 1997): 67–74.

"Reflections on Philosophic Recovery." In *The Recovery of Philosophy in America*, edited by Thomas P. Kasulis and Robert Cummings Neville. Albany: State University of New York Press, 1997, 1–10.

"American Philosophy's Way around Modernism (and Postmodernism)." In *The Recovery of Philosophy in America*, edited by Thomas P. Kasulis and Robert Cummings Neville. Albany: State University of New York Press, 1997, 251–68.

"John E. Smith and Metaphysics." In *Reason, Experience, and God: John E. Smith in Dialogue*, edited by Vincent M. Colapietro. New York: Fordham University Press, 1997.

"Political Tolerance in an Age of Renewed Religious Warfare." In *Philosophy, Religion, and the Question of Intolerance*, edited by Mehdi Amin Razavi and David Ambuel. Albany: State University of New York, 1997.

"Comments on 'Is There a Metaphysics of Community? A Continental Perspective on American Philosophy' by Hermann Deuser." *The Journal of Speculative Philosophy* 11.2, new series (1997): 97–100.

"Reply to Serious Critics." *American Journal of Theology and Philosophy* 18.3 (September 1997): 281–94; replying to "The Culture of Metaphysics: On Saving Neville's Project (From Neville)" by David L. Hall, "Neville's Theology of Creation, Covenant, and Trinity" by Hermann Deuser, "Neville's 'Naturalism' and the Location of God" by Robert S. Corrington, and "Knowing the Mystery of God: Neville and Apophatic Theology" by Delwin Brown, in the same volume.

"A Paleopragmatic Philosophy of History of Philosophy." In *Pragmatism, Neo-Pragmatism, and Religion: Conversations with Richard Rorty*, edited by Charley D. Hardwick and Donald A. Crosby. American Liberal Religious Thought. New York: Peter Lang, 1997, 43–60.

"Is There an Essence of Human Nature?" In *Is There a Human Nature?* edited by Leroy S. Rouner. Notre Dame, Ind.: Notre Dame University Press, 1977, 94–109.

"A New Confucian Lament for Alienation." In *Loneliness*, edited by Leroy W. Rouner. Notre Dame, Ind.: University of Notre Dame Press, 1998, 258–72.

LIST OF
CONTRIBUTORS

GEORGE ALLAN is Professor of Philosophy Emeritus, Dickinson College. He is the author of a number of works in philosophy and education, most recently *Rethinking College Education*.

DELWIN BROWN is Harvey H. Potthoff Professor of Theology and Dean, Iliff School of Theology. Author of a number of essays and books in theology, he has most recently written *Boundaries of Our Habitation*.

J. HARLEY CHAPMAN is Professor of Philosophy and Humanities and Dean of the Liberal Arts Division, William Rainey Harper College. Author of several essays in metaphysics and theology, he has written *Jung's Three Theories of Religious Experience*.

CHUNG-YING CHENG is Professor of Philosophy, University of Hawaii at Manoa. Editor of the *Journal of Chinese Philosophy*, he has written *New Dimensions of Confucian and Neo-Confucian Philosophy*.

PATRICIA COOK is Assistant Professor of Philosophy, Loyola College in Maryland. She has edited *Philosophical Imagination and Cultural Memory* and is the author of *Forgetting in Plato's Dialogues* (forthcoming).

ROBERT S. CORRINGTON is Professor of Philosophical Theology, Drew University. Author of a number of books in semiotics and philosophical naturalism, he has recently published *Nature's Religion*.

HERMANN DEUSER is Professor of Systematic Theology and Philosophy of Religion, Johann Wolfgang Goethe-University of Frankfurt am Main. A scholar in Kierkegaardian studies, he has recently published *Gott: Geist und Natur. Theologisches Konsequenzen aus Charles S. Peirce's Religionsphilosophie* and also edited and translated Peirce's writings in the philosophy of religion.

LEWIS S. FORD is Louis I. Jaffe Professor of Philosophy Emeritus, Old Dominion University. Author of numerous essays in process philosophy and theology, he has published *The Emergence of Whitehead's Metaphysics*.

NANCY FRANKENBERRY is John Phillips Professor of Religion, Dartmouth College. She is the author of numerous articles in empiricism, pragmatism, process thought, and feminist philosophy of religion, and *Religion and Radical Empiricism*.

DAVID L. HALL is Professor of Philosophy, University of Texas at El Paso. Author of numerous articles in philosophy of culture and Chinese philosophy, he has written *Rorty: Poet and Prophet of the New Pragmatism*.

GEORGE R. LUCAS JR. is Professor of Philosophy at the United States Naval Academy and is Executive Director of the American Academy for Liberal Education. He is the author of numerous articles and *The Rehabilitation of Whitehead*.

ROBERT CUMMINGS NEVILLE is Professor of Philosophy, Religion, and Theology, and Dean of the School of Theology, Boston University. Author of numerous articles and books in philosophy, theology, and religion, he has written *The Truth of Broken Symbols*.

SANDRA B. ROSENTHAL is Professor of Philosophy, Loyola University, New Orleans. She is the author of numerous articles and books in pragmatism and phenomenology and, most recently, *Charles Peirce's Pragmatic Pluralism*.

MARJORIE HEWITT SUCHOCKI is Ingraham Professor of Theology, Claremont School of Theology. Author of a number of essays and books in theology, she has written *The Fall to Violence: Original Sin in Relational Theology*.

CARL G. VAUGHT is Distinguished Professor of Philosophy, Baylor University. Author of essays in philosophy and religion, he has most recently written *The Quest for Wholeness*.

EDITH WYSCHOGROD is J. Newton Rayzor Professor of Philosophy and Religious Thought, Rice University. She is the author of a number of essays and books, most recently *An Ethics of Remembering: History, Heterology and the Nameless Others*.

INDEX